REPRESENTING THE RACE

REPRESENTING THE RACE

The Creation of the Civil Rights Lawyer

KENNETH W. MACK

HARVARD UNIVERSITY PRESS
Cambridge, Massachusetts
London, England
2012

Library of Congress Cataloging-In-Publication Data

Mack, Kenneth Walter, 1964–
Representing the race : the creation of the civil rights lawyer / by Kenneth W. Mack.
p. cm.
Includes bibliographical references and index.
ISBN 978-0-674-04687-0 (alk. paper)
1. African American lawyers—Biography. 2. Cause lawyers—
United States—Biography. 3. Civil rights movements—United States—
History—20th century. I. Title.
KF372.M33 2012
340.092'2—dc23   2011040342

For my father, Jesse Mack,
my late mother, Readymae Mack,
and Gwendolyn and Carlton

Contents

Contents

REPRESENTING THE RACE

Introduction:
The Problem of Race and Representation

He had been in close contact with the best element of . . . white people, and naturally acquired their habits of thought and action and imbibed their self respect and innate feeling of perfect equality with all mankind.

P. B. S. Pinchback, on the nineteenth-century black lawyer
John Mercer Langston

There are circumstances which compel one to question what is a representative man of the colored race. . . . I have in mind a young man in Baltimore, Bernard Taylor by name, who to me is more truly representative of the race than half of the "Judges," "Colonels," "Doctors" and "Honorables" whose stock cuts burden the pages of our negro journals week after week.

Paul Laurence Dunbar

DECADES after he began practicing law in his native Baltimore, Thurgood Marshall remembered the 1935 case that desegregated the University of Maryland Law School as encapsulating his early career as a lawyer. Marshall recalled that even while he was studying law at the historically black Howard University, "my first idea was to get even with Maryland for not letting me go to its law school." Skipping lightly over his early years in private practice, Marshall remembered the Maryland victory as the first step on a road that would lead directly to his most famous accomplishment, the decision in *Brown v. Board of Education.* The story fed into local legend and was picked up by news accounts, reference works, and biographers, and even made it into the one-man theatrical production about Marshall's life that has played to enthusiastic audiences in recent years: The defining feature of Marshall's professional life was his application to, and rejection by, his segregated local law school. He went to Howard with a chip on his shoulder and returned to Baltimore determined to seek his revenge in the form of a desegregation impulse that would take him to *Brown*. Out of that one decision to exclude a young black man who simply wanted to study law in his hometown would come a challenge to the legal underpinnings of segregation in America.[1]

The problem is that there is no historical evidence to support the local legend. Surviving records contain no mention of Marshall ever applying to Maryland. His biographers divided among themselves on the subject, with the author of the leading academic account of his career refusing to take sides on the issue. Yet even those who conclude that he did not apply still take pains to accept Marshall's story that his inability to attend was the shaping fact of his career.[2]

In Marshall's telling, the story of race relations in modern American history begins with a simple act of segregation, backed up by law. The act defined him as it would the black lawyers of his generation. Race and professional status inexorably pointed them toward desegregation work as their principal professional challenge. For Marshall, the story of his rejection by his hometown law school—regardless of its truth or falsity—folded seamlessly into the larger narrative. Marshall, as everyone around him knew quite well, was a powerful storyteller. By the 1950s, his recollections, and those of his generation of African American lawyers, began to play a key role as these lawyers wrote their own professional lives into the core narrative of American history. To oral historians, biographers, scholars, and the public at large, the experiences of these men and women seemed to provide a transparent window into the world of black life under the Jim Crow legal regime, forgetting, of course, that past experience is often opaque and always filtered through memory, culture, and the imperatives of present-day politics.[3]

Thurgood Marshall, like most black Americans of his time and place, chafed under segregation and fully understood that most southern institutions, including the University of Maryland, were closed to him. But he also self-consciously framed the story of his past, and by extension the story of race relations in the twentieth century, through a lens that looked forward to *Brown* and the civil rights acts of the 1960s. He had plenty of help in this process, and indeed, many of the leading shapers of America's public memory of race were his allies. The eminent historian C. Vann Woodward helped popularize the expression "Second

Reconstruction" to describe the civil rights victories of the 1950s and 1960s, tracing a direct connection to the unfulfilled promise of the Reconstruction-era constitutional amendments that Marshall sought to mobilize as an NAACP lawyer. Woodward's *The Strange Career of Jim Crow,* which Dr. Martin Luther King Jr. publicly invoked in service of his own objectives, reads like a historical brief in support of Marshall's litigation project, which it was. Its first draft emerged in the wake of Woodward's participation in the *Brown* litigation along with other influential scholars such as Kenneth Clark.[4]

In their hands, the dominant story of race relations in modern America began to take shape. The story began with the legal construction of Jim Crow in the late nineteenth century, continued with the founding of the NAACP and its early school-desegregation cases, and reached its zenith with the social movements, litigation, and legislative victories of the 1950s and 1960s, which finally wrote back into law what had been taken away in the late nineteenth century. Nearly twenty-five years after *Brown,* that interpretation was so settled that works like Eric Foner's magisterial history of Reconstruction, subtitled *America's Unfinished Revolution,* invited its many readers to trace a direct line of precedent from the unfulfilled promises of Reconstruction-era citizenship to the still-unfulfilled ones of the 1960s. Guided by Marshall, his allies, and their successors, the tracks of legal precedents that had been mobilized to secure courtroom victories now became historical precedents that were used to remember the past. Memory shaded into history, and then into a nation's public recollection of its racial past. Looking back from *Brown,* the Maryland law school desegregation case became a starting point for both legal precedent and history.[5]

The story that follows is a collective biography of a group of African American civil rights lawyers during the era of segregation, but it tells their story by putting aside the segregation-to-integration narrative that Marshall and others planted as the core narrative of American race relations. It puts aside, as well, the stories that accompany that narrative— stories of protest and accommodation, heroes and villains, assimilation and black separatism, movement building and backlash, progress and retrenchment—that are the usual subjects of race-relations history in the post–civil rights era. It also declines the invitation to recover the agency of oppressed people living under slavery and segregation—a project that has nourished several generations of race-relations historians.

There will be progress and retrenchment, agency and powerlessness, and movements and countermovements enough in the pages that follow, but it is not the main purpose of this story to recount them.

Instead, the story presented here begins with an enduring paradox of race relations. From their beginnings, Americans imagined that they inhabited a country composed of distinct racial, ethnic, and religious groups that somehow constituted a unified nation—an idea that, for some, is encapsulated in their historic national motto, e pluribus unum.[6] Just as assuredly, since the time of the nation's founding Americans have imagined that certain minority groups fit uneasily, or perhaps not at all, into the national whole. Among the most prominent of these groups have been African Americans, and what has connected this particular minority group to the larger nation has been its representatives—those who claimed to speak for, stand in for, and advocate for the interests of the larger group.

The usual story of black civil rights lawyers in American history is that these lawyers represented the interests of a unified minority group that wanted to be integrated into the core fabric of the nation—or, as more-recent accounts have described them, perhaps these lawyers failed at their task of representation.[7] But the story was not so simple as either of these accounts would have it. Rather, from their beginnings, black civil rights lawyers were people caught between the needs and desires of the larger, white-dominated culture, and those of their own racial group, and there was no simple way out of that dilemma.

Whenever leaders of minority groups have stepped into the larger world of public life, as lawyers like Marshall did in the early twentieth century, the first question that arose was whether they represented the cultural values of the larger group, or those of the minority. Being a prominent black person has often meant that prominent whites must recognize you as one of their own. During most of American history, access to the upper reaches of wealth, power, and public notice depended on resources outside the control of the minority group. The idea of the "representative man" was one response to the problem. A representative man (or perhaps a representative woman)—to use the term that came into common usage in mid-nineteenth-century America—was a person who encapsulated the highest aspirations of his racial or cultural group, in terms of education, professional advancement, and intellectual ability. The very existence of such persons was a potent argument for inclusion of marginalized peoples in the larger fabric of American life.

But the problem of the black lawyer as racial representative was not simply a case of the larger society demanding one thing and the minority group demanding another. Both blacks and whites were unsure of exactly what they meant when they demanded that civil rights lawyers be "representatives" of the minority group. In an era when segregation limited what most African Americans could accomplish in the world, a representative black person often had to be as unlike most members of the minority group as possible. Black Americans themselves often took great pride in the achievements of atypical members of their race. At the same time, however, both blacks and whites often demanded that the representative be an "authentic" black person—someone as much like the masses of black people as possible. From the middle of the nineteenth century onward, Americans spoke often of the "representative colored man," or later the "representative Negro." But no one knew which of these two senses of representation they meant when they casually applied the term to prominent African Americans, often lawyers. In fact, people often spoke of representation in both senses at once. There was no escaping that tension in the nineteenth and twentieth centuries, and it still lives with us in our own time. Americans have always needed—and still need—the representative Negro, even though they have always been unclear about exactly what that meant.[8]

African American civil rights lawyers have been a prime example of this larger phenomenon at work. Historically, law was different from other lines of work. In the early years of the Republic, lawyers reinvented their profession as a route to success in business and public life that was open to any ambitious young man—and later woman. After the Civil War, law opened itself nationally to blacks as well as whites, thus creating an opportunity for a black person to cross racial lines like few other African Americans could, simply by deciding to become a member of the bar. Legal professionalism supposedly had no racial identity. In reality, though, law was a field dominated by whites. Inside the courtroom, where most black lawyers made their livings, none of the decision makers would be members of their own race. There was usually little chance of appearing before African American judges or jurors until relatively recent times. To succeed in law, a black person labored publicly under the gaze of white observers as in no other field.

Lawyers like Marshall represented their race in the ordinary sense of lawyers representing clients and advocating for group interests, but they also represented the larger minority group in the eyes of observers, then and now, who read into these lawyers' experiences the hopes and dreams of an entire race. Simply by becoming a lawyer and coming to court, a black person stepped outside his individual identity as practicing lawyer and, for blacks and whites alike, seemed to stand in for the masses of African Americans who could never come to court and interact with whites as equals. But to be a successful lawyer, one had to also represent the core identity of what was a white-dominated profession. Early black lawyers pioneered the questions that would be asked of succeeding generations of African American leaders as the civil rights era finally put black figures into politics, corporate boardrooms, the judiciary, and other places in public life.

What does it mean to represent a race? The familiar notion of civil rights representation took root as a dominant idea only in the 1950s, when lawyers of Marshall's generation began to remember their pasts as the story of unproblematic group representation in the struggle against segregation. That protest theme meshed well with the intellectual trends of the two succeeding decades, when social historians called attention to the question of agency—the humanity and protests of oppressed people living under the regimes of slavery and segregation. Racially subordinated peoples preserved their humanity and fought the system even in its worst manifestations, many scholars argued, reinforcing the choice between accommodation and resistance that had helped define the emerging field of African American history. The civil rights narrative fit easily into this framework, for that narrative was, at its core, the struggle of "discrete and insular minorities," as the Supreme Court famously named them,[9] fighting for recognition in the larger world of American politics. The story of civil rights became the story of a race—represented by its lawyers in courtrooms across the country—crafting the legal precedents that would restore the lost promise of the civil rights laws and constitutional amendments of the Reconstruction era.[10]

The search for agency remains a powerful idea and has pushed civil rights historians to embark on their own search for the true representatives of a race. More-recent work in the field has turned away from the NAACP lawyers and leaders, liberal Supreme Court justices, and well-known figures like Martin Luther King Jr. who dominated the first wave of writing and remembering. Admirable as they are, such figures seem too respectable in a world driven by the need to find agency in the authentic voice of protest among the masses of African Americans themselves. Some found that voice in the ideas of black parents who dissented from the views of the integrationist civil rights establishment and simply wanted good schools for their children, whether integrated or segregated. Others found it in what Lani Guinier has called an "eerie nostalgia for the feeling of community that was destroyed" in the push for desegregation. For others, the authentic voice of protest lay in the left-labor movements of the 1930s and 1940s, bravely working to unite black and white workers in a social democratic vision of America's future. Others found it in the middle-class activists and intellectuals who sought to speak for African Americans by linking their struggles to the anticolonial movements and the language of human rights during the 1940s and 1950s. Others kept their focus on lawyers, but identified dissenting constitutional traditions that might have helped bring about black freedom but were crowded out by liberal traditions in the second half of the twentieth century.[11]

Still, the call of grassroots protest and authenticity has remained the strongest impulse in civil rights history, leading many writers to focus on the organizing traditions of local southern black communities that developed their own organic forms of protest far outside the confines of the civil rights establishment. Waves of new writing in this area have emerged over the past several decades, each announcing its rejection of what was now called the "top-down" approach of earlier scholarship in favor of bottom-up history of grassroots protest. As scholars shifted their focus ever more downward to the politics and organizing traditions of local communities and individuals, they continued the search for the story of the real civil rights movement, as told by the people themselves, or more accurately, by their representatives.[12]

Among the central claims of the story that follows is that law constructs race, or more accurately that lawyers construct race. Racial identity varies with social context, and historically part of the work of a successful black lawyer was to demonstrate this fact. In every action that black lawyers took in their professional lives, but particularly so in their performances inside the courtroom, they remained powerful symbols of the fragility of racial boundaries in a nation committed to maintaining them. The idea of race deployed here is captured well by W. E. B. Du Bois's quip that "I recognize [black] quite easily . . . the black man is a person who must ride 'Jim Crow' in Georgia."[13] Even in the era of segregation, racial identity could be fluid and malleable. It was often determined by who had access to public space and what kinds of things they could do and say once they got there.

Black women lawyers fit uneasily into the American narrative of minority group representation, and their struggle to figure out where they belonged in that story would help create sex discrimination as a modern category of American law. Black male lawyers often confounded the expectations of everyone around them by coming to court and being treated like white men, but that was not a viable option for African American women in the first half of the twentieth century. When women lawyers came to court, it was often in woman-identified venues like domestic relations and probate courts, where they rarely practiced in front of a jury. What happened when a woman tried to join the fraternity of lawyers and come to court? Philadelphia lawyer Sadie Alexander struggled with this question all of her life. She became a nationally known figure in civil rights politics, but she did not litigate civil rights cases. That type of work was the province of her husband, Raymond Pace Alexander. What exactly it was that kept her out of the civil rights courtroom she found it impossible to tell.

Pauli Murray, however, was sure of the answer. It was sex discrimination. Murray came to believe that separating people by sex was often just as objectionable as separating them by race—a fringe position in the middle of the twentieth century. That position grew out of her own consciousness of herself as a person who never quite fit in in a society that was bent on segregating its black citizens from its white ones, and separating men from women. In a society that required people to identify as men or as women, Murray felt as though she were something else. That feeling of discomfort would emerge full-blown when Murray decided to become a civil rights lawyer and wanted to come to court. Out of that sense of constantly being out of place, Murray would help write sex discrimination into the fabric of American law.

The story that follows is a multiple biography of a group of African American lawyers whose intersecting lives have come to encompass the story of the civil rights lawyer for many Americans. They range from famous figures, like Thurgood Marshall, to lawyers who have recently become of interest, like the feminist civil rights lawyer Pauli

Murray, to those whose accomplishments were well known in their own time but who have been largely lost to history, such as Los Angeles lawyer Loren Miller. Some of them, like Marshall, had a profound effect on how Americans remember the conventional story of the civil rights lawyer, and this book takes that as an invitation to rewrite the story that they told about themselves. They are all African American, but that is not intended to slight the accomplishments of white lawyers who did civil rights work. It is merely to suggest that these lawyers shared many important characteristics, and that their story can be seen as a coherent whole which illustrates a larger narrative arc of American race relations. What they had in common is that they began practicing law in northern, western, and border-state cities after World War I, in an era when African Americans began migrating out of the rural South in large numbers. It has become commonplace to observe that that migration altered the country's racial history in many ways.[14] The migration also created the civil rights lawyer, in that it made it possible for a large group of black lawyers to believe that they could support themselves at the practice of law. Many of these lawyers could now devote sustained attention to civil rights matters. What these lawyers also had in common was an important professional ancestor—acknowledged by some of them but largely forgotten today—John Mercer Langston's tragic story begins this book, and his struggle with racial representation would set the stage for the subsequent struggles of Thurgood Marshall and others.

It is immediately evident that certain groups of black lawyers are largely absent from this story. The rank-and-file lawyers who sometimes worked part time, did little-to-no civil rights work, scratched out a living, and often could not support themselves at the practice of law are not represented here. Theirs is a very different story and deserves to be told on its own terms. Where possible, the personal papers of a few that survive, like Baltimore's Dallas Nicholas, and oral interviews with others provide a contrast to the lawyers who form the subject matter of this book.

In addition, southern black lawyers, particularly those in the Deep South, are also largely absent from the core narrative of this book, although some of their story appears in its early chapters. For black lawyers, the South was indeed another country. Large parts of the South were no-go areas for black lawyers, and those who practiced were sometimes placed in mortal danger for pursuing the type of civil rights advocacy that their counterparts to the north could do as a matter of course. Although some prospered in southern cities, they were few in number, and they experienced a set of professional circumstances that were vastly different from those of their counterparts in other parts of the country. By the late 1940s, one study showed just three black lawyers serving a population of one million African Americans in Alabama, while Washington, D.C., with a black population of just 220,000, had 136 black lawyers.[15] Those few black lawyers who persisted in places like Mississippi and Alabama, and the greater numbers who made a go of it in places like Atlanta, Nashville, Durham, and southeastern Virginia, inhabited a world markedly different from that of their peers in other parts of the country.

The story told here focuses on two main racial groups—blacks and whites—but the way that it unfolds has been deeply shaped by recent writing that acknowledges that "the color of America has changed," as the historian Mark Brilliant has recently argued. It has become a commonplace observation that America's racial composition is being transformed in an unprecedented way, with the controversy over which categories the United States census should record just one element of a larger debate. One strand of recent writing in civil rights history has explicitly acknowledged this change and begun to focus on more than one minority group at once—blacks and Japanese Americans, for example, or African Americans and Mexican Americans. Although driven by differing impulses, what that work often shares is a focus on the messiness of racial categories and complexity of group identity.[16] What follows might be termed an invitation to rework perhaps the foundational story of race in American history—the story of the evolution of slavery and freedom in African American life—using insights drawn from those who have sought to transcend it.

Half a century ago, the memories of veteran civil rights lawyers helped cement in American national consciousness what remains the core narrative of race relations in modern history—a continuous journey from slavery and segregation to freedom and equality, led, in part, by lawyers with firsthand experiences of life as second-class citizens. It was a heroic narrative formed at a time when the struggle for equal citizenship was paramount in African American life, and it understandably focused on agency, resistance, and organized protest. It also made the question of just what it meant to represent a race during the era of segregation seem unproblematic, buried by the conditions of a society intent on separating white from black. That narrative has entered so firmly into the national mythos that many modern debates about the politics of race—for instance, those over affirmative action, urban inequality, and education—are often fought out over who has the better claim to civil rights history.[17]

Yet, often obscured by the seeming consensus on that story (if not on its application to present-day public policy), questions of racial representativeness remain unresolved. Periodically such questions rise to the surface, as they did when younger activists began to challenge the representativeness of the older civil rights generation during the 1960s, and during the debates over racial authenticity during the culture wars of the 1980s and 1990s, and again during the more recent discussion of whether the life story of the nation's first black president—himself a black lawyer—accurately represents the experiences and history of the mass of African Americans. In each instance, the authors of those debates have styled themselves as exploring something new in America's struggle with race, when in fact the question of representativeness is as old as the struggle to define freedom in a society founded on racial inequality.

Indeed, each of these moments, from the civil rights protests of the 1960s to the election of an African American president, symbolizes the larger movement, structured, constrained, and channeled by law, of Americans across the color lines that once divided them in the public places where they worked, shopped, lived, learned, and voted. It was a movement fraught with contradiction, incompleteness, frustration, and irony—feelings that would have been quite familiar to the nation's black lawyers as they began their professional lives in an era of segregation.

The Idea of the Representative Negro

IN 1925, a young black lawyer named Raymond Pace Alexander stepped gingerly but forcefully across the color line in his hometown of Philadelphia, when he rose to give a speech before a local white civic group. Only two years had elapsed since his graduation from Harvard Law School, but he was already racking up a string of improbable courtroom victories that would soon make him one of the best trial lawyers in the city, regardless of race. That year, he also won his first major civil rights case, which broke the color bar at a Center City movie house. His fellow lawyers would soon elect him president of the John Mercer Langston Bar Association, the local professional group for black attorneys. He had much to explain to his white listeners, and he started in fast. Alexander asked the audience to empathize with the plight of "[t]he American Negro of education and high social standing in his group," who was having more and more difficulty finding "a place to live in keeping with his means and standing." What hope is there for harmonious race relations, he asked, "when there is no opportunity for *your people* to know *my people* of means, responsibility and position"? Very few whites, argued Alexander, come into regular contact with "the Negro of high training and education, the man of letters, the successful man in business, the artist—the professional man." The tragic result of irrational white prejudice, argued Alexander, is that racial issues are driven by the influence of "our most unrepresentative persons."[1]

Three months later, he went before a black audience and delivered a message that was entirely consistent with what he had said on the other side of the color line. Speaking before the middle-class congregation of

Union AME Church in North Philadelphia, he urged his listeners to get behind an effort to stamp out the segregation that was still openly practiced in the city's elementary schools. He offered the usual explanations. Segregated education was unconstitutional; it psychologically harmed black children; it resulted in unequal school facilities and resources. But he went further. American society, he argued, "has as its standard of supremacy the white man—his acts and achievements, his precepts and examples, his law and government." If black Americans wanted equal rights and fair treatment, "we must study and train up to that standard . . . we must—of necessity—ape the white man, or consider him our preceptor, if only for the selfish purpose of gaining what he has to give us or teach us." School segregation, he concluded, robbed segregated black children of the contacts with the white social and cultural standards that provided the benchmarks for measuring their progress on the road to responsible citizenship.[2]

Although they ring uneasily in modern ears, Alexander's remarks were not the voice of accommodation to white mores in an era of segregation. Nor were they the words of a prosperous lawyer with little contact with those for whom he spoke. In fact, Alexander had only recently arrived in the comfortable middle class, after an upbringing that often brought him perilously close to poverty. Raymond Alexander's remarks expressed, instead, a common enough 1920s-era worldview among the men and women who, two decades later, would do much to teach their fellow Americans about the meaning of integration. They called themselves representative Negroes, and they occupied an often-uncomfortable space between white desires and black hopes. One can find traces of their story in many eras of American history, including our own.

A Black Lawyer in a White Man's Profession

The story of the representative Negro goes at least as far back as the time of the man whom Philadelphia's black lawyers claimed as their progenitor—John Mercer Langston—and to the moment when Langston placed himself between two racial groups simply by deciding to become a lawyer. Langston is only faintly remembered today, although some have tried to claim him as a model for the nation's first African American president. In the nineteenth century, however, it was a different matter. Langston was one of the leading public figures of his day, rivaling Frederick Douglass for preeminence in black politics and earning the trust of whites in ways that would seem noteworthy in almost any era of American history. Born in 1829 in Virginia and raised in Ohio, Langston graduated from Oberlin College and was admitted to the bar in an era when his fellow Ohioans weren't even sure that African Americans deserved basic citizenship rights. He then somehow persuaded a steady stream of white clients to beat a path to his door. In 1855 he wrote Douglass to announce something that seemed unprecedented. Langston had been elected to local office in an all-white township. He became a popular speaker in the 1850s and won election as president of the Equal Rights League at a national black convention in Syracuse, New York, in 1864. After the Civil War, he threw himself into Republican politics and as a result was named as the inaugural dean of Howard Law School, as acting president of Howard University, and as the United States minister to Haiti. He would cap his career when he won a seat in Congress, representing his native Virginia.[3]

Langston was the quintessential nineteenth-century representative black man. To abolitionist-minded whites, he was a person in whom they could see a darker reflection of themselves. For them, Langston seemed to personify everything that the colored race might become once it threw off the shackles of slavery. But to black and white observers he also seemed to personify the struggles of a poorly educated mass of enslaved and free African Americans with whom he had little in common other than white racial prejudice. Langston's improbable journey began with his decision to become a lawyer. It gave him confidence in his role in public life, and an ease among whites, which he would later put to good use. But to become a lawyer, the figure who believed that he could stand in for the aspirations of blacks would first have to prove that he was a white man.

Langston shared an important characteristic with Frederick Douglass and Booker T. Washington, the only two nineteenth-century black Americans who outclassed him in national influence: he was the product of a biracial parentage. John Mercer Langston was the son of a white Virginia slaveholder who lived openly with a formerly enslaved woman named Lucy Langston, and who sent their young son to Ohio to be educated after his death. (He was also the great-uncle of the poet Langston Hughes.) Langston bore a complexion that reflected his multiracial heritage, and it would smooth his path in the world, as it would for his successors at least through the era of Thurgood Marshall. But that did not necessarily exempt him from the reach of Ohio's Black Laws, which, among other things, had excluded the state's free black population from jury service, testifying against whites, the state militia, and the public schools. Voting was also limited to white males. Although the Black Laws were liberalized somewhat in 1849, black Ohioans were far from full citizens of that state.[4]

No law made whiteness a requirement to join the bar, but such a prerequisite was a simple extension of what had been done in other areas. But there was one loophole. Under the relevant Ohio precedents, persons of African descent could be classified as white if they were "of more than half white blood." Many among Ohio's free black population actually voted through the subterfuge of being classified as white, depending on the sometimes capricious decisions of local voting officials who scrutinized the complexion of each prospective voter to see if he seemed to have more than one-half white "blood." The decision to allow a black Ohioan to vote probably depended on appearance, general reputation, and how one acted in the presence of whites. By the time he was ready to apply for admission to the bar, Langston would have been quite familiar with what it took for a black person to be recognized as an equal citizen under the laws of Ohio.[5]

Simply becoming a black lawyer and practicing one's trade was a civil rights claim in a nation still unresolved on the subject of full black citizenship. In that respect, at least, the autobiographical story that Langston fashioned for himself was true. That story began on the afternoon of September 13, 1854, when Langston and Philemon Bliss, an abolitionist lawyer who had trained him, went before a panel of judges in Elyria, Ohio, to break the color barrier among that state's bar. As Langston's bar application sat before them, the judges openly discussed their dilemma about what to do next. Here was a black man indistinguishable from the best white applicant who could appear in their court, save for his somewhat darker complexion. That, it turned out, supplied the answer. Bliss and a local white lawyer stepped in and suggested the solution. "Where is Mr. Langston?" the chief justice inquired. "He sits within the bar," the local sheriff replied. The chief justice bade him to stand up, then assessed his light brown skin and thin features, and without further comment swore him in as a white lawyer. It was a sign of how Langston would begin to rise in the world. Key to the beginning of his career was his ability to make whites believe that he was, as near as possible, one of them.[6]

Langston's entry into the legal profession placed him at a dividing line within his state, and indeed within the country as a whole, on the subject of race and American citizenship. To set oneself on the path to law in Ohio, or indeed throughout the antebellum North, was to decide to enter a white man's profession. Many northern states had only recently completed the transition from slavery to freedom. White northerners had gradually emancipated their slaves after the American Revolution, but that took decades and still left a small number of African Americans living as slaves or indentured servants in the North as late as the 1840s. Black children were initially barred from many northern public school systems and then segregated when they were finally admitted. Some local communities, however, allowed them to attend school with whites, and Massachusetts banned school segregation by statute in 1855. Segregation of public accommodations—hotels, restaurants, and theaters—was pervasive. In most of New England, black residents possessed the right to vote on the same terms as whites, and in several other states they possessed limited voting rights. In the rest of the country, they were barred from the polls. Langston had the good sense to make his home in Ohio's Western Reserve, located in the northern part of the state, which had been settled by New Englanders and was one of the most abolitionist areas of the country. Southern Ohio, by contrast, was a hotbed of antiblack sentiment.[7]

Langston wasn't the first person to place the question of black lawyers on the country's agenda. Langston's former tutor, George Boyer Vashon, was rejected by the Allegheny County, Pennsylvania, bar upon conclusion of his legal studies in 1847. Bar admission authorities ruled that since suffrage was limited to white men in that state, law practice was also. A disappointed Vashon was soon admitted in New York and decamped for Haiti. Only in New England abolitionist circles had black lawyers done better, beginning with Macon Bolling Allen, who was admitted in Maine in 1844 and promptly moved to Boston. When Boston lawyer John S. Rock decided to apply for admission to the Supreme Court bar in 1863, it produced more than a year of maneuvering that eventually drew in the abolitionist senator Charles Sumner and Chief Justice (and former treasury secretary) Salmon Chase, culminating in the black lawyer's admission one day after Congress approved the Thirteenth

Amendment. The timing was no accident. Rock's application drew such high-level interest because in admitting him, the Court could implicitly repudiate former chief justice Roger Taney's infamous ruling in *Dred Scott* that black Americans could not be citizens of the United States. As Sumner put it, "Admission of a colored lawyer to the bar of the Supreme Court would make it difficult for any restriction on account of color to be maintained anywhere."[8]

To become a black lawyer was to cast one's lot in with the mainstream of American life, and indeed it was a turning point for Langston himself. In deciding to become an attorney, Langston put aside his youthful fling with black nationalism. For half a decade, he had flirted with Martin Delany's controversial endorsement of emigration to another land, where American-born blacks could have equal citizenship rights. At an 1849 Ohio black convention, he told his fellow African Americans that "I for one, sir, am willing, dearly as I love my native land, (a land which will not protect me however,) to leave it, and go wherever I can be free." By August of 1854, however, Langston had experienced a change of heart. At a black emigration convention in Cleveland, he publicly broke with Delany. Arguing that "[a] colored man of science, learning and industry" could "be as much respected here as the white man," he rejected all calls to leave the United States. America's Constitution and its Declaration of Independence were "for freedom," he declared, and Langston informed the delegates that he intended "to work out my destiny in Lorain County, Ohio." Three weeks later he began that journey when he became the first black lawyer admitted to the bar outside of New England and its environs. It remained to be seen whether Langston's admission as a white lawyer, instead of a black one, was a validation of Delany's pessimistic stance on black citizenship, or of Langston's own more hopeful one.[9]

Bar admission was certainly a triumph, but actually practicing law was another matter. There were no black judges or jurors, and free black communities in the antebellum era often made the sensible decision to shun members of their own race when looking for a lawyer who could be effective in the courts. Such communities had little paying business to sustain a lawyer in full-time practice, in any event. George Boyer Vashon, back from Haiti and practicing law in Syracuse, made so little money that his own father confessed that "I made a *woful* mistake in educating my son [to be] a lawyer." John Rock declared that "[e]ven in Boston," the colored professional "has no field for his talent." After becoming a lawyer, he quickly obtained an appointment as a justice of the peace. His fellow black Bostonian Robert Morris had brought the precedent-setting school desegregation case of *Roberts v. City of Boston* along with Charles Sumner, and became a militant leader in the protests against the Fugitive Slave Act. But Morris was also known as the "Irish lawyer," since he was sustained in practice by a poor white clientele. He married a Catholic woman, converted to her faith, and soon joined the exodus of Boston's black leadership to the suburbs. To be a practicing lawyer and a leader in the black community, one had to earn the trust of a class of white people who often had little sympathy for the dream of black-white equality. So, too, it would be with John Mercer Langston.[10]

Langston's story of how he came to be a successful lawyer was a standard tale that one could hear from his contemporaries like Morris. One could hear a version of it even a century later, from lawyers like Raymond Pace Alexander. It usually involved a high-profile case, an experienced white opponent, and a local community that was skeptical of the black lawyer's abilities. For Langston, that narrative began soon after his admission to the bar, when he purchased a farm in all-white Brownhelm Township and set himself up as a gentleman farmer (probably with his inheritance from his father), complete with a white tenant who presumably did most of the actual farmwork. About two weeks after Langston arrived in the township, an inexperienced local lawyer named Hamilton Perry came to the farm asking for help in an upcoming trial. Perry was defending a client in a land dispute and had the misfortune to be going up against Stevenson Burke, a sharp and popular lawyer who was very good in the courtroom. Perry needed all the help he could get and told Langston that if a black lawyer took on a case involving such a popular opponent, it would confer "prestige and influence" and a "very large professional advantage."[11]

Langston, never one to let an opportunity pass, was delighted to accept, and one week later the biracial defense team made their unprecedented appearance in the local township court. So many people showed up to watch the spectacle that the judge moved the trial to a nearby barn to accommodate the crowd. The trial began at 1:00 P.M., with Perry initially handling the cross-examinations with Langston's help. But the white lawyer soon deferred to the superior expertise of his black assistant. Langston continued the defense alone, finished the cross-examinations, and put on the defense's case. The proceedings dragged on until nine o'clock at night, with spectators still crowding the barn. After Langston and Burke's dueling summations and the judge's instructions, the jury apparently ruled for Langston's client without even retiring to deliberate. Even four decades later, Langston recalled the overwhelming rush of emotions he felt after the jury verdict. "Never did [an] American lawyer leave a court house with more grateful feelings in his triumph" than Langston's as he exulted in his victory.[12]

Langston's was a common enough story, and its details were almost certainly embellished, but it captured something that would be true until at least the middle of the twentieth century. In law, success for a black person depended on the recognition of whites. It also required luck, which Langston possessed in abundance. He was fortunate enough to begin practicing just as Ohio's temperance movement—which Langston heartily endorsed—was moving aggressively against local liquor dealers under the state anti-liquor law. When desperate local dealers began looking for any lawyer who could help them, Langston's recent performance, helped along by the racial ambiguity that would follow him all his life, made him the natural focal point of their efforts.[13]

Like Robert Morris in Boston, Langston was sustained in practice by the loyalty of poor whites who often found their home in the Democratic Party—hardly the type of people to endorse black equality. He was good in the courtroom and was skilled at convincing whites with his words. Within two years he was making enough money at his craft to move to nearby Oberlin, accompanied by a wife who was as much like him as possible. Caroline Wall was the biracial daughter of a North Carolina slaveholder and had been educated at Oberlin College. (The descendants of Wall's abolitionist brother, O. S. B. Wall, would later pass over the color line and become white Americans.) With his new wife and his growing reputation, Langston quickly became one of Oberlin's most respectable citizens. When state politics heated up in the late 1850s over the twin issues of slavery and equal rights for blacks, Langston threw himself into the black convention movement. He traveled around the state delivering speeches before black and white audiences, arguing for equal citizenship rights and the protection of fugitive slaves.[14]

Langston was evolving into what would soon be called a "representative colored man." It was a term that would be bandied about everywhere in the second half of the nineteenth century, as it would be in the early part of the twentieth. For whites and blacks alike, these representatives seemed to encapsulate "the best the race had to offer," according to historian Nell Irvin Painter. They were black Americans "who spoke to whites in a language they could readily understand." These were the lucky few who had attained enough education and training to become doctors, dentists, schoolteachers, ministers, and lawyers. Their mere existence was an effective argument for equal citizenship. If the most common principled argument against full citizenship was that blacks lacked the intellectual capacity and character to be entrusted with such rights, then the representative colored man seemed to refute that proposition like nothing else. It was exposure to prominent black Americans like Frederick Douglass during the Civil War, for instance, that helped persuade Abraham Lincoln to abandon his belief that enslaved blacks should be colonized in another country upon emancipation, and to finally concede that full citizenship rights, including voting, should at least be "conferred on the very intelligent, and on those who serve our cause as soldiers."[15]

If Langston encapsulated the representative ideal, his life also seemed to expose the paradox that lay at its heart. Did Langston owe his success to the grudging recognition that his fellow black Americans had the potential to equal the achievements of whites in every respect, or did he owe it to the fact that his contemporaries tended to see him—as the Ohio courts defined him—as a white man? Or did they see him, perhaps, as some intermediate category between black and white? Langston himself could not be certain of the answer.

Americans were never sure which of these ideas of "representation" they had in mind when they casually used the term to apply to people like Langston. It was a problem that would attach itself to every black person who became a successful lawyer. The *New York Tribune*'s correspondent recognized it when he reported on the admission of John S. Rock to the Supreme Court bar. After exulting over the fact that Rock had interred "the corpse [of] the Dred Scott Decision," the paper went on to note that "the Black man was admitted. Jet black, with hair of an extra twist—let me have the pleasure of saying, by purpose and with premeditation, of an aggravating 'kink'—unqualifiedly, obtrusively, defiantly 'Nigger'—with no palliation of complexion."

As the correspondent saw it, no one could mistake Rock for a white man, and no one could pretend that this was anything other than an acknowledgment of full black equality. Not so with Langston, and with so many of the representative Negroes of his era. Even in Rock's case, aside from his color, he seemed so much like the prominent whites among whom he moved that one biographical account called him "Boston's Black Brahmin."[16]

Langston recognized the paradox as he rose to prominence in the late 1850s, and he sternly rejected the idea that his unusual pedigree marked him off as different from other African Americans. At this point in his life, he rejected the idea that representative men should speak for black Americans—at least if those representatives were white. In two 1858 speeches, for instance, he traced the evolution of the antislavery movement as a movement of whites who, of necessity, spoke for blacks who had little voice, to one led by the masses of uneducated colored men themselves. The movement, he conceded, had once been guided by "Representative men—men who have been its advocates, its Champions and its Heroes." But, as Langston noted, invoking the nationalist pride of his younger years, with the Haitian Revolution the movement passed from a peaceful one led by "Heroes and Representative men" to one full of "blood, carnage and death" that was firmly in the hands of *"colored men themselves."* Langston's brother had recently been a participant in the celebrated Oberlin-Wellington rescue, where a group of armed black and white locals rescued a fugitive from slave catchers, and he took it as proof that blacks were exhibiting sufficient manhood to be citizens. He imagined that full citizenship rights would be won not by the efforts of representatives like himself, but by the combined effort of black Americans, slave and free. He would soon get his wish.[17]

With the outbreak of the Civil War, Langston felt his own struggle for recognition in American life merge with that of his entire race. He helped raise three black regiments to support the Union and kept up a vigorous schedule of travel, speechmaking, and recruitment throughout the war. By its close he believed that the battlefield performance of thousands of black troops offered the strongest proof yet that equality should now be the rule. He took the argument to New York's Cooper Union in early 1865: "Another argument against the negro was his ignorance—all nonsense!" scoffed Langston, according to the report of the speech. Langston "demanded the franchise because the colored people were men" and "the negro had fully proved his manhood" upon the battlefields of the war. As he would phrase it in a speech to a black convention in Indiana later that year, "[t]his right is not created by constitutions simply, nor is it uncreated by them. . . . It is a constituent element of manhood." For adult males at least, Langston would brook no compromises on the question of full equality, including voting rights.[18]

The Making of a Representative Man

With the onset of Reconstruction, the story of the black lawyer suddenly became a national one. Although the Supreme Court declined to hold that the newly ratified Fourteenth Amendment conferred a right to practice law, most southern states quickly admitted black lawyers to the bar. These lawyers were drawn particularly to places like South Carolina and Mississippi, centerpieces of black political power during Reconstruction. Many of these new attorneys came from outside the South, as few southern-born blacks had received the type of education necessary to prepare them for legal study. Robert Brown Elliott, for instance, who was most likely born in England, arrived in South Carolina by 1867, was admitted to the bar, and quickly became one of the most powerful politicians in the state. Elliott was joined by a group of northern-educated black lawyers who came south with the onset of Reconstruction and often threw themselves into electoral politics. In Mississippi, according to one study, eleven black lawyers were admitted to the bar before 1880, but only three of them were born within the state. George Boyer Vashon, who had returned to Pittsburgh after his unsuccessful attempt to practice in New York, was admitted in Mississippi in 1875, although it is unclear whether he actually practiced law. The ebb and flow of the black bar was a mirror of the nation's commitment to racial equality, and by the early 1870s it was clear that that commitment would be measured by the progress or failure of the pioneering figures in the South who sought to join what had always been a white man's profession.[19]

Langston, however, would not be among them. The most prestigious black lawyer in America had headed south even before the close of the Civil War, en route to Nashville to commemorate the second anniversary of the Emancipation Proclamation in 1864. He encountered a region he had not seen in thirty years and a people he had long spoken for from afar. It was a disorienting and an emotional experience, which he freely admitted. Stopping off in Louisville, Kentucky, he prompted quizzical stares from Union military personnel. They wondered who exactly was this strange man passing through the state only two weeks after Union troops, including black soldiers, had destroyed a Confederate army at Nashville. One asked him for a pass, telling him: "Sir, I don't know whether or not you are a colored man." Langston quickly "called on a black man to testify" to his authenticity as a Negro, and he was let through. That odd encounter was about more than skin color. Langston's complexion was not light enough, by itself, to raise questions about his race in Louisville. But combined with his aristocratic bearing and his customary dress on the lecture circuit—"blue or brown frock coat, black doeskin pants, a fancy silk or satin vest, and a black cravat"—it made him hard to place. Racial identity was sometimes as much about how one acted and what one did as it was about complexion, and Langston was used to performing like a white man. In the courtrooms of Ohio, Langston's way of moving through the world was a requirement for success, but in the South it could make him seem positively alien.[20]

Langston's southern trip was a turning point as momentous as his admission to the bar a decade earlier. Speaking at an AME church in Louisville, he was direct. "Now is the time," he argued, "for you to assert your manhood and to convince the world that you are worthy of a place among free men." Over the next several years, he would return again and again to his native region as an inspector for the Freedmen's Bureau—the temporary federal agency charged with integrating the former slaves into free society—and an organizer for the Republican Party. Traveling through the South and the Middle West, he gave speech after speech seeking to uplift a people who seemed both familiar and strange to him. In late 1865, at a black convention in Indiana, he repeated his standard mantra that the right to suffrage "is a constituent element of manhood." But now he added a new element, telling his listeners that black men deserved voting rights because "we have made surprising advancement in all things that pertain to a well-ordered and dignified life," such as the establishment of schools for freedmen and freedwomen, black civic organizations, and success in professional occupations. For a decade, Langston had dismissed all talk that black Americans might not be prepared for the ballot as "nonsense," but now he was not so sure. While his fellow black lawyers were staking their careers on the political strength of the freedmen in the South, Langston held back.[21]

Langston's trip South was also a turning point of another sort, for it set in motion a series of events that would bring him into national politics. Like Frederick Douglass, he would eventually settle in Washington, D.C., and become a fixture in Republican political circles. The nation's capital was undergoing a short-lived experiment of its own with home rule, strong civil rights protections, and local voting rights for blacks. Both Langston and Douglass found new opportunities there, and the two rivals would "keep a wary eye on each other for the rest of their lives," according to Douglass's leading biographer. Southern blacks sometimes kept a wary eye on the two of them as well. As one Nashville man later put it:

> Neither Douglass nor Langston are leaders; they are nobody but Douglass and Langston. Whenever they go among the colored people they charge them well for it. All those fellows that lay around Washington City and represent that they are the power of the colored nation are frauds and false.

Nonetheless, Douglass had an important advantage over his well-educated rival. He had been enslaved for twenty years, and spoke with a power and common touch that would always place him a step ahead of Langston in the contest for racial authenticity.[22]

Langston's status as a lawyer, however, carried some advantages of its own. He had come to prominence in law because of his skill at speaking to whites in their own language. Now he found an important listener in Union general O. O. Howard, the head of the Freedmen's Bureau. Langston became the bureau's inspector of schools. When traveling through the former slave states, he emphasized the duties that freedmen would have to perform to justify any grant of equal citizenship rights. "Ape the virtues of the white men," he told them. "[B]e economical and saving, recollecting that the higher your pile of greenbacks the loftier your position will be." From Mississippi, Langston wrote to General Howard—nicknamed the "Christian General" for his religious piety—that he had urged his colored brethren to put away their "tobacco and whiskey." "I shall do all I can, both in precept and example, to induce them to put away their filthy and expensive practices." It was the kind of advice that would soon lead the general to recommend Langston for the inaugural deanship of the law school at Howard University, the newly founded institution that would grow into the nation's most famous historically black university.[23]

Although Langston's tenure at Howard proved stormy, he could take credit for ensuring the survival of a law school that would later play such an important role in the careers of lawyers like Thurgood Marshall and Charles Houston. Some of his first students "had only a year before been unable to read and write," according to a contemporary account. Langston's school educated many who had recently been enslaved, and stressed memorization, practical skills, and moral fitness for the bar. Reporting back to General Howard, who was now president of the university named in his honor, he noted that his students were "obedient, teachable, and faithful." With Howard's strong endorsement, Langston became acting president of the university when the general resigned his post amid scandal over the university's finances. The university's board, however, passed over Langston for the permanent job.[24]

Despite the disappointment, Langston continued to rise in black and white politics. He later served as U.S. minister to Haiti, the requisite appointment (which Douglass would later hold) that generally went to a well-placed African American in national politics. After giving up that post, he returned to his native Virginia in 1885, for a two-year stint as president of the Virginia Normal and Collegiate Institute. At the conclusion of that job, he decided to run for Congress from Virginia's mostly black Fourth District in a state that had never elected any black candidate to that body. Langston's Democratic opponent initially claimed the victory in the fall of 1888 amid allegations of voter fraud, but after a long protest, Congress finally decided to seat Langston in September of 1890.[25]

In becoming a congressman from the South, Langston finally sought to represent, in a more direct way, those for whom he had long claimed to speak. He did so at a contentious moment. White supremacists were beginning to purge blacks from the polls throughout the South, claiming that freed slaves and their descendants were unprepared to vote responsibly. One of their favorite means was the imposition of an easily manipulable literacy test that would give voting officials wide discretion to bar black citizens from voting. Mississippi led the way with an 1890 state constitutional amendment that produced a new requirement that voters be able to "read and write any section" of the state constitution to the satisfaction of local voting officials. In response to the growing calls for disfranchisement, Republicans pushed bills in Congress that would allow the United States government to supervise federal elections, but that effort came to naught in 1891.[26]

Langston eagerly joined the voting rights debate during his brief period in Congress, but it would cost him dearly. His term was dogged by allegations that he was, in reality, a representative of the Republican elite in Washington, where he maintained a home, rather than of the Fourth District, where blacks struggled to hold on to basic citizenship rights. And there was more. While in Congress he introduced a joint resolution to amend the United States Constitution to place federal elections under the control of Congress, provided, however, that those who "cannot read and write the English language" would be barred from the polls. It was a compromise proposal. Federal supervision was anathema to white southerners, while the literacy requirement, even if enforced properly, would fall most heavily on black voters, although not on those of Langston's class. An aging Douglass used that concession to get in one last shot at his rival. The old abolitionist publicly denounced Langston and accused him of proposing to "limit suffrage to the educated alone." Langston, he charged, was "very learned, very eloquent and very able" but had taken leave of his senses. "Much learning has made [him] mad," he fumed.[27]

Langston had conceded something he had spent his entire adult life defending, although he still sometimes spoke of suffrage as a natural right of manhood. That concession was more than a simple accommodation to the desires of a society bent more and more on relegating its black citizens to second-class status. For Langston, it was a direct outgrowth of a tension that he had papered over for three and a half decades, ever since he had been admitted to the bar as a white lawyer. As a successful black lawyer in a white world, he had always been torn between conflicting expectations that he speak to whites and be the authentic representative of blacks. Now he beat a hasty retreat from the conflict. His service in Congress over, he would retire to a cottage that he had built near Howard University, to practice a bit of law and work on his memoirs. Long after his death in 1897, a gathering at the Langston home each year would still mark the beginning of the social season for Washington's colored aristocracy. In spite of himself, he had become a representative man.[28]

Racial "Progress" in an Era of Segregation

In April of 1904, Robert Terrell, a well-known Washington lawyer and judge, along with over a hundred "representative colored men," as he called them, gathered in the Old Senate Chamber of the Capitol building, where the Supreme Court then heard its arguments. They stood and sat uneasily, facing the justices. The crowd spilled over into the Capitol Rotunda, with those who could not make it into the packed chamber represented by the black luminaries inside. "Never before had so large a number of colored men and women attended a session of this national tribunal," Terrell wrote of the gathering. (Apparently women could be representative men, too.) They included the register of the United States Treasury, the District of Columbia recorder of deeds, a former state governor, two local judges, several Howard University professors, and a host of others. What brought them there were two cases that challenged the Virginia State Constitution of 1902, which, through a variety of subterfuges, was designed to eliminate black voters from the polls. The audience that had gathered to listen to what the justices had to say was "composed mostly of colored men and women, modestly but well dressed, well behaved, thoughtful, intelligent people." They would soon be disappointed. Three weeks later, the Court handed down a pair of decisions, ruling that since the contested election had already taken place and the victors had been seated in Congress, there was nothing more for it to do. A quarter century earlier, people like Terrell would have come to the Court brimming with confidence in their natural rights as free American citizens. Now they were reduced to making the case with their mere physical presence, which attested to "the splendor of the progress and attainments of the Negro," as Terrell put it. The justices were unmoved by that impressive display, but perhaps others might be.[29]

The events which brought Terrell to that unhappy conclusion had been in motion for a quarter century, and they marked a turning point in the story of representation. In the South, the population of black lawyers—always an index to the strength of black citizenship claims—had waxed and was now on the wane. Even after the close of Reconstruction, black southerners had continued to vote and hold political office until the end of the nineteenth century, and their lawyers continued to prosper after a fashion. A new group of lawyers had come to the bar in the 1880s. They were mostly native southerners who had often been born into slavery or were one generation removed from bondage, and had acquired sufficient education to study for the bar. Some attended the short-lived black law schools that cropped up throughout the South. Others went to Howard or to northern institutions, given that the mainstream law schools in the South were generally closed to them. In an era when one could still become a lawyer by "reading law"—private study with an experienced practitioner—some pursued a path similar to that of Thomas Calhoun Walker of Gloucester County, Virginia. The formerly enslaved Walker persuaded a former Confederate major to train him in law, so long as the would-be lawyer promised to "let those devilish politics alone." Walker and most others heeded that advice, and began to focus on practicing law, although many continued to hold low-level elective office.[30]

This new group of southern lawyers usually set up their offices in areas with large concentrations of black residents. Indeed, to practice in other places was often to put one's life in danger due to enraged local whites. In areas where they were well known, however, many had little difficulty being accepted in court and finding clients. Some, like Walker, and Wilford H. Smith of Galveston, Texas, even earned enough respect to attract white clients. The 1910 census recorded about four hundred black lawyers in the southern region, with large concentrations in Virginia, Oklahoma, Tennessee, and Texas, although census figures somewhat overstate the number of those who were actually members of the bar and practicing. With the hardening of Jim Crow, however, there was a distinct movement toward urban law practice. Cities like Charleston, South Carolina, and Galveston supported active groups of black lawyers well into the twentieth century. In the coming decades the population of black lawyers in the Deep South would shrink to almost nothing, save for a few who persisted in cities like Atlanta.[31]

Those who continued to endure the hardships of life as lawyers in the South often saw themselves as bridgeheads to the white world—a role that Thurgood Marshall would reprise a generation later. Walker recalled that he was perhaps the only person in his local community who could communicate with both angry whites and fearful blacks when an African American was accused of a serious interracial crime. In one typical case involving a black murder defendant, the intrepid

Walker reasoned with a white mob, and cooperated with the local judge and sheriff, to keep the accused man out of the hands of lynchers and get him into court. There, he was "brought in guilty and given the full penalty of the law." In Little Rock, Arkansas, Scipio A. Jones was also ambassador to the white community, although in his case he backed that up with an active civil rights practice. Jones was so well respected by local whites that he was twice elected as a special judge in the local courts. He was known among his contemporaries for having "conducted himself in such a way as not to offend" white judges and jurors. He also had many white friends, including the Progressive-era Arkansas governor George Donaghey. It also helped that the light-skinned Jones was rumored to be the son of a white man who paid for his education.[32]

Oklahoma lawyer Buck Colbert Franklin believed that he had enough influence with local whites to have averted the famous Tulsa Race Riot of 1921, where whites burned down the African American section of the city because of a rumor that a black man had assaulted a white woman. Franklin recalled that, shortly before the riot, he single-handedly dispersed a black mob that was talking about burning white homes in retaliation for what whites were preparing to do. He also heard a white lawyer express doubts as to whether the sexual assault had actually happened, and to the end of his life Franklin regretted that he failed to follow up with his fellow lawyer. "[T]he decent element of the [two] races," he believed, could have gotten together to "nip this trouble in the bud." A. T. Walden, of Macon, Georgia, transferred his practice to Atlanta after World War I, where he became the core of what a recent account calls a "bi-racial elite" of black and white moderates who carefully managed race relations in the so-called "city too busy to hate" for the next four decades. Many of these same lawyers had active civil rights practices and litigated cases up to the appellate courts, notably Walden, Jones, Wilford Smith of Mississippi and Texas, Florida's S. D. McGill, and Maryland's W. Ashbie Hawkins. Such men, however were few and far between.[33]

The future of the African American civil rights bar was clearly in cities outside the South, like New York, Washington, and Chicago. In the North, however, to be a successful black lawyer, one often had to live most of one's professional life among whites. In Boston, for instance, old abolitionists trained black lawyers, who then established offices located downtown and served an interracial clientele, including Irish Democrats. A number, like Harvard Law School graduate William H. Lewis, were elected to office by an overwhelmingly white electorate. In Cleveland, prospective white immigrant lawyers served as apprentices to their more established black counterparts. Chicago's Ida Platt established a real estate and probate law practice in the 1890s and used her fluency in French and German to attract a clientele of European immigrants. Her fellow Chicagoan Edward H. Morris developed such a reputation that he was tapped to defend a former United States senator against serious criminal charges. Washington, D.C. lawyer Charles Houston must have had such relationships in mind when he wrote, in the late 1920s, that "[a]ll of the older lawyers who have made any considerable success in the North directly out of the law have done so out of a white clientele. They have offices in the white business districts, very often have white stenographers, and do not cater to Negro clients."[34]

At the turn of the century, an ambitious young man named Robert Abbott sought out the help of one such lawyer—his fellow Chicagoan, Morris. For his efforts, the young Abbott received the advice that he was "a little too dark to make any impressions on the court in Chicago." Abbott would go on to found the *Chicago Defender,* one of the country's leading black newspapers, instead. By that time, a studied racial ambiguity often seemed to be a prerequisite for a black person who wanted to make a successful career of law. Chicago lawyer Ida Platt was so light-skinned that, after the city celebrated her 1894 bar admission as a breaking of race and gender barriers, she slowly slipped out of the consciousness of the city's black community and ended her life as a white lawyer. Boston's William H. Lewis so resembled the whites around him that a Harvard alumni publication had to identify him for its readers in an old sepia-toned photo of Lewis and his white teammates on the university's football team. Gaius Bolin of Poughkeepsie, New York, the city's first black lawyer, was of partial Indian descent and married a white woman, as did his brother. Bolin's multihued family prompted perplexed stares as they walked the streets of their small northern city. All those things helped him draw a white clientele to his firm and eventually cap his career by being elected president of the local bar association. Even Raymond Pace Alexander claimed descent from a white slave-owning grandfather who held his own sons (Alexander's father and uncle) in bondage in Virginia until Union troops arrived during the Civil War.[35]

Washington, D.C., with its social segregation and its opportunities for black advancement, was the crossroads of these southern and northern trends, and no figure better exemplified that fact than Judge Robert H. Terrell. The 1884 Harvard College graduate had earned his LL.B. and LL.M. at Howard Law School and had set himself up as a lawyer and later as the principal of the prestigious M Street High School in Washington. He married Mary Church, the Oberlin-educated daughter of Robert Church Sr., the biracial Memphis businessman who had been born a slave in Mississippi. In 1901, Terrell secured a breakthrough appointment, with Booker T. Washington's help, as a judge of the District of Columbia police court, which had recently been elevated to a regular court staffed by lawyers and judges.[36]

After several years in his new position, Terrell struggled to explain his success in a post where he had to preside over whites in a segregated city. "[T]act and good judgment" were the main requirements for success, he concluded—"elements without color and without racial identity." At a banquet in his honor, Terrell told his black audience that he had "the good sense to meet in the proper spirit the many delicate situations peculiar to the courtroom." His own success was just one more step toward equal citizenship rights, he argued. "In this century the Negro must prove that he is equal in every particular to the demands and requirements of American civilization." And Terrell could offer no better proof than to make whites aware of persons like himself. "[A]t this period in our development," he concluded, black Americans needed to have "all of our best and ablest men and women . . . brought in contact in one way or the other with the men and women of the white race who own and control large business enterprises." Only in this way, he believed, could public sentiment be altered such that his race would achieve its proper due. His own humble service as a lawyer and judge, he believed, was a small but exemplary step in that direction.[37]

Terrell's prominence in law brought him face to face with the dilemma of representation. His own complexion, education, and ability to interact with whites in a segregated world placed him among "our best and ablest men and women," as he called them. Terrell, who was now the most prominent black lawyer in the land, spoke of duties rather than rights when talking about black citizenship, and of the hard work that African Americans were doing to demonstrate their fitness for citizenship. In that respect, he was not alone. In 1913, William Lewis

commemorated the fiftieth anniversary of the Emancipation Proclamation with a speech before the Massachusetts legislature. Half a century earlier, John Rock had appeared before that same body and pleaded
for his race in the language of natural rights. But now times had changed.
Lewis told his white listeners that the Negro "has increased his numbers
nearly threefold. . . . He has reduced his illiteracy to thirty per cent. He
owns nearly $700,000,000.00 worth of property including nearly one
million homes. He has shown that his tutelage in American civilization
has not been [in] vain." A decade later, Philadelphia lawyer John Asbury would appear before the Pennsylvania legislature to argue for a
civil rights bill. "[W]ho are these people that are asking for adoption of
this bill?" he asked rhetorically. "They are a people with a population
of four million in this country fifty years ago and today are a population of twelve millions. They are people whose percentage of literacy fifty
years ago was three percent, and today it is seventy-eight percent."[38]

"Progress" was the watchword in this new rhetoric of civil rights.
Black lawyers talked endlessly about the progress that the Negro had
made, as if by repeating the statistics on literacy rates, property ownership, and population growth over and over again, they could finally
convince their fellow white citizens, and themselves, that the country
was on the path to racial equality. Even Langston had joined in with
the new rhetoric of progress in the last decade of his life. When over one
hundred "representative colored men" gathered at the Supreme Court
in 1904 to show the justices the "progress" of the Negro, as Terrell put
it, they were simply making perhaps the only argument left to them in a
nation that, for the most part, seemed to have stopped listening.[39]

To focus on "progress" and "representative Negroes" as a civil rights
claim was to make the mere existence of the black lawyer into a potent
argument for equality. In no place was this more true than in public
accommodations and public space—restaurants, theaters, social clubs,
swimming pools, amusement parks, hotels, and other public places
where people might have cross-racial contact. The biracial Los Angeles
lawyer Loren Miller, for instance, was born near an Indian reservation
and raised in Kansas and Nebraska. Miller recalled that "I learned about
segregation at college." Growing up, he was somewhat conflicted about
his racial identity—that is, until he came to the University of Kansas.
"Negro students couldn't play on the athletic teams; they couldn't swim
in the pool; they couldn't attend class parties." "I went to college an

American," he recalled, but "I emerged a Negro." Miller acknowledged that his upbringing was atypical, but his method of learning about race, he believed, was not. Once he became a civil rights lawyer, he put that belief into practice; one of his first cases involved two black men who were turned away from a lunch counter.[40]

New Jersey's Robert Carter remembered that his first civil rights protest occurred when he jumped into his high school pool after hearing about a court ruling that public pools had to desegregate. He couldn't swim and held on to the side of the pool "for dear life," but he had made his point. Philadelphia's William Coleman began his auto-biography by noting that he grew up in "the sheltered comfort of a middle-class family" and that one of his first encounters with "Yankee-style racism" happened when his high school eliminated the swim team rather than let him into the pool. Chicago lawyer Truman Gibson met his future wife when she sought his legal counsel after being turned away from a Greek restaurant. He won both the case and the heart of his future spouse. Philadelphia lawyer John Asbury sparked a decade-and-a-half of lawsuits and agitation by local African Americans over the humiliating treatment he received when he arrived to take his seat at the opening of a new Center City theater in 1921.[41]

The origin stories that northern black lawyers told about their own civil rights advocacy were often stories of public accommodations, but their subtext was representation. Philadelphia lawyer Sadie Alexander, for instance, recalled that the source of her "interest in better race relations" lay in incidents like one that she and her future husband, Raymond, experienced in college in the late 1910s. It began when she and Raymond, who were both attending the University of Pennsylvania, decided to go on a double date to a performance at the Shubert Theater with another black couple, one of whom attended Penn and the other Cornell. Raymond's male friend, who "was fairer than Raymond[,] and I suppose if you just passed him by you wouldn't know whether he was colored or not," went to the theater to pick up the tickets for the four of them without incident. When the two couples arrived for the performance, however, theater personnel told them that they had the wrong tickets and turned them away. It wasn't the first time such a thing had happened, and the four improvised a response on the spot. Each began speaking a foreign language. "Raymond was more fluent in Spanish than he was in French. I was more fluent in French. And my friend was very good in German." The manager, who didn't understand any of it, finally remarked "they're not niggers" and let them in. Alexander and her future husband learned fast, and by the time that they began practicing law in the mid-1920s, their standard method for convincing skeptical whites to desegregate downtown theaters, restaurants, and hotels involved black plaintiffs who seemed as much like whites as possible. It began with three "very refined young colored women, school teachers in the Philadelphia public schools," who provided Raymond with his first victory as a civil rights lawyer when he broke the color line at the Aldine Theatre in 1925.[42]

That victory was an outgrowth of Raymond Alexander's first major civil rights controversy, which took place while he was still in law school at Harvard. In the early 1920s, a small number of black graduate students began to study there, and many would go on to have careers as important civil rights figures, including future NAACP lawyer Charles Houston; future Justice Department Civil Rights Division lawyer Maceo Hubbard; Jesse Heslip, who would go on to serve on the NAACP's National Legal Committee; and Alexander himself. What held that small group of students together, initially at least, was the Harvard Negro Club, later renamed the Nile Club—the campus black student group that Houston helped organize in the early 1920s. From all appearances, the Nile Club was a paper organization, with a few formal meetings and dues payment constituting its main activity. What it needed was a purpose, and almost inevitably, that purpose was supplied by a controversy involving public space.[43]

Harvard's administrators unintentionally gave its small black student group an additional reason for being, and sparked a national debate, when they made dormitory residence compulsory for freshmen in the mid-1910s and barred black students from living there. There was little organized opposition to the policy until the fall of 1921, when five black freshmen were admitted to Harvard and three of them applied for dormitory residence and were turned down. That decision sparked a letter-writing campaign by black and white alumni, which soon spilled over into the popular media. Harvard's president, A. Lawrence Lowell, wanted to compel everyone (except black students) to live in the dormitories to break down ethnic and social class distinctions among students. This effectively made the dormitories public space—places that anyone who was admitted to the university expected to enter. Somewhat paradoxically, Lowell defended race exclusion on the same basis: that "we have not thought it possible to compel men of different races to reside together." The exclusion policy was inevitably linked to Lowell's contemporaneous push to impose a quota capping the number of Jewish students at the university. Lowell defended the quota as necessary to prevent Harvard's New England culture from being overwhelmed by those who did not share in it.[44]

If culture supplied the terms of the debate, then it would also provide the means for the black students to fight back. Led by Raymond Alexander, now president of the Nile Club, and Houston, the black student group found its purpose. The members organized and confronted Lowell on campus, but failed to get him to change his mind. The Nile Club eventually took its protest to the public in the pages of the Urban League's journal, *Opportunity,* in an essay authored by Alexander.[45]

The article was Alexander's first piece of civil rights advocacy directed to a national audience. It was titled "Voices from Harvard's Own Negroes" and presented itself as an encapsulation of the debates that had thus far taken place inside the black student group. It began with a somewhat pretentious quotation from speech given at Harvard by the former secretary to former British prime minister David Lloyd George, and a detour into the formal logic behind Lowell's decision. But it hit its stride when Alexander turned to perhaps the most potent argument for nondiscrimination in the dormitories. It was the five black freshmen themselves. With evident pride, Alexander noted that they came from "very representative Negro families." Their presence at Harvard, he argued, attested to the "social progress of the Negro students." Their fathers included a physician, graduates of Yale and Harvard, and a prominent Boston lawyer. Alexander spent considerable time educating his readers on the background and family history of men who, outside of the rarefied circles of the black aristocracy, remained unknown to most of the American public. "It is probably fair to conclude," he continued, "that no half dozen men picked at random among the Harvard freshmen class could present any better family history or training." In fact, "a great deal of the public sympathy with the Negro on this issue, and popular support, may be directly traceable" to the students' family backgrounds. Just as his broadside went to press, the public outcry had its intended effect. The university's governing body ruled that no one could be "excluded by reason of his color" from the dormitories, but also that "men of the white and colored races shall not be compelled to live and eat together." Most observers hailed it as a reversal of Lowell's policy.[46]

Alexander believed that he and his fellow black students had given a full answer to Lowell's objectionable policy, but his essay raised as many questions as it answered. The students' ticket for admission to the segregated dormitories was their membership in "very representative" black families. It was a variant of the strategy that would win Alexander his first civil rights case as a practicing lawyer. But no one seemed to know exactly what that phrase meant, including Alexander himself. The essay explicitly distinguished the black students from what he called "the middle or working class of people" who made up the bulk of the black population in Cambridge. In explaining why the freshmen could not just board with local blacks, he claimed that locals weren't used to taking on boarders, and "where board can be got" there was also "the striking lack of unwholesomeness [*sic*] of the food and culinary art in its preparation." As Alexander presented them, the students represented the best of the elite white culture that Lowell wanted to preserve. But "representation" certainly did not mean that one longed to be white. Indeed, one of Alexander's favorite rhetorical devices as a practicing lawyer was to merge his presence in court with that of "[t]he four hundred and fifty thousand colored people of this State," who, he constantly reminded his white listeners, stood metaphorically just outside the courtroom.[47]

Two decades earlier, a group of representative Negroes had gathered in the Capitol with nothing but their mute bodies to present to the Supreme Court justices as proof of their capacity for full citizenship; but as the 1920s dawned, a new group of young race leaders moved out into the world with words and ideas to back up their civil rights claims. Those words were buttressed by the little-known state civil rights statutes that guaranteed nondiscriminatory access to public accommodations in many northern cities, and provided lawyers like Raymond Alexander and Chicago's Earl Dickerson with their first victories as lawyers for their racial group. They were buttressed, as well, by a powerful idea that had taken hold at the turn of the century. It was an idea that caused lawyers like Robert Terrell, who in his youth spoke forcefully in the language of natural rights, to turn in his mature years to the duties of a responsible citizen. Where equality had once seemed like the natural inheritance of all Americans regardless of race, now it seemed to turn on the existence of representative men, and women, whose progress provided the opening wedge for civil rights claims in the new century. Where representative Negroes might lead, perhaps an entire race might follow. In that respect, these lawyers were truly the descendants of the man Alexander claimed as his professional ancestor: John Mercer Langston.

At the turn of the century, Detroit lawyer David Augustus Straker had called Langston "the *paterfamilias* of the Negro lawyers in America," and indeed he was. Langston's life and career encapsulated the tension that would attach itself to black lawyers even a half century after his death. To be a successful black attorney, one often had to practice a studied racial ambiguity in a society bent more and more on establishing clear lines between black and white. Law was different from other lines of work for members of an insular minority group. Unlike the challenges faced by a doctor, a teacher, or even a college professor, the early life lesson that Langston learned in Ohio's Western Reserve was that a black lawyer had to make a way in a profession where one had to speak a language that whites could understand. Judges, jurors, and just about everyone who had power in the legal system were white, as they would be for the next century. Speaking that language, paradoxically, gave one a claim as an authentic leader among blacks—a representative of one's race.

Who was the representative Negro? It was the black person who crossed racial lines, and often shook up the expectations of a segregated society. It was an African American whose formative experience with race came in an encounter with segregated public space. It was also—on many occasions—a black person who was as unlike the rest of his race as possible. A segregated society often demanded that representative Negroes be racially ambiguous. But that society also demanded more. It required that they be authentic representatives of those who would never be allowed into Harvard, or the Aldine Theatre, or the Supreme Court's hallowed space. It was an experience fraught with deeply conflicted emotions and desires. Langston eventually gave up trying to solve that problem and spent his last years immersed in his gardens and the memories of his youth. It was a problem that he would bequeath to his professional descendants.

2

Racial Identity and the Marketplace for Lawyers

IN AUGUST of 1929, C. Francis Stradford, president of the National Bar Association (NBA), the black lawyers' professional group, delivered his farewell address at the bar group's annual meeting. The Chicago lawyer would later come to national prominence as a member of the legal team that took the well-known restrictive covenant case, *Hansberry v. Lee*, all the way to the Supreme Court. As one might expect, Stradford told his fellow black attorneys that "[l]awyers need have no fear of championing human rights," but he also added that "[a]ll history attests that such efforts have brought fame, distinction, [and] often wealth and power." Stradford noted that "[p]articipation in civic and social movements will give to the lawyer invaluable and unpurchaseable publicity. In short it will sell him to the people." Jesse Heslip, after becoming NBA president in 1931, likewise urged his fellow lawyers to do public service work for their personal benefit, so that they could get behind "a constructive program from which they, themselves, will reap large benefits as individuals and as members of the bar."[1] Three years later, NAACP lawyer Charles Houston advised his young protégé Thurgood Marshall that desegregation work might redound to the benefit of Marshall's paying client base: "You can get all the publicity from the N.A.A.C.P. work but you have got to keep your eye out for cashing in."[2]

At the beginning of their careers, three of the most important black lawyers of the post–World War I era had merely noted what would seem obvious to any casual observer of the civil rights politics of that time. High-profile antidiscrimination work had cash value, as Houston put it—sometimes in monetary terms, and always in terms of the prestige and social standing that defined race and professional identity in America. In taking on important cases, a black lawyer represented not only individual clients but also the aspirations of an entire race. Grateful African Americans, Houston and his fellow black lawyers were pointing out, might respond in kind with the thing that these lawyers desperately needed to survive—money, or perhaps at least social status that would allow them to attract more paying clients.

The postwar era marked a break from the past in the nation's civil rights history. For the first time, a large number of black attorneys could hope to represent their fellow African Americans in the conventional sense of lawyers representing clients. In the coming decades, many of them would become well-known civil rights lawyers. But there was one problem, they told themselves over and over again. It was the central problem of representation that went all the way back to the time of John Mercer Langston. In the minds of most African Americans, they believed, the ideal lawyer—the true representative of their race in its everyday legal battles—was a white man. As ever, black lawyers found themselves in an in-between space, caught at a boundary line that was supposed to mark off one racial group from another.

A Marketplace for Black Lawyers

Success in the marketplace for lawyers, rather than civil rights advocacy, was the principal way for African American lawyers to represent their race during the 1920s. The main reason for this was the migration of African Americans out of the rural South, which accelerated during World War I. As the migrants went north and west, the nation's black bar went with them, and began to grow at an unprecedented rate. The total number of black lawyers in the nation jumped 22 percent from 1910 to 1920, and by almost a third during the next decade, reaching a temporary peak of 1,247 in 1930. The new black lawyers typically lived in cities—Philadelphia, Chicago, Washington, and others.[3]

Early twentieth-century black lawyers sensed that their lives were embedded, for the first time in their history, in the market for law work. Charles Houston noted that "[t]he recent war with its shift of population and greater distribution of wealth among Negroes marks the

entrance of the Negro, and hence the Negro lawyer, into the field of business in large numbers." More migrants meant more accused criminals
to defend, more wills to draft, more divorces to broker, more small business matters to handle, and more opportunities to go to court, at least
as an aspiration. As Houston remarked, "the great improvement in the
position of the Negro lawyer is due to the large practice he has picked up
from the Southern migrant Negro. The Southern Negro . . . has pointed
the way to the Northern Negro in conferring patronage upon the Negro
lawyer."[4]

If these New Negro lawyers depended on clients for their livelihoods, a newfound hardening of racial barriers ensured that these
clients would be almost exclusively black. The world of the turn-of-the-
century black lawyers who lived their professional lives among whites
was rapidly fading away by the 1920s. In Cleveland, where black lawyers had once been partly integrated into the white world, now they found
themselves relegated to an overwhelmingly black clientele and had their
offices in African American districts rather than downtown. In Chicago,
Earl Dickerson practiced with Edward Morris, the dean of the black Chicago bar, in his early years as a lawyer but could not replicate Morris's
success in attracting prestigious white clients to his firm. By that time,
the light-skinned lawyer Ida Platt had been nearly forgotten by the
city's black community. Boston's white voters had long ceased their former habit of electing black lawyers to public office. The last one, William H. Lewis, had won election to the state legislature in 1902. Lewis's
mode of being a lawyer was one that would remain closed to the black
bar for another half century, until the election of Edward Brooke as Massachusetts attorney general and later to the Senate signaled the return
of that state's long tradition of electing racially ambiguous black lawyers to office.[5]

In the early twentieth century, race consciousness was the order of
the day for the nation's black lawyers. Their numbers grew like never
before. They sold their services in a newly created market of potential
African American clients. At the same time, what it meant to be a black
lawyer was limited like never before to a world bounded by race. An
index to all these trends was the formation of black bar associations by
lawyers who were excluded from, or unwelcome in, the white ones,
in migration-era Chicago (1914), Washington, D.C. (1916, 1925), Detroit

(1918), Cleveland (c. 1918), Baltimore (1921), St. Louis (1922), Indianapolis (1925), Philadelphia (1925), and Harlem (1926), as well as the National Bar Association (1925). In Baltimore and Chicago, the white bar associations even delegated disciplinary duties for black lawyers to their African American counterparts.[6]

During the 1920s, a new generation of black lawyers latched on to one of the oldest dreams of the American bar—that becoming a lawyer could be a route to success in life for a young man (or perhaps a young woman) of ambition and talent. But for them, that dream was based on a potential, rather than actual, thriving black client base. Earl Dickerson vividly remembered his first encounter with Chicago's black lawyers. They were his co-workers holding down the night shift at the post office while picking up what practice they could during the day. Dickerson found postal work so disheartening that he abruptly quit, and vowed that if he ever became a lawyer he would avoid that fate at all costs. Black graduates of even the most prestigious law schools could expect no jobs in white law firms, while Houston reported that "I do not know of any [black law] office available which has practice enough to justify employment of a law clerk . . . at a living wage." Most black law firms consisted of two or more lawyers who shared office space but not profits, and had little extra business to give to an inexperienced lawyer.[7]

Even those lawyers who were lucky enough to have their own firms could often barely support themselves at the practice of law. Middle-class black clients regularly turned to white lawyers with their important work, and in many cities black lawyers made do with part-time practice and the government jobs that Dickerson found so disheartening. It was a common practice for them to depend on their spouses, who often worked as schoolteachers, to provide a steady income—a circumstance that would persist into the 1950s. The process varied a bit from city to city. Chicago's large black lawyer population was nurtured by the growing black political power that provided jobs as salaried government lawyers. In Baltimore and Washington, clerical jobs provided the mainstay of support for many part-time practitioners. In Philadelphia, where government jobs were fewer and political opportunities relatively scarce, the black bar grew at a glacial pace. The result, however, was the same. For the nation's black lawyers, reliance on the rough-and-tumble of law work left them poorer than even the white ethnic lawyers who had once served as their predecessors' apprentices. Idealistic dreams helped draw African Americans into law, but in practice law often seemed to promise nothing more than a life of financial distress and dependence.[8]

Stories of Upward Mobility

The self-styled leaders of the black bar practiced in a world that produced an intense need to explain—both to themselves and especially to a black public whom they yearned to represent—how immersion in the market could be an experience of upward rather than downward mobility. Many of them drew on the standard narrative of the self-made man, a common enough American archetype that middle-class black men appropriated for themselves in this period.[9] In fact, Raymond Pace Alexander's and Charles Houston's abilities to explain market success would make these young lawyers into the most influential black attorneys in the country by the end of the 1920s.

Born in Washington, D.C., in 1895, Houston seemed to enter life already immersed in the story of the market. Three years before Charles's birth, his father, William LePre Houston, had received his law degree from Howard University. Over the next two decades, the elder Houston would claw his way up from a position as a government clerk to a career as a successful practicing lawyer and a part-time instructor at Howard Law School. He sent his son to Washington's segregated M Street High School, one of the best high schools in the country, and then on to Amherst College, where Charles earned a Phi Beta Kappa key and graduated in 1915. William taught his son the story of the self-made man by example. He was a stern taskmaster and forced young Charles to submit a detailed budget and justify every expense during his college years, even objecting that his son had spent fifty cents rather than twenty-five on sock garters. After serving as an army officer during World War I, Charles entered Harvard Law School, where he became the first black student selected as an editor of the *Harvard Law Review* before graduating in 1922. He stayed on at Harvard and wrote a thesis for his S.J.D. degree (1923) on the scope and powers of the emerging administrative state.[10]

After studying in Spain for a year, Houston returned to Washington, D.C., in 1924, where he joined his father's law firm and taught part time at Howard Law School. It was a comfortable enough life, but the younger Houston was restless. At Harvard, he had come under the influence of proto–Legal Realist professors Roscoe Pound and Felix Frankfurter, who urged him to apply social science methods to the study of law. In 1927, he obtained a grant from the Laura Spelman Rockefeller Memorial and began an empirical study of the status of the African American legal profession. The following year he would complete several drafts of a report that offered his initial thoughts on the past and future of his chosen profession.[11]

Houston interviewed black lawyers from around the country for his 1928 report and captured their aspirations, and his own, in writing up his findings. The report is sometimes cited as a first draft of a program for civil rights lawyering. Yet desegregation litigation received nary a mention in the document, save one or two brief commendations of lawyers who took on "case[s] of discrimination or oppression" and legal aid for the indigent. The obsession that pervaded the piece, rather, was mere survival. Houston had good reason for this focus. His own law practice didn't produce enough income to be his primary means of support. The majority of black lawyers he interviewed for the report were in similar or worse shape, and in the conclusion of his report he defined his subject matter, appropriately, as "the hardships of the Negro lawyer in practice." Houston's report incorporated the standard black middle-class rhetoric of the period, arguing that the solution to the problem of survival lay in the development of bigger and better black businesses. His main focus in the report was the challenge of getting black lawyers to service those businesses. As business rose to new heights, he predicted, black lawyers would rise with it. For Houston, it was a program that ensured his own social mobility at least. His research stimulated his interest in reforming the curriculum at Howard Law School, and one year after finishing the report, he was appointed vice-dean, and de facto head, of the nation's largest producer of black lawyers.[12]

Houston's transformation of Howard law into the training ground for lawyers like Thurgood Marshall is a well-known story. It has been written into the American legal imagination as a modern-day civil rights project through the recollections of Marshall and others, remembering back in the decades after *Brown*. Houston closed the night school, required full-time study, increased the standards for admission, and created the institution that would educate many future NAACP lawyers. Yet if Houston imagined that he was creating a school of civil rights

lawyers whom he expected to work a revolution through reform litigation, he failed to mention that goal in his extensive public and private
writings from the period, which document the transformation. Indeed,
one year earlier, when thinking about the new black lawyer that a transformed law school would produce, he had written that "[i]t is not my
idea that such a man would go into his community and proceed to dic-
tate a solution of the race question." Instead, he would

> move about in the courts and the community—just doing his routine
> professional work—he would be a bulwark of community strength and
> solidarity. Then as he gained the respect and confidence of the commu-
> nity, he could whittle away on the immediate concrete local problems
> of the mixed community life: better schools, improved streets, specific
> abuses of justice, and so forth.

Contrary to popular belief, Howard Law would not add its famous course
in civil rights law until several years after Houston had left Howard for
a position at the NAACP, and over half a decade after Marshall had
graduated. Houston returned to Howard and taught the course several
years after its introduction. Howard's transformation into a laboratory
for civil rights work began in 1933, two years after Houston had announced that his reform program was complete. It started when NAACP
head Walter White began to seek out Houston's assistance with the organization's legal matters, and Houston in turn began to rely on his students, including Thurgood Marshall, for help. Still, the change of direction proved controversial. At one point, Houston's students began to
complain publicly that his busy schedule of civil rights activities was
distracting him from the practical work of overseeing the training of
lawyers at Howard.[13]

At Charles Houston's law school, one did not learn to be a civil
rights lawyer. That development would come later, after he was no longer vice-dean, when Howard introduced its civil rights course and began to supply materials and student support for the NAACP's Supreme
Court litigation. Houston fully endorsed that change, and indeed he
took the first steps that would usher it in during his last two years at his
post. His evident passion—that black lawyers should work to advance
the race rather than serving the status quo—showed itself in almost everything he wrote and did at Howard, but that passion ran along chan-
nels that simply did not map to modern distinctions between civil rights

lawyering and the ordinary business of practicing law. Indeed, one year into his own law school studies, Houston had explored the possibility of transferring out of law entirely and entering the Harvard Business School.[14]

Once ensconced as vice-dean at Howard law, he argued that the purpose of what he called the "functional teaching of law" was to prepare his students for the pragmatic challenges of succeeding at the everyday work that was desperately needed in helping to improve the status of African Americans. Houston planned an experimental criminal law laboratory and a course in psychiatry. In 1933, he set out his grand vision of reform for Howard in a memorandum to Mordecai Johnson, the university's president. Arguing that "[l]aw cannot be separated from government and business," Houston proposed that Howard's law school, its commerce and finance department, and its government department be combined into "one big school" with a unified course of study. In fact, the only major curriculum reform to emerge from Houston's vice-deanship was an overhaul of its business law offerings, inspired by the scholars belonging to the Legal Realist movements at Yale and Columbia. What Houston wanted to explain and demonstrate during his years at Howard was how to give the black lawyer what he called "the dignity of independence which unquestioned professional competence would give." Independence and competence were the watchwords of Charles Houston's generation—necessary components for success in a world in which the very idea of the black lawyer was being reconstructed from the ruins of its nineteenth-century origins.[15]

Raymond Pace Alexander, like his friend and former Harvard Law schoolmate Houston, also rode the market for lawyers to a position at the pinnacle of the black bar. Alexander's precipitous rise in status was a testament to his success in speaking to the deepest anxieties of his fellow lawyers. Indeed, it explains the most unlikely triumph of his early career as a lawyer—his election to the presidency of the black lawyers' professional group, the National Bar Association.

Alexander had been born in Philadelphia in 1897 to a formerly enslaved father who ran a livery stable and a mother who died in his youth. He set himself on a path to better things when he excelled at the city's elite public school for boys, Central High School. Even as a young man, the tall, lanky, and extremely loquacious Alexander made a strong impression on most white observers—a quality that would serve him well as a lawyer. He went on to the University of Pennsylvania, where he met his future wife, Sadie Tanner Mossell (Alexander). The two would marry in the fall of 1923. While attending Harvard Law School, he came under the influence of Pound and Frankfurter, like many black Harvard law students in that period. Following his graduation in 1923, he began practicing law in Philadelphia and quickly prospered. Alexander built a reputation as an accomplished litigator, and by 1928 he ran what was probably the only black law firm in the country that could afford to hire salaried lawyers onto its staff.[16]

Despite his success, Alexander struggled with the common perception that a black lawyer could not be an effective representative of his race in a profession dominated by whites. He used two early cases to work through the perception, and to place himself in a position to aspire to national prominence among the black bar. In the first case, he represented Walter Rounds, a black man accused of attempting to rape a southern white woman aboard an elevator in Philadelphia. Despite exculpatory testimony from white witnesses and allegations of police brutality, Rounds was convicted, sentenced, and shipped off to prison with such unusual rapidity that even a local white newspaper reported that court observers were "bewildered" by the speed of the proceedings. A visibly angry Alexander shouted that "I will reverse you in the Supreme Court" and asked the NAACP's national office to support an appeal and a possible retrial. After initially agreeing to help, the NAACP officials backed away, questioning both his effectiveness in court and the usefulness of a second trial.[17]

His second major case produced a better result. There, he got an acquittal in the headline-grabbing case of Louise Thomas, a black woman accused of murdering her lover, a local police officer. Thomas, as one might expect, hired a white lawyer for her first trial but was convicted and sentenced to death. The death verdict prompted local African Americans to raise money for a defense fund. They convinced Alexander to handle the appeal but asked him to partner with Thomas's experienced trial lawyer. On appeal, the state supreme court ruled that Thomas should get a new trial, because the trial judge had allowed the jury to hear improper character testimony. Thomas's original lawyer abandoned the retrial as hopeless, according to the *Philadelphia Tribune*, and Alexander pushed ahead by himself. He persuaded Thomas to refuse a plea bargain, and got the unexpected acquittal after an emotional argument that his client had acted in self-defense. The courtroom erupted in a raucous celebration, and the *Tribune* sternly editorialized that the result was a signal accomplishment: "NEGRO BUSINESS MEN EMPLOYING WHITE LAWYERS, TAKE NOTICE!"

Alexander had served notice that he was as good as any white lawyer in the city, and that the doors of his firm lay wide open for any black business owner who wanted to walk through them. With the Thomas victory firmly behind him and a growing practice, he felt ready to take on the challenge of becoming the leader of the national bar.[18]

Still, the National Bar Association presidency was a challenge he was not likely to overcome. Despite the name, the organization was anything but national. Founded in 1925 in Iowa, the NBA was essentially a midwestern organization. It usually met in that region, and midwesterners dominated its leadership. At the 1929 convention in Detroit, the usual crowd was in attendance, and NBA president C. Francis Stradford expected to have little trouble handing off the job to his fellow Chicago lawyer William Haynes. Regional blocs often determined outcomes of elections to the presidency, and what would come to be known as the "Stradford machine" was the most powerful bloc. In a surprise move, however, the 1929 meeting elected Alexander as the first easterner to win its presidency—a triumph that seemed so unlikely that nearly five decades later, Sadie Alexander remembered it as "[o]ne of my happiest memories" as a lawyer. In an unprecedented move, the NBA returned Alexander for a second term as president the next year. The Chicago faction boycotted the bar association's activities during Alexander's first year in office. Nonetheless, under his leadership, the NBA would finally live up to its national aspirations by drawing in lawyers from all over the country, and Alexander remained the most influential member of the organized black bar for the next two decades. It was as unlikely a rise in status as any black lawyer could expect in that era, and naturally he interpreted it by filtering his life story through the standard self-improvement narrative.[19]

The key to Alexander's triumph in the face of the Chicago machine was the speech he gave at the 1929 convention. Like Houston, Alexander told his fellow lawyers that their future lay in the consequences of the Great Migration, which provided the opportunity to build more and larger black business. As a result of these developments, he continued, an African American law firm might easily encounter a variety of clients on the same day: a woman needing a divorce; a man seeking to incorporate a taxi company; a group of people desiring to self-insure; a contractor fired from his building project; a mother needing to get her son out of jail; and a "middle-aged lady in black, with tear-moistened eyes," who had been willed a $50,000 estate. Specialized roles for individual lawyers within a black law firm, he argued, remained the only way to get and keep such a clientele. The lawyers there knew exactly what he was talking about. Probably only one black firm in the country resembled what he had described—his own. In early twentieth-century America, specialized practice was what distinguished wealthy white lawyers from the mass of ordinary practitioners. His speech was, in effect, an invitation for his listeners to dream of joining that elite group of whites, and they accepted.[20]

It was reputation and perception that Alexander sold to his clients, and sold again to his fellow black lawyers at the 1929 NBA convention. By the time of the convention, he had been at work for years on the story that he would so effectively deploy in his NBA speech. In fact, the roots of that 1929 speech can be traced back about half a decade, to an essay that he wrote after only a year or two of practice, titled "A Short Biographical Sketch of the Life of Raymond Pace Alexander, Philadelphia's Young Colored Lawyer."[21] The sketch was probably the first of a series of ghostwritten anonymous articles that emerged from his pen over the next several decades. Alexander developed into a skillful ghostwriter as well as a very good lawyer, and planted articles chronicling his cases, practice, and accomplishments in a wide variety of newspapers.

Alexander's "Short Biographical Sketch" ran to twenty-six single-spaced, handwritten pages. It was narrated not by Alexander, but rather by an anonymous writer who had been told the story by a similarly anonymous black businessman who had heard the story from Alexander. "All my life I have used white lawyers," the businessman began, telling his story through the narrator. A short while earlier, however, while waiting for a case to be called in the Court of Common Pleas, the businessman happened to be in court when a young black attorney began his case against the Philadelphia Rapid Transit Company before Judge Stern. The case involved an assault on a black passenger aboard one of the transit company's trolley cars by an intoxicated white rider.[22]

Raymond Pace Alexander, representing the black passenger, remained calm and confident throughout the proceedings, even after it became evident that the transit company was represented by a white lawyer, that all blacks would be stricken from the jury, and that the transit company's case would be based on the testimony of five white witnesses while Alexander could only rely on his client's testimony and that of two other black passengers. Alexander simply proceeded with his evidence, exposed the contradictions in the white witnesses' stories, and won the case for his client. The businessman was ecstatic, feeling that his "[r]ace had achieved a great victory." The whites in the courtroom complimented Alexander's performance, and then even the judge "paid deference to him." The businessman's interest was piqued because he had been "obsessed with the idea that only a white person could gain the recognition and respect of the court and jury, an idea which so many of our people have cultivated."[23]

Curious about this young lawyer, the businessman decided to visit his office, although it took three visits to meet with him because of the volume of his clientele. It was a Saturday before he finally got a chance to sit down for an extended conversation with the interesting young man. Alexander told him an extraordinary tale of a self-made man—the story of his life. His mother having died in his youth, Alexander remarked, at eight years of age he began selling newspapers before and after school to help lighten his father's financial burdens. Young Alexander subsequently held an assortment of odd jobs, generally beginning work at 5:00 A.M. before school and returning to work once the school day was done. On Saturdays he arrived at the waterfront at 5:00 A.M. to begin work there, and he worked Sunday evenings too until his aunt forced him to reserve Sundays for church obligations. Upon entering Central High School, Alexander found a job in the cloakroom at the opera house. There he met the great opera stars of the day and made the acquaintance of the city's leading citizens, many of whom would make small financial contributions to support his ambitions. Alexander's studies at Central, his work at the opera house, and his years of hard labor among the masses had produced "a young man, with a balanced concept of life, a knowledge of the world, an appreciation of art, [and] an acquaintance with every class of people."[24]

That story of pluck and luck would eventually lead Alexander to a successful career as a lawyer—at least according to the biographical sketch. At the University of Pennsylvania, he kept up a similar grueling schedule of daytime study and night/weekend work at a café. His good fortune continued when, in his senior year, he met the noted lawyer John R. K. Scott, who happened to be eating at the café. Scott inquired about the background of his black waiter and was surprised at his educational accomplishments. Impressed by this and a subsequent meeting, Scott encouraged him to apply to law school and offered him a job in Scott's own office upon graduation. At Harvard Law School, Alexander worked as hard as ever—part time as a teaching assistant in the economics department, and summers as a redcap, while establishing a solid record at the school. A sure sign of his impending success was his marriage, following his graduation, to Sadie Tanner Mossell, daughter of two prominent black Philadelphia families, who had recently earned her doctorate in economics at the University of Pennsylvania.[25]

At the conclusion of Alexander's story, the businessman was impressed. He understood for the first time the secret of Raymond Pace Alexander's success—his common touch, supplemented by his years of training and refinement. These elements had allowed him, at only twenty-seven years of age, to build a "large & lucrative practice," as well as earn the "respect of the bench and bar." Alexander's successes would increase the confidence of the "people of all races, which constitute his clientele[,] not only in his ability but also in the capabilities of Negro attorneys." The most surprising result of the whole affair, thought the businessman, was that "I[,] a hardened advocate of white lawyers[,] take pride in being his client."[26]

How to read this strange essay? Many of its details were almost certainly false, but that fictionalization itself gives a clue to the work the words did in their context. The essay drew on stock narratives of success in the market economy to explain how a black lawyer could prosper when so many were failing. The story of the poor boy who, after the death of a parent, rises to middle-class respectability through chance encounters with influential benefactors and exposure to highbrow culture was a standard trope of Horatio Alger's fiction, which was still common reading for schoolboys of Alexander's era. Alexander's first autobiographical essay immersed him in the core project of the black lawyer in the 1920s, as well as the larger stream of America's cultural history.[27]

Alexander's unlikely climb to the pinnacle of the black bar rested on his ability to show his fellow lawyers how they could dream of representing an expanding black clientele, and the image of the self-made man was key in that process. Other black attorneys also fastened on to that same American archetype. Alexander's friend Earl Dickerson, for instance, a well-known Chicago lawyer, also told an autobiographical story in which several fortuitous patrons appeared at critical moments in his life to ensure his rise from humble origins (for him, in Mississippi) to economic and professional respectability after the death of his father. In one episode, a college professor happened to meet a youthful Dickerson, who was scrubbing steps to pay his keep, and found out that the industrious youth planned to attend a mainly black high school. His newfound patron quickly arranged for him to get a scholarship to an elite private school in Evanston—a city where a "new world" soon opened to him. There, he plunged into an incredible routine of manual work to support himself and lay the groundwork for his future.[28]

Pluck and luck also played a role in the autobiographical tale that William Houston, Charles Houston's father, spun out near the end of his life. According to William, as a young man he was coming home one day soaking wet after falling in the river, but stopped to help out a woman who was trying to hitch up a horse. She turned out to be the wife of a distinguished white lawyer, and gave the earnest young man a dime as well as a job. Her husband loaned him a law book and encouraged him to become an attorney. With the book tucked into his travel bag, he set out for Washington, D.C., with nothing but his dream of becoming a lawyer, taking his first step on the path to a prosperous career marked by hard work, saving, and perseverance.[29]

In the standard self-improvement narratives, the poor boy who rises is self-educated, in contrast to Alexander and his colleagues, who were formally educated, often at some of the most elite universities in the country. Yet even here, Alexander's wife, Sadie T. M. Alexander, supplied a needed modification of the common story. One of her earliest surviving pieces of writing, entitled "The Doom of the Self-Made Man," celebrated the replacement of self-taught doctors, lawyers, and businessmen with elite-trained professionals. A close reading reveals its text to have been lifted from a contemporary article of the same name by Richard Walsh, who was well known for updating the common self-improvement narrative for an era in which university training was becoming the means to rise in status.[30]

The Selling of the Black Lawyer

Alexander and his colleagues relied on the story of the self-made man to make sense of their struggles to represent black clients in a profession dominated by whites, and that marked yet another turning point in the history of the black lawyer. Previously, the standard origin story that successful black lawyers told about themselves involved a high-profile case, an experienced white lawyer, and a courtroom full of white observers who doubted the competence of the African American lawyer. That story made sense in a world where ambitious black lawyers dreamed of representing white clients. By the 1920s, however, that world had fallen apart. Alexander and his colleagues told the same origin story of the breakthrough courtroom case, but with one crucial difference. Now the core audience of potential clients was black, and those black clients desired, most of all, that a white lawyer represent their race.

The most common complaint of early twentieth-century black attorneys was that local black communities desired whiteness in a lawyer. Raymond Alexander's "Short Biographical Sketch," for instance, presented the same common elements one could find in the writings of black lawyers from as far away as Oklahoma, Florida, and New York: a judicial system dominated by whites, the competent black attorney, the less competent white attorney, and the potential black client harboring the mistaken assumption that the white lawyer's influence in the white-dominated system was more valuable than the black lawyer's skill. As Charles Houston would write: "In the past it very frequently happened that a Negro lawyer would make connections with a white lawyer as a sort of protector and adviser, and use the white lawyer to try all his cases." Once cases became important enough to make it to court, even black clients often expected whites to take over.[31]

This was a complaint that went all the way back to the antebellum era, and would carry forward at least to the 1960s, when the Black Panther Party co-founder Huey Newton employed a white lawyer in his famous murder trial, provoking outrage among members of the black bar. But the problem was particularly acute during the Great Migration era, when the dream of social mobility for black lawyers hinged on their ability to hold the core client base of black businessmen, organizations, and middle-class individuals.[32]

In the world of the black lawyer, it was essential to be able to go to court and win to move up to better things in life. These lawyers typically worked their way up from low-level criminal court work to more remunerative practice. As Washington lawyer and judge Robert Terrell reported, "Whatever conspicuous success has come to the Negro lawyer has been though what is known as criminal practice," which, if successful, would lead to "a corresponding increase in that better and more lucrative practice of the Civil side of the Court, where matters involving rights of property and business interests are adjudicated and settled." Houston likewise observed that "the Negro lawyer probably knows more about criminal law than any other branch . . . and perfects and argues his appeal with a view to making a reputation in the community." As far south as Atlanta, A. T. Walden advised his black colleagues to take up court cases for poor defendants, which would provide "excellent practice as well as a means for becoming known to the great body of our people who frequent our criminal courts."[33]

Alexander's victory in Louise Thomas's criminal trial had been just such a reputation-making moment. Even years later, as he would recall, "when it is realized that in 1924 [1925] the public regard for the Negro lawyers was low, the spectacular results obtained in this case were a turning point in the general attitude of the white and Negro population toward the Negro lawyer." Reputation was what drew clients to lawyers, and lifted attorneys into the world of the propertied classes.[34]

W. E. B. Du Bois described the problem quite well in assessing the inability of black lawyers to succeed in turn-of-the-century Philadelphia:

> This failure of most Negro lawyers is not in all cases due to lack of ability and push on their part. Its principal cause is that the Negroes furnish little lucrative law business, and a Negro lawyer will seldom be employed by whites. Moreover, while the work of a physician is largely private, depending on individual skill, a lawyer must have co-operation from fellow lawyers and respect and influence in court; thus prejudice or discrimination of any kind is especially felt in this profession.

Carter G. Woodson put it more bluntly: "In places where Negro physicians and dentists flourish Negro lawyers may starve."[35]

Going to court was simply different from anything else that a black professional might do in the era of segregation. In Philadelphia, Sadie Alexander's uncle, Nathan Mossell, responded to discrimination within the medical profession by starting an African American hospital. The creation of separate black schools within the city's school district served the needs of black schoolteachers who would not be allowed to teach white children. Black ministers presided over black churches. The list goes on. There would be no separate African American legal system for black lawyers, however. Very few black lawyers could prosper without the personal injury cases, high-profile criminal work, and small-claims matters that required an appearance in court. Many subsisted on low-level criminal representation. If they were to thrive, it would be by gaining a degree of recognition and respect from the courts and their clients.[36]

The basic problem of the black lawyer was that success in the market for black clients depended on coming to court, but inside the courtroom they performed under the gaze of whites. Along with the conventional legal services and dollars that circulated in the marketplace for legal services, what also circulated was reputation, perception, and the ability to make connections with those who made the decisions in the legal system. Success in the market could make a black lawyer seem whiter, and paradoxically made black clients more likely to hire them—or so the lawyers imagined. All around them, it seemed, was irrefutable evidence for this proposition. Consider, for example, the fates of four lawyers who began practicing during the 1920s and whose professional worlds intersected: Dallas Nicholas, Charles Houston, Earl Dickerson, and Raymond Pace Alexander. The relative success of each man, in his early years as a lawyer, was defined by the relationship between racial identity and the market.

Baltimore lawyer Dallas Nicholas is someone almost unknown to history, and for good reason. For three decades following his death in 1966, Nicholas's papers lay undisturbed and unwanted in the attic of the building that housed his firm until they were discovered, covered in dust and exposed to the elements, by a graduate student. The papers provide a picture of a lawyer who bravely persisted at the margins of the legal profession, following his graduation from Howard Law School in 1926. He was unable to make it into court much or even to support himself at the practice of law.[37]

Nicholas made his living at office practice—matters that rarely required an appearance in court. He set up his practice in one of the city's two black lawyer enclaves, and probably picked up referrals from other black lawyers in the city. He also did some repeat business for clients and families, and received a steady stream of referrals from his Philadelphia friends, Raymond and Sadie Alexander, when they needed a Baltimore lawyer. Some of his cases barely required the skills of an attorney. In one set of "cases," he negotiated payment schedules for working-class Baltimoreans who had fallen into debt during the Depression. He did personal injury work, but a typical dispute involved an exchange of perfunctory letters with a possible defendant until a standard, modest, settlement was agreed upon. Nonetheless, within his realm of expertise he was an exceedingly competent attorney, and the Alexander firm relied on him for his learned expositions on the latest developments in Maryland law. Such expertise made him little money. His 1941 tax returns, for instance, reported a modest income of $3,805, which seems consistent with what he had made in earlier parts of his career. Most of his income, however, came from activities other than practicing law. His wife's salary as a schoolteacher accounted for about two thousand dollars of his reported income, and real estate holdings accounted for a substantial portion of the rest. One contemporary remembered that Nicholas made much of his money in real estate.[38]

Nicholas rarely came to court and thus lived his professional life behind a veil that marked him off as a member of a separate and unequal part of the bar. He did office practice of a kind that made him into a low-status lawyer. Sadie Alexander, for instance, reported that the men at her law firm considered Nicholas's type of office practice to be "principally bookkeeping . . . which afforded them no opportunity to display their forensic ability before a jury." Even the most successful of Baltimore's office practitioners, Roy S. Bond, who years later was still fondly remembered by older black lawyers in the city for supporting himself on what one called "ninety-nine dollar divorces," remained almost unknown outside Baltimore. Raymond Pace Alexander, the country's best-connected black lawyer, would casually misspell Roy Bond's name as "Barnes" when trying to think of a Baltimore lawyer who did divorce work during the mid-1940s.[39]

Charles Houston, by contrast, entered life as a lawyer with a reputation already made, but he still made little money at his craft. At age nineteen, he had already been written up in *The Crisis,* the NAACP's organ, for his academic performance at Amherst College. He then made history by receiving two degrees from Harvard Law School and becoming the first black editor selected to the prestigious *Harvard Law Review.* His father was already an established lawyer, and he left law school assured of "a desk in my father's office" in Washington, D.C., as he later remembered. Houston's father told him frankly that "your opportunities have been better than mine," but Houston's earnings from his early years of practice were not much different from Dallas Nicholas's. The problem lay in the professional world that his father, William Houston, had created for him. The elder Houston had learned the trade in Chicago from the venerable Edward Morris, who made his reputation defending the city's gambling fraternity. Upon returning to Washington, however, William eschewed criminal work. While his mentor was teaming up with Clarence Darrow to defend future congressman Oscar De-Priest against corruption charges in Chicago, William settled into office practice and low-level courtroom work. Along with his salary as a professor at Howard Law School, it provided a comfortable enough income, and indeed was a safe choice given the political and cultural differences between Morris's Chicago and Houston's Washington, D.C. But it also assured that the world of his mentor remained forever closed to him.[40]

In his early years, Charles Houston practiced within the bounds set by his father. In his first decade as a lawyer, he devoted almost half his private practice to debt collection and trusts and estates work. Almost a third of his remaining work involved real estate practice. The only significant category of work that promised serious courtroom time was civil suits in tort, but even here much is suggested by the fact that Houston found so much commonality between his own practice and Nicholas's that he later sent Nicholas sample forms to be used in personal injury, divorce, and other cases. Even the platform of his father's established practice could not net Houston more than $1,000 in profits per year during his first two years in office practice. Houston was apparently kept afloat by his $1,200 salary as an instructor at Howard Law School and his wife's slightly higher salary as a teacher in the public schools. Not coincidentally, this was very nearly the same financial situation in which Dallas Nicholas found himself in Baltimore. Even Houston's reputation and the platform of his father's practice could not lift him out of the race-defined world of the black lawyer. Houston's patient work in Washington received little notice outside African American circles until the following decade, when courtroom work for the NAACP brought him a public reputation commensurate with his actual skill as a lawyer.[41]

In Chicago, Earl Dickerson had been horrified by the part-time practitioners he met in the post office, but was saved from a similar fate only by the black machine politics and African American businesses that offered a few lucky Chicago lawyers a chance to prosper. Born in Canton, Mississippi, in 1891, Dickerson migrated to Chicago and earned his college degree at the University of Illinois. He served as an army officer during World War I, and graduated from the University of Chicago Law School in 1920. Dickerson opened his law office in 1921 and specialized in civil practice, but his meager earnings from that activity paled in comparison to the salary he received after his political connections earned him a job as an assistant corporation counsel, and later as an assistant attorney general. Like William Houston, he practiced for a short time with Edward Morris. But Morris soon moved on, and with him went Dickerson's chance to trade on the prestige of his experienced colleague. In addition to his government jobs, what saved Dickerson's career as a lawyer was a chance meeting that landed him in a job as the general counsel of the newly formed Liberty Life Insurance Company (later Supreme Liberty Life). The company would become one of the largest black businesses in the country, eventually providing Dickerson with a steady source of income and an institution to call home. He would eventually win election as the president of the National Bar Association and the National Lawyers' Guild, but only after taking an important racially restrictive covenant case to the Supreme Court. His rise to the top of the black bar was testament to his keen intelligence, talent, and grit, but if he had been cast to the fortunes of the market for lawyers, all signs indicate that he would have foundered.[42]

Raymond Pace Alexander, by contrast, showed his colleagues how to succeed in a world where reputation made race and courts made reputations. A key figure in that success was the white lawyer who appeared in Alexander's "Short Biographical Sketch"—John R. K. Scott (although Alexander fictionalized the circumstances of their meeting). Scott gave Alexander his initial training in law practice, but more importantly showed his young black protégé how to make a reputation inside the courtroom. Shortly before Alexander apprenticed in Scott's office,

John Scott took on the case that made his career as a lawyer. He represented a Philadelphia woman who shot her husband and his female stenographer in a jealous rage. Scott's argument in the lurid murder trial—that his client was a helpless woman driven insane by her husband's infidelity—reportedly brought tears to the jurors' eyes during his summation. His client was acquitted, and that made him one of the highest-profile lawyers in the city.[43]

Within three years, Scott's former apprentice won his own career-defining case in defending Louise Thomas against the charge that she had murdered her lover. Not coincidentally, Alexander also painted his client as a helpless pawn of a man and reduced jurors to tears. Twice more, in the ensuing years, Alexander would win a landmark case that replicated his mentor's example. During the succeeding decade, Alexander won an improbable acquittal for two white women who were accused of being part of a ring of "poison widows" who murdered their husbands for insurance proceeds, after the initial defendants all pleaded guilty or were convicted and sentenced to death. A little more than a decade later, he achieved international fame in getting an acquittal for two black youths initially sentenced to death for the murder of a white storekeeper in Trenton, New Jersey. The reputation quickly translated into profits. Within four years of the Thomas acquittal, he reported over $18,000 in profits from his private practice. At that time, by contrast, Charles Houston's practice netted the Washington lawyer only about $2,000.[44]

John R. K. Scott provided the model for Alexander's career, and Alexander, in turn, used that model (and some creative fiction) to rise to the top of the organized black bar by the end of the 1920s. Oddly enough, it was a white attorney who taught Alexander how to dream of representing the aspirations of his fellow black lawyers, and by extension, his entire race. Yet there still remained the question of whether the figure of the white lawyer—present just about everywhere in the world of the black lawyer—remained a help or hindrance in that process. Alexander's "Short Biographical Sketch," for instance, remained at its most opaque at the points where its narrative touched on his emulation of whites.

Alexander, like Dickerson and William Houston, constructed a life story in which fortuitous white benefactors were the key to his success. In his biographical sketch, paternalistic whites intervened at crucial points in his life to give him access to places usually occupied by white persons—from the opera house patrons who contributed toward his studies, to the college professor who arranged for his teaching assistantship, to John R. K. Scott. The role of the most important of them, Scott, lay behind perhaps the deepest layer of fiction and obfuscation in the entire piece. In Alexander's other autobiographical essays, more fortuitous white benefactors would appear. In one story, the principal of Central High School gave him the "thrill of a lifetime" when he encountered a young Alexander shining shoes for a living and told him that he would be awarded a scholarship for college. In another, the Philadelphia opera house manager encountered a malnourished young Alexander selling newspapers and, upon hearing his life's story, offered him his job at the opera. It was the classic story of the self-made man, but Alexander, like his black contemporaries, made it into a potent weapon in navigating the pitfalls of life along the color line.[45]

Throughout his career (and in his biographical sketch) Raymond Alexander would oscillate back and forth between contrasting ideas of racial representation. Sometimes he stated publicly that he was never known as a "Negro" attorney. At other times, he told both blacks and whites that he could stand in for the life experiences and desires of the thousands of poor, rural African Americans who were streaming into Philadelphia. Which one of these stories was true? Both, of course, captured parts of a key tension the pervaded the life of a black lawyer in the early twentieth century. It was a paradox of representation that Alexander could never escape.[46]

By the end of the 1920s, a little-noticed phenomenon was at work in urban black communities throughout the North, and in border-state cities like Washington, D.C. It would alter the nation's civil rights politics in the coming years. A new generation of black lawyers had entered firmly into the market for legal services. They were learning, and teaching their colleagues, the means to achieve success in a world that could not have been imagined by nineteenth-century lawyers like Robert Morris and John Mercer Langston. In the new world of race and lawyers, a black attorney could dream (often only dream) of earning a living from an all-black clientele. Some could now dream, as well, of doing civil rights work as a significant part of their practice. In the coming years, lawyers like Thurgood Marshall, Raymond Pace Alexander, and Earl Dickerson would trade on those dreams to become nationally important civil rights lawyers.

Some things, however, had not changed. Successful black lawyers practiced their trade in a place where all the decision makers—judges, juries, courtroom personnel—would be white. But when they stepped into the courtroom, they yearned to represent—in all senses of the word—their entire race. In a nation more and more intent on drawing the color line, North and South, this relatively small group of lawyers constituted one of the few groups of Americans who found themselves astride a permeable boundary line between two racial groups. They practiced in a world where blacks and whites seemed to want them to be both like and unlike the rest of their race. That conflict would remain unresolved even after they moved out into the world of civil rights law during the next decade, and it would provide the opening wedge for a critique of their efforts that would almost derail them.

3

The Role of the Courtroom in an Era of Segregation

IN THE spring of 1932, a black youth named William E. (Willie) Brown went on trial for murder in a Philadelphia courtroom so fraught with racial and sexual fear that Brown seemed destined for the electric chair, even without the added burden of a black lawyer for the defense. A month and a half earlier, the police had begun "one of the greatest manhunts in the history of the city," according to a local paper, after the sexual assault and murder of Dorothy Lutz, a seven-year-old white girl. Near-panic gripped the section of the city where the murder took place, as fearful parents kept their children indoors. There were no witnesses to the crime, but police picked up Brown when his family—thinking he had no connection to Lutz—reported him missing after he stayed away overnight. After about thirty-six hours in police custody, Brown signed a written confession to the heinous crime.[1] As a dazed Brown arrived at the scene of the coroner's inquest, a "mob gathered around the doorway leading up to the cellroom." It took half an hour for police to clear the crowds so that he could exit the proceeding safely. The local media reported that "a heavy guard of extra police" escorted Brown to his subsequent trial, as unruly crowds began to gather again. By this point, an unlikely figure had entered the story. It was Philadelphia lawyer Raymond Pace Alexander, who, assisted by Robert N. C. Nix, agreed to take on the seemingly hopeless task of defending Willie Brown.[2]

To modern eyes, the image of a black lawyer defending an African American client in a high-profile criminal case seems unremarkable, but that was not so in the 1930s. In fact, Alexander's entry into Brown's case was one important point from which one can date the emergence of the African American civil rights lawyer. Before that time, a defendant like Brown would have wanted, most of all, to be represented by a white lawyer. In a trial where no African American could expect to participate as a judge or juror, hiring a lawyer of his own race would have seemed tantamount to suicide. Law, it seemed, was a white man's profession, as it had always been, and this was particularly so in racially charged cases. In a trial with civil rights implications, only a white lawyer could be an effective representative of African Americans.

Alexander, however, had one thing going for him, and it was the same phenomenon that had allowed an earlier generation of black lawyers to make their livings out of a white clientele. If his race made him an outsider in the courtroom, then the solution to his dilemma was to push back against the bounds of racial identity and convince his white lawyer colleagues and judges that he was, as nearly as possible, one of them. As the Depression decade began, a black lawyer could finally dream of entering the civil rights courtroom as an authentic representative of his entire race, but it would be a black attorney who, as much as possible, seemed like a white lawyer. At the center of it all lay the singular role that the courtroom played in the lives of lawyers living behind the veil of segregation.

Courtrooms as Public Space

Courts occupied a unique place in American life as the world of segregation began to be extended to the North, for courtrooms remained open to the crossing of racial boundaries in a way that most other public places were not. The question of whether race was a barrier to pleading in court had been quickly settled after the Civil War, when black lawyers were admitted to practice in all sections of the country. These lawyers entered a profession that was shedding its aristocratic pretensions and becoming more democratic and easier to join. Even as barriers began to go up again in the early twentieth century, competence and character rather than race or ethnicity remained the only formal requirements, and the profession made no overt distinction between classes of lawyers.[3]

As other public spaces were closed off with the expansion of Jim Crow, and southern law schools shut their doors to African Americans, it was still possible to find black lawyers appearing in court from Maine to Mississippi and from New York to Los Angeles. Surprisingly, most reported little overt unequal treatment in the courtrooms where they regularly practiced. Two decades after his admission as Delaware's first black lawyer, for instance, Louis Redding reported that "I can honestly say that I have never encountered from any judge any overt display of racial prejudice." Although things varied the farther south one went, even in Jackson, Mississippi, one was still quite likely to find a black law-yer making a report like this: "Negro lawyers, of course, actually try cases here in court in some form or another almost daily. White and colored lawyers work amicably together in the same case, although there are quite a few lawyers here who would not try a case with a Negro associ-ate." As late as the 1940s, many southern black lawyers said that they received a remarkable degree of fairness in court in the cities that were often the only safe places for them to ply their trade, although in a few states, such as Mississippi and South Carolina, whites appeared to be de-termined to prevent any more of them from being admitted to the bar.[4]

When black lawyers stepped into the courtroom, they entered a venue where things seemed to happen that simply did not happen in most other places. Consider the following exchange between Raymond Pace Alexander and a white police detective in a murder case in Phila-delphia. Cross-examining the witness, Alexander verbally browbeat the detective, eliciting a staccato drumbeat of "No, sir," "Oh, no sir," "I made a mistake, I think, sir," and "They didn't find anything there, Mr. Alexander." The exchange might seem unremarkable, save for the fact that a few hundred feet away Alexander would struggle to be served a sandwich in downtown Philadelphia, while the detective could claim a customary entitlement to use most public spaces as a matter of course.[5]

In a segregated world, racial identity was defined by one's treat-ment in public space. Even in northern cities, Americans maintained the uneasy boundaries of racial identity through the treatment they accorded to different people in public spaces such as restaurants, the-aters, hotels, and schools. Sadie Alexander, for instance, wrote eloquently of the almost daily insults, exclusions, and reminders she received of her subordinate racial identity in the public places of early twentieth-century Philadelphia. Just trying to get lunch, to board a trolley, or to see a movie in Center City was often a humiliating experience. In the courtroom, however, public space played the opposite role. There was only one class of lawyer, and in court a black lawyer could inhabit a professional role that demanded a type of formal respect accorded to an elite member of society. This was something African Americans could receive almost nowhere else.[6]

Courts were important places for the reimagining of racial identity, for inside the courtroom black lawyers inhabited a public space where words and actions often conformed to a social script. In court, they experienced a world in which forms of address, patterns of deference, and professional acts crossed racial lines, within some limits at least. If public social interaction helped make race, then by appearing in court a black lawyer performed a racial identity that was solely associated with whites in almost every other public place.

Black lawyers imagined that, by coming to court, they could change even the language in which race was spoken about. Baltimore lawyer Dallas Nicholas, for example, roused himself from behind the veil of office practice that walled him off from the white world to mount a rare verbal indictment of one of his colleagues after hearing him use the word "darkey" to refer to a black witness in court. The white lawyer had received a previous warning about the practice from the city's black bar, and Nicholas angrily reminded his colleague that "we are all human and all entitled to courtesy and respect." Chicago lawyer Irvin Mollison devoted one of his few interjections in the restrictive covenant case of *Hansberry v. Lee* to the sly observation that he had no objection to his opposing counsel referring to blacks as Negroes, "as long as you make it very plain [by pronouncing it] with the 'e.'" Mollison's objection helped set off successive rounds of discussion among the lawyers and witnesses on the appropriate racial language to be used in court, culminating in one white witness apologizing for using the term "niggers" in court, even when repeating verbatim an out-of-court statement made by an admitted racist.[7]

Even in the Upper South, black lawyers sensed that by coming to court, they could disrupt the social interactions that helped define race. NAACP lawyer Charles Houston, for instance, treading dangerous ground in a high-profile Virginia case where it was feared his client might be lynched, nonetheless took the time to launch a formal protest against a local judge after hearing him use the word "darkies" in court—an admonition that would have been unthinkable outside the litigation process. Nashville lawyer Z. Alexander Looby recalled that even judges would routinely use the words "nigger" and "darky" in court during the 1920s, but that the practice changed once black lawyers came to court and objected on the record. Raymond Alexander remembered traveling south to represent an African American client who had struck and killed a white child with his car. Needing a local lawyer to move for his admission to practice in the courts, Alexander telephoned a fellow Harvard alumnus, who agreed to sponsor his admission. Upon meeting Alexander, the lawyer was shocked to learn that he would be associating with a black person in public. The professional role of the courtroom lawyer, however, crossed racial lines, and the white lawyer had little choice but to appear alongside his fellow Harvard graduate and move for his admission "in almost inaudible tones," although neglecting to call him "Mister." Alexander eventually negotiated a settlement in the case.[8]

The public scrutiny that came with the entrance of a black lawyer into a courtroom could alter racial interaction even outside the courthouse. In one of Charles Houston's early Virginia cases, a black reporter observed the change that occurred once the Howard vice-dean came to town. "Crowds of rough, unkempt natives gather on the street corners and in the stores" at night, he reported. "Come up behind them and you hear lots of 'nigger this' and 'nigger that.' But let your presence be discovered and a hush envelops them." Although black residents would say nothing publicly about the arrival of the first African American lawyer that locals had ever seen, whites felt it keenly. Pauli Murray also sensed a change in atmosphere outside the courthouse after two black NAACP lawyers appeared in court to represent her when she was arrested for getting into a dispute with the driver of a segregated Virginia bus. After the trial, she boarded another bus to continue to her destination, and happened to get the same driver who had shoved her and used abusive language during their first encounter. Now she reported that he was "the 'epitome' of courtesy," and Murray believed that the change in his language and actions was brought about because of what had happened in court.[9]

The distinctive nature of courtroom interactions helps explain Thurgood Marshall's well-known penchant for the proper observance of lawyers' decorum with opposing attorneys. Robert Carter, Marshall's principal deputy at the NAACP, often found himself puzzled in his early years as a civil rights lawyer when he saw Marshall assume a deep southern accent and an extremely courteous persona when dealing with

opposing lawyers in the South. After a while, the younger lawyer understood that his mentor was simply sticking to the courtroom script that
bound lawyers together regardless of background or position. "[A]lthough
we were on opposite sides . . . we were lawyers representing our clients
and had no personal quarrel with each other," he remembered. Carter
soon began to mimic Marshall's example, "albeit without the Southern
drawl."[10]

Black lawyers reacted with vigor to marked departures from the
courtroom script that defined the most distinctive feature of their professional lives. Pauli Murray, for instance, during a brief stint in Los
Angeles, read a report that a local judge had compared African Americans to "sleek, fat dogs" in court. She immediately confronted the jurist
and obtained a public clarification of the judge's views on proper forms
of racial address in court. The black bar as a whole erupted in outrage
when a Pennsylvania judge, Benjamin Atlee, sentenced a black defendant for attempting to seduce two white girls and warned him in open
court that "[h]ad they [white citizens] lynched you they would have
been justified." The National Bar Association bristled with rage at the
breach of courtroom etiquette and organized protest actions, while
NBA member (and state legislator) Homer Brown petitioned the legislature to impeach Judge Atlee. Raymond Alexander coordinated with
the local and national NAACP to prepare for a hearing in the legislature,
prompting even a white Philadelphia newspaper to call for the jurist's
ouster. A chagrined Atlee eventually made a public apology before the
state legislature.[11]

The racial script of the courtroom did not fit within any fixed idea
of how people should talk to and interact with one another. Instead,
it was improvised on the spot, and emerged from repeated encounters
with the same opponents and allies, with the terms of interaction shifting markedly over time. Despite their urban locations, most of the
nation's black lawyers still practiced in relatively small, inbred legal
communities—at least by modern standards—that could produce striking recurrences of personnel during the course of a lawyer's career. Alexander, for instance, cut his teeth in courtroom practice in John R. K.
Scott's office alongside a young lawyer named Michael A. Musmanno,
as both men negotiated the bounds of race and ethnicity that defined
their respective professional lives. While the two lawyers began their
careers as relative equals, the relationship between the men changed in

successive encounters over the years. Musmanno rose through the white ethnic world to become a nationally known activist for Italian American ethnic pride and a famous state supreme court justice, while Alexander stayed within the black one. Their relationship culminated in the justice's two vigorous lone dissents in favor of Alexander's clients in a landmark school desegregation case during the 1950s. Chicago lawyer Earl Dickerson was bonded to the first Jewish governor of Illinois, Henry Horner, by the ties formed years before when Dickerson was a young lawyer practicing in front of Horner in the probate court. After Judge Horner rose to become the Depression-era governor of his state, Dickerson used their relationship to press the governor into service in support of Dickerson's legal maneuvers that saved the nation's first black insurance company, Supreme Liberty Life, from insolvency.[12]

If black lawyers imagined the courtroom as a space where racial identifications slipped their ordinary bounds, they also claimed that their clients remained oblivious to this fact. Indeed, the supposedly fixed views of black clients toward the work that race did in the courtroom became a staple of their professional talk. Their standard answer to the problem of black client perceptions was to emphasize the competence and skill of the black lawyer, which, they constantly told themselves, would trump the ability of white lawyers to connect with judges and juries. Courtroom work made the black lawyer into a figure with a deeply malleable identity.

One of Thurgood Marshall's many colorful stories of his career as a lawyer involved a lecture he received from a court clerk while in law school. The clerk noted that he could "look at a pleading filed by a lawyer and tell from looking at it whether it was done by a white or a Negro lawyer." This was not true, of course, and the clerk later told him so. Nonetheless, Marshall recalled that "it stuck; from that day until I stopped practicing law, I never filed a paper with an erasure on it. If I changed a word, it had to be typed all over." In subsequent years, Marshall developed into a lawyer who was also known for his exacting manner of dress and his polished diction when appearing in court—qualities he shared with contemporaries such as Alexander and Loren Miller. Listening to an oral history interview with Miller, for instance, one is immediately struck by the extremely careful diction and the sometimes old-fashioned terminology—"Middle West" instead of "Midwest," for instance—used by the Nebraska-born lawyer who spent the latter portion of his career in the courtrooms of California. Marshall, by contrast, used a different script in court than he did elsewhere. One of his former secretaries from his days in Baltimore later remarked: "I bet he still speaks in court like the man who wrote the grammar book and yet commits felonious assault on the King's English in private."[13]

The most famous advocate of competence as a way to bridge the barriers of race was Marshall's mentor, Charles Houston. He was a feared and respected figure during his time as vice-dean of Howard Law School. Writing to the Carnegie Foundation's Alfred Z. Reed in 1931, Houston argued that his reforms at Howard would create a "representative Negro student body"—a group that could stand in, metaphorically, for the rest of their racial group. Students like Marshall and Oliver Hill called him by nicknames such as "Ironpants" and "Cement Shoes" because of his compulsive professionalism. Houston was well known for his sometimes-brutal assessments of his fellow black lawyers. As a young lawyer, he had dismissed most of the older established black attorneys with the offhand comment that "[t]hey do not know how to study and are too shiftless to learn." Houston defended his view of professionalism by arguing that "[e]very educational advance that Howard University is able to make has a practical and a spiritual value to the Negro first, and then to the nation at large." He imagined Howard as a public stage where one could change the racial perceptions that attached to a black lawyer.[14]

Courtrooms were public marketplaces where black lawyers bought and sold prestige and social standing as well as money and legal services, and therein lay the source of one of their most intractable problems with the bounds of race. The courtroom work that brought both high-level prestige and a unique chance to serve the race was often that of the NAACP, but the organization preferred white lawyers for its most important work. From its earliest cases, the association found itself in conflict with local black lawyers who staffed its cases. NAACP officials questioned the competence of black attorneys and accused them of using courtroom work to make money. As the organization's treasurer, Oswald Garrison Villard, stated during the 1910s: "It is an unfortunate fact that the colored lawyers, as we have learned to our cost in the Pink Franklin case, usually take advantage of philanthropic interest of this kind to make money for themselves." Even a decade later, NAACP leaders such as Walter White were apt to dismiss members of the migration-era black bar as simply "trying to gobble all the fees and the credit" when they were brought in to participate in an important case. The leaders of the nation's premier civil rights organization accepted at face value the sometimes questionable assertions of its white lawyers that they had nothing to gain from NAACP work.[15]

As Houston acknowledged, high-profile antidiscrimination work presented black lawyers with the prospect of "cashing in"—sometimes in monetary terms, and always in terms of social standing within the race-inflected world that defined one's place in the legal profession. When it came to NAACP work, however, their dreams of success on the same terms as white lawyers—in the marketplace for law work—were turned against them. Raymond Alexander experienced it in one of his earliest high-profile cases, when the national NAACP backed away from an initial promise of support because of a lack of confidence in his abilities. That story was echoed in places like Indianapolis and Baltimore, where the NAACP asked black lawyers to step aside in high-profile cases, amid accusations of incompetence and self-interest. Even Charles Houston had to wait to assume his historic place at the head of the NAACP's civil rights program until the organization had first offered the job to Columbia law professor Karl Llwellyn, an eminent white law scholar whose main qualifications for the job were his race and social standing.[16]

The civil rights courtroom—at least in important NAACP cases—was the most visible public space that remained off-limits to the racial work that was done inside the court process. Yet, by the end of the 1920s, there were distinct signs of movement on that score. With the migration of African Americans out of the rural South, the growth of the black bar, albeit uneven, was unmistakable. Charles Houston would note that "with the greater Negro population and wealth flowing into the North, the younger Negro lawyers . . . are devoting their attention toward pushing their Negro practice ahead as rapidly as possible." While most still struggled to make a go of it in practice, by the end of the decade it was becoming harder to deny that at least some possessed the experience to take on important cases. Then, in 1929, Moorfield Storey and Louis Marshall, the NAACP's principal white lawyers, passed away within months of each other. Clarence Darrow, who had also done important work for the organization, was visibly aging. Shortly afterward, National Bar Association president Jesse Heslip observed that "white men of the type of Morefield Story [*sic*], Louis Marshall, [Arthur Gar-field] Hayes and Darrow are rapidly falling away; they extend to us, Negro lawyers, their torch of able service."[17]

Despite Heslip's exhortations, little of what black lawyers did in court came to the attention of whites. Alexander's outsized annual profit from practice was testament to his skill and his ability to market himself to blacks, but even locally he remained largely unknown to white Philadelphians. Houston's work at Howard came to the attention of law school deans and legal reformers nationwide, but his own law practice remained mostly of the office kind; neither effort translated into general respect for the black lawyer in the eyes of whites. Farther west, the University of Chicago's first black law graduate, Earl Dicker-son, remained in practice with another African American lawyer and dabbled in local black politics but had yet to distinguish himself from the masses of local black lawyers who did similar work. What was needed was an appearance by a black lawyer in a well-publicized case with civil rights implications. That opportunity presented itself when, in early 1932, Philadelphia authorities decided to put a black youth on trial for a terrible crime.

A New Public Space: The Civil Rights Courtroom

Raymond Pace Alexander stepped into unknown territory when he came to court to convince a jury that Willie Brown should not die for the assault and murder of Dorothy Lutz. Brown's case seemed quite dif-ferent from the racially charged trials of the previous decade, where—in several cases involving black women murder defendants—local African American lawyers had done well by playing on early twentieth-century forms of sentimentality. Alexander brought the jury to tears in one such case, but at Brown's trial the tears that jurors shed would all be invoked by the prosecution. The dominant image of Brown was that of a sullen-looking youth, "with his gray felt hat at a jaunty angle and his overcoat upturned rakishly." Report after report presented the defendant as emotionless and uncaring throughout the proceedings, even when pre-sented with the most ghastly evidence of the crime and its effect on the victim's family. By contrast, the deceased Lutz was represented by an angelic photo of herself in life, and by her gaunt mother, dressed in black, whose composure on the witness stand slowly melted with grief for her daughter. It did not help matters when the case was assigned to Judge Harry McDevitt, a controversial local judge known as a "loyal champion of police against all complainers" and a scourge of violent criminals. Coupled with Brown's confession and several pieces of circumstantial evidence linking him to the crime, it seemed like enough to make Brown's fate a matter of certainty. The Willie Brown courtroom seemed like the last place that an African American lawyer would want to appear.[18]

Yet, there were also reasons—self-interested as well as altruistic—to champion Willie Brown. While the high-profile race cases of the previous decade had registered only dimly in the consciousness of most whites, whoever defended Brown would do so in front of an interracial audience of unprecedented proportions for a black lawyer. That audience was only increased when leftist radicals began to charge, in the local media, that Brown's prosecution was motivated by racial prejudice, drawing fire from the prosecutor and the trial judge. White newspapers across the state covered the case, while black outlets with a regional or national circulation such as the *Pittsburgh Courier*, the *Norfolk (Va.) Journal and Guide*, and the *Baltimore Afro-American* also picked up the story.[19]

Moreover, many local African Americans were appalled when charges circulated that police, lacking suspects and needing a scapegoat to tamp down public outrage, picked up Brown at random and obtained the confession through thirty-six hours of beatings and other physical abuse, starvation, sleep deprivation, and threats that he would be handed over to a lynch mob. Brown's upcoming trial seemed like a distended replay of the Walter Rounds case of the previous decade, where the treatment accorded to a black man accused of an interracial sex crime had led Raymond Alexander to shout defiance at the trial judge at the end of the proceedings. By the time of the coroner's inquest into the Lutz murder, Alexander, assisted by Robert Nix, announced his entry into the case. Brown soon found other supporters, prominent among them the *Philadelphia Tribune*, edited by black lawyer E. Washington Rhodes, while the national NAACP closely monitored the proceedings. The defense team announced that it would take the case without charging a fee.

By refusing any fee, the lawyers sent a signal to the public that they were motivated by racial loyalty rather than self-interest. "In this case [the defense lawyers] are backed by an element much greater than fees—the voice of popular approval," the *Afro-American* newspaper noted approvingly. Black lawyers regularly claimed that they never earned a fee in any of their civil rights cases during the Jim Crow era, but this was not exactly true. By the 1930s, the NAACP had established a policy of paying the lawyers who represented it—at least if they were not members of the association's National Legal Committee. It was money well spent, because most black lawyers struggled to earn enough to make a living at their trade; a lawyer in small-firm practice might have to close up shop and refuse to take on paying work for weeks to do a civil rights case. In Brown's case, the lawyers were telling the truth about their refusal of fees, because the NAACP's national office did not officially back the controversial defendant.[20]

The strange logic of early twentieth-century public media ensured that the racial identities of both Alexander and his client would be front and center when Willie Brown went on trial. If most whites had never heard of Alexander before, now they read daily reports that often designated him as "Raymond Alexander, Negro lawyer," or "the colored lawyer for the defense," while almost never identifying the race or ethnicity of any white person involved in the case. If they needed any reminders, "Willie Brown, 16, a Negro," or "Willie Brown, 16-year old negro," invariably made the defendant's racial designation clear to the white newsreading public. The *Pittsburgh Courier* congratulated the white dailies for showing restraint by mentioning Brown's race only in the body of their articles rather than in their headlines, as they had done in the past with black defendants.[21]

When Brown's murder trial opened on March 28, Alexander entered a courtroom that was ill-suited for the type of performance that would become emblematic of the black bar leadership. He faced a difficult audience in the form of an openly hostile judge and an all-white jury when, as he probably expected, all blacks were struck from the jury. His charges of police brutality were a tough sell at a time when white Americans were just waking up to the racial inequities in the southern, rather than northern, criminal justice system. Moreover, he faced a prosecutor who was also pushing against the bounds of race and ethnicity in the courtroom. Clare Fenerty had been an assistant district attorney for only a few years when the Willie Brown case began, and two years later he would ride the notoriety of the case to a seat in Congress.

In less than a decade, he would become a judge on the Court of Common Pleas, where he would serve for the rest of his life.[22.]

Fenerty made the most of the opportunity that Willie Brown presented. Images of masculine neglect circulated around Dorothy Lutz's murder and fed into the prosecution's case. In the panic that had ensued after the discovery of Lutz's body, mothers had stayed indoors with their children while "fathers and brothers joined the police" to search for those who remained away from home. "Little Dorothy Lutz," as the newspapers often referred to her, was wandering without parental supervision when she disappeared. It soon became public news that Lutz's father had died about a month before her murder, and Mrs. Lutz was accompanied to the coroner's hearing by two male friends. Stories of parental carelessness ran in the newspapers. The prosecution and defense agreed to exempt women from the arduous duty of passing judgment on Willie Brown, while the media prominently reported the marital status of the men who composed the jurors on the case.[23]

At trial, Fenerty exploited his chance, emphasizing the horrific nature of the crime and the evidence—multiple alleged confessions as well as a ring found near the body that may have belonged to the defendant—that pointed to Brown's guilt. In an emotional fifty-one-minute closing argument, Fenerty "fairly screamed" when exhorting the jurors to exact harsh vengeance on Brown, according to the *Daily News,* causing some members of the all-male jury to weep openly. Making their duty clear, he told them that "if there had been one or two men at the scene of this crime, we never would have had this case here today."[24]

Alexander, by contrast, struggled to find his footing during three days of proceedings in a hostile courtroom. Race and gender conventions worked against him (unlike in the Louise Thomas case), and he built few of the bonds with white onlookers that would become the trademark of the black bar leadership. He spent most of his time clashing with the judge, police witnesses, and Fenerty over his own main theory of the case—that Brown had been arrested and brutally beaten into confessing because of race prejudice. Much of his questioning seemed less geared toward persuading the jury than expressing cynicism about a legal system proceeding inexorably toward his client's certain execution. An argument with assistant superintendent Joseph LeStrange that police rushed to judgment about Brown's guilt produced the following exchange:

Alexander: What you mean is that you were completing your case
    against him before you even gave him a hearing.
LeStrange: Well, when you have a smart lawyer, you have to cover all
    the ground.
Alexander: He had no smart lawyer.
LeStrange: He has one now.

To most whites, Alexander seemed like a "smart [Negro] lawyer" who was trying to save a patently guilty client because of racial loyalty. Brown's testimony about the beatings, as well as his mother's testimony that the two were at the theater at the time of the murders, could be easily disbelieved. Alexander's closing argument, which reminded the jurors that "219,000 colored people [in Philadelphia] are waiting for this verdict," fell flat. In any event, Judge McDevitt interrupted his closing to rebut his charges of police brutality, and criticized various aspects of the defense case in his jury charge. After this, there was little suspense. After little more than an hour of deliberation, the jurors decided that Brown was guilty and should be put to death.[25]

Alexander's role in Willie Brown's trial seemed to bolster the conventional understanding that the public space of the high-profile civil rights courtroom was no place for a black lawyer. The prosecution made its case using images so charged with implicit (and explicit) calls for white male protection of vulnerable women and girls that the local black newspaper likened Brown's trial to a lynching, only done through the courts.

It was a different case, however, when the appellate proceedings began in the same building where the trial had taken place, but eight months later. In Willie Brown's appeal, one can see a new public space begin to open up for the black lawyer, and for the reworking of racial boundaries in a world where segregation remained a fact of life even in cities like Philadelphia.

A Fraternity of Lawyers

When the Pennsylvania Supreme Court heard Alexander's appeal on behalf of his client in late November, "the utmost calm" prevailed, according to the *Pittsburgh Courier.* "Counsel were extremely courteous to each other," and local lawyers crowded the courtroom, listening intently as the language of interaction—always a marker of racial identity—changed markedly from the trial. Alexander referred to his opponent as "[m]y friend," while Fenerty returned the compliment by emphatically referring to his adversary by the formal "Mr. Alexander." Gone were the stark racial and sexual images that had dominated the trial. At one point, Alexander even disavowed any intention of questioning Fenerty's trial tactics and pronounced them markedly fair to the defense. His main complaint, he told the court, was based on the prejudicial comments of Judge McDevitt. At the conclusion of the arguments, "[b]oth lawyers were warmly congratulated by members of the bar in the audience." It was a performance that had an immediate impact on state supreme court justice George Maxey. "You addressed your argument to the Supreme Court," the justice later told him, "with clarity and vigor, and with fidelity to the prescriptions of good taste."[26]

The Willie Brown appeal confirmed Raymond Alexander's membership in a fraternity of the bar that extended across, and in fact redefined, the boundary of race. No longer "Raymond Alexander, Negro lawyer," or the "smart [Negro] lawyer," Alexander in the appellate courtroom seemed to blend seamlessly into a brotherhood of lawyers whose most defining feature was their own connection with one another.

What accounts for the marked change between the trial and the appeal? The most obvious factors were the passage of time—the Brown case no longer dominated the headlines, and passions had cooled—and the new judicial venue. Moreover, the formalities of the legal process now put Alexander on the offensive—Judge McDevitt had given him a clear appeal issue by interrupting his closing and disparaging his case in the jury charge. Hovering about the case, however, was a process by which Alexander began to renegotiate the bounds of the profession.

In the appellate stages of the case, Alexander began to build bonds with lawyers and judges that would make him a repeat player in the legal interactions that built community among the local bar. Take Justice Maxey, for example. The justice and the black lawyer were hardly unknown to each other. In fact, Alexander had corresponded with Maxey the previous year when he distributed the National Bar Association's proceedings to local judges and lawyers in an effort to raise the profile of the black bar with influential whites. Alexander knew his audience well. Earlier that year, Maxey had been named to the "Honor Roll for

1931" at the liberal magazine *The Nation* for a vigorous dissent, on free speech grounds, from a decision upholding an injunction that prevented a union organizer from urging factory workers to join a union in violation of their yellow-dog employment contracts. Alexander, most likely, knew about the *Nation* article, and he would soon put that knowledge to good use.[27]

When the state supreme court came to a decision overturning Willie Brown's conviction in early 1933, the decision was written, as Alexander almost certainly hoped, by George Maxey. Maxey largely accepted Alexander's reading of the trial, concluding that Judge McDevitt had disparaged Alexander's theory of the case and offered his own testimony concerning police brutality, in violation of the state constitutional right to be heard by counsel. Maxey's opinion cleared the way for a retrial, which ended with an agreement in which Brown pleaded guilty in exchange for a life sentence. Brown's defenders would hail it as an improbable victory under the circumstances.[28]

The encounter between Alexander and Maxey in that city hall courtroom in late 1932 was the beginning of a series of public and private interactions between the two men that would help validate Alexander's place in the profession. Following the decision, Alexander's publicity machine kicked into full gear. Five days after the decision was handed down, he ghostwrote an article for the *Norfolk Journal and Guide* that praised the decision and compared Maxey to Benjamin Cardozo, Oliver Wendell Holmes Jr., Louis Brandeis, and other famous judges. This was no accident, since Maxey himself had cited Holmes, Cardozo, and other liberal heroes prominently in his dissent in the yellow-dog case of the previous year. Alexander undoubtedly had a hand in other articles that soon appeared in the black and white press noting, and often celebrating, the decision. He also restarted his correspondence with the justice within twenty-four hours of the decision. The young black lawyer expressed gratitude from "[t]he four hundred and fifty thousand colored people of this State" for the opinion and noted that "[i]n the short space of one day scores of lawyers have commented [to me] on the liberal philosophy throughout your opinions." Maxey at first responded by merely claiming that he had followed the dictates of judicial duty, but Alexander continued writing and sent him the laudatory news articles, some of which he had ghostwritten himself. After receiving a clipping from *The Nation*, Maxey finally confessed his liberal political views (and that he was a weekly subscriber) and his distaste for the "gross injustices" that African Americans had been made to suffer.[29]

Following Maxey's confession, the state supreme court justice and the young black lawyer developed a strong alliance in the state's liberal Republican politics. Within two years, Alexander opened up his North Philadelphia home for a dinner in Maxey's honor, and invited local and out-of-state lawyers to celebrate the justice's (and Alexander's own) status and reputation. When Alexander sought to break the color bar at the American Bar Association a decade and a half later, it was Maxey who lent his prestige to Maxwell's application by sponsoring it. The relationship between the two men was permeated, no doubt, by a good deal of paternalism. Maxey, for instance, once told Sadie Alexander that he was signing a letter to her "with the pen Abraham Lincoln used in signing the Emancipation Proclamation." The jurist added that "[t]he last occasion I used it was in signing a check for a colored college in North Carolina." Nonetheless, it was a form of paternalism that Raymond Alexander relied on time and again as a validation of his place at the center, rather than the margins, of the legal profession.[30]

Much the same process soon kicked into gear with Clare Fenerty, Alexander's opponent in the Willie Brown case. It was Alexander and Fenerty's lawyerly camaraderie before the state supreme court, rather than the vicious combat of the trial, that would define the relationship between the two men as the years passed. As Fenerty's post-trial fame propelled him to a seat in Congress and a judgeship, he and Alexander found themselves on the same side of many racial disputes. The same man who had mobilized images that were associated with lynching to get Brown's conviction would later be cited by NAACP secretary Walter White for his strong support for antilynching legislation.[31]

Nothing was more emblematic of the intertwined fates of the former opponents who rose to prominence in the glare of the Willie Brown trial than the controversy that erupted over an extradition request for a black criminal suspect in 1942. In July of that year, Thomas Mattox kicked up a firestorm in Elberton County, Georgia, when he cut a white youth with a knife while defending himself and his sisters from a brutal assault. Mattox quickly fled to Philadelphia to escape local reprisals. Back in Elberton County, local authorities incarcerated his sisters and a brother and threatened them with lynching, while white men beat his mother bloody, in order to learn his whereabouts. The Georgia authorities soon arrived in Philadelphia to demand that Mattox—who was being held in the county prison—be extradited to stand trial for assault with intent to kill the white youth. Despite fears that Mattox would never live to stand trial if sent back, it was an extremely difficult request to deny. Generally, courts had to presume that an extradited person would get a fair trial when sent back to the requesting state, and could only inquire into technical aspects of an extradition request. But Mattox had the good fortune to get Raymond Alexander as a lawyer, and the additional good fortune—surely not a coincidence—to have Alexander get his habeas corpus petition in front of Common Pleas judge Clare Fenerty.[32]

The Thomas Mattox extradition controversy became a textbook example of the professional ties that bound the two former opponents together in ways that pushed back against racial division, the bounds of precedent, and even the ethical limits on out-of-court contacts between lawyer and judge. Fenerty—now safely ensconced as an experienced judge following his retention election to a full ten-year term—adjourned the hearing on the habeas petition for three months, while Alexander mobilized the testimony of Mattox's Georgia relatives about the pervasive violence surrounding the case. When Fenerty went on vacation late that summer, Alexander contacted the jurist to ensure that he would not allow the matter to be decided in his absence by "any other Judge, since it was originally heard before you." When Georgia officials wrote a letter questioning the judge's impartiality because of his endorsement of antilynching legislation while serving in Congress, Fenerty turned it against them and concluded that the letter itself was evidence that the officials condoned extrajudicial violence against black criminal defendants.[33]

That fall, Judge Fenerty decided that Thomas Mattox should go free. Needing to craft an opinion justifying his action, the judge telephoned his old friend Alexander to ask for a supporting memorandum that would help him write it. Fenerty issued an opinion that stretched the governing legal doctrines to their limits in concluding that the required presumption that Mattox would get a fair trial in Georgia could be, and had been, rebutted. A few months later, the same process played itself out again, when Georgia authorities arrived with an arrest warrant for a young black woman charged with stealing from her employer. Once again, Fenerty adjourned the proceedings until Alexander could marshal evidence that the woman's employer was using the local justice system to keep her from fleeing the peonage-style conditions of her Georgia employment. Fenerty and Alexander, the two onetime adversaries who had once clashed angrily over their differing perspectives on racism in the criminal process and extrajudicial violence, now made common cause against them.[34]

Fenerty's was not the strangest professional association to emerge from Alexander's role in the Willie Brown case. That label could be reserved for the young black lawyer's relationship with the trial judge, Harry McDevitt. Alexander's appeal on Brown's behalf had earned McDevitt a public rebuke from the state supreme court, and decades after the judge's death, Alexander would remember him as "violently anti-black" in his judicial role. But that did not stop the feared jurist from appearing onstage shortly after the final resolution of the case at a rally sponsored by Alexander and members of the local black bar in support of legal aid. Two years later, McDevitt would address a meeting of the John Mercer Langston law club, the local black lawyers' group, where he urged the assembled lawyers to believe that the court system was fair to black lawyers and their clients.[35]

The judge had a paternalistic soft spot for low-level criminals and those whom he thought were reformable, and Alexander soon exploited it. By the latter part of the decade, Alexander had such confidence in his rapport with the judge that he approached McDevitt on behalf of a prisoner seeking parole and predicted—based on that rapport and his knowledge of McDevitt's tendencies—a favorable outcome "if you will be a good girl and obey the prison rules and regulations carefully and readily." Carefully parsing the judge's words and predispositions, he told his client that McDevitt "would favorably consider your case after you have served a period of a little more than one year." In Harry McDevitt's case, professional ties bound the two lawyers together not only in a relationship where racial difference marked off one lawyer from one another, but one where race prejudice did as well.[36]

Relationships like these would eventually produce the courtroom victory that confirmed Alexander as one of the best trial lawyers in the city, regardless of race. Surely, only his connections to white lawyers and judges can explain the chain of events that landed him in perhaps the most unlikely situation for a black lawyer, when a white client with a seemingly hopeless case asked Alexander to represent her. It began when, as he later remembered, Common Pleas judge Eugene Alessandroni sent for him unexpectedly and asked, "Raymond, how is your trial schedule for the next three weeks or so?" Alexander had tried many cases before Alessandroni, and the judge wanted him to defend a woman named Stella Alfonsi.[37]

Alfonsi was accused of being part of a gang of Italian American "poison widows" who murdered their husbands for the insurance proceeds. The case transfixed the city, and amid the public outcry all the initial defendants were tried and sentenced to death, or chose to plead guilty in the hope of avoiding the electric chair. Alfonsi's case, however, was assigned to Alessandroni, the city's first Italian American judge, who reportedly confided in Alexander that he was "thoroughly disgusted" by the unfairness of the previous trials and wanted the best possible defense. Shortly before trial, Alfonsi unexpectedly rose in open court, dismissed her inexperienced white counsel and—perhaps at the urging of the judge—asked that Alexander represent her.[38]

Thus far, defense lawyers in the poison widow cases had struggled in the face of hostile judges and jurors, but Alessandroni's courtroom turned out to be an entirely different venue. The judge gave Alexander room enough to mount a vigorous defense that focused on lack of motive (Alfonsi had allowed her insurance policy to lapse) and the fact that prosecution witnesses testified in exchange for leniency. The jurors were convinced by both arguments, and after thirteen hours of deliberation they found Alfonsi not guilty. It was an improbable victory for a lawyer of any race. Even Alexander—never one to minimize his abilities—confided to his friend Charles Houston that "I could not honestly say to you that . . . I was expecting any such result."[39]

Yet one month later Alexander did it again, in a case that most observers thought was even more hopeless than Alfonsi's. This time, he represented Rose Carina, nicknamed the "kiss of death" widow because of the suspicious deaths of three husbands in a row. Carina's case was tried before Francis Shunk Brown Jr., an old correspondent of Alexander's. Like Alessandroni, Brown gave him room to put on an aggressive defense of his own choosing. The wily defense lawyer reduced jurors to tears by relying on the trademark tactic—honed during his early years of practice—of presenting his client as a helpless pawn in the hands of overbearing men. He argued that browbeating police officers, who had little evidence to convict her, had nearly driven her to commit suicide following her arrest. This time the jury only deliberated five and a half hours before delivering a verdict that shocked the city.[40]

The poison widow courtrooms produced stark images that signaled that something new was at work in the politics of racial identification in Philadelphia. The *Philadelphia Tribune* reported that after Carina's acquittal, the attractive young woman "collapsed in the arms of Alexander," an act that carried substantial racial and sexual freight in a city where a dubious charge that a black man had improperly touched a young white woman had produced a quick conviction and harsh sentence a decade and a half before. Following the victory, the Alexander firm's lobby quickly became "crowded with Italians, friends and relatives of the accused, seeking to secure his services to save a loved one from death or life imprisonment." When he escorted his client back to prison to await further proceedings, both white and black inmates erupted in cheers of "We want Alexander, we want Alexander!" for nearly an hour while they banged their cups against the prison bars and walls. Other potential clients also took notice. A secretary who joined the office in the early 1940s reported that by that time, a quite substantial portion of his clientele was white. By the middle part of the decade, Alexander claimed that he was "rarely referred to, and never in the press, as a 'Negro' attorney." It had all been set in motion by Alexander's success, a decade before, in the most prominent public space that remained off limits to the black lawyer—the civil rights courtroom.[41]

The Willie Brown case had been the first step in a chain of events that pointed directly to the victory in the poison widow trials, as well as to the most important marker of racial identity for a black lawyer—being retained by white clients. At Brown's trial, Alexander had assumed the role expected of a black lawyer in a world where exclusion from public space helped define African American identity. In that courtroom he had been marked by race as an outsider to the court process, and vainly struggled against a system in which his own racial identity remained a burden to his client. In the appellate courtroom, however, he began to latch on to the professional script that, formally at least, marked lawyers as members of a fraternity that crossed the color line.

The key to Alexander's success was his ability to demand, and receive, the scripted public courtesy that marked him as a member of a profession cemented together by repeat encounters with the same allies and opponents over time. White lawyers and judges helped his career along because he seemed to represent the core values of their profession, as well as the aspirations of his own racial group. It was often formal courtesy, to be sure, that they extended to their black colleague. Many of his professional relationships carried subtexts of paternalism and even race prejudice, and contrary to his public statements, newspapers still referred to him as a "Negro attorney," even after his greatest victory to date in the poison widow cases. Nonetheless, time and again, his formal relationships with fellow attorneys provided him with a distinct advantage that allowed his evident courtroom skill to work its magic with judges and juries, and eventually with white clients as well.

Alexander wasn't the only one among the black bar to notice the value of the civil rights courtroom in remaking racial boundaries. At the time of the Willie Brown case, his friend Charles Houston still did much of his work outside the notice of the white public, within the bounds of his father's law firm and at the head of Howard Law School. Houston had achieved his goals for the transformation of Howard and was wondering what he should do next. Alexander's early victories had a powerful effect on both Houston and on a young Howard law student named Thurgood Marshall and helped inspire both men to dream of bigger things. Houston would give the Willie Brown case its denouement in a prominent write-up in the Urban League's journal, *Opportunity,* where he lauded Alexander as "one of the finest young lawyers the Negro race has produced." Within six months, Houston would get his own chance to represent a black defendant in a high-profile, seemingly hopeless case, and to write the next chapter in the story of racial representation.[42]

4

A Shifting Racial Identity in a Southern Courtroom

IN THE fall of 1933, Charles Houston stepped into a Virginia courtroom to defend a black man named George Crawford against a murder charge, and placed himself at the center of an intense debate over the meaning of race in the American South. The story had begun almost two years before, when the murder of Agnes Ilsley, a wealthy socialite, and her maid in Loudoun County, Virginia, made national headlines. Local authorities immediately declared Crawford the prime suspect and indicted him, and many feared that he would be lynched before being brought to justice. A nationwide manhunt finally netted Crawford in Boston a year later. While the NAACP publicized the case and organized a wide network of supporters to prevent him from being extradited to Virginia, federal judge James A. Lowell ratcheted up the case's national profile by ordering Crawford's release after a habeas corpus proceeding. Lowell reasoned that a trial in Virginia would be unconstitutional because African Americans had been excluded from the grand jury that indicted Crawford. Judge Lowell's ruling produced an impassioned debate on the floor of Congress about the fairness of southern justice; the House of Representatives voted to have its Judiciary Committee launch an investigation of Lowell's conduct. After Lowell's ruling was overturned on appeal, *Richmond Times-Dispatch* editor Virginius Dabney noted, with trepidation, that "the entire country will be watching" when Crawford went on trial in Virginia. Houston's entry into the case as Crawford's attorney, at the head of an all-black defense team backed by the NAACP, offered him the biggest stage yet presented to a black lawyer, as well as a venue previously off-limits to his peers—a southern civil rights courtroom in a case of national importance.[1]

The racial ideas and perceptions of a wide network of observers would attach themselves to the body of a relatively young and inexperienced Charles Houston when he came to court that fall to defend George Crawford. The trial was one of those flashpoints—like the case of the so-called Scottsboro Boys two years before in Alabama and that of the black Communist Angelo Herndon earlier that year in Atlanta— that focused international attention on race relations in the American South. In the imaginations of everyone from European leftists to U.S. Supreme Court justices to southern white moderates, the trials became markers of just what race meant in an American region that openly fostered disfranchisement, segregation, and lynching. The NAACP's choice to field an all-black defense team in the Crawford case introduced a new element into the story. If the trial began as a contest over what kind of justice a black criminal defendant could get in the South, observers quickly began to focus their energies on the novel question of what a black lawyer would be able to do and say in court, in a place where nobody had ever seen one before.

When Houston came to court to defend Crawford, most people saw him as something more than a lawyer representing a client or a cause. Houston seemed to personify the aspirations of African Americans all over the South who were excluded from meaningful participation in the criminal justice system. In the trial, a set of tensions would emerge that would play out over the next several decades as a small group of lawyers became known in their local communities, and sometimes nationally, as the authentic representatives of African Americans. These were the same set of tensions that lay just beneath the surface in Raymond Alexander's handling of the Willie Brown case, but here they would emerge on a much larger stage. As the proceedings wore on, Houston seemed more and more to represent the values of the local community of white southern lawyers in which he now found himself. The surest way to remain the authentic representative of blacks, it appeared, was to seem more and more like a white lawyer. That was a paradox that would arise again and again in the succeeding decades, as lawyers like Houston, Thurgood Marshall, and Leon Ransom came to court with novel civil rights claims as well as a shifting racial identity that sometimes overshadowed them.

The Racial Space of a Southern Courtroom

Houston's arrival in rural Loudoun County in October of 1933 set in motion a chain of events that would eventually make his own racial status as much an issue in the upcoming trial as that of his client. In coming to court, he challenged the social etiquette of a community where both language and public space helped make racial identity. Even in Upper South communities like Loudoun County, courtrooms were segregated, with seating, restrooms, and refreshment facilities marked black and white. The formal space of the courtroom, where judges and jurors sat, was a whites-only preserve. In the front of the courtroom, black witnesses had to be addressed by their first names, as they were in other public places. There was harsh retribution for deviation from the expected script. Philadelphia lawyer David Levinson, for instance, found this out when defending a black murder suspect in a nearby Maryland county, where a reporter told him that "[w]e don't call any niggers Mister down here and I am sure your case is lost beyond redemption." Farther south, Samuel Leibowitz helped transform himself from an idle curiosity to the object of an entire community's wrath in the Scottsboro retrial when he interrupted the prosecutor's examination of a black witness to say, "Call him Mr. Sandford please." Nearly two decades later, Houston vividly remembered the struggle over that one word, "mister," as one of the most significant accomplishments of that controversial proceeding.[2]

The presence of a black lawyer in court only intensified the problem. How should a southern community respond when a black man came to court and wanted to do what any lawyer should be able to do as a matter of course—cross-examine white witnesses, interact with his professional equals, amnd participate in local governance? No one quite knew. Theoretically, black lawyers could claim a common professional identity that should allow them to do anything in court that whites did, even if the same kinds of things were forbidden just outside the courthouse. In some parts of the South, particularly white rural counties, locals solved this problem by simply invoking custom to forbid black lawyers from practicing in the courts. Some black lawyers had to address witnesses from the segregated spectator section of the court rather than occupy the space inside the bar with white lawyers, judges, and jurors. Many others, particularly those in cities, often reported that they encountered very little racial prejudice in an entire lifetime of courtroom practice.[3]

In places where they were welcome, black lawyers still walked a fine line between the social deference that a lawyer could expect and the subservient role reserved for African Americans. Florida lawyer S. D. McGill observed that "[h]ow to contact him [a white man] in court whether he be Judge Bailiff, Clerk . . . is one of the most perplexing problems confronting the negro lawyer in the south." Galveston, Texas, lawyer Thomas Dent learned that "we should make our objections to the judge in a high-toned and flowery language, and avoid trouble that way." Cross-examination could sometimes be dangerous. As Ben Davis recalled of his native Georgia: "Imagine a Negro attorney exposing some white attorney or a white woman—Heaven forbid!—as a liar. It would no longer be a matter of legal procedure but a case of mob violence."[4]

Sheriffs and other nonprofessional white men often meted out harsh treatment to those who broke with these conventions, while white judges and lawyers sometimes made common cause with their black counterparts. NAACP lawyer Leon Ransom found this out when, after an amicable interaction with his peers at the bar in a Tennessee case, a former deputy sheriff attacked him just outside the courtroom. Mahala Dickerson recalled that she was "ordered to the back of the courtroom by an armed sheriff" upon her first appearance in a segregated Alabama court, until local women lawyers and the judge interceded on her behalf. In Mississippi, Willis Mollison learned the dangers of cross-examination when a judge abruptly cut short his questioning and ruled against his client. The judge explained afterward that the witness's brother was about to hit the black lawyer in the head with a club. Yet, in the strange negotiations that made the identity of a black lawyer in the southern courtroom so ambiguous, the brother later became the black lawyer's client.[5]

During the Jim Crow era, the appearance of a black lawyer in court was a performance that cut against the grain of normal racial interaction in a manner so striking that a good portion of the local community might turn out to watch. NAACP lawyer William Hastie found that out in mid-1933 when he arrived in Durham, North Carolina, to represent a black man named Thomas Hocutt, who was suing for admission to the University of North Carolina's school of pharmacy. Hastie was the NAACP's logical choice to represent Hocutt because he had followed almost exactly the career path of his mentor, Charles Houston. The Knox-ville, Tennessee, native had been valedictorian of both Dunbar High School (formerly M Street High) and Amherst College before earning a law degree at Harvard, where he became one of Felix Frankfurter's protégés. Hastie settled into a comfortable life teaching at Howard Law School and practicing at the Houston law firm before returning to Har-vard for his S.J.D. degree. Following that, the NAACP tapped him to head up Hocutt's legal team. Charles Houston recommended Hastie for the job, and the claim by the impeccably credentialed Hastie that he should be treated like any other lawyer quickly became the central drama of the trial. Hastie found the Durham courtroom "packed like a sardine box" with local African Americans, as most of the black and white local bar turned out to watch his performance.[6]

Inside the courthouse, Hastie was immediately struck by the electric effect of the racial perceptions that fastened onto the body of a black lawyer in a southern courtroom. He reported back to the NAACP: "Town agog. . . . Incalculable good done whatever the outcome." He found a sympathetic judge who continually sustained his objections to his opponents' tactics, while black spectators laughed out loud at the sight of Hastie doing something that could be done nowhere else in the city. At one point a prominent white lawyer in the audience "extended his hand to Mr. Hastie and congratulated us with feeling, on the way the case was conducted," according to his local black co-counsel.[7] Has-tie's initial impression proved to be correct. While he lost the case and recommended against an appeal, years later what most participants would remember about the trial was the powerful impact of Hastie's performance of a role that, save for the fact that his opponents would not refer to him as "Mister," made him seem like a white lawyer.[8]

By the following decade, experiences like Hastie's were becoming common for black NAACP lawyers and the communities where they tried their cases. Thurgood Marshall, for instance, described the thrill brought on by an aggressive cross-examination in an Oklahoma county that had never seen a black lawyer before. Even though Marshall even-tually lost the case, he reported that the white witnesses "all became angry at the idea of a Negro pushing them into tight corners and mak-ing their lies so obvious. Boy did I like that—and did the Negroes in the Court-room like it." NAACP lawyers Robert Carter and Constance Baker Motley had a similar experience when they arrived at the Jackson,

Mississippi, federal courthouse in the late 1940s to try a teacher salary equalization case. According to Motley, local African Americans thought that it was "the greatest thing that had happened in Mississippi since Emancipation" to see the white superintendent of schools being "sharply questioned" by Carter, and being made to speak up so that the black lawyer and others could hear him. She recalled that Carter's performance played to a packed audience in the courtroom, and afterward a crowd gathered at a local black barbershop while an African American patron mimicked the extraordinary scenes that he had seen in the courtroom. On the first day of trial, black spectators had segregated themselves by standing at the back and sides of the courtroom, but after Carter told them that no segregation was required in the public space of the federal court, they took the whites' seats. The whites left in disgust at the reversal of the usual markers of racial identification.[9]

The breakthrough moment for such performances was Charles Houston's arrival at the Loudoun County Courthouse in the fall of 1933 to argue a motion challenging the racial composition of the grand jury that had indicted Crawford. He was greeted by "[s]ix hundred spectators, half of whom were Negroes," who "filled every available seat in the court room while scores of others milled about the courthouse," according to the *Washington Post*. Houston had been greatly influenced by Hastie's performance in the Hocutt trial some months before, but translating the professional script that had worked so well in relatively urban Durham to a courtroom in rural Virginia would prove difficult.[10]

Houston's client, George Crawford, had been accused of murdering the socially prominent Agnes Ilsley and her maid in a county whose movers and shakers still styled themselves part of the aristocracy. The principal alternate suspect, never questioned by the authorities, was the murdered woman's equally prominent brother, Paul Boeing, who discovered the bodies, acted strangely afterward, and was said to be a beneficiary of an insurance policy on Ilsley's life. Local authorities had already invested much in proving Crawford's guilt. The county prosecutor had obtained what he said was Crawford's signed confession to the crime and was also amassing witnesses to rebut Crawford's principal claim of innocence—that he was in Boston at the time of the murders. Added to this was the fact that Houston's own race constituted an attack on segregated public space, as did his principal legal argument—

that the exclusion of African Americans from grand and petit juries in the county was unconstitutional. It had the makings of an explosive combination, and even the sympathetic newspaper editor, Dabney, would concede that "there was considerable speculation as to how Loudoun County would react" to Houston's presence in court.[11]

Loudoun's whites struggled mightily to map their ordinary under-standings of race onto a lawyer the likes of whom they had never seen before. Gender conventions were the greatest source of unease, and one local white man advised that the NAACP would be "damn fool . . . to bring colored lawyers in there." "I don't know," he speculated, "if a Negro lawyer gets to cross questioning a white witness, particularly a white woman, I don't know what might happen." Everything about Houston seemed to throw local whites into confusion. As one white man remarked after laying eyes on him at the trial: "He ain't black and he ain't white. I can stand a thoroughbred n––, but I can't stand these mongrels." Even the local prosecutor, John Galleher, was thrown out of sorts by Houston's arrival. As local citizens whispered that the young white prosecutor might need some help in facing such a well-credentialed black rival, Galleher fumed in the local newspaper, "At the present time I see no need for assistance. If, as the trial progresses, I feel assistance is necessary I will let that fact be known." Yet, when facing his black ad-versary for the first time at the grand jury hearing, even ordinary things like racial language became sources of unease. The prosecutor searched for the proper terms to be used inside the bar of the court, veering between the offensive "nigger" and the less offensive "nigra," and the proper "Negro."[12]

There were evident reasons for that discomfort, for the Crawford grand jury hearing produced racial images of a type never before seen in the county. The massed interracial audience saw a black lawyer come to court and cross-examine none other than the local circuit judge himself, J. R. H. Alexander. The venerable judge was referred to by one part-time local resident as a "well educated gentleman" who was among the "gentry" who still thought of themselves as the natural leadership class in the county. Houston had filed a motion charging that African Americans had been excluded from the grand jury that indicted Craw-ford, and Judge Alexander had picked the jury. Alexander disqualified himself from hearing the motion, and Judge James L. McLemore was brought up from Suffolk County as a replacement. Houston then called

Alexander to the stand as his principal witness in the hearing on his motion. Houston got permission to treat the patrician jurist as a hostile witness and peppered him with questions like: "Did you or did you not consider the Negro population" in picking juries? The judge answered evasively, stating merely that he picked jurors from those he knew to be responsible.[13]

Houston hammered away at those responses in his closing argument to Judge McLemore. Calling Alexander a "slow and reluctant witness," he all but said that the circuit judge was lying, and that Alexander's present testimony differed from past statements he had made to Houston privately. Arguing that the only questions at issue were whether qualified African Americans existed and whether they were excluded from jury service because of their race, Houston "shouted affirmative answers to both questions," according to the press. He charged that judge Alexander was perpetuating a caste system designed to mark African Americans as inferior: "Judge Alexander has been revolving around a closed circle—a wheel excluding all Negroes. In other words, a caste system is prevalent in Virginia and the South."

"'Why all this fight unless, deep down, there is something solid that makes Southern courts exclude Negroes?' Houston shouted," according to the local paper. He kept at it even after Judge McLemore rejected his grand jury motion. Houston fought back, asking McLemore for a more explicit ruling on race discrimination in local grand juries, and finally wringing an admission from McLemore that "[w]e're perfectly conscious that the social caste is well marked in Virginia. I have nothing to add to my decision."[14]

Houston's performance at the grand jury hearing was at once radical and respectable, and only his identity as a lawyer inside the courtroom enabled him to negotiate it. He had helped to shape the atmosphere that greeted him at the hearing by announcing, like so many of his black lawyer peers, that he believed in the fairness of the court system in which he found himself. "Every present circumstance leads us to believe that Crawford can and will obtain a fair trial in Loudoun county," he stated, in publicly declining to seek a change of venue. White observers invariably viewed his performance as courteous and respectful, even when he was telling the county's patrician leaders, face to face, that they were perpetuating a system of white supremacy.

As a local white man would comment after viewing one of Houston's spirited arguments at the subsequent trial: "You got to give it to him. He knows what he is doing even if he is a nigger."[15]

All this was occurring while Houston was putting local authorities on notice that he would take his challenge to its logical conclusion, even if it provoked violence. He announced after McLemore's ruling that he would appeal it all the way to the Supreme Court, and that he viewed the grand jury hearing as the first skirmish in a long and costly battle to gain equal rights for black southerners. At a subsequent rally in Washington, D.C., he argued that "[t]rained Negro leaders must be ready to make the fight," in Virginia and elsewhere in the South, "even to the extent of getting their heads cracked."[16]

The image of cracked heads was a metaphor for the unyielding resistance that the eminent black lawyer had expected to encounter at the local courthouse, although that metaphor would soon be replaced by another. Initially, both Houston and NAACP officials concurred that Crawford's defense ran up against not only a stone wall of racial superiority, but one embedded in class and sexual anxiety as well. Hints of a desire unnameable (at least among the local upper class) circulated around the case in the person of the principal alternate suspect, Paul Boeing. Boeing was the only other person in the house on the night of the murders, was reported to have quarreled with his murdered sister over money, and acted strangely after discovering the bodies. A local magistrate called him a drug addict and a "pervert," and "the queerest man I ever knew." "He is effeminate," the magistrate said, and Boeing reportedly had brought another "queer sort of man back to America" from a visit to Paris. Like Boeing and Ilsley, many of the county's aristocracy hailed from out of state and moved to the area to experience its upper-class social scene and country living.[17]

NAACP investigators had no trouble finding local whites of ordinary means who doubted Crawford's guilt and whispered that an embarrassed local gentry was protecting one of its own. Houston initially thought the case had the trappings of class warfare with its basis in a "certain feudalism on the part of the landed gentry." He fully expected the local lawyers to support the gentry. Indeed, he initially despaired of even finding sympathetic local counsel, given that "reputable attorneys will probably be identified with that class of people apparently anxious for Crawford's conviction."[18]

Representative Men, Black and White

In later years, what must have been most surprising to Houston about his first appearance in a southern courtroom in a major civil rights case was how much it confounded his expectations, and those of so many whites, about the role that race played in the public spaces of the South. Instead of a place filled with race prejudice and sexual anxiety, what Houston ultimately found in Loudoun County was a courtroom occupied by white opponents whose self-identity, in many ways, mirrored his own. They called themselves by a familiar name: "representative men." As the trial approached, the local press announced to the public that a group of men variously styled as "representative white men of the county," or "representative business men" or "representative men of the county," would have firm control of the proceedings.[19]

The idea of the representative man was something that crossed racial lines, as it had since the nineteenth century. Since John Mercer Langston's time, a group of whites who called themselves "representative men of the South," and similar names, had long emphasized their own role as sober-minded citizens in a region marked by racial division and violence. As Crawford's trial approached, local representative white men, and those elsewhere in the state, stepped in to take charge. They talked about the prejudices of their poorer brethren and the media attention being lavished on Virginia, and argued that only their presence could banish emotionalism and appeals to racial loyalty from the trial. Like most ideas of racial representation, theirs was based on a paradox. They claimed to stand in for poor whites who supposedly had little interest in a fair trial. At the same time, they also wanted to reach out to outsiders, including the NAACP, and to convince them that the trial was fair. Judge McLemore, for instance, would later state that if he himself "had been counsel for Crawford, [he] could not have been more solicitous to see that everything that could be done for him was done." Representative whites claimed to be committed to white supremacy in Virginia, but some of them eventually pledged to include blacks on grand and petit juries. They blanched at the possibility of "one or more crackers," as one put it, being seated on the jury—"the kind of white man in which resentment against the Negro grows in direct proportion to the intelligence and ability of the Negro." At the same time, they would eventually welcome Houston into the Loudoun County courts with open arms. Representative whites claimed to stand in for the mass of white Virginians who could never be entrusted with power over race relations in that state, but how exactly they represented these poor whites they could never explain.[20]

To representative white men, Houston's own presence would come to stand in for the larger tensions at play in Crawford's trial. Taking control of the proceedings, they made sure that the courtroom atmosphere at the grand jury hearing was far different from the one that Houston had expected. For instance, the first local judge Houston faced in Loudoun County had freely used the term "darkies" in court, prompting a protest letter from the black lawyer. But things changed markedly once Judges Alexander and McLemore took charge. With the national press in attendance, Judge McLemore banned the customary practice of segregated seating in the courtroom, ordering that blacks and whites could sit together at the grand jury hearing. While McLemore denied Houston's grand jury motion, afterward the judge asked local authorities to add blacks to the trial jury pool. At the trial, one of McLemore's first acts was to condemn a newspaper article that had misquoted Houston's "heads cracked" remark in an inflammatory way. "The Commonwealth and the counsel for the defense have the same rights in the courtroom," he announced, "and if they [the Negro lawyers] conduct themselves properly, I have no doubt they will be treated like white men." The tradeoff was clear. If the out-of-town black lawyers acted like local representative men in court, they would be folded into the local bar and treated exactly like those white men. Acting like a white man in court essentially made one white, at least in the eyes of the lawyers and judges inside the courthouse.[21]

It was no accident that Houston would face a judge who was committed to the proposition that performing like a white man was an act that changed one's racial status. Representative whites were worried that Crawford's trial would be a replay of the infamous Scottsboro proceedings, where the retrials had opened earlier that year after the Supreme Court invalidated the initial death sentences and no end of that controversy seemed to be in sight. If Scottsboro provided an opportunity, then Houston, along with NAACP head Walter White, quickly seized on it. They recruited two prominent white Virginians to their cause. Virginius Dabney, editor of the *Richmond Times-Dispatch* and author of *Liberalism in the South,* and Douglas Freeman, the *Richmond News*

Leader's editor, both arranged for favorable coverage of the NAACP's defense effort in their newspapers. The two editors grew concerned when the racially moderate Judge Alexander had to recuse himself, and Freeman consulted with the governor to make sure that a jurist of similar disposition was brought in to replace him. McLemore fit the bill. If the trial judge hadn't already gotten the message, Freeman took the jurist aside in advance of the trial to explain "what Virginia expects at his hands."[22]

Local lawyers, too, seemed to see something in Houston that made them view their black counterpart as a reflection of themselves. That development was helped along by Loudoun County's own small-town version of the inbred local legal communities that still populated early twentieth-century America. Lawyers in Loudoun County knew each other well. In fact, just about everyone who was involved with the case seemed to have served as the local commonwealth's attorney at one time or another. Judge Alexander, for instance, hailed from a prestigious local legal family and used that as a stepping-stone to a judicial career that would eventually make him one of the most influential judges in that part of the state. Not coincidentally, the person who occupied the post of commonwealth's attorney before Alexander was a lawyer named Cecil Connor, who used the position as a launching pad to election as a state senator. Connor joined the prosecution team in the Crawford case after local citizens began fretting that John Galleher was not up to the task of opposing Houston, and pooled their resources to hire some additional firepower. Locals also decided to retain Frank Wray, a prosecutor from a neighboring county who had the misfortune of not having served as Loudoun commonwealth's attorney. But Wray was "well known in Loudoun, having several times appeared as counsel in cases at the local bar," including one recent case where he had pitched in to support the local prosecutor. Galleher himself was the lawyer who succeeded Alexander as the local commonwealth's attorney. At the time of the Crawford case, he was "a young, ambitious lawyer . . . whose entire career is in front of him," according to one press report. "The Crawford case can 'make' him." But just how it might make him was not yet clear.[23]

It was Judge Alexander who sent the signal to the local bar that they should close ranks to welcome their black counterpart into their insular community. J. R. H. Alexander would become a revered figure in Loudoun County and the vicinity, and was influential in setting the standards of conduct for lawyers in the entire area. His actions in Crawford's case were a prime example of the phenomenon. The turning point in the attitude of the local bar toward Houston was the black lawyer's aggressive cross-examination of the well-known jurist. When Judge Alexander failed to take umbrage at what he endured at the hands of the lead lawyer for the defense, he signaled to the local bar that the script for racial interaction inside the courtroom had changed. Galleher quickly got the message. The young prosecutor had used racially offensive language at the grand jury hearing, but he soon changed his tune once it became clear what was expected of him. Galleher and Houston got to know each other after the grand jury hearing, as they cooperated in the preparations for the trial. Within a month their relationship was such that Houston stated that his opponent was showing "rather extraordinary courtesy" toward the black defense team. In fact, the intertwined fates of the two young lawyers, bound together across the borders of race and thrust into public prominence by their first major case, resembled the relationship that was developing between Raymond Alexander and Clare Fenerty in Philadelphia.[24]

If the local lawyers were coming to a consensus about how to treat the well-credentialed black lawyer for the defense, the NAACP's southern white moderate allies still needed to be convinced that race was not a bar to pleading Crawford's case. Here, the key factor was the decision of local representative men of the bar to accept Houston as one of their own. The NAACP desperately needed the support of influential figures like Dabney and Freeman. But these men stuck to their position that Houston had to partner with a white lawyer, or perhaps bow out completely, for Crawford to have an effective defense. Writing to Walter White just before the grand jury hearing, an apprehensive Dabney opined that "I have become still more convinced that the appearance of a Negro lawyer in the case might have a bad effect on the jury." That attitude changed markedly in the aftermath of Houston's performance at the hearing. Within days of its conclusion, White wrote to Freeman to say that influential representative men, especially "Judge McLemore and Prosecutor Wray . . . who assisted Mr. Galleher, stated to me after the trial that they thought it would be a very serious mistake if we

replaced Mr. Houston for the criminal trial." The community of lawyers had spoken, and Freeman quickly conceded the issue. The last barrier to the appearance of a black man as chief counsel to Crawford had
fallen.[25]

The prospect of Houston's entry into the case prompted a ground-
swell of excitement within the African American bar itself. Only one
year before, Walter White had traveled to the National Bar Association
convention to promise an increasingly impatient and skeptical group of
lawyers that in the future "we can turn to you and you to us whenever
problems of mutual interest arise." As the prospect of a black lawyer
appearing in Loudoun County loomed, enthusiasm began to grow even
before the announcement of an all-black defense team, particularly
among the students at Howard Law School. Houston reported that "[t]he
men here feel that if Crawford could be defended by all Negro counsel
it would mark a turning point in the legal history of the Negro in this
country." A wave of sentiment was cresting among the faculty and students, and it would soon engulf the vice-dean himself. Houston resisted
it at first, but his eventual change of heart was brought about by "the
position I find myself in as heading up Negro education for the bar,
which I have been preaching as self-sufficient and able to stand on its
own feet."[26]

For half a decade, figures like Houston and Raymond Alexander
had told their fellow black lawyers, African American communities,
and any whites who would listen that their own professional dreams
stood in for those of the rest of their race. Only two years before, Houston had boasted that Howard's "representative Negro student body"
would "demonstrate what the mass of Negroes can accomplish." Now,
he believed, he had a chance to prove it before a national audience, as
he assembled an all-black defense team composed of faculty and former
students at Howard Law School. His own autobiographical story was
encapsulated in the upcoming trial, and it would shape what the public
believed was truly at issue in that courtroom. As Houston himself confessed: "I am enmeshed in my own propaganda."[27]

Propaganda was not too strong a word, because Houston's performance in the Loudoun County courts was one of such power that it
helped change the perceived stakes of Crawford's trial. At first, most
observers thought that the trial was a test of how much justice a black

defendant could get in a southern courtroom. The test, it was assumed, would focus on the issue that Houston planned to push hardest—the exclusion of blacks from southern grand juries. Only months before, white Alabamans had dug in their heels on this issue and others in the Scottsboro retrial, producing a second death verdict, and many observers feared that Loudoun would follow that example. Even the local sheriff and court clerk told the defense team to seek a change of venue because of the small chance of getting a fair trial in Loudoun County. That sentiment, however, would soon change. The precipitating event was Charles Houston's arrival in the county to argue his grand jury motion.[28]

Though Houston lost the grand jury challenge, a new story of what was at issue in the case quickly emerged. A local white man announced the new point of view when he told Walter White that even though the defense had lost the motion, "he thought we had done a remarkable piece of educational work in demonstrating that there is a Negro of Dean Houston's type with the ability and manner which he showed." As the trial date approached, the Crawford case took on a double meaning in the eyes of many observers. Houston encapsulated it clearly, in explaining to Freeman his decision to forgo white co-counsel: "I am trying to see whether this case can be lifted above racial prejudice either at the bar or at the counsel table." The problem of a black lawyer in a southern courtroom would now take its place as one of the central issues that would define the meaning of the case.[29]

The new symbolic meaning of the trial would now move to the forefront. Houston announced the new view in a public letter to the *Richmond News Leader*. Explaining why he would not ask for a venue change, Houston noted that he had "received every professional courtesy at the hands of the County officials and attorneys for the Commonwealth." In fact, the local press cited Houston's meeting with "representative white men of the county" in explaining his change of attitude. Houston stated that if Crawford "could get a fair trial in Loudoun County [it] would demonstrate to the world that there are places in the South where a Negro can get a fair trial no matter what crime he is charged with." As for the issue of discrimination in jury service that had once seemed like evidence of a racial caste system, even that could now be displaced from the trial. "The court and the Commonwealth take a different view from ours on the question of the omission to consider Negroes for jury service," Houston announced in the media after losing the grand jury motion. "[B]ut that difference of opinion," he continued, "will not be permitted to embitter the trial. We will settle the jury question in an orderly fashion in the appellate court."[30]

Once a sign of entrenched racial inequality, jury exclusion now became an issue on which lawyers could take differing good-faith views. The lawyers now had a common cause: ensuring that cross-racial professionalism would govern the conduct of the trial. As Houston told reporters after losing the grand jury motion: "I wanted this trial conducted on such a high plane that it would serve as a model for future cases involving potential racial antagonisms." Lawyerly interactions at the Crawford trial would now provide the model for how representative blacks and whites could work together in seeking racial equality in the South.[31]

The Work of Race in a Virginia Courtroom

George Crawford's trial proceedings opened on a mid-December day at the Loudoun County Courthouse amid an outwardly calm but "mighty tense" atmosphere, according to White. "You could almost feel the electric waves." Much of the anxiety was focused not on Crawford, but on the defense team, "in sharp contrast to the amicable feelings displayed by counsel and court officials" at the grand jury hearing, according to one press account. Tensions rose as four black lawyers marched past the statue of a Confederate soldier that guarded the entrance to the courthouse and took their seats at the defense table: Houston ("Dean Houston," as the press called him), Leon Ransom, who was a professor at Howard Law School, and two recent Howard law graduates, Edward Lovett and James Tyson. They were flanked by NAACP executive Walter White. Local observers "who had previously been extremely tolerant toward the defense were impatient" as Houston examined witnesses during a challenge to racial exclusion in the trial jury pool. One news account reported that while Crawford was in little danger, his lawyers were. Ever-present was the question of how whites would react to black men cross-examining white witnesses. "[T]hey had better be careful how they examine commonwealth witnesses" the paper warned. Judge

McLemore later admitted that he came to court with "fear and trembling" at the possibility of "the race question coming up," and the trial opened with a phalanx of state policemen guarding the courthouse, armed with tear gas and submachine guns.[32]

Outwardly, the defense team seemed to be taking up just where they had left off after the grand jury motion, but behind the scenes almost everything about the case had changed during the previous month. Publicly, the defense had announced that the principal issue in the case was whether the prosecution could prove that Crawford was in the county at the time of the murders. At the extradition hearing in Boston, seemingly trustworthy witnesses had testified that Crawford was in that city at the relevant times. The purported confession, elicited by Galleher while Crawford was in jail in Boston, was assumed to be the product of coercion. Crawford remembered that he had a cellmate in Boston named Herbert Finch, who could testify that Crawford had been forced to sign the confession. Moreover, as the NAACP hinted in its press releases, there was another suspect to the crime. Roy Seaton, a local magistrate who investigated the case, was cooperating with the NAACP and claimed that local authorities were covering up for Paul Boeing. By the time of the trial, all these bases for the defense had been undermined.[33]

In the month and a half between the grand jury hearing and the trial, the moral clarity that underlay the black defense team's approach to the case slowly began to evaporate. First, the defense found out that several local African Americans, some of whom were subpoenaed by Galleher and interviewed in his office, stated that Crawford had been in Loudoun County at or near the time of the murders. To verify the story that Crawford had been in Boston instead and that his confession was coerced, Houston had sent two members of the defense team, Ransom and Tyson, to that city. The two lawyers were supposed to interview the alibi witnesses, track down Finch, and get a copy of the confession. But Houston made the fateful decision not to go with them because of transportation difficulties. For reasons that were never made clear, Ransom and Tyson never located the alibi witnesses, even though subsequent investigators found them easily. After making some effort, the two lawyers concluded that they could not locate Finch. They did, for the first time, see a copy of the purported confession, which Galleher had never provided to them. In it, Crawford appeared to confess to robbery, although saying that a fellow robber committed the murders while Crawford was outside the house.[34]

Back in Virginia, the defense lawyers endured further setbacks. They learned that magistrate Seaton had been dismissed from his post for either financial irregularities or his sympathy to the defense, and was "leaving very shortly" for another part of the country. In addition, Houston decided to soft-pedal the theory that Paul Boeing had committed the murders. Houston told the prosecution, during an amiable pretrial conference, "that I did not want to spread muck unless there was real justification for involving Paul B." Boeing had left the county sometime after the murders, while his wealthy relatives retained their own investigators and provided information to the NAACP that seemed to support Crawford's guilt. When Boeing did return to Loudoun to attend Crawford's trial, it was in the company of a New York lawyer. There were periodic rumors of a libel suit over the NAACP's public hints about Boeing as a possible suspect and his unorthodox lifestyle. Finally the defense learned, two weeks before the trial, that despite McLemore's recommendation, no African Americans would be called for the trial jury pool. Faced with the need to assemble more witnesses to support a motion challenging the trial jury, Houston recalled Ransom and Tyson from Boston to concentrate on the motion and on trial strategy.[35]

But the most important reason for the behind-the-scenes maneuvering that redefined the defense's case was provided by George Crawford himself. As the debate about the case raged from Boston to the federal appellate courts to the floors of Congress, and ultimately to Virginia, Crawford had come to symbolize many things to many people without doing much speaking himself. When he communicated at all, he seemed like the embodiment of unlettered innocence. For instance, he wrote one letter telling his NAACP supporters that "God know all thing and he know I am inser [innocent] if the people dousen [doesn't] believe me." Then, in the weeks before trial, Crawford began to speak up more clearly, albeit in the privacy of his consultations with his defense team. What he actually said was difficult to figure out, either for contemporaries or from the vantage point of history. The confidentiality of lawyer-client communications made Houston circumspect about what had happened, while Crawford never testified at his subsequent trial.[36]

What can be established is that, with the evidentiary basis for their case shifting and with only two or three weeks left before the trial, the defense lawyers began to pressure Crawford about the truth of his story. And the story changed. On the eve of the trial, White wrote, cryptically, to Roy Wilkins that "much has been uncovered during [the] last fortnight which C. had not told his attorneys." White would later assert, after coming under heavy criticism for the NAACP's handling of the case, that Crawford admitted his complicity in the crime. Houston was more cautious in both public and private, later confiding to close associates that "Crawford abandoned the Finch confession story at the end." Houston said little at the time about the defense's eroding case, but based on his later statements it seems that the Howard vice-dean came to court that December believing that he was defending a client who had been complicit in murder. That placed Houston in a situation that he had not anticipated, for as he admitted to White months earlier, he was not an experienced criminal lawyer.[37]

To the assembled onlookers, Houston's most surprising act at the trial was his choice not to speak. After the trial jury motion and some preliminary proceedings, he fell silent for long periods of time. Galleher's opening statement quickly summarized the prosecution's main evidence—local witnesses who claimed to have seen Crawford near the time of the murders, and the alleged confession. Houston responded with a terse "The defense waives its opening statement." Likewise, as the prosecution put on its key local witnesses during the first two days, Houston often replied with an even more terse "No questions," or posed a few perfunctory queries that did not exculpate Crawford from participation in the crime. Some witnesses claimed to see Crawford under questionable circumstances—at night or from a distance—and Houston reportedly "knew that four or five of those who were swearing away Crawford's chances had recently served prison terms themselves for offenses ranging from dope peddling to violent assault." The veracity and recall of black witnesses as well as white ones went largely unchallenged, even though at least one person had informed the defense team that Galleher was threatening local African Americans to induce them to give evidence for the prosecution. Only a few days before, Houston had announced that he would put the Boston alibi witnesses on the stand, but he soon admitted that none would appear. The *Washington Post* summarized the views of many surprised observers when it noted that Houston "entered no defense whatsoever" to most of the prosecution's case.[38]

Tensions mounted as the key witness, Paul Boeing, stepped up to testify. When the "dapper, high strung, athletic" brother of Agnes Ilsley came forward to swear to tell the truth, there was a "murmur in [the] courtroom." No one knew what he would say. Even the white onlookers must have wondered if he had been complicit in his sister's murder. "Spectators leaned forward to catch every word" as Boeing took the stand for the prosecution, and "a pin falling to the floor could have been heard" as he testified about his actions on the night of the murders and his discovery of the bodies the next day. As the anxieties built to a crescendo, a window fell shut in the back of the courtroom, and everyone jumped at the noise. On cross-examination, Houston stepped gingerly around rumors that Boeing had acted strangely before and after the murders and had motive to commit them himself. Instead, the black lawyer used his questions mainly to establish Boeing's actions around the time of the crime without any implication of suspicion. The murdered woman's brother smiled at Crawford when asked to identify him in the courtroom, while the defendant jumped up and bowed in homage to his patron. The tension in the courtroom quickly dissipated.[39]

With regard to Houston's lawyerly interactions with the prosecution and witnesses, however, things could hardly have been more different. Here the black lawyer and his assistants continued their assault on local racial mores. As the trial wore on, Houston continually, and sometimes aggressively, showed up his white opponents. Galleher quickly displayed his inexperience, producing an early rebuke from McLemore for leading one witness and laughter from the audience for flubbing a line in his opening statement. Houston soon pounced on his adversary, and repeatedly interrupted Galleher's witness examinations as tedious and duplicative of evidence that the young prosecutor had introduced before. At one point, as the prosecutor was asking a witness to describe Crawford (who was sitting in front of him) based on a past meeting, Houston interjected sarcastically: "If he knows him, there he is," prompting Galleher to do the obvious—simply get the witness to say that the man he was looking at was Crawford. Even the veteran prosecutor Frank Wray, brought in to back up Galleher, was shown up by his black adversary. Wray, too, came in for one of Houston's interpositions when he tried to qualify a witness as an expert, only to have the defense team interrupt his questions, successfully, as wearisome and redundant. At one point Wray had difficulty reading a letter written in Crawford's unorthodox syntax and deferred to Houston, who read it easily. The room fairly "hummed" with discussion of a black lawyer reading a document when his white colleague could not. White summed up the surprise of many when he wrote that Houston had demonstrated that he was "easily [the] most brilliant man in [the] courtroom."[40]

A shift in language, too, marked a break in the rules that governed race relations in southern courtrooms. Houston provoked it early, beating back objections from Galleher and Wray and aggressively challenging the local jury commissioners in his trial jury motion. Houston left one commissioner, C. A. Whaley, so confused in trying to explain his jury selection methods that one audience member whistled in amazement. The flustered commissioner began to answer him "No, sir" and "Yes, sir." Another commissioner, after opining on the low intelligence of potential black jurors, sat in embarrassed silence after Houston offered him a list of voters, and it became evident that he could not read it. Once Houston began to show up his prosecution adversaries at trial, even Galleher, the local coroner, and some white witnesses began to slip up and call the black lawyer "sir" in response to questions. As always, most of the apprehension focused on examination of white women witnesses. By the second day of trial, the black defense team was sure enough of itself to call a local white woman who lived near the murder victim as its witness to testify that she heard no disturbance on the night of the murders. Answering Houston with a crisp "Yes, sir," and "No sir," she testified without incident and completed the process that, as Judge McLemore had announced before trial, resulted in Houston being able to act almost like a white man in court. As Houston stepped firmly into a role that would be denied him anywhere else in the county, whites and blacks broke with tradition to sit side by side in the courtroom.[41]

It was a striking thing for the interracial audience to see a black lawyer performing like a white man inside the Loudoun courthouse, but that performance had two elements—aggressiveness in professional interactions, and deference on the question of Crawford's guilt. Both came together in the argument over the admissibility of the alleged confession. Galleher had obtained it when he visited Crawford in his Boston jail cell, and the statement remained the only direct evidence connecting the defendant with the murders. Even the local press admitted that without it, the state "undoubtedly would have been without a case." In the alleged confession, Crawford indicated that he had tried to rob Ilsley's home with an accomplice, Charlie Johnson, and that Johnson had committed the murders while Crawford waited outside unaware that any violence would ensue. There was just one problem. The transcript of the confession came in two parts. The first part, entitled "Statement of George Crawford," seemed to show Crawford adamantly resisting entreaties by Galleher to confess and denying even being in Virginia at the time of the murders. "He can't say that and be telling the truth," Crawford says on the last line of this part of the transcript, denying that any honest person could contradict his story. Immediately after that, the second part, titled "Additional Statement of George Crawford," begins:

Q: (by Attorney Galleher) You are willing to make this statement
    freely and without hope of reward?
A: Yes, sir.

After that, he confesses to the crime.[42] The transcript itself gave no clues to explain the disparity between the two parts. Galleher, put on the stand by the prosecution, testified that he showed Crawford a picture of Ilsley and her house during the interview, which induced Crawford to begin to cry and then to quickly (and wordlessly) shift from adamant denial to contrite confession. For almost the first time during the trial, Houston aggressively cross-examined the prosecution's witnesses, and got Galleher and others to admit that not everything that transpired in the jail cell was recorded on the transcript. After vigorous arguments by both sides, the judge ruled that the alleged confession could be read to the jury.[43]

Yet even the spirited arguments over the confession served to reinforce the process that separated the black defense team from the cause of Crawford's freedom. Houston's sole chance to free his client was to create some doubt in the minds of McLemore or the jurors about just what Galleher had done in the time separating the two transcribed statements. He had to argue (or at least imply) that Galleher had used some improper coercion, threats or illicit promises, not recorded on the transcript, to produce Crawford's seemingly implausible change of

heart. But to do that would be to conflict with the cross-racial professional norms that had evolved into the most surprising feature of the
trial. Houston did not do it. Instead, he argued that the confession
was tainted by a simple mistake by Galleher, but not any bad intention
or explicit coercion. Houston contended that the prosecutor used the
wrong words in getting Crawford to confess and thus violated the technical requirements for the admission of confessions. This was not
enough, in the eyes of the judge or the jury, to make it inadmissible or
unreliable as evidence. After the judge's ruling, a despondent Walter
White admitted that the day's proceedings were "the worst yet for the
defense." Crawford's conviction and execution seemed certain.[44]

The defense lawyers' apparent concession drew Galleher and his
associates, as well, across the bounds of race and power that had once
seemed to separate the lawyers on the two sides of the color line. To the
surprise of the audience, Galleher began his statement to the jury by
thanking the "very able and learned counsel who represent the defendant" for their "courtesy and consideration." Wray followed him with a
closing that amounted to a dry recitation of the evidence without any
of the implicit or explicit references to race or the protection of white
womanhood that onlookers had expected.[45]

The converging views of the lawyers began to transform what the
jurors, and the public, viewed as the stakes behind the trial. After first
congratulating Wray for "one of the most unusual and one of the fairest
arguments I have ever heard," Houston pleaded with the jury to spare
his client from the electric chair. He painted Crawford as an obedient
"homeless hungry dog," noting that his client had saved the life of one
former white patron and had risen in deference and bowed when the
patrician Paul Boeing had testified. If the jury believed the confession,
he argued, it meant that Charlie Johnson, not his submissive client,
had gone into the house alone and done the killings. If Crawford were
executed, then no one would be left to testify against Johnson once the
killer was caught. A "murmur of approval" swept through the courtroom audience at Houston's surprising argument. Silence reigned when
he sat down, as people "coughed and shuffled uneasily." The cry of a baby
finally broke the tension. When Connor finally rose to deliver a half-
hearted rebuttal, he confessed that Houston had "touched my feelings."[46]

The jury was out only a short time before it delivered a verdict that
gave something to both sets of lawyers. The prosecution, as expected,

got its conviction. But, as onlookers registered "considerable surprise," the defense was rewarded with a sentence of life imprisonment for Crawford. Houston quickly offered to plead his client guilty to the murder of Ilsley's maid in exchange for a second life sentence. In the aftermath, jurors confessed that Houston's closing argument had convinced them to forgo the death sentence that was expected for a black man who was involved in the murder of a southern white woman. Crawford, too, seemed to radiate happiness with the verdict, at least initially. After all, given the evidence produced at trial, there is a good likelihood that he was complicit in the double murder, and he had escaped death by either lynching or legal execution. Houston had apparently either concluded that his client was guilty and did not deserve a vigorous defense, or that the best he could accomplish given the weakening of his case was a conviction and life sentence. For the moment, his client seemed to agree.[47]

The lawyers viewed themselves as heroes of the affair, and both sides now imagined that their own actions inside that courtroom had been representative of how their entire racial group should go about improving race relations in the South. As the lawyers gathered to await the jury's verdict, Judge McLemore told his colleague that he had seen a "new vision of what can be and what ought to be the atmosphere of every criminal trial." Both McLemore and Judge Alexander had already endorsed the NAACP's contention that blacks were qualified for jury service. They were soon reportedly joined in this endorsement by the assistant prosecutor and local state senator, Connor. Houston, who a few months earlier had told McLemore that his jury rulings perpetuated a caste system, now pronounced them "absolutely fair." Houston told McLemore and his opponents that he was now glad to have lost his jury motions, for if he had won them the trial would have been transformed into a "battle of wits" between the lawyers instead of a cooperative endeavor. The same man who had once called on his fellow African Americans to get their heads cracked to get blacks on juries now told his white counterparts that "we can only rise by convincing you that we are entitled to and are able to share in your institutions without endangering them." For Houston, Exhibit A in this process was the unexpected professional interactions of the lawyers at trial. Indeed, the end of the case produced so much bonhomie among the gathered members of the bar that one newspaper titled its summary of the case's conclusion, "Crawford Case Ends in Legal Love Feast."[48]

As the general public struggled to understand the unexpected denouement of what had once promised to be a pitched battle over race prejudice in the southern justice system, they picked up on the lawyers' interpretation of the trial. Two days after the lawyers' exchange of courtroom sentiments, the NAACP's Walter White began drafting an article for the organization's journal, *The Crisis,* to interpret the case's resolution for its puzzled readership. Originally drafted before the trial by the organization's staff, the article had begun as an indictment of the local justice system for railroading Crawford in order to protect Boeing. White now penned a new draft, which argued that the principal benefit of the trial was that it impressed onlookers with Houston's brilliance, and that it showed the ability of black and white lawyers to interact as equals in public. The *News Leader*'s Freeman endorsed the same view, writing that the case "performed a large education function in showing the South that there are Negro lawyers of the type of Mr. Houston and his associates." The *Times-Dispatch*'s Dabney highlighted this point in informing the *New York Times* readership that the trial's outcome "pleases Virginia," while the *Washington Post* made Houston's end-of-trial statements the centerpiece of its argument that the NAACP had learned the proper means to triumph over southern prejudice. For the NAACP leaders, their moderate allies, and the press, Houston's actions inside that courtroom were truly representative of how African Americans as a whole should go about seeking equality.[49]

As the national press congratulated itself on the resolution of the case, behind the scenes a tension lay unresolved that had been in the air for quite some time. From the moment he set foot in Loudoun County, Houston seemed to stand in for southern blacks who often had no voice in the judicial system. But what it meant to represent his race in that courtroom was an open question. Initially, Houston thought that he spoke for the masses of blacks who believed that southern justice perpetuated what he had called a "caste system." After all, it remained true that significant exculpatory evidence still existed (the Boston alibi witnesses), and that the confession was likely tainted by the off-the-record actions that Galleher took to get it. Moreover, regardless of Crawford's guilt or innocence, Houston had demonstrated that Loudoun officials excluded blacks from the grand and trial juries that decided Crawford's fate. Only one year before, the highest court in neighboring Maryland had overturned a criminal conviction because of racial exclusion from juries in a case much like Crawford's, and two years later the Supreme Court would do the same thing in the second round of Scottsboro appeals.[50]

Houston had not been entirely wrong in his initial belief that Crawford's trial was further evidence of a local caste system, and in believing that representing his race meant speaking out against that caste system even if it resulted in violence. But as the trial wore on, the question of caste came to focus more and more on Houston himself. Now it seemed that he would represent his racial group (and perhaps keep his client from being executed) by insisting on equal treatment for black lawyers in a southern courtroom. The surest way to represent black people, it seemed, was to be treated like a white man. That even extended to adopting the consensus views of the Loudoun lawyers on the outcome of the case, and in suppressing the racially divisive issues that once seemed to define the meaning of the trial. For the moment, all seemed well as the lawyers converged on the story of the trial.

The emerging consensus launched the trial lawyers into new roles. Houston, buoyed by the new interpretation of Crawford's case, would soon move to New York to become the first African American to serve as chief lawyer for the NAACP. Galleher rode the publicity surrounding the case to a position in the Department of Justice. Once he was ensconced there, one of the first things to come across his desk would be a brief written by Houston and his assistants in support of federal action in the NAACP's antilynching effort.[51]

Houston's new status reflected, as well, back on Loudoun County, where his enhanced profile would make him a repeat player in local civil rights cases. He had made quite an impression on the white Loudoun citizenry. One upper-class local woman reportedly confessed that "[a]fter hearing that brilliant man, I can no longer hold the views I previously held of the Negro." He remained a familiar presence in the county over the next decade and a half. When local black citizens needed help getting a modern high school to replace their run-down one-room school, they called on Houston. He entered into polite but firm negotiations with the school authorities, backed up by the explicit threat that he would bring his considerable courtroom skills to bear in a lawsuit challenging the inferior black facilities. That intervention was backed by pressure from both local African Americans and from Dabney, who coordinated with Houston to produce favorable coverage of the dispute in the *Times-Dispatch*. The school authorities soon acceded to the request.[52]

By the end of the decade, Houston's credibility was so high in Loudoun County that he returned there to take on another case that supposedly could not be won. It involved a black man who was falsely accused of attempting to rape a white woman. A defendant in such a case could be saved from execution in Virginia, as recent research has shown, and Houston proceeded to show how it could be done. He found himself in familiar territory when he appeared before Judge Alexander and was nominally opposed by the current commonwealth's attorney, Charles Harrison. After the jury's decision, as expected, was conviction and death, Houston held a series of conferences with Alexander and the reluctant Harrison (it was an election year) and persuaded them to support a different result. Judge Alexander and the prosecutor made it clear to officials statewide that they were ready to go public with their views to prevent the execution. Before they could make good on that promise, the state Supreme Court of Appeals unexpectedly stepped in to overturn the verdict, calling the testimony of the alleged victim and her husband "so contrary to human experience . . . as to be totally insufficient to justify the verdict." With that political cover, Harrison declined to recharge the defendant, and Houston quickly arranged for him to be spirited out of the state. Even the besieged prosecutor had thought such a result impossible, and the court's decision can only be attributable to the credibility of Houston and the influence of the local legal community in convincing their brethren in Richmond to produce a result that was difficult to achieve in Loudoun.[53]

Perhaps the most significant reflection of the events in the Loudoun County Courthouse, however, lay in their effect on the black lawyers' imagination of what it meant to represent a race. This was particularly so in the centerpiece of that representation project, the newly transformed Howard Law School, where the law school community's excitement had pushed Houston into the controversial decision to employ an all-black defense team. Houston's most promising former student from Howard had undoubtedly followed the proceedings closely from his home in nearby Maryland. While he had helped out with the Boston extradition proceedings, Thurgood Marshall was still hard at work getting admitted to the bar and setting up his law practice in Baltimore as the Crawford case proceeded toward trial. Houston did not ask him to do the time-consuming work of preparing the case. Instead, with significant help from his mentor, Marshall would spend the next few years in Baltimore working through the same set of tensions that hovered just beneath the surface during the extraordinary events that had just taken place in Loudoun County.

5

Young Thurgood Marshall Joins
the Brotherhood of the Bar

THURGOOD Marshall's life as a lawyer is preserved in American memory as a story that moves quickly from the beginning of his law practice in Baltimore in 1933, to his first major civil rights case two years later that desegregated the University of Maryland's law school, and then to his move to New York to work for the NAACP on the litigation that would lead to *Brown v. Board of Education.* His life as a young lawyer struggling to build a reputation in Baltimore evokes little interest, save as an example of his neglect of, and lack of interest in, the ordinary work of an attorney in private practice. Yet Marshall's Baltimore practice files, long available to researchers but little used, paint a picture of a lawyer who was about as successful in drumming up clients as contemporaries like Dallas Nicholas. Like his fellow Howard graduate Nicholas, Marshall set up his practice in one of the city's two black lawyer enclaves, at 4 East Redwood Street. Like Nicholas and so many of his contemporaries, he made his living mostly in office practice—small business affairs, divorces, real estate, probate, and similar matters. Like them, he held down a side job to make ends meet. Marshall worked part time as a government clerk. For the most part, his private practice was a typical one for black lawyers in places like Baltimore and Washington, D.C., straight through the 1950s.[1]

What set Marshall apart was his ability to do something most of his contemporaries could not—get into court in a few high-profile cases that made his reputation on both sides of the color line. Marshall came to prominence as a lawyer because, for blacks and whites alike, he seemed to represent something much larger than himself. White lawyers and judges tended to see the young, confident, impeccably trained black lawyer as someone much like themselves. Black Marylanders did, too. The authentic representative of African Americans in the courts, both groups told themselves, was a black lawyer who seemed as much like his white colleagues as possible. But each group wanted something different from the youthful lawyer whose presence in court seemed so disruptive of local racial mores. White lawyers seemed to desire, most of all, a person who could explain to a skeptical black public that the legal system treated them fairly. Blacks seemed to want an African American lawyer whose acceptance by whites gave him the power to call out racial inequity in the system. Marshall walked a fine line in his early years in practice, and the key to his success as a civil rights lawyer was his ability to convince each group that when he stepped into the courtroom, he represented its particular point of view. It was a paradoxical position, but that balancing act was the foundation for the stunning victories that marked his early years as a lawyer, including the one that desegregated the University of Maryland's law school.

Reversals of View: Law and Lawyers

More than anything else, Thurgood Marshall's formative years as a lawyer were shaped by the fact that he began practicing law in the shadow of the Crawford case. Baltimore's white lawyers and judges, like their counterparts throughout the South, were well aware of the events that had taken place in nearby Loudoun County, and of the interpretation that the lawyers had stamped on the trial's unexpected end. In fact, the leaders of the city's bench and bar were in the midst of their own controversy about race and criminal justice. Two of the leading figures in that controversy would play key roles in Marshall's early career. The first one, Judge Morris Soper, was already on his way to a career as one of the most respected federal circuit court judges in the country. As a younger man, however, he had opposed his state's leading lawyers by carrying a black voting rights case all the way to the Supreme Court, where it became one of the famous "Grandfather Clause" cases of 1915. Soper also incurred the displeasure of the local bar association by his unsuccessful effort to get it to admit black lawyers to membership. The second figure who would make a difference in Marshall's career was Baltimore City circuit judge Eugene O'Dunne. Earlier in his career,

O'Dunne had also risked his reputation, and his life, in defending a black man accused of an interracial rape on the state's then-remote Eastern Shore, after a mob of thousands had tried to lynch him. O'Dunne succeeded in getting the original trial invalidated because it had taken place in a mob atmosphere, and got the retrial moved to Baltimore County.[2]

Soper and O'Dunne were members of a prestigious group of Baltimore lawyers, many of whom had attended the state's flagship law school at the University of Maryland. In the early 1930s, that group was locked in a struggle with local communities in outlying areas of the state. The controversy began with a series of interracial criminal cases that had led to the lynching of two black men in rural parts of the state, and had caused several others to be transferred to the custody of the Baltimore legal community to preserve their lives. The conflict between law and lynching weighed heavily on the minds of the leaders of the state's white bar, and for many of them Thurgood Marshall would come to personify the means to resolve it.[3]

Marshall was drawn into the conflict indirectly, but it would make his reputation as a lawyer. Born in Baltimore in 1908, Marshall grew up in a middle-class household in the city's respectable Druid Hill Avenue neighborhood. His father was a dining car waiter, his mother a schoolteacher, and his brother became a doctor. After graduating from Lincoln University, the well-known historically black institution in Pennsylvania where he attended school with the poet Langston Hughes, Marshall got married and entered Howard University in the fall of 1930. Commuting by train from Baltimore, he graduated first in his class in 1933. His academic performance placed him among the group of top Howard students and professors, including Edward Lovett, James Tyson, and Leon Ransom, who Charles Houston called on for help as Houston became more involved in NAACP matters that year. Marshall was perhaps the best example of the success of Houston's program of turning out confident and extremely competent black lawyers and sending them back to their own communities to practice. But the Baltimore native had the misfortune to graduate as the Great Depression was reaching one of its lowest points, so clients were few and profits hard to come by, even for local lawyers with established reputations like Nicholas. Marshall also began practicing just as the lynching controversy was putting the city's small group of black lawyers in the spotlight.[4]

At the time, it seemed unlikely that any black lawyer could come to court and represent an African American defendant who had been accused of a serious interracial crime, particularly in the state's rural areas. In fact, the state's leading black civil rights lawyer, the aging W. Ashbie Hawkins, had been booed and hissed by a crowd of African Americans at a forum two years earlier, after a speaker charged that local black lawyers had failed to respond to the controversy. White lawyers had taken the lead in the cases, in particular a radical Baltimore lawyer named Bernard Ades. In a case involving Euel Lee, a black man accused of murdering a white family on the Eastern Shore, emotions ran so high that Ades had to take refuge in the local jail for seven hours while a mob surrounded the building and threatened him with violence. Nonetheless, in 1932 Ades had convinced Maryland's highest court to invalidate Lee's conviction because blacks had been excluded from the jury pool—the same precedent that inspired Houston to make that issue a centerpiece of his Crawford defense. But Ades's aggressive tactics and combative language in several of his cases landed him in federal court in Baltimore on disciplinary charges. Ades asked Houston to defend him in the disciplinary proceeding, and Houston, in turn, brought Marshall into the case.[5]

There was a delicious irony in Houston and Marshall coming to court to defend a white lawyer against disciplinary charges in Maryland, and Ades knew it. In Maryland, state and local bar groups excluded black lawyers from membership, as did the institution that bound the leaders of the white bar together—the University of Maryland Law School. Ades's fate at the trial would turn on the question of whether he had performed like a reasonable Maryland lawyer in defending Lee and other criminal suspects. But everyone knew that the real question—given the racially exclusionary character of the bar's disciplinary groups—was whether he had performed like a reasonable *white* lawyer. In Baltimore, black and white lawyers were so separate that by the end of the decade each group would have its own bar group with segregated disciplinary proceedings. In Ades's case, however, African American lawyers would come to the federal courthouse in Baltimore to prove that he had performed like a white lawyer in court. Ades enjoyed tweaking the racial consciences of his fellow Maryland lawyers, and asking two black lawyers to defend him would have appealed to the young radical lawyer's rebellious streak.[6]

Ades was lucky, for his disciplinary hearing was moving forward just as Houston was making national headlines with his impeccable performance—like a white man—at the pretrial hearings in Crawford's case. As the Crawford trial date was approaching, Houston announced that his next case would be Bernard Ades's defense. Houston promised to bring in "all my associates" from the Howard defense team, but the task ultimately fell to him and Marshall alone. Marshall did the preparatory work for the disciplinary hearing, and the strangeness of two black lawyers appearing in a southern courtroom to defend a white lawyer was not lost on the people around them. One typical contemporary account described Ades as "bushy-haired and wild-eyed," which contrasted strongly with how observers described his black defense team. That assessment can only be reinforced by viewing a photograph of a hatless and gloveless Ades emerging from court in winter weather, while beside him stood his fedoraed, bundled, and trim duo of black defense lawyers.[7]

In the disciplinary hearing to come, it would be Houston and Marshall who seemed, to all around them, to be performing like white lawyers, while Ades marked himself as an outsider. That juxtaposition was reinforced by Ades's membership in the Communist-affiliated International Labor Defense. ILD lawyers openly condemned regular legal proceedings as akin to lynchings in the South. This was exactly the stance Ades took in Euel Lee's case, and one that caused him to be nearly lynched along with his client. Nonetheless, Ades's aggressive tactics had kept his client alive and out of the hands of rural mobs for two years and through two appeals to the Maryland Court of Appeals, until Lee was finally convicted and sentenced to die in Baltimore County. When Ades applied to the federal court for a writ of habeas corpus, the judges suspended him from practice before that court because of his controversial rhetoric and tactics. After Ades lost his final appeal to the state's highest court, Lee's luck ran out and he was executed.[8]

The radical lawyer added fuel to the already considerable fires he had started when he claimed that Lee had written a will giving him custody of his body. Ades planned to take it to New York for a leftist demonstration. Judge O'Dunne, in an emotional ruling from the bench, enjoined Ades from claiming the body and instructed the sheriff that he was "justified in shooting to kill" members of any group that interfered with Lee's burial in Maryland, in order to ensure the "preser-

vation of law and order." O'Dunne believed that he and his fellow Baltimore lawyers were essential to that preservation. But it wasn't clear who
exactly he believed was the greater threat to law and order—the Eastern
Shore lynchers or the radical lawyer who opposed them in the courts.[9]

Houston and Marshall's appearance on behalf of Bernard Ades in a
packed federal courtroom in March 1934 seemed to throw just about
everyone out of sorts. The two black lawyers arrived in court to defend
a member of the University of Maryland's prestigious law alumni group,
as one of Ades's fellow Maryland law graduates sat in judgment. The defense team set up a meeting with the leaders of the state's whites-only
bar association, while Marshall pushed forward with an audacious proposal to throw their newfound prestige behind an effort to persuade the
local federal judges to remove Judges Calvin Chesnut and William Coleman, who had originally suspended Ades, from the case. Within a month,
Houston announced with evident satisfaction that "Coleman and
Chesnut are out" and that "Soper will try the disbarment proceedings." Judge Soper's selection put the black attorneys in front of a judge
whose public racial liberalism dated back to his participation in the
Grandfather Clause cases.[10]

As Houston took the lead inside the courtroom and Marshall
supplied the research, the black lawyers mounted a spirited defense of
Ades's controversial words and actions. With their help, Soper found
ample reason to dismiss the most serious charge against Ades: that he
had inserted himself into several cases before his clients agreed to hire
him. However, with regard to Ades's attempt to obtain Lee's body for
a demonstration in New York, Houston stepped out of his role as an
advocate and into a new role as a member of the state's legal fraternity.
Reportedly stating that he was speaking "not as Ades' attorney, but as
man to man," he told Soper that a reprimand would be appropriate.
The judge agreed. Citing "the decisive action of Judge O'Dunne" in pre-
venting Ades from getting Lee's body, Soper ruled that the leftist attorney had gone too far. In a compromise result, Soper delivered a formal
reprimand to Ades but reinstated him to practice before the court.[11]

By the time the proceeding was over, it was Houston and Marshall,
not Ades, who seemed to personify the professional values of Maryland's
leading white lawyers. In fact, in Ades's disciplinary proceedings, the
Howard defense team's actions in another case became the standard by
which Ades's own conduct was to be measured. It was the case of Page

Jupiter, a black man who was brought to Baltimore just ahead of a lynch mob after being accused of murdering a white woman in southern Maryland. Charles Houston and Edward Lovett had been involved in the case at first but withdrew once they were convinced that Jupiter would get a fair trial with adequate counsel. Ades, by contrast, continued to accuse Maryland's legal community of effecting a lynching. Houston vigorously resisted the comparison between the black lawyers' restraint and Ades's aggressive tactics, but Judge Soper found it compelling. The actions of "leading members of Jupiter's race," wrote Soper in his opinion, stood in stark contrast to Ades's incendiary tactics. After Soper's ruling, the Jewish and radical Ades continued his journey to the margins of the local bar when state authorities began their own ethics proceedings against him. Ades followed that up with a run for governor on the Communist Party ticket and eventual exile from his home state and its legal community.[12]

With Judge Soper's help, Marshall and Houston had emerged from the disciplinary proceeding both as "leading members of Jupiter's race"—representative Negroes—and as exemplars of the core values of the white bar. Those two somewhat contradictory assessments were just about the only things that Maryland's lawyers concurred on at the end of that controversial proceeding. Many lawyers thought that Ades should have been sanctioned more harshly or even disbarred, while others thought that he was being disciplined for his political views and for defending an unpopular client. As local lawyers continued to argue over the result, one of Ades's Maryland law school classmates wrote to Houston to tell him that during his ten years of practice in the local courts, he had "never seen a cause so ably defended as this one." "[N]o matter what the decision might have been, everyone of the numerous persons with whom I discussed the case," he gushed, "agreed that your conduct of the case was faultless in every respect."[13]

Larger, unresolved issues of race, justice, and extralegal violence swirled around Depression-era Maryland courtrooms, but Houston and Marshall's exemplary conduct temporarily pushed those issues to the background. It remained true that a high-profile black defendant who escaped lynching in the outlying areas of the state was still likely to be convicted and executed after a trial in Baltimore City or County, as had Euel Lee. While the elite Baltimore lawyers and Maryland's black residents concurred in their opposition to lynching, they agreed on little else. For the moment, however, that conflict was put to the side. Houston returned to his law school duties in Washington, while Marshall slipped back into the office practice and part-time legal work that marked off black lawyers as a race and profession apart in Maryland. Years later, even Ades would remember him as "young Thurgood." Marshall remained a low-status lawyer in Maryland. But longer-term trends in Maryland law and politics would soon push him back across the racial divide within the profession. Chief among them was the continuing dispute between Baltimore's lawyers and outlying communities about black men accused of serious interracial crimes.[14]

As a Baltimore lawyer, Thurgood Marshall was a member of a profession that had a great deal of influence on how its fellow Marylanders responded to cases of serious cross-racial crime. In those cases, Maryland's black defendants often took advantage of the state's long-standing practice of allowing defendants to waive jury trials. Black criminal defendants preferred to put their fates in the hands of judges and lawyers rather than those of presumably hostile all-white juries. The same situation probably prevailed in neighboring Virginia, where two black lawyers reported that they also waived jury trials in criminal cases. By the early 1930s, it had become quite common for black Maryland defendants in interracial cases to be transferred to the Baltimore legal system for safekeeping, and sometimes for trial, where their fates lay entirely in the hands of that city's legal community.[15]

The city's leading white lawyers tried to save these black defendants from lynch mobs, but had far less to say about the racial caste system that made conviction and a death sentence the expected outcome in many cases, even in Baltimore. As a young lawyer, Eugene O'Dunne had even joined the armed groups of local citizens who pursued one of his black clients after the man broke out of jail to escape a lynch mob— after being duly deputized as part of a legally constituted posse. After capture, a trial, and a retrial in Baltimore County, his client was executed, and O'Dunne had the man's possessions sold out from under his family to pay the lawyer's fee. As a judge, he was incensed at Ades's charges of systematic bias in regular legal proceedings. By the early 1930s, however, the radical lawyer's charges were being taken up by black communities in outlying areas of the state, and Marshall's new role drew him back across the color line and into the heart of the dispute.[16]

Marshall's ability to perform like a white man in court was key in resolving a series of disputes where black and white Maryland communities differed markedly in their views of courtroom proceedings. An interracial crime could produce profoundly differing narratives of exactly what happened in a trial. In the case of Alexander Jones, for instance, accused of raping a young white woman in Montgomery County in 1934 and held in Baltimore to guard against mob violence, the area's white dailies dispassionately reported what appeared to be an orderly progression through indictment, sober mobilization of evidence, conviction, and a death sentence after an unbiased trial held in Rockville. The *Baltimore Afro-American,* by contrast, lamented that "[e]vidences of prejudice were rampant around the court." Jones sat "emaciated, and evidently cowed by armed authority hemming him in," in a racially segregated courtroom where black Marylanders felt unwelcome even as observers. His white lawyers, according to the *Afro-American,* offered little evidence and even waived their closing argument. In lieu of argument, the defense attorneys pronounced themselves "satisfied with whatever the court decided to do." After the presiding judge "almost shouted" the death verdict at the cowering defendant, his lawyers thanked the judge for a fair decision. They quickly announced that there would be no appeal.[17]

How would the arrival of a black lawyer in court alter those contrasting interpretations of justice in Maryland? That was the question that Marshall confronted in the aftermath of the Ades proceeding, when his enhanced reputation made it only natural that the state's black and white leadership would turn to him for resolution of their contrasting views of law.

Joining the Fraternity of Lawyers

A few months after the Ades hearing, Marshall began to move to the center of the controversy about race in Maryland courtrooms when a neighbor came to him with a difficult case. James Gross was being held in Baltimore for his safety for allegedly being part of a gang that pulled off a series of robberies, assaults, and burglaries in Prince George's County that ended with the murder of a white shopkeeper. Marshall's arrival in Upper Marlboro in July of 1934 to defend his client was an event so striking that black newspapers halfway across the country took notice. The *Chicago Defender* called him "the first Race lawyer to try an important case here in the memory of court attaches." The self-assured, gangly, light-skinned black lawyer had arrived in court in a place where no one had ever seen anyone like him before. For James Gross, however, the novelty of Marshall's presence mattered little. Marshall forged lasting bonds with the local judges and prosecutor, but it was not enough to save his client. Gross was quickly convicted and later executed, leaving Marshall's file notation of "convicted 1st degree—hang" as a terse record of his reaction to the decision.[18]

Marshall got another chance when a minister approached him in December about James Carter, who was being held in Baltimore amid rumors of lynching after being accused of attempting to rape a white woman in a park in Frederick on Halloween night. Local black citizens didn't trust Carter's court-appointed counsel and suspected that his upcoming trial would be a sham. They turned to Marshall for an independent investigation of the facts and of the fairness of the trial. He promptly enlisted the support of the *Baltimore Afro-American* and kept the NAACP's national office apprised of the case. After interviewing possible defense witnesses, Marshall was inclined to agree with local black sentiment. He concluded that Carter, most likely, was not present at the time of the alleged attack, had been drunk when he signed a written confession to the crime, and might be mentally incompetent.[19]

The young black lawyer's views of the case changed markedly after he interviewed the local judge, the prosecutor, and Carter's defense lawyers. Instead of a small, white-dominated community bent on excluding blacks from influence in the criminal process, he found a community of lawyers and judges who were willing to extend "every courtesy" to their black Baltimore colleague, as he reported back to the NAACP. Marshall noted with apparent surprise and approval that the defense lawyers even "offered to enter my appearance in the case." The prosecutor had "expected that the case would attract outside attention," but "Court and Counsel have a good opinion of the N.A.A.C.P. and seem to know about it"—almost certainly because of the Howard defense team's work in Crawford's case. With the lawyers' help, Marshall continued investigating and decided that the local bar and bench's unified opinion was correct. He concluded that the stories of black alibi witnesses could not be verified, and that Carter was in the park on the night of the assault and was guilty of the heinous act. The young Baltimore lawyer accepted his colleagues' invitation to sit in at the trial, which would be closed to the public to protect the victim.[20]

At first, Marshall thought he would come to court to represent the views of a skeptical black community to the white legal fraternity, but it now became Marshall's job to present that fraternity's views to his fellow African Americans, who, along with the rest of the public, were barred from the trial. With Marshall in attendance, Carter's trial proceeded to the expected conviction. However, in what was perhaps a compromise result, he was sentenced to life in prison rather than death. The young black lawyer emerged from the closed courtroom to announce in the African American press that Carter had been treated fairly by the local courts. To the NAACP, he reported that Carter "received an exceptionally able defense by his counsel." Privately he told his mentor, Houston, with evident satisfaction, that "he is guilty as the devil and has been sentenced to life." Marshall's pronouncement appeared to end the sustained agitation within the local black community, and he now pushed that community to refocus its energies on establishing an NAACP chapter.[21]

Yet, a more complicated view of the trial lay just beneath the surface, even within the *Afro-American*'s write-up, which had been based on Marshall's own report of the trial. The *Afro* subtitled its article on the case "William Carter Is Sentenced after Trial Lasting Only 12 Minutes." The paper told its readers that the defense put Carter on the stand, where he admitted that he was in the park that night but contended that he was drunk and couldn't recall his actions. Even the *Washington Post*, not noted for its sympathy for black criminal defendants in that era, reported that "[t]he defense used only ten minutes, nine of which" were taken up by Carter's futile testimony. Moreover, according to the *Afro*, another man had been initially arrested for the crime and was held for a month before police focused their efforts solely on Carter, and at least one witness at trial indicated that the defendant's confession had been obtained under duress. Nonetheless, the paper gave Marshall the last word on the case, which he used to compliment the defense lawyers on a job well done, and on what the paper called the "courtesy" they had extended to their black colleague.[22]

Six months later, Marshall returned to Frederick for another interracial rape case, and he could sense that something had changed.

"[T]hey knew what I was there for," he reported back to the NAACP. He was now so well known to lawyers and judges there that they were not surprised at his arrival. They welcomed it. Marshall was soon face to face with two of the judges who had participated in the Carter trial. The case involved James Poindexter, who had already been tried and sentenced to death. Poindexter was a codefendant of Alexander Jones, the black man whose rape prosecution the previous year had so stirred the *Afro-American* to condemn the case as an exercise of prejudice and browbeating white authority. Poindexter had gotten his story out to a national black audience by writing a letter that was published in the *Pittsburgh Courier*. He contacted the NAACP, which sent Marshall to investigate.[23]

Marshall quickly found himself in agreement with the Frederick-based judges who had presided over the trial in neighboring Montgomery County. He reported that they spoke with him "very freely and frankly" about the case, and told him that "[t]hey consider the case one of the most horrible they have ever judged." With their permission, he read all the testimony in the case. Ultimately he recommended that the NAACP not get involved, although he wrote the governor a letter requesting clemency "not because of the trial or the record but on the basis that the death penalty seems to be for Negroes alone." The NAACP's Roy Wilkins wrote back to thank him for "the excellent report and recommendation" and recommended that the organization have nothing more to do with Poindexter's fate.[24]

When Marshall arrived at the Baltimore City Circuit Court in the middle of 1935 for a trial that would desegregate the University of Maryland's law school, he was no stranger to the judges who would resolve the issue. The story that brought him to that courtroom had been unfolding for over a year, ever since he and Houston had walked into the federal courthouse just across the street to defend Bernard Ades, and the integrity of the white bar. In fact, what would happen in the University of Maryland suit was a direct result of Baltimore's own version of the inbred local legal communities that were so important in the careers of Raymond Alexander in Philadelphia and Charles Houston in his Loudoun County cases. It was no coincidence that sitting in front of the courtroom was a figure who was a core player in Marshall's story— Circuit Judge Eugene O'Dunne, the liberal judge who had presided over Euel Lee's trial and prevented Ades from taking Lee's body to New

York. Only months before, the young black lawyer had asked for the judge's advice in a police brutality case in Prince George's County, which O'Dunne gave freely.[25]

When Marshall filed the Maryland law school suit, he found himself in the middle of a community of lawyers for whom the young black lawyer had come to represent something larger than himself. Marshall was a quick study, and he immediately took advantage of the professional capital that he had built up over the previous year. He personally asked Judge O'Dunne to hear the case, and it was assigned to him. Now O'Dunne had to decide whether the state's practice of excluding black students from its state law school and paying their tuition to go out of state to study law violated the Fourteenth Amendment. The out-of-state scholarship fund, it turned out, was administered by Judge Morris Soper, yet another figure who was mightily impressed with Marshall's efforts in the Ades disciplinary hearing. Ultimately, the issue of the law school's racial policies lay in the hands of the Maryland Court of Appeals, since whoever lost the suit was sure to appeal. There the issue would be resolved by Chief Judge Carroll Bond. Bond himself was a personal reminder to all involved that, within living memory, blacks and whites had studied law alongside one another at the university. The chief judge had attended the University of Maryland Law School only a few years after the school had instituted its whites-only policy and expelled its last black students, including W. Ashbie Hawkins, in 1890.[26]

Even before Marshall had begun practicing law, well-educated black Baltimoreans were pushing to reverse the state university's whites-only policy. A group of young African Americans, including local activist Juanita Jackson, began to apply for study in several of the graduate programs at the university. Nine prospective black students would apply to study law at the university between 1933 and 1935. As early as December 1933, Jackson was eager to file suit, and Marshall had become interested in joining the fight. Marshall expected help from the aging Hawkins and other senior local black lawyers, but wound up pushing the cause forward himself. One year later, Amherst College graduate Donald Murray applied to the law school. Other than his race, he more than met the requirements for admission, which were two years of college and upright moral character. After Murray's application was rejected, Marshall consulted with Houston and filed suit in Baltimore. In June of 1935, the two black lawyers came to court to get Murray admitted to law school. Accompanied by their client, the NAACP team would face off against Maryland Assistant Attorney General Charles LeViness.[27]

Again and again during the subsequent trial and appeal, judges and opposing lawyers went out of their way to suggest that there was something special about Marshall and Houston appearing before them in this type of case. Even before the case came to trial, O'Dunne signaled to his fellow lawyers that the black lawyers' claims should be embraced. When LeViness came to court to ask for a routine delay in the start of trial, the judge called Marshall over and gave him some confidential, friendly advice: "When the attorney general asks for [an] adjournment, object." It was not the first time the judge had given him pointers on his civil rights litigation, so Marshall did as he was told. To LeViness's surprise, O'Dunne put the case on for trial the next day. When Marshall moved that Houston be admitted to practice in the Baltimore court at the start of the proceedings, the judge broke the tension by joking that he had heard of law school deans moving the admission of their former students, but never the reverse. Even during opening arguments, O'Dunne pointedly expressed skepticism about LeViness's case, and interrupted to point out that the out-of-state scholarship fund seemed inadequate to meet Murray's true expenses if he chose to take advantage of it.[28]

At the trial, O'Dunne gave every indication of having been persuaded quite early by Marshall and Houston's meticulous assembly of evidence that Murray was qualified for admission and that the alternatives Maryland provided for him—a segregated university system with no black law school, or an uncertain out-of-state scholarship fund— were constitutionally inadequate. Marshall opened the evidence with Murray's testimony, which established his clear qualifications to attend the state law school and the hardships of attending school elsewhere. As his main witnesses, Houston called the president of the University of Maryland and its law school dean, mainly to establish the poor alternatives available for Murray's legal studies, both in and out of state. As LeViness called several state officials to establish that the segregated higher education system provided equal opportunities to blacks and whites, O'Dunne seemed to grow bored. At one point, he told LeViness that his evidence was irrelevant and that "I won't even be awake" when the state's witnesses were testifying.[29]

Before the day was over, O'Dunne had decided that there was little justification in keeping people like Murray, or Houston and Marshall for that matter, out of the state's elite legal fraternity. LeViness had, too. In case anyone had missed the point, Houston noted in his closing argument that "[r]ight here in this courtroom white and colored persons are sitting together." If people could interact across racial lines in court (at least in the city of Baltimore), they could certainly do it as law students. All the lawyers in the room had seen the evidence, and in fact the black NAACP lawyers had provided it by their own presence. During LeViness's closing, O'Dunne again took the initiative and pressed the state's lawyer on the need for blacks to go out of state to study law. He finally elicited the tepid defense that exclusion was defensible since few blacks would apply. The judge had heard enough. Noting that Maryland provided segregated railroad cars even though few blacks rode the trains, he interjected sarcastically, "How would you let them ride, in an ox cart?" The courtroom broke up into laughter. After Marshall, Houston, and LeViness finished their arguments, the assistant attorney general asked for an adjournment to give O'Dunne time to reflect before making his decision. The judge once again signaled that Marshall should object, and then, to the NAACP lawyers' surprise, O'Dunne issued an oral decision requiring the university to admit Murray. LeViness was so overcome by the symbolism of the moment that he shook hands with Murray in court and told the audience that "I wish to be quoted as saying that I hope Mr. Murray leads the class in the law school and graduates as valedictorian."[30]

As the case made its way to the Court of Appeals, the NAACP's Walter White noted that "there is a certain psychological value of having a Negro lawyer appear in a case of this character." The NAACP executive secretary was fending off the inevitable objection that a white lawyer should now be brought in because of judicial prejudice. He was stating what now seemed obvious to all those closely connected to the case: while Marshall and Houston's thorough preparation and courtroom work provided the groundwork for O'Dunne's ruling, perhaps their most potent evidence had not been presented in court that June, but rather had been assembled during the past year and a half of Marshall's interactions with his white colleagues at the Maryland bar. When the objection was raised again, White reiterated that "[t]here will be certain strategic advantages in a Negro arguing against educational discrimination against Negroes." Black lawyers' own presence in court had become the most important proof in support of their claims, particularly when the law school's own alumni controlled the litigation process.[31]

When Marshall and Houston appeared in the state Court of Appeals that fall, they received a collegial reception. LeViness went out of his way to second Marshall's motion that Houston be admitted to practice in the Maryland court. The white prosecutor told the judges that he took "great pleasure" in endorsing the admission of his esteemed black colleague. A vigorous, but respectful, oral argument ensued, and federal judge Morris Soper later took Marshall aside to tell him how "very much impressed" Chief Judge Bond of the Court of Appeals had been with the black lawyers' appellate argument. A month after that, Bond authored an opinion that affirmed O'Dunne's ruling that Murray should be allowed to go to the state law school.[32]

As significant as the Maryland law school victory had been, one last stumbling block remained for the black lawyer in a Maryland courtroom, and that block was the jury trial. Even Walter White doubted that someone like Marshall could make headway against entrenched racial perceptions when juries rather than judges rendered the verdict. Not even in the city of Baltimore, thought White, were black lawyers ready to take on this work. Yet even that barrier was being broken as White rendered those sentiments, and Marshall's brothers at the bar would play a key role in its removal.[33]

The breakthrough came in a seemingly unlikely place. It was a police brutality trial in then-rural Prince George's County—a place where, as Marshall reported, the general sentiment was that "a Negro lawyer could not try a case." Not until 1950 would a black lawyer open an office there. The case involved Kater Stevens, who had been shot and killed after a traffic stop while fleeing a police officer named Charles Flory in Bladensburg, a small locality that had a reputation for police abuse of black motorists. Washington lawyer Belford Lawson came out to Bladensburg for the coroner's inquest and found that the proceedings took place in a "prejudiced and tense atmosphere" and that "the whole town turned out" amid heavy police presence to keep watch over the hearing. The coroner's jury failed to determine even the cause of death, and prosecution seemed unlikely. The local prosecutor, Alan Bowie, was sympathetic but cautious. Ten years before, he had indicted four police officers in the fatal shooting of a black man, but now he was worried about fanning white resentment with an election coming up.[34]

Only months before, Marshall had challenged racial mores in Prince George's courtrooms simply by showing up for his first major criminal case amid rumors that his client, James Gross, might be lynched. The mere fact of a black lawyer's arrival in previously off-limits territory had made headlines in the national black press. Marshall's client was convicted of murder and would soon be executed, but the young black lawyer had formed useful bonds with Bowie and with J. C. Mattingly and William Loker, the local judges who heard the case. When Marshall returned to the county for the Kater Stevens controversy, the prosecutor proved to be a friendly but reluctant ally, but Marshall found more reliable ones in the judiciary.[35]

Back in Baltimore, Judge O'Dunne helped him come up with a legal theory that would allow local judges to appoint Marshall and Lawson as private prosecutors to take charge of a manslaughter trial for Flory. Marshall had already met with Prince George's Judge Mattingly, whom he found to be "wealthy, independent," and responsive to his fellow lawyers rather than electoral sentiment. With the assurance of a friendly hearing before Mattingly, he began to push forward with O'Dunne's proposal. Bowie now reluctantly agreed to prosecute, after Marshall promised to campaign with him for black votes during the next election.[36]

At the manslaughter trial the white prosecutor served as the amanuensis for his black colleagues. Marshall worked up a set of memoranda that supplied the material for Bowie's trial strategy, and the two black lawyers sat next to him at the prosecution table. When the jury rendered a not-guilty verdict, Marshall and Lawson went ahead with a civil suit on behalf of Stevens's widow. They found themselves in friendly territory when they once again appeared in Judge Mattingly's courtroom. In a result that Marshall pronounced "beyond our fondest hopes," they won the case and got a judgment for $1,200 from a jury of eleven whites and one African American in October 1935. In the rush of victory, Marshall told his NAACP contacts that the key element in the unexpected result was the racially tolerant atmosphere created by Judges Mattingly and Loker.[37]

In the aftermath of the victory, Lawson sent Marshall a note, gushing that the two black lawyers had earned unprecedented credibility on both sides of the color line in Prince George's County. Marshall quickly put that credibility to good use. A few months later, he found himself back in the county when, as now seemed inevitable, yet another sex crime allegation placed him in the middle of Maryland's racial politics. Dubbed the "Maryland 'Scottsboro' case" in the local black press, the controversy involved four black youths who were being held in Upper Marlboro in connection with an alleged assault on a white woman in a remote section of the county. When no hard evidence of their involvement emerged, Alan Bowie had the youths arrested and held incommunicado for four days. All that changed when Marshall showed up to begin his own investigation. After one day of interviews with the police, the youths, and local whites, Marshall caucused with Bowie and got an immediate agreement that the youths would be released the next day.[38]

As one of his last significant cases before his evident skill and effectiveness resulted in a move to New York to work full time for the NAACP, the Maryland "Scottsboro" case effectively bookended Marshall's career in that state. It brought him to the scene of his first major criminal case—where his client had been convicted and executed—and to a place where a year and a half before no one thought a black lawyer could come to court. It also brought him back into contact with the same lawyers he initially encountered there. They now received him, unevenly of course and with many remaining slights, but recognizably as a brother.

When Marshall and his colleagues came to court in southern civil rights cases, everyone saw them as much more than lawyers representing clients. To see a black man interact with whites in public—albeit with the cover of the lawyerly courtroom script as a justification—was an emotional experience for many white southerners. Representative white men looked across the courtroom and saw—or desired to see, at least—black lawyers who were their mirror images. Influential lawyers and judges like Morris Soper and Eugene O'Dunne saw in Marshall's performances an answer to a vexing problem of how exactly a lawyer should conduct himself when figures like Bernard Ades tried to blur the line between legal trials and lynching. In Virginia, Judge McLemore called the cross-racial lawyerly interactions in the Crawford trial an "oasis in a desert" and declared that he was ready to call for blacks to be put on juries when he returned to his home county. He also took the time to write a letter to the editor of *The Nation* praising Houston's conduct in his courtroom. Virginius Dabney, the influential molder of public opinion in his state and author of *Liberalism in the South*, came to see the black defense team as encapsulating his hopes for racially moderate progress in his region of the country. Even the newly elected governor of Virginia praised the Crawford trial as a model for continued racial progress in his inaugural address. These same cross-racial interactions that white moderates hailed as symbols of the South's racial future would have been impossible only a few steps outside the courthouse door.[39]

For black observers as well, the image of a black lawyer in the courtroom continued to invest itself with both drama and danger when measured against interracial social contact in other places. As black lawyers took over the NAACP's southern civil rights cases, lawyers like Leon Ransom, Constance Baker Motley, Robert Carter, and Marshall himself would experience the electric atmosphere that sometimes caused large portions of southern black communities to turn out when they came to court. Houston and Marshall's early cases were just the beginning of a story that would continue to unfold as late as the 1960s, when civil rights protesters fashioned constitutional claims out of courtroom segregation and the refusal of whites to address black lawyers and witnesses by their full names, and carried those challenges all the way to the Supreme Court.[40]

By that decade a new corps of civil rights attorneys had appeared in places like Alabama, where lawyers like Solomon Seay and J. L. Chestnut Jr. would cut their teeth by facing down white sheriffs in counties that had never seen a black lawyer before, or perhaps pausing for a chat or a drink of liquor with local authorities in unexpected moments when professionalism trumped race. Seay and Chestnut would marvel in their autobiographies about walking a fine line between actions that might inspire violence from local officials and those that might get them to "sit down and talk to you, not quite as equals but with a kind of acceptance not given to most blacks," as Chestnut put it—or "almost as if you was a white man," as a local sheriff instructed Seay.[41]

The early southern successes affected civil rights politics in other parts of the country. Coming on the heels of the Willie Brown victory in Philadelphia, the southern trials finally settled the question of whether black lawyers would appear in northern courtrooms in important NAACP cases. The fact that a black lawyer could sometimes perform like a white man in a southern courtroom helped launch the careers of a new generation of civil rights lawyers in other parts of the country. In the succeeding decades, lawyers such as Raymond Alexander, Chicago's Earl Dickerson and Irvin Mollison, and Los Angeles's Loren Miller would become local and nationally important figures in the American politics of race.

The lives of these civil rights lawyers later became part of the core American narrative of the nation's racial history. These lawyers seemed to be authentic representatives of their racial group in the journey from Jim Crow to equal rights. But that was only half the story, because what happened in those southern and northern courtrooms was part of a more conflicted, unsettling story that stretched back at least to the time of lawyers like John Mercer Langston. Americans had always wanted contradictory things of figures like Langston, Houston, and Marshall. The partial folding of black lawyers into the fraternity of the white bar placed them at the center of a racial divide, because to be an authentic representative of your race—in the eyes of blacks and whites alike—was often to be seen, as much as possible, as a white man. It remained true that black and white communities often constructed profoundly different narratives out of the same set of observations of what happened in a courtroom. Indeed, those contrasting views of law and race were now thrusting themselves to the fore with a vengeance, just as the leaders of the black bar were coming to believe that their roles as representatives of a race were finally secure.

The elegant, biracial lawyer John Mercer Langston seemed to confound all that nineteenth-century Americans believed about racial identity. That was the reason for his rise in American politics, and also a reason he always stood second to his rival Frederick Douglass.

Brady-Handy Photograph Collection, Library of Congress.

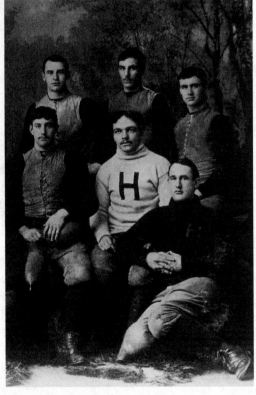

William H. Lewis and teammates on the Harvard football team. Lewis is wearing the white sweater. The Boston lawyer had many prominent white clients in the early twentieth century, and that helped make him a respected leader among African Americans.

Courtesy of the Harvard University Archives.

Washington, D.C., judge Robert H. Terrell, at his desk with the Supreme Court justices pictured behind him. Terrell and over one hundred "representative colored men" gathered in the Capitol building in 1904 to face down the justices. Nonetheless Terrell advised that "tact and good judgment" were the main requirements for success as a black judge, "elements without color and without racial identity."

Courtesy of the Archives Center, National Museum of American History, Smithsonian Institution.

Raymond Pace Alexander clasping hands in victory with Stella Alfonsi, one of the "poison widow" defendants who were charged with murdering their husbands for insurance money. It was the most important case of Alexander's early career and pushed him past the barriers that separated him from the mainstream bar.

The University of Pennsylvania Archives.

Charles Houston and his Howard Law School defense team in the George Crawford murder trial in Loudoun County, Virginia, joined by NAACP executive Walter White in 1933. Their own racial identity quickly overwhelmed the other issues at the trial. *Left to right:* White, Houston, James Guy Tyson, Leon A. Ransom, and Edward P. Lovett.

Prints and Photographs Division, Library of Congress.

In a famous but obviously posed photograph, Thurgood Marshall, *left,* with his client, Donald Murray, *center,* and his mentor, Charles Houston, preparing for the case that would desegregate the University of Maryland Law School. Marshall looks as if he is auditioning for something, and he was: membership in the whites-only fraternity of lawyers.

Prints and Photographs Division, Library of Congress.

Everyone seemed to think it was a breakthrough to have New York Domestic Relations Judge Jane Bolin in the front of a courtroom, but people had trouble saying exactly why. Observers were fascinated by her poise and beauty.

Courtesy of the Library of Congress.

Sadie T. M. Alexander enjoying herself at a 1947 National Bar Association luncheon, surrounded by current and former NAACP lawyers, *left to right,* Judge James A. Cobb (glasses), Leon A. Ransom (bow tie), Thurman Dodson, and an unidentified man. By then she was serving on President Truman's Committee on Civil Rights, but she still struggled to name what it was that kept her out of the civil rights courtroom.

The University of Pennsylvania Archives.

A startling physical transformation helped write sex discrimination into the fabric of American law. Pauli Murray in her 1927 high school graduation picture *(left)*, where she appears as a conventional example of Jazz Age femininity, and how she looked some years later *(below)*, when people sometimes mistook the passionate, waifish woman for a teenaged boy.

The Schlesinger Library, Radcliffe Institute, Harvard University.

Communist lawyer Ben Davis Jr. speaking at a rally at Madison Square Garden in 1945. He was forever divided from colleagues like Thurgood Marshall and Charles Houston by what happened in his first civil rights case.

Courtesy of the Library of Congress.

The biracial Los Angeles lawyer Loren Miller was born near an Indian reservation in Nebraska, adopted a black cultural identity in college, and later went to the Soviet Union with Langston Hughes. Miller became a fierce critic of his fellow black lawyers, but later joined them and argued in the Supreme Court alongside his former opponent, Charles Houston.

The Huntington Library, San Marino, California.

John W. Davis, *left,* was a believer in separation between blacks and whites, except if the black person was a lawyer like Thurgood Marshall. The friendly but complicated relationship between the two opposing lawyers in *Brown v. Board of Education* would serve as a metaphor for postwar race relations.

UPI / Corbis-Bettman.

Chicago lawyer Earl Dickerson, *center,* with labor leader Ferdinand Smith and the chairman of the War Production Board, Donald Nelson, during World War II. Dickerson broke racial taboos through his angry confrontations with whites as a member of the wartime Fair Employment Practices Committee, even as his position in Chicago black politics was eroding.

Courtesy of the Library of Congress.

By the early 1950s, Americans were fascinated with both Third Circuit Judge William Hastie and "Mr. Civil Rights," Thurgood Marshall. Hastie *(above)*, speaking beneath a portrait of Chief Justice John Marshall, subsequently faded so much from view that Kennedy Justice Department officials thought he was a conservative Republican. Marshall *(left)*, seated beneath a portrait of Justice Louis Brandeis, reworked the role of a black judge in a way that even his successor on the Supreme Court, Clarence Thomas, found irresistible.

Courtesy Historical & Special Collections, Harvard Law School Library, and Library of Congress.

In the early 1960s, Philadelphia's Rev. Leon Sullivan, *right*, began a movement for black economic empowerment that helped define the community-based racial politics of the 1970s and also threatened to consign his own traditional parishioner, Raymond Pace Alexander, to irrelevance.

Courtesy of Temple University Libraries, Urban Archives, Philadelphia.

Philadelphia lawyer Cecil B. Moore. Behind the bombastic rhetoric and provocative imagery, he wanted the same thing as his competitors— desegregation. His only complaint was that his rivals were no longer representatives of their race.

Courtesy of Temple University Libraries, Urban Archives, Philadelphia.

Thurgood Marshall, *center*, and his slightly less urbane number two on the NAACP's legal staff, Robert L. Carter, *right*, in happier times. The two men would grow into rivals, because of differences of personal style and political views. Carter was less comfortable with whites, but more attuned to the mood of the race-conscious young African Americans of the 1960s.

UPI / Corbis-Bettman.

Attorney General Robert F. Kennedy, *center*, with some of the older lawyers he helped to displace as race leaders: Raymond Pace Alexander, *far left*, and Judge William Hastie, *far right*. Along with President Kennedy, the attorney general helped write the beginnings of a new story of racial representation by bringing a young generation of black lawyers to Washington to staff the federal bureaucracy.

The University of Pennsylvania Archives.

6

A Woman in a Fraternity of Lawyers

ON JULY 22, 1939, New York mayor Fiorello La Guardia took a break from his duties at the city's World's Fair building to conduct a routine swearing-in of a local judge, and quickly saw his actions splashed across the pages of black newspapers from coast to coast. The story even made it into the white dailies in New York and Los Angeles, and for good reason, because the appointment made a little-known assistant corporation counsel named Jane Bolin into the nation's first black woman judge. When Bolin assumed her duties on the city's Domestic Relations Court the following week, the excitement had barely subsided. Reporters trailed her for days before she took up her post, and groups of well-wishers applauded as she took her seat in the Manhattan branch of the court. Flowers and telegrams crowded her desk, and a veteran judge introduced her to the crowd with an emotional speech hailing her appointment as an example of why "[p]eople come here from the four corners of the world" to make new lives for themselves. Black judges were not unknown in the city. Nor were women judges a complete novelty there. But observers around the country seemed to invest special significance in the appointment of the thirty-one-year-old Yale Law School graduate to the bench, and this would continue until Bolin's death in 2007. For blacks and whites alike, Bolin's appointment made her something not seen before on the American landscape—a black woman lawyer as representative of an entire race's aspirations.[1]

Black women lawyers meshed uneasily with the American narrative of minority group representation, and their struggle to figure out where they belonged in that story would eventually help create sex discrimination as a modern category of American law. Certain well-educated black women had long been claimed as "representative women of the race," but the story, for the most part, centered on what nineteenth-century Americans had called "representative colored men." Of late, lawyers like Charles Houston, Raymond Alexander, and Thurgood Marshall had inserted themselves into that narrative by performing like white men in court and being folded into the local fraternity of white lawyers. Common professional norms held local fraternities of lawyers together, and that provided a space for black men to cross over into the white world and stand in for something much larger than themselves.

Bolin's appointment to the municipal court prompted two up-and-coming black women lawyers to take up the question of just how they fit into the fraternity of lawyers. Philadelphia lawyer Sadie Alexander found enough inspiration in Bolin's achievement to begin drafting an article about the struggles of black women lawyers and to rededicate herself to a career that would see her become a nationally important civil rights leader. Yet, if Alexander took inspiration from Bolin, she read her own successes, for the most part, as a story of racial advancement. The language of modern feminism would remain foreign to Sadie Alexander to the end of her days. In New York, a twenty-eight-year-old black woman named Pauli Murray also took inspiration from Bolin's success, as well as from Houston and Marshall's early courtroom victories, and decided to cast her lot in with law. She would soon enter law school at Howard University and wanted nothing more than to perform like a white man in a civil rights courtroom. Like Alexander, Murray would find law to be a disorienting profession for a black woman lawyer. But Murray would connect that sense of displacement to a nascent feminist consciousness that two decades later would make her a pivotal figure in the creation of sex discrimination as a category of modern American law.[2]

Alexander, Murray, and their black women lawyer peers have been claimed by history as race women fighting against discrimination, conventional players in the emerging Cold War conflict, "new women" of the post–World War I period, dissenters from conventional civil rights politics, and warriors in the equality debates of the mid-1960s.[3] They were all of these things, and none of them, for the most important thing in their lives was something else. They became lawyers, and after that the whole world seemed slightly askew.

Who Is the New Negro Woman Lawyer?

Just about everyone was sure that the sight of Jane Bolin sitting in the front of a courtroom stood in for the potential of the rest of the race, but no one could quite say why. Jacob Panken, the veteran judge who spoke on Bolin's first day on the bench, invoked his own immigrant past to understand the significance of the day. News reports, by contrast, tended to focus on Bolin's appearance and dignified persona in court. "Fashionably smart in a beige sheer wool two-piece suit, an aquamarine blouse, russet brown shoes and a large natural straw hat," noted one account. Another emphasized what it called her "keen, penetrating glance" as she surveyed the courtroom. Others wrote about her hobbies and vacation interests, and what she did on a typical day from the time she got up to when she went to bed. The black reading public ate up the reports and hungered for more. Some readers took note of her light complexion (Bolin's mother was white) and the fact that she employed a European maid. *Ebony* magazine rated her as one of the most beautiful people in the United States. Bolin herself found it difficult to explain what was significant about becoming a judge, merely commenting that she hoped her appointment would inspire young women to study law. Nearly two decades after her generation of black women lawyers had begun appearing in courtrooms throughout the North, everyone (including themselves) still struggled to figure out what it all meant.[4]

One thing at least was clear: the legal profession was a fraternity, and that made all the difference in the lives of women like Bolin, Alexander, and Murray. Black women of their educational levels typically chose law over more conventional, and safer, careers for women. To decide to become a lawyer was by definition to rebel against established gender mores among blacks as well as whites. Sadie Tanner Mossell Alexander, for instance, was born in 1898 and hailed from two of the most educated black families in America, where graduate degrees were the norm. Still, after she earned a Ph.D. in economics at the University of Pennsylvania and worked for a time at a North Carolina insurance company, teaching beckoned as an obvious career choice. But she couldn't get a job in the Philadelphia schools, since no black teacher could be hired to teach in the secondary schools (where they would have white pupils). With the encouragement of her husband, she chose law school as an alternative. Ruth Whitehead Whaley turned away from a teaching career to enter Fordham Law School, at the urging of her lawyer husband. A few years later, Smith College graduate Eunice Carter transitioned from teaching and social work to the night law school program at Fordham, disregarding the advice of her mother. Carter's mother was herself an independent spirit who was active in Pan-Africanist circles and had dragged her young daughter off to Europe for study, but she urged Carter to make a more conventional choice. Edith Spurlock Sampson felt crushed after she learned that no black teachers could be hired by the public schools of her native Pittsburgh. She turned instead to the New York School of Social Work at the urging of local patrons, and held fast to that choice even after she made the highest grade in a law class taught there by former Columbia law dean George Kirchwey. After marrying and moving to Chicago, she finally gave in to Kirchwey's entreaties and began studying at John Marshall Law School. Jane Bolin had to buck up against her father's expectation that she would become a teacher after she finished Wellesley College. After her appointment to the bench, a reporter asked her: "Most little girls go through various stages of wanting to be teachers, nurses, doctors, and even actresses, didn't you?" "No," answered Bolin confidently. "I always wanted to be a lawyer."[5]

To enter law was to make something visible that was harder to see when women like Bolin pursued more conventional careers, and even when they followed less conventional ones like medicine. Ruth Whitehead Whaley, for instance, struggled with the changing contours of gender roles as she entered Fordham Law School in the early 1920s. New York's black and white papers avidly followed the career of the black woman whose academic record topped her class. Writing autobiographically in 1923, Whaley pleaded for acceptance of what she called the "New Negro Woman" who was traveling "outside her sphere." "Woman's emancipation is strangely parallel with the Negro struggle," she wrote, but the New Negro Woman presented an even greater challenge. "[H]er closed doors are of the thickness of two—she is first a woman, then a Negro. May the fates be kind to her!" One year earlier, Zephyr Abigail Moore, who transitioned from Howard University's teachers college to its law school, wrote that finishing her legal studies had made her a member of "the most conservative of all professions" with regard to women. Bolin saw something in her father for the first time when he complained that a career in law would involve her in "too indelicate a profession for a woman." Gaius Bolin, as the first black lawyer in Poughkeepsie, New York, had battled race prejudice all his life, but his daughter convinced him to accept her unconventional career choice by telling him that he was showing "prejudice of another kind."[6]

Still, something unsettling remained about law as a career for these women, and the effort to define that something would continue for the rest of their lives. Commenting on the experiences of women like herself in the legal profession, Sadie Alexander wrote that "[t]he discriminations which we feel are so subtle that it is difficult to state them with any assurance." At the University of Pennsylvania Law School in the mid-1920s, for instance, Sadie Alexander found the dean, a Virginian named William Mikell, to be a "very prejudiced man" who would not speak to her in the halls and ordered the women law students to exclude her from their club. When Alexander's grades earned her election to the law review after her first year, she recalled that the dean ordered the editors to deny her membership. The same thing happened after her second year, even though a black man, Robert B. Johnson, was elected to the review without protest. She took her rightful place only after the editor-in-chief threatened to resign if she was not appointed.[7]

Ruth Whaley, too, found law school to be an experience that defied easy description. A year after she published her "New Negro Woman" essay, for instance, Whaley sparked a controversy when she finished law school with an A-plus average, believing that this made her the winner of a contest sponsored by a law book company that would award a prize to a high-achieving student. When school authorities asked her to re-take an exam to avoid a controversy over the award, Whaley went public with her allegations that "this Catholic school" was doing something that echoed the practices of the "Ku Klux Klan and other anti-Catholic organizations." Fordham withheld her degree for a time because of the controversy, but exactly what had happened to Whaley, no one really knew. Black newspapers played up the dispute, and school authorities charged that the law book company was to blame, while Whaley, the first black woman to finish Fordham law, held fast to her allegations of race discrimination. Five years later, she spoke somewhat differently, claiming that "the law school is . . . still a man's institution" and that black and white women had similar experiences in the profession. But Whaley, like Alexander, was not ready to assert that the incident was motivated by prejudice against what she called the New Negro Woman who stepped out of her bounds.[8]

When they finished law school, Whaley and her peers entered a profession that seemed profoundly different from the one that lawyers like Raymond Alexander encountered. Describing New York's legal community in the mid-1940s, Pauli Murray used words that would have applied with just as much force two decades before. The surest way to " 'hustle up' clients" and build a practice, she wrote, was "joining a local political club, becoming active in many community organizations, or hanging around courthouses waiting to be assigned criminal cases." The courthouse option was surely the toughest of the lot. It was the proverbial way that lawyers like Raymond Pace Alexander came up through the ranks, but to pursue it meant to wait outside the most disreputable public places in the city, scaring up gamblers, thieves, violent men and women, and sometimes even prostitutes in the hope of "making a reputation in the community," as Charles Houston wrote of the 1920s. A generation later, Dovey Johnson Roundtree would make her way at the bar through rough-and-tumble criminal practice in Washington, D.C., but this was not an easy route at the time.[9]

The public was the problem for black women lawyers. Lawyers got ahead by establishing a reputation in public, but there was no easy way to do that for these attorneys. The surest route was politics, since they tended to practice in cities like New York, Philadelphia, and Chicago, where black political strength was becoming significant for the first time. "I started off with some measure of publicity because of my school work, my speaking, and my political affiliations," remembered Whaley. The same year that she graduated from law school, she also joined the Harlem branch of New York's Tammany Hall organization, and used that connection to draw clients to her office. Eunice Hunton Carter and Jane Bolin, both trying to gain some traction as lawyers in Depression-era New York, ran for the state assembly as Republican nominees. Both soon leveraged those connections into appointments as government lawyers. Carter secured an appointment on the staff of special prosecutor Thomas Dewey, while Bolin got a job in the corporation counsel's office. Elsie Austin came to the attention of the black public when she was selected as an editor of the *Cincinnati Law Review*. She then bootstrapped black political power in Ohio's Democratic politics into an appointment in the state attorney general's office. In Chicago, Edith Sampson joined other black women lawyers like Sophia Boaz Pitts in serving as a staffer in the juvenile courts until she could transition to full-time private practice. Sometimes politics sought these women out instead of the other way around, as when Lena Trent Gordon, a faithful party worker in Philadelphia's Republican machine, learned of Sadie Alexander's admission as the first black woman to practice law in Pennsylvania. Gordon stopped by Alexander's house and introduced her to the local ward leader, who connected her with the mayor, who arranged for her appointment as assistant city solicitor.[10]

Whatever their route to practice, what defined these lawyers' careers was the same thing that gave people so much trouble trying to interpret Jane Bolin's breakthrough: their presence in the courtroom. As it was with their male peers, courtroom victories were a sure route to success in the profession, but from the moment they stepped into that space, they could sense something that had barely registered before. In a 1931 interview, Whaley said that her unexpected success in practice could be symbolized by one thing: "I never speak in court with my hat on." In those days, men doffed their hats in court, while women kept them on. What was a woman lawyer to do? That simple conflict became a standard story that many of them told about their sudden realization of what was different about law. Sadie Alexander recalled her rude introduction to the profession when she arrived in court to be admitted to the bar.

> When I had approached the Bar of the Court, I heard a voice say: "Take off that hat!" I wondered what male neophyte came to be sworn in and kept on his hat. A few minutes later, I heard the command repeated in a more angry and louder tone, only to realize that I was being told to remove the hat, for which color and price I had combed the stores. I tore it off in so doing dropping my copy of the Code of Professional Responsibility and lost the correct page. I was the only woman in the group but not a man attempted to retrieve my book.

Women lawyers had struggled with that problem since the nineteenth century, and stories of inexperienced women lawyers, black and white, being introduced to the profession by being told to take off their hats in court would persist into the 1960s.[11]

Bodies, too, taken for granted when the courtroom was an all-male domain, immediately became visible when these women came to court to practice. For instance, it is quite easy to find out (because so many people commented on it) that Ruth Whaley, Jane Bolin, and Pauli Murray each stood just over five feet tall, and were extremely petite and attractive. Everyone seemed to want to know what these women looked like who had taken on such an unusual public role. Whaley, "a mere slip of a girl, with her fluffy bobbed hair and her ready smile," prompted colorful descriptions from women and men alike. Observers tended to view Edith Sampson, by contrast, as a rather buxom woman. Press accounts mentioned both her dress size and her love of cooking, and she joked publicly about her girth.[12]

A black woman's body in court could also be a discomforting presence, so much so that it produced a crisis in Alexander's early career. It began when, soon after receiving an appointment as assistant city solicitor, she learned that she was pregnant. Her husband thought that she should resign her post as soon as the pregnancy showed, but Alexander believed that remaining in the position would set a precedent for those who followed in her footsteps. She was the first black woman lawyer, and the second woman, ever to hold the post, and there were few precedents to guide her. She prevailed upon her embarrassed husband to speak with the Orphans' Court's presiding judge, Curtis Bok, who was known for his racial liberalism, and the two men conferred over lunch about the propriety of a pregnant woman appearing in court. Bok endorsed her choice, commenting that "I don't think there is anything more beautiful than a pregnant woman." Alexander stayed on the job.[13]

Competition, however, was the word that most accurately described the feelings evoked when a woman came to court, and black women lawyers produced even more of it by the added fact of their race. Coming to court was a direct assault on the masculine norms that governed the most public of the institutions of law, and jury trials were the site of greatest controversy. Alexander remembered that when she joined her husband's firm, the men there wanted an "opportunity to display their forensic ability before a jury" and kept her away from this line of work. As soon as male lawyers found out that she was their opponent, they invariably began "laying roadblocks, such as absolutely unnecessary interrogations, preliminary objections, depositions" and similar obstructions. Once she made it to court, she found that "[j]udges get irritated the minute they see a woman lawyer." In the rare cases where women lawyers got jury trials, it remained true that "many jurors do not like women lawyers, but perhaps before the case is over they can be won."

Victory might provoke an even stronger response, such as when one lawyer lost a case and then cursed Alexander outside of court. Her reply summed up the stakes behind that reversal of normal courtroom perceptions: "I should give you my skirt and you give me your pants." Ruth Whaley found that "[t]he attitude of the man toward a woman lawyer is generally skeptical—he will generally try to take advantage of her" until she proves her mettle. Jane Bolin's breakthrough judicial appointment, notably, came in a court that often dispensed with lawyers' services, as well as normal adversary proceedings, in favor of a clinical approach to the social problems of families.[14]

Women lawyers of all races struggled with courtroom practice in the early twentieth century. Contemporary surveys showed that by the 1920s, women attorneys had made little progress in practice areas—such as criminal and personal injury law—that required courtroom appearances. Overwhelming percentages of women were engaged in general office practice, specializing in probate, real estate, and domestic relations law. Many practiced with their husbands, where they took charge of the firm's office work, research, and brief writing while the men appeared in court. Some of these wives even became office managers, handling the firm's record keeping, typing, and other day-to-day support tasks. Observing the situation in the mid-1940s, Pauli Murray commented that many black women lawyers "worked for Negro male attorneys as glorified clerks, doing legal drudgery with little chance for advancement." Office practice and office management went hand in hand with the emerging idea that women were particularly well suited for routinized and detailed tasks.[15]

Still, private practice and courtroom work remained at the top of the pyramid for black women lawyers, and they defined themselves by their ability to succeed in that all-male venue. Most of them preferred what they called "independent practice" to salaried government positions where they often did not make it into court. Chicago lawyer Barbara Watts Goodall commented harshly that "[t]here are just a few women who have the nerve to remain in the field to practice and not accept a job." Edith Spurlock Sampson observed that "[t]here are many successful women in independent practice but the majority have salaried positions." Eunice Carter told Sadie Alexander that she knew of only five other successful black women lawyers in New York. There were more, of course, but these women were of little note since they were "not in active practice." Alexander was thrilled to hear that Carter was doing "actual trial work" and even supervising other attorneys: "I cannot say too much for the ability that you have shown as well as the diplomacy which you must have exercised to have obtained such a position." Elsie Austin wrote to Alexander to tell her that the two women lawyers in the Ohio attorney general's office did "general opinion work," and added with regret that "[n]either of us were given much trial work."[16]

Thus black women lawyers of the early twentieth century faced a paradox. Their choice of law as a career marked them as dissenters from what their communities, and sometimes even their relatives, expected of them. They made their way in a profession where a public persona was key to getting ahead in the world, but their appearance in that public was so overlaid with race and gender perceptions that no one could sort them all out. Some, like Whaley, took comfort from analogies to what was then called the "race question," but even she was uncertain about whether this was the right way to look at the problem. At the same time, they valued what they called "actual practice" or "independent practice" as the measure of success in their chosen field, even though few of them would ever quite realize that ideal. The problem was neatly encapsulated in the career of the lawyer who counted herself among the most successful of them, and who did so much work to connect these women with one another in the late 1930s—Philadelphia's Sadie Tanner Mossell Alexander.

"Independent" Practice

Like most of her contemporaries, Alexander could never quite put her finger on exactly what had happened when the first black woman lawyer entered the courtrooms of her state. As she remembered it later, her career as a lawyer began with a story that she would tell for the rest of her life, although the details shifted over time. It started soon after she joined the Raymond Pace Alexander law firm, and involved an encounter with Judge Thompson of the Philadelphia Orphans' Court. The judge presented her with what she regarded as "a most exceptional opportunity." He called her into his chambers and told her that he noticed that she had a substantial volume of business before the Orphans' Court. Alexander was the first black woman to practice before the court, and Judge Thompson wanted to make sure that none of his fellow judges would question her competence. The judge arranged for all her court filings to be referred to him, and every Friday he called her to his chambers to go over her pleadings and ensure that they were in the proper form. Alexander "gratefully accepted" his offer of help, and for four months or more she "had the privilege, once a week, of personal tutoring by a master in Orphans' Court law and practice." One Friday he told her that she was ready to go out on her own, but reminded her that she could always come back for more tutoring if she needed it.[17] Forty-five years later, in her signature essay on her experiences at the Philadelphia bar, she took time to thank the judge for his kindness and solicitude. Alexander wrote that she could only hope that the quality of her work had been "such as fully to indicate the depth of my appreciation of Judge Thompson's concern for me and [his] unselfish contribution to my career as a lawyer."[18]

The story, however, was never as simple as Alexander wanted it to be. No other lawyer would have received the kind of tutoring given to her, and a skeptical reader might see Judge Thompson's actions as, at best, an example of a benevolent patriarch trying to offset the prejudices of his fellow judges. At worst, the incident might reveal that the Orphans' Court judges simply had no confidence in her abilities and worried that she would be an embarrassment. Even Alexander harbored a more conflicted set of feelings about this experience than she let show in public. Five years after publicly thanking the judge in her essay, she gave substantially the same description of her tutoring in an unpublished interview.[19] "However," she added at the end of the account, "as I reflect upon what was done, I'm wondering whether the judges didn't get together and decide that . . . she's coming in and we don't want to be tangled up with some woman, because they did have one woman in particular, who never knew what she was doing. And they thought, well they'd straighten me out from the beginning." Reflecting a bit more, she then recalled a case in which Judge Thompson had appointed guardians for boys who had been badly injured in an accident. Looking over the amounts that the boys had been awarded for their injuries, the judge turned to his tipstaff and muttered, "What do you think of these niggers getting over a $100,000." Maybe this was more evidence, Alexander thought, that the judge had given her special treatment simply because he didn't want to get "tangled." "Anyway," she concluded, "it was a great value . . . what he did."[20]

In the eyes of Thompson and others, Alexander was indeed a representative woman of her race—a person whose success or failure in the law stood in for a host of larger issues. Many of her colleagues at the bar doubted that she would succeed as a lawyer in the face of the obvious hardships, so much so that at her law school graduation ceremony, when it was announced that she had now received four degrees from the University of Pennsylvania, someone shouted: "What degree is Sadie going to get next?" The reply was immediate: "Mamma! Mamma!" Others simply didn't know how to place her, and no other Orphans' Court judge showed anything like Thompson's solicitude. The judge's special concern for her, including his decision to break with the practices of some of his brethren and invite her into his chambers, was indeed of "great value" to her career. But it was also treatment that highlighted what made her different from every other lawyer to practice in that court, including the first white woman to appear there. Was Judge Thompson a benevolent paternalist, or a judge who harbored deep-seated racial and gender prejudices? He was, of course, both, and that was the contradiction that the appearance of a black woman in his courtroom laid bare.[21]

For Alexander, to begin practicing law was to enter a world where a simple act like coming to a judge's chambers brought unprecedented complications, and nowhere was that more evident than in the most important professional relationship of her career—that with her husband, Raymond Pace Alexander. Raymond, of course, gave her a start in practice. "[I]t never occurred to [Raymond] or me that I would not join his staff," she recalled. The Raymond Pace Alexander law firm was a showcase of black economic progress by the late 1920s. It hired only Ivy League law school graduates, and Sadie Alexander's educational qualifications stood head and shoulders above those of the men who practiced there. The firm was perhaps the only black law practice in the country that hired salaried lawyers onto its staff. There were women lawyers at other firms in the city, but when Raymond proposed that Sadie join his own firm, one of the other lawyers objected strongly, saying that he would not work with her. Raymond gave the lawyer the choice of leaving the firm or staying and working with his wife. The lawyer stayed, and Sadie Alexander joined the practice. But even this turned out to be a more complicated victory than it first appeared.[22]

When Sadie Alexander joined the firm, the question of what she would actually do there immediately arose. It was one thing for male lawyers to agree to work with her, but it was quite another for her to do the kind of work that competed with their own. For reasons that were not then apparent to her, Raymond quickly petitioned the city's Orphans' Court for her admission to practice before that body, and she was admitted in October 1927. Soon afterward, she learned the reason why. The Orphans' Court had jurisdiction over probate matters, and the firm had a substantial amount of undone trusts and estates work that needed immediate attention. The men in the office didn't like this work, which, according to Alexander, "they considered principally bookkeeping." Bookkeeping was women's work in early twentieth-century America, and, by tradition, jury trial work was a masculine preserve. There were no jury trials in Orphans' Court, where practice required mastery of the technical details of pleading and procedure. Sadie Alexander was the first black woman lawyer in the state, one of only fifteen women lawyers in Philadelphia, and fortunate to have a job practicing law. "[I]n order to get your foot in a firm, you had to take what was offered to you," she later remembered.[23]

Sadie Alexander quickly got the chance to display her skill at detailed work in her other area of specialization—domestic relations and divorce law. Her divorce docket began in the fall of 1926, during her third year of law school, when she worked part time in her husband's firm, and continued after she joined the firm full time. In a typical case she collected a twenty-five-dollar or fifty-dollar initial fee from a plaintiff seeking a divorce from a spouse who lived across town, out of state, or sometimes at "address unknown." The court usually appointed a local attorney as master, to receive evidence and report back with a recommendation, which the presiding judge adopted as a matter of course. Few of the cases were contested, and often the defendant was notified of the final divorce decree by publication. Pennsylvania courts granted divorces only for fault, and one common ground for divorce was desertion without reasonable cause for two years. By the time Sadie Alexander joined her husband's firm, its reputation was familiar to the city's African American population, and uncontested divorce plaintiffs simply walked in the door and were steered to her. Defendants did not contest cases, because they did not know or did not care about the result, providing Alexander with the same claim, often the same evidence, and the same procedure repeated over and over again. There was money in this type of work, to be sure, due to the volume of cases, but it probably held little interest for the men in the firm. As rote and repetitive work, it was hers to handle.[24]

Alexander captured the attention of the local black community when, in 1928, she got an appointment as the second woman ever to work in the city solicitor's office. But, as she would advise Elsie Austin a decade later, it was hardly a route to prominence for a black woman lawyer. After a high-profile announcement of the appointment, she found that she had an office and a salary but no duties. This was too much, even for someone who tolerated many slights in her profession, and her protests finally earned her an assignment. As she might have anticipated, she became the city's representative in Orphans' Court, helping to oversee audits of the accounts of decedents' estates. Office practice would be her lot once again. This meshed well with her work at the firm, where she continued to work while serving as an assistant solicitor for two more years, and for four subsequent years in the late 1930s. This was a far cry from the independent practice that she envisioned for herself.[25]

Independence is what black women lawyers defined as their goal (and the quality that scholars sometimes use to measure success for women lawyers of their generation). But, for them, independence was a complicated idea. Many of them were in companionate marriages— unions with an unusual degree of gender equality—often to other lawyers. These types of marriages are often seen as a marker of women's independence in that era. Though women like Bolin and Alexander credited their husbands for supporting their unconventional career choices, that did not lessen the expectation that women lawyers should also manage their households. Ruth Whaley put it this way: "The community accepts her adventurous role but scrutinizes closely whether she is making her normal contribution to it as a woman." By the mid-1930s, after the birth of two daughters, Alexander found herself almost overwhelmed by conflicting responsibilities. Writing about her dilemma to a local columnist, she lamented:

> It is a hard job trying to be a mother, a lawyer and a good wife. I am not at all too certain that the three can be successfully combined. At times I think it is impossible and that I must devote my entire time to my husband and children; then I think of the sacrifice that my mother made to train me and of the number of clients who seem to depend upon me. I then try to find strength to serve all of the interests.

She hired a nurse to help her, but she was not always optimistic about her future in the profession: "When it seems to me that the children will need more of my care I feel quite certain that I shall have to withdraw from such active practice."[26]

Family responsibilities, which were almost never mentioned in the correspondence of their male peers, helped limit these black women's expectations—particularly the expectation that they might represent their race in court. Early in her career, Edith Sampson suddenly found herself burdened with two young children when her sister died and she was appointed their guardian; nonetheless, Sampson boasted that she always remained self-supporting because of her law activities and real estate investments. Jane Bolin began raising her young child with the assistance of her maid, since Bolin's husband, also a lawyer, had a job with the postal service in Washington, D.C. He died not long after the child was born. Bolin, like Alexander, speculated that if given the chance she would have taken an extended leave of absence from her judicial post to care for her child. Whaley packed her two young children off to North Carolina to live with their grandmother during each school year, as she built up her law practice in New York. Eunice Carter, somewhat unhappily married to a dentist and pursuing her own career opportunities, sent her young son off to live with relatives in Barbados for five years just as her career as a lawyer began to take off. Carter advised black professional women that if their careers eclipsed those of the men in their lives, they should downplay this fact and instead act like conventional wives and mothers: "Women must never forget that men should dominate the race." "I believe in the independence of women, nevertheless," she added.[27]

For these women, independence was a word so hedged by societal expectations and family duties that it sometimes made situations like Alexander's into a boon rather than a burden. In fact, for many of them, professional life was barely a step up from the social work jobs that were their obvious alternative. In Chicago, lawyers like Georgia Jones Ellis, Sophia Boaz Pitts, and Edith Spurlock Sampson all maintained staff positions in the city's Juvenile or Domestic Relations courts, which often dispensed with lawyers and resembled social work agencies as much as they did courts. Jane Bolin took time off from her efforts to establish herself as a lawyer and worked for a year as a social worker in

Depression-era New York before her breakthrough appointment in the corporation counsel's office. Even that appointment as a lawyer placed her in a court that styled itself partly as a social work agency. Eunice Carter could name only six practicing black women lawyers in New York, of whom four were in government posts or specialized areas of practice like real estate or landlord-tenant law. Carter's own breakthrough came when she got a job that few men probably wanted, supervising pro forma low-level prostitution cases that involved the same fact patterns over and over again, repeat encounters with the same lawyers, and resulted in few convictions. Of the small number of black women lawyers who could claim to be actively practicing their trade in northern cities, Whaley was one of the few who could claim what they called independent practice.[28]

Office Practice as a Route to Respectability

By the middle of the 1940s, Sadie Alexander hardly resembled the lawyer who had speculated about giving up her marginal stake in the profession. She was evolving into a tough negotiator who could bring wealthy institutional clients like black churches to the Alexander firm. She battled with clients and opponents, and placed her own stamp on legal proceedings, so much so that a young male lawyer at the firm called her the "darling" of the Orphans' Court judges. She was getting to be well known locally. Along with liberals such as the University of Pennsylvania's Clark Byse, she would soon help found an organization that evolved into the local ACLU affiliate. Alexander had also become secretary of the National Bar Association, and there was a movement afoot (resisted by many lawyers) to position her to become president of the group. President Truman would soon appoint her to his Committee on Civil Rights, which would cement her in the national firmament of race leaders. She was now optimistic that little could stand in the way of her success in the profession. "When I hear the white women lawyers complaining about their lot, it is amusing to me," she told an acquaintance. "[I]t is the same problem I have faced all my life and it is no longer a problem to me." The source of that changing viewpoint was an unexpected one: the work that once defined her as marginal within her husband's firm.[29]

Alexander later recalled that "if you got five dollars to go to court, you went to court for five dollars. . . . You were gaining experience, and you were building a reputation so you counted all that in."[30] By the 1940s, after more than a decade of slow and uncertain reputation-building, Alexander's divorce docket began to change. Aided by the improving economy, she was beginning to take on cases that would tax her skills as a lawyer and negotiator. In 1943, she began to represent Mary Goode in a divorce proceeding that was hardly pro forma. It dragged on for two years, through negotiations with a succession of attorneys for Goode's husband, William, and through a series of court filings that finally ended with a court order for William to pay both parties' legal fees.[31] At about the same time, Annie Sterling came to Alexander to negotiate her divorce. What might have been a brief proceeding soon turned into a year and a half of miscommunication. During a long separation in the couple's thirty-six-year marriage, Sterling had married another man, with whom she had two grown sons. Sterling and Alexander never quite connected with one another after that revelation, resulting in a succession of letters and meetings in which the two could not agree on the appropriate defense strategy or the desired result. The master eventually recommended that the divorce be granted, without alimony.[32] Messy domestic quarrels and disagreements with clients and opposing counsel came to occupy a good portion of Alexander's divorce docket by the 1940s, and her job as a lawyer often required her to sort out complicated family disputes.

A similar thing happened to Alexander's probate practice in the 1940s, and she was probably warming to her bigamous clientele when Dorothy Rolle walked into her office. Rolle's husband, Tony, had died, and his estate, including a $5,000 war risk insurance policy, was being probated in the Orphans' Court. Three women claimed to be Tony's widow, but after learning that Rolle had married him first, Alexander cheerfully told her client: "I expect you will collect."[33] It turned out, however, that Tony wasn't the only one with multiple spouses. Dorothy had also been married before. When her first husband disappeared, she and Tony decided to marry without going through the trouble of having her file for a divorce. Apparently, Tony was so fond of this process that he moved to Virginia and repeated it, then repeated it again before he died, resulting in a web of serial unions. A flood of correspondence and factual investigations in two states ensued, after which Alexander concluded that Rolle's case was hopeless, and she reluctantly withdrew the claim.[34]

It was the James Windsor case, however, that probably convinced Alexander that she was no longer in the world of bookkeeping. When Windsor died in 1942 leaving no will, the Orphans' Court appointed Alexander as the administrator of an estate that included $5,000 in bank accounts, a home, and a variety of securities and rental properties. She immediately went to work collecting rents, evicting tenants, paying taxes, managing the properties, and preparing to divide the assets among a geographically scattered extended family. What had looked like a simple job soon turned into six years of contentious negotiations with jealous relatives. By 1943, the relatives were already accusing one another of stealing from the estate. Soon they accused Alexander herself of theft, and much of the dispute came to center on Jackie Windsor, James's sister, who hired her own lawyer. Alexander soldiered on for four more years as heirs variously died, were shipped overseas during the war, and continued their accusations of fraud. During this process, the scattered heirs seemed to be in contact with each other only through Alexander's persistent letters, urging them to trust one another (and herself), and to cooperate to resolve the matter. In 1947, Alexander finally gave up and had the property partitioned by the court a year later, with the remaining $22,000 in assets apportioned among the still-divided Windsors.[35]

By the mid-1940s Sadie Alexander's growing negotiation skills and fame placed her in the position to land perhaps the most desirable client for a law firm like hers—the black church. Churches were different in kind from clients like the Windsors, whose cases were essentially one-shot deals. Individual clients didn't regularly return for business, and courts rarely referred matters to the firm. The Alexanders, like most lawyers, yearned for organizational clients that brought larger fees and recurring business with them. Black churches existed in even the poorest of communities and inevitably brought with them real estate transactions, tax matters, and church schisms that could be grist for the mill of an enterprising attorney. By the mid-1940s that spirit of enterprise was evident at the Alexander firm when Sadie Alexander brought in the AME Church, the largest and best-organized black church in America. Its founding branch, Mother Bethel AME, was located just outside the city's traditionally black Seventh Ward. Alexander's grandfather, a prominent AME figure, had published its quarterly review. When disgruntled church members filed a lawsuit in 1944 challenging the legitimacy of the pastor of St. John AME, one of the church's Philadelphia branches, the AME church turned to the Alexanders for its defense.[36]

The Alexander firm had expertise in handling this kind of case. It was a type of lawsuit that grew out of the titanic struggles that periodically reverberated through black churches when differing factions within a church, or the minister and deacons, fought each other for control of the institution. The losing parties might be put out of the community that meant most in their lives, and the winners gained control over both the institution and thousands of dollars in property. For ministers, defeat meant the loss of their livelihoods, so the stakes were high and the parties frequently wound up in court. There they secured injunctions and counter-injunctions until a judge could appoint a master to examine the church's bylaws and if necessary supervise a vote of church members to decide the winner. Black Baptist churches, with their congregational autonomy, were particularly vulnerable to such power struggles, and Raymond Alexander made a specialty of handling these cases when they arose. Sadie and Raymond worked on St. John AME's case jointly. They divided up their expertise, with Raymond drafting the pleadings and motions and Sadie corresponding and negotiating with opposing counsel and the master. When the master recommended the case's dismissal, the Alexanders gained powerful new allies within the church hierarchy. By the time that Sadie negotiated a resolution to a contract suit against the church, she was stating publicly that she was the AME Church's legal representative in Philadelphia.[37]

Landing the AME Church as a client brought Sadie Alexander real estate, tax, and other business matters as her most common form of church representation. Churches were the wealthiest property owners in many black communities and could generate large fees for their lawyers. For example, when Monumental AME had trouble purchasing some Center City property for a church mission, Alexander helped it get clear title to the land. When AME bishop John Jefferson needed help purchasing a church building in Harrisburg, the state capital, he asked her to oversee the transaction.[38] These types of church representation were also a means of advertising one's services to the pastor and

the congregation. Alexander, for instance, handled a real estate transaction for the Reverend Julius Langhorne in 1942, followed by a criminal case (handled by Raymond) for a church member in 1943, and
negotiations over settlement in an automobile accident for Langhorne
the following year. A simple nonprofit incorporation for the Saints of
Grace Church in 1950 generated more business when Sadie Alexander
realized that the pastor's wife, Mrs. Groomes, held title to the church's
property and owed back taxes on it. Over the next sixteen months, she
arranged for taxes to be paid and for Mrs. Groomes to deed the property to the church, which was now incorporated as a separate entity
and exempt from further taxation.[39] Repeat business and access to additional networks of potential clients made churches a coveted clientele
for black lawyers, and by the mid-1940s Sadie Alexander was bringing
many such clients to the firm.

At midcentury, Raymond Alexander remained the public face of
the firm, but that masked substantial changes that took place inside
the downtown art deco building that housed their law practice. The Alexanders' practice took on a dynamic that resembled those nineteenth-
century law firms that invented the divide between office practice and
courtroom advocacy. In such firms, one partner would become the
courtroom lawyer, while the other was the "office man," as legal historian Williard Hurst named him, who focused on advice-giving, negotiation, and the managing of clients' private affairs.[40] For Sadie Alexander,
being a lawyer now required her to dispense advice to a client who
might want guidance in collecting money, getting a divorce, or managing real estate, but it never stopped there. Her job evolved into a liaison
role between rival familial claimants to a will, or multiple spouses in a
divorce, or between sacred and secular obligations in a church case. She
dispensed advice about how clients should arrange their private affairs
as easily as she did legal guidance. It was a role that was consistent with
longer-term traditions in the legal profession, where office practice and
institutional clients were becoming a route to greater prestige than courtroom litigation.

Woman of the Year

In 1948, the National Urban League published a comic book for children that hailed Sadie Alexander as "Woman of the Year" and used her

career as an inspiration for black youth. It was an appropriate enough moment since, according to the census takers, the population of black women lawyers would double during that decade. By 1950, Alexander, Edith Sampson, and Jane Bolin would emerge as the troika of black women lawyers who had acquired a national profile. But curiously, after noting that Alexander was the first black woman to practice law in her state, not one picture in the colorful display showed her inside a court-room, interacting with other lawyers, or doing anything that the public associated with practicing law. Instead, the magazine presented young readers with stories of traditional women's uplift activities, and showed Alexander guiding youthful advisees on to responsible careers. What she did in her own career remained a mystery to readers. The magazine did highlight Alexander's service on President Truman's Civil Rights Committee, but it showed her doing research and writing work rather than anything associated with the public role of a lawyer. Two decades after her generation of black women lawyers began practicing, the na-tional organization whose raison d'être was to get African Americans into the job market had difficulty describing what a black woman lawyer might actually do in the world.[41]

Alexander herself struggled to explain how the world looked dif-ferent from the perspective of a black woman lawyer. Often she tried to fit her story into the comfortable tracks of hard work triumphing over race prejudice, but she had trouble sticking to that story. Writing to an acquaintance in 1946, she stated that "I do not feel that the position of the Negro woman lawyer differs from that of the man lawyer." "Natu-ral prejudice" against outsiders was the problem, and it differed little for black men and black women, or for white women lawyers, for that matter. "The prejudices that the white woman [lawyer] suffers are the same prejudices which the Negro as a whole has suffered." "In spite of it," she asserted confidently, "I must succeed." The main barrier to suc-cess, she believed, was getting "into the courts where they have an opportunity to distinguish themselves as trial lawyers," and Alexander proudly stated that she was almost unique in that she was able to "handle my own cases from the first court of jurisdiction to the Supreme Court of our State." Yet an ambiguous reality lay behind Alexander's story of over-coming simple prejudice against outsiders. Writing to an acquaintance two years earlier, she confessed that "although I have been at the Bar for more than fifteen years, today was the first time I have handled a case in

the criminal Courts. I always felt incapable of measuring up to the requirements of a criminal lawyer. However, Raymond insisted that I must
handle this case." At the Alexander firm, criminal law, like civil rights litigation, remained a masculine preserve, and the courtroom practice that
Sadie Alexander so proudly asserted was her most significant accomplishment was taken up, for the most part, by the Orphans' Court cases
that the men did not want.[42]

Edith Sampson, too, acquired a strong public profile that masked
an ambiguous relationship to courtroom practice. Sampson had worked
her way up the clerical hierarchy in Chicago's Juvenile Court before
opening her own practice and specializing in divorce law. After returning to government as an assistant state's attorney in 1947, she shot to
international prominence during a tour sponsored by the radio forum
America's Town Meeting of the Air. During a stop in New Delhi, she gave a
speech aggressively defending American democracy—including domestic race relations—against the political systems of Communist states,
and became an instant celebrity. That speech earned her government-
sponsored trips overseas to speak out for Americanism, accolades from
the likes of Justice William O. Douglas and Senator Hubert Humphrey,
and a call from the White House to serve as a delegate to the United
Nations. Sampson was on her way to a career that would see her become
an elected judge in Chicago. But at the height of her prominence, she
confessed that, as a practicing lawyer, she had found courtrooms to be so
inhospitable that she suffered from stage fright when she went to trial.
She often waived jury trials in her cases, she said, preferring to face the
judge alone.[43]

Sadie Alexander yearned to tell a conventional life story of prejudice and perseverance, but the story of the black women lawyers who
talked of independence was never so simple. Women like Alexander,
Bolin, and Sampson emerged on the public stage as the civil rights era
dawned, but something unsettling remained about their choice of law
as a career, and even Alexander, in her less guarded moments, acknowledged it. Ruth Whaley did also, near the end of her quarter-century career as one of the nation's few black women lawyers in general private
practice. As Whaley prepared to round out her career as secretary of the
New York Board of Estimate, she returned to the themes she had first
outlined in her 1922 essay on the New Negro Woman. Putting aside
some of the bravado that she had expressed in earlier interviews, Whaley

wrote with the forthrightness of someone who no longer needed to attract clients to her firm. The world did look different through the eyes of a black woman lawyer, she confessed. "More is required of a Negro woman who is a lawyer by her colleagues, the courts and the community," she observed. In addition to the competition and increased scrutiny that accompany all women lawyers, she argued, "Negro women are more easily identified, they are less in number and are more recent invaders." Clients accepted her, once she proved her worth, but on a "more highly individualized basis" than any other lawyer. She was "an exception" to whatever perceptions attached to black or women lawyers. A black woman at the bar was truly sui generis, she asserted, something without precedent, and the stakes behind her success at her profession were profoundly political. "After over 20 years in active practice," she asserted, "there is no sweeter music to my ears than: 'Hear ye, Hear ye, His Honor the Justice of the Court—all persons hav[ing] business of the Court draw near.'" "This is Democracy's battle cry," she concluded. Democracy, of course, was the language evoked by civil rights movement activists as the nation emerged from World War II, and Whaley sought to wrap the unique circumstances of the black woman lawyer in that larger movement.[44]

It would be Ruth Whaley's protégée, however, who would do more than any other among the nation's black women lawyers to connect their special circumstances to the larger civil rights movement. As Whaley handed off her clients to an up-and-coming lawyer about a decade her junior, she handed off as well an engagement with the questions that had bedeviled her ever since the beginning of her law studies. Pauli Murray was already coming to the realization that, as she later confessed to her diary, "I am 'unique,'" and "I seldom fit into accepted modes of thinking and patterns of operation." Becoming a black woman lawyer would both reinforce that tendency and help her to translate it into a new kind of civil rights politics.[45]

7

Things Fall Apart

FOR TWO generations, stretching from John Mercer Langston to Robert H. Terrell to Raymond Pace Alexander, to be a prominent black lawyer was to occupy an uncomfortable space in a nation that was deeply conflicted about what it expected of its minority group representatives. Suddenly, in the middle of the 1930s, the tension that was at the heart of that discomfort broke into the open. In Baltimore, local African Americans vented their displeasure when W. Ashbie Hawkins, perhaps the most experienced civil rights lawyer in the South, tried to speak at an open forum held by the local Elks. At a raucous civil rights rally in North Philadelphia, a young black speaker denounced lawyers like Alexander as the audience "shook the very rafters with the reverberations" of their cheering. In New York, Charles Houston faced hecklers among the invited guests, and even within the host committee, when he appeared at the podium at a testimonial dinner for NAACP national legal committee chair Arthur Spingarn. Atlanta lawyer A. T. Walden worried publicly about the turn of events that had caused his young colleague, Ben Davis Jr., to forsake mainstream civil rights practice in favor of the radical left. In Los Angeles, Loren Miller had abandoned the practice of law entirely for a new life as a nationally syndicated columnist and public speaker, where he remade himself into a fierce critic of his own professional training. Struggling to explain the turn of events that, in only a few short years, had produced such reversals, Charles Houston helped draft a statement for the NAACP that declared that the source of the controversy was "a difference in point of view."[1]

Lawyers like Houston, Alexander, and William Hastie had shot to national prominence earlier in the decade on the strength of their ability to interact with whites as equals in some of the most contested public spaces in the country. It was a delicate balancing act, but the civil rights lawyers believed that they could stand in for the masses of African Americans, and at the same time represent the viewpoint of the communities of white lawyers in which they found themselves. But that story was one told from the vantage point of these representative men. Suddenly, other views were coming to the fore, putting new questions on the table. Could a black lawyer really represent his race and at the same time be folded into the larger community of lawyers? Was it really possible to practice one's trade in a world where both blacks and whites seemed to demand that the lawyers be at once both authentic and atypical? These were questions that raised larger and more diffuse issues than the well-chronicled Depression-era movement of civil rights politics to the left. It was a crisis in the very idea of representation. One question remained on the lips of an increasingly vocal set of critics of the black bar in the early 1930s. It was: "Who do you represent?"

Three sets of causal forces exposed the contradiction at the heart of racial representation. The first was one of the most familiar causes of historical change: generational conflict. In the early 1930s, a younger set of black lawyers came to occupy center stage in civil rights politics. Lawyers like Loren Miller, Ben Davis, and John P. Davis were only a few years younger than figures like Houston, Hastie, and Alexander, but that made all the difference. The older generation had spent the 1920s dreaming of prosperity in the migration-augmented cities of the North. Younger lawyers who began practicing at the end of the decade, or the beginning of the 1930s, often believed they had little reason for such optimism. The main reason for that lack of optimism—the Great Depression—was the second thing that fueled the controversy. Black Americans felt the reverses of the Depression far more than the white communities around them, and their lawyers felt it even more keenly. For lawyers whose formative years coincided with the stunning economic reversals of the Depression, dreams of prosperity seemed fanciful. Most, like Thurgood Marshall, muddled through the lean years while struggling to build their reputations, but some broke out in active revolt against their elders.

But the most disruptive force that set in motion the crisis of represen- tation happened, as one might expect, in the civil rights courtroom. The controversy that would set it all in motion did not take place in any of the places frequented by black lawyers, but rather in a small town in Alabama where nine black youths went on trial for their lives in early 1931.

Arguing about Law

It affected civil rights politics like nothing else ever had. Raymond Alexander offered to "put the whole machinery of the National Bar As- sociation to work" in his role as president of the organization, to "avoid the wholesale slaughter of human flesh that is contemplated by these Alabaman bloodhounds." The Cook County Bar Association, the na- tion's largest and best-organized local black bar, similarly volunteered the full resources of Chicago's black lawyers to the defense. To the ends of their lives, Charles Houston and Loren Miller would cite it as the defining moment in the evolution of their political consciousness. The case was that of the so-called Scottsboro Boys, nine black youths accused of raping two white women aboard a train near Scottsboro, Alabama, in March of 1931. When the youths received quick trials and eight of them got death sentences, white Alabamans congratulated themselves that the defendants had not been lynched. As the NAACP held back, the Communist-affiliated International Labor Defense took control of the case. The leftist organization's cries that the trials were a sham—simply lynchings by another name—soon made the case an international cause célèbre. Protests and violence broke out in places as far away as Africa, Asia, and South America as disparate groups rallied around the con- demned youths. When ILD representatives offered to speak that fall at the National Bar Association's usually staid annual meeting, the bar group's leaders gave their enthusiastic assent to the appearance of "two well known lawyers in New York, attorneys for many of the big radical movements."[2]

Twenty-five hundred people packed the opening session of the NBA convention that fall, where they witnessed something few of them had expected: a white attorney claiming that he was the representative of poor African Americans, while black lawyers remained on the defen- sive. The white lawyer was the ILD's chief attorney, Joseph Brodsky.

The affable Brodsky moved easily between the worlds of black protest and white paternalism, Yiddish-language politics and leftist activism, and working-class protest and electoral politics in his adopted hometown of New York. Like his ILD colleagues David Levinson of Philadelphia and Bernard Ades of Baltimore, Brodsky came to court confident of his place in public space and free to give vent to his radical impulses. Brodsky was part of a growing crop of low-status, mostly night-school-educated Jewish lawyers who existed uneasily, but firmly, on the white side of the color line in Depression-era America. Everything about him seemed different from the respectable white lawyers who made such a difference in the early careers of figures like Marshall, Houston, and Alexander. It was Brodsky's message, however, more than the messenger, that would most provoke his listeners at the NBA convention.[3]

Brodsky claimed, somewhat audaciously, that he represented the masses of black Americans, or more accurately the masses of black and white workers. His organization, the ILD, had been founded as a leftist defense fund in the aftermath of the post–World War I red scare, and was led by members of the Communist Party USA (CPUSA). Its lawyers believed that trials of poor or working-class defendants were simple manifestations of class repression. Out of the Scottsboro controversy, ILD lawyers and activists fashioned a story in which southern criminal trials were often the equivalent of lynchings, staged in order to divide black and white workers: "Lynch the Negro, or if is more convenient, bring him to trial and get him sentenced to death on the chain gang or in the electric chair. There is no fear that the courts will fail you." In response, they fashioned a legal strategy that they called "mass defense." "The correct policy," they contended, "is to secure the services of competent lawyers and, by combining their work in the court room with organized publicity and protest, to transform court trials of workers into propaganda demonstrations in which the capitalist persecutors are put on trial before the working class."[4]

The idea of the courtroom as theater was not a new one when the ILD latched on to it; the fiery abolitionist John Brown and others had used it to great effect in the nineteenth century. But the radical group's innovation was to remake trials into scripted performances that, they believed, would generate direct action by potential supporters in the working class. When he came to court, a lawyer like Brodsky saw himself

as a representative of the masses of poor southern blacks (and whites)— .
not because he resembled those masses, but because he stood at the
vanguard of an inchoate movement of workers and farmers.

When black lawyers stepped inside the courtroom, they experienced something entirely different—a place where, under proper circumstances, blacks and whites could interact as equals. Even in the
South, many black lawyers imagined courtrooms to be nonracial spaces.
Tennessee lawyer Webster Porter, for instance, told his colleagues at the
NBA that "when you go into the fact that you are standing before the
Courts, forget that you are black. I am a lawyer and not a Negro lawyer,
and let them shoot me if they want." Scipio A. Jones of Arkansas pro-
fessed to believe in the nonracial character of courtroom practice, even
after he had gone all the way to the Supreme Court and struggled for
years afterward to free a group of African American men sentenced to
death after a trial in an atmosphere of threatened mob violence. Half a
decade later, Jones would state that "I have found generally that the
courts of the South have sought to be fair and impartial in the administration of justice." Southern judges, argued Jones, "are of the Southern
aristocracy. . . . Being thus endowed and motivated, they are unwilling
to break the great chain of precedents . . . just to do injustice to the cases
espoused by the black lawyer."[5]

Lawyers like Porter and Jones were under no illusions about racial
inequity in the justice system, or about the dangers that they sometimes
faced by appearing in that system. They simply referenced the cross-racial
professionalism that made their interactions with white lawyers and
judges seem like the most distinctive feature of their lives. They harbored
a profound belief in the power of lawyers in ameliorating the harsher
aspects of the Jim Crow system.

It was that strongly held set of beliefs that caused the NBA leadership to invite Clarence Darrow to address the opening session of their
1931 convention. Darrow was a hero in black communities across the
nation. Half a decade earlier, the famous labor lawyer had gotten a
mistrial and then an acquittal in the Ossian Sweet murder trials, where
a group of African Americans had been indicted for murder for shooting into a mob that had assembled after they moved into a white neighborhood in Detroit. The NBA leaders thought that Darrow's opening
address would reinforce their own perspective on law. They were mis-

taken. Darrow would scandalize the convention, while Brodsky would throw it into an uproar.[6]

The convention opened on a hot, dry August day, as an overflow crowd braved the heat and packed Cleveland's historic St. John AME Church to see Darrow speak that evening. There they would hear many things they did not expect. Decades of defending labor radicals in the courts had given the aging and iconoclastic Darrow a healthy skepticism about law, and he vented those doubts when he followed Washington, D.C., municipal judge James A. Cobb to the podium. Cobb, the former NAACP lawyer who had succeeded Robert H. Terrell in the most prestigious judicial post held by an African American, delivered a dry address on the constitutionality of a federal antilynching law. That provoked a sharp rejoinder from Darrow. "I was interested in the address of my friend [Cobb], but I don't think it amounts to much," he said. Focusing in on the courtroom advocacy that marked his black colleagues in so many ways, he noted that "you may have all the laws in the world and the judges will set them aside." "You might just as well ask the Lord to help you as the judges—and neither one of them will." Darrow told his black listeners that African Americans were "lynched in courts" daily, even in northern cities like New York.[7]

The lynching metaphor was the ILD's core idea, and as the audience paused to take in Darrow's unexpected remarks, Brodsky jumped in to ratchet up the tension even further. The radical lawyer took to the stage to say that Darrow "preaches a doctrine of no hope" and urged the conference to give the ILD more time on the program to explain mass defense as an alternative.[8]

By the time Brodsky returned to speak the next day, the convention was already in the midst of a contentious debate over Darrow's unexpected remarks. Cobb took the floor to accuse Darrow of "appeal[ing] to force" rather than to law, while younger lawyers like C. Francis Stradford and Charles Houston came to the podium to extol the professionalism of black and white lawyers as the antidote to tyranny and race prejudice. Brodsky, typically, stirred the pot even more. "I wish I could come to a conclusion that the law profession is what Mr. Stradford said it was or could be," lamented the radical lawyer at the beginning of the speech. Launching into a full-throated exposition of mass defense, Brodsky said that the white lawyers Stradford had praised were simply servants of capital, and he castigated the NAACP for its faith in courts. The ILD, on the other hand, was organizing black and white workers around the world into a protest "that will be heard inside those jail doors at Scottsboro, Alabama, and will force those doors of this jail open to these boys." Referencing the controversy that had gotten him invited back for a second speech, he closed by saying that "I heard Judge Cobb last night, and I agreed with Darrow's view of the Judge's talk. But Darrow's doctrine in my opinion, was even more dangerous." Instead, he called on the black lawyers to join him in "a doctrine of struggle, a doctrine of fight," which would unite black and white workers in a struggle against the capitalists and their lackeys in the judiciary.[9]

Nothing like that had ever been said at a National Bar Association convention, and anger and resentment lay just beneath the surface for the rest of the proceedings. The tension boiled over when an NBA committee proposed a resolution that would criticize the Scottsboro verdicts, praise the efforts of the ILD, and request that the NAACP cooperate with the radicals. When the draft resolution was read, the *Pittsburgh Courier* reported that "[i]mmediately about ten lawyers leaped to their feet." President Alexander, controlling the floor, recognized an ILD critic, who moved that the proposed resolution be rejected. An hour and fifteen minutes of intense discussion and argument ensued. Initially speeches were limited to five minutes, then three minutes, then one, and finally each speaker got only ten seconds to make a point. Judge Cobb and others denounced the ILD and supported the motion to reject. Still others urged that the ILD be thanked, since it was fighting for African American rights. The motion to reject the original resolution lost, as did another that would send the resolution back to the committee for rewording, and the entire convention deadlocked over the issue. No one knew how to proceed. Finally, after much wrangling, the lawyers passed a substitute resolution endorsing "the lawful efforts of all organizations and their lawyers to reverse the verdict," which gave each side part of what it wanted, since many attendees had characterized the ILD's methods as unlawful.[10]

As the lawyers scattered to communities around the country with the close of the convention, they had endured what was probably the most divisive debate in the organization's history. Despite the agreement on the resolution's language, they remained stalemated on the basic is-

sues that Darrow and Brodsky had raised. Instead of conferring legitimacy on their young bar association, their white colleagues' appearance raised and left unresolved the central questions that had so riled
their convention. Exactly what was the relationship between courtroom
space and race? Did black lawyers really stand in for the rest of the race
when they made common cause with their white counterparts? Brodsky and Darrow were both white lawyers, and their dissenting views
could perhaps be dismissed as unrepresentative of what black people
really wanted. However, the same questions would soon reemerge with
renewed force, voiced this time not by outsiders but by clients, local communities of African Americans, and even by those within the respectable black bar itself.

"A Difference in Point of View"

In the half decade that succeeded the black lawyers' gathering in Cleveland, two opposing trends grew up side by side in American civil rights
politics. In a series of high-profile cases, the larger public become aware
of a new phenomenon, as the power of a black man interacting with
his white peers in the courtroom had a profound effect on many white
observers, and a greater effect on the black lawyers themselves. But it
remained true that blacks and whites might draw entirely different narratives out of the same set of facts in a criminal case involving an African American defendant, as they often did in Thurgood Marshall's native
Maryland. Racial representation depended on one's point of view, and
beginning with the 1931 NBA convention, something came to the fore
that had been papered over ever since middle-class African Americans
had created the representative Negro in the middle of the nineteenth
century. For many, the very same cases that put lawyers like Raymond
Alexander, William Hastie, and Charles Houston on the map seemed like
something far more ambiguous than the triumphs that the black lawyers believed them to be.

It began in earnest only months after the National Bar Association
convention, when Willie Brown was placed under arrest in a city transfixed by the assault and murder of young Dorothy Lutz in early 1932. If
Brown had been arrested for a similar crime in February of 1930 or
1931, he would have probably gone to the electric chair with little fan-
fare, and Raymond Alexander would have remained behind the veil

that separated the city's black and white bars. But his case arose in 1932, when in Philadelphia and cities around the world people had been hearing stories of Scottsboro for nearly a year. Brown's story, as it emerged in a statement released to the press by Alexander, was that he had implicated himself in the crime only after the police "told him that if he did not confess they would let loose the 'howling mob' that surged around the station house." The local black newspaper, the *Philadelphia Tribune,* connected the dots immediately for its readers in a headline that read: "Lynch Threat Used in Lutz Case Grilling." Like the Scottsboro defendants, the implication went, Brown had confessed with the sincere belief that the alternative of mob violence lay in the background. His upcoming trial for a heinous crime against a white girl would take place in an atmosphere of such racial and sexual fear that its result was a foregone conclusion. It was simply a means of producing the same result as that imagined violence, only now done with the imprimatur of law.[11]

Reports on the latest developments in Brown's case and those on the ILD's Scottsboro advocacy regularly ran side by side in the *Tribune,* published E. Washington Rhodes, a prominent black lawyer. After the expected conviction and death sentence, the paper threw off all restraint, given that the prosecutor had openly exhorted the white male jurors to protect their women and daughters, and that Judge McDevitt's evidently biased jury charge had removed any remaining doubt about the outcome. The *Tribune* now ran editorials about Scottsboro and Willie Brown right next to each other, denounced the Scottsboro verdicts as a "legal lynching," and used some new language to refer to the Philadelphia proceedings. Adopting the ILD's framework, the paper invoked images of southern mob violence to refer to what awaited Brown: "The State will now, perhaps, have its 'burning party.' "[12]

As the Brown case headed to the state supreme court with the *Tribune* still chronicling its developments alongside Scottsboro, white lawyers and judges also began to struggle with the analogy between the fevered proceedings in Brown's trial and what had happened in Alabama. For them, the comparison had become difficult to avoid, as the two cases moved to their final appeal stages at the same time. But to acknowledge it threatened to invert everything the lawyers and judges believed about their own court system. The prosecutor, Clare Fenerty, was evidently on the defensive about the analogy. Under pressure during his oral argument, he was forced to acknowledge the elephant in the room. When Fenerty finally confessed that he had chosen not to mention Scottsboro at the trial, reportedly in order to "avoid racial prejudice," it was a statement tinged with more irony than truth.[13]

Willie Brown's case divided that city's black and white populace like no other before it, but during the appellate stages of the case, white lawyers and judges began to see hopeful signs for common ground in the actions of Raymond Pace Alexander. In his opinion reversing Brown's conviction, Chief Justice Maxey wrote eloquently of cases that cried out for vengeance but where neither judge nor counsel "departed for an instant" from the " 'calm spirit of regulated justice.' " Maxey took the latter quotation directly from the recent United States Supreme Court opinion in *Powell v. Alabama*, which was the Court's opinion in Scottsboro, handed down only two months before. There, the justices had invalidated the first trials because the defendants had not been given adequate counsel; but everyone understood that the real issue was the circus atmosphere that pervaded the Alabama trials. Lawyers' professionalism was the thing that separated law from lynching in Maxey's world, and the judge soon wrote to Alexander to compliment him on his "poise, dignity and skill" in the face of the racially charged proceedings of the trial. As the relationship between the white judge and the black lawyer grew and matured in the aftermath of the case, Maxey would find those initial impressions reinforced.[14]

Maxey's opinion earned Alexander and his colleagues a temporary reprieve from the questions that had dogged them since the NBA convention, and Charles Houston used it to present the black bar's standard view of courtroom practice to the national readership of the Urban League's journal, *Opportunity*. Houston explained the outcome of the case that constituted the best evidence so far of the young black bar's claims to race leadership. Disregarding the larger issues that swirled around the case, Houston wrote that both Scottsboro and Brown's case had simply raised clear-cut legal issues that the appellate courts had now resolved. As such, he contended, Maxey's opinion "confirms our faith in the independence and integrity of our courts."[15]

Yet, another perspective constantly threatened to intrude on the professional bonds that allowed Alexander, Maxey, Fenerty, and even

Judge McDevitt to disregard what had once seemed to divide them. The ILD used the Willie Brown case to stir up vociferous support for itself among the city's African American population. The leftist organization contended that the bonds between the lawyers remained the problem rather than the solution to the problem of race prejudice in the legal system. Indeed, only weeks after Brown's arrest, the ILD organized a raucous North Philadelphia rally, which featured Blanche Brown herself, Willie Brown's mother, as well as the mother of one of the Scottsboro defendants. When one black speaker charged that both the Scottsboro defendants and Willie Brown were "being railroaded to prison and [the] electric chair by Negro reformists and Negro newspapers," Alexander and his fellow lawyer and newspaper publisher E. Washington Rhodes were the obvious targets of the criticism.[16]

Maxey's opinion and Brown's subsequent life sentence helped mute some of the criticism but did not silence it. In fact, as the proceedings on remand moved toward a guilty plea and life sentence, ILD lawyer David Levinson showed up in court to announce that he had "grave doubts" about Brown's guilt. The ILD stirred up such a ruckus with public statements and telegrams charging that the lawyers had colluded to serve their own class interests that the trial judge felt the need to announce, in open court, that "[t]here have been no conditions made to invite this plea of guilty." Still, Alexander felt the pressure. Within months of the Brown case's resolution, he broke with the NAACP's national office to ally himself with the radicals in building a local mass movement behind a school desegregation fight in the nearby suburb of Berwyn.[17]

Fundamentally, the issue that Levinson and his colleagues raised was one of representation. Alexander had saved his client's life; but lost amidst the growing cross-racial camaraderie of the lawyers was Brown's original contention, backed by the *Tribune* and the large crowds of African Americans who had rallied to his defense, that he was innocent and had been railroaded to confess by threats of lynching. After more than a year of fierce activism that linked Brown's case to Scottsboro, it was now impossible to separate them. Even *Opportunity*'s editors struggled with it. In introducing Houston's write-up on the case, they lumped Philadelphia in with the Deep South's criminal justice system in questioning whether there was any difference between law and lynching, even in the North.

"Is lynching decreasing?" they asked of both Scottsboro and Willie Brown's case. "Or is the technique of lynching improving?"[18]

For his part, Willie Brown remained silent on the question of whether he was receiving justice, because of his understandable fear of cross-examination at trial or any possible retrial until the case reached its final resolution. Outside of his trial testimony, Brown's interactions with the public were almost entirely nonverbal, save for his public expressions of affection for his mother, which reinforced her role as his spokesperson. Blanche Brown stood in for her son at many public gatherings. News reports noted what they took to be her extreme shyness, but that seeming reticence allowed her to present entirely different images to the disparate groups that sought to represent her son. The words uttered in the unresolved debate over Willie Brown would be mostly those of the lawyers and activists. When the next chapter began in the dispute that had emerged at the 1931 NBA convention, it would involve a working-class defendant who stated clearly what he wanted to happen inside the courtroom, and how he wanted his lawyers to represent him.

From Philadelphia, the attention of the black bar leaders turned southward to an unlikely location, Atlanta, and to a lawyer whose own biography seemed to encapsulate the frustrations of a generation of lawyers only a few years younger than Alexander and Houston. Benjamin J. Davis Jr. was part of the group of notable black figures who often roomed with or near each other, argued about politics, and formed lasting ties while they studied at Harvard in the late 1920s. The group included future civil rights lawyers William Hastie and Louis Redding, as well as the lawyer and political activist John P. Davis, historian Rayford Logan, future Nobel Peace Prize winner Ralph Bunche, and Robert Weaver, who would go on to become the first black cabinet secretary. They were a very different group from the black students who had studied at Harvard earlier in the decade. While Charles Houston had believed himself radical when he hosted the Pan-Africanist leader Marcus Garvey at a Harvard reception earlier in the decade, by the late 1920s conversations among the Harvard graduate students strayed to topics like Marxism and economic theory. These were not unusual topics for black college students of Ben Davis's generation. As far away as the University of Kansas, Loren Miller debated Marxist dialectics with his friends during the late 1920s before deciding to become a lawyer.[19]

Ben Davis received his law degree from Harvard in 1929, and after a short stint in the publishing business he returned to Atlanta to practice in the midst of the Great Depression. It was not an auspicious time to become a black attorney. Suddenly, lawyers who had imagined a universe of expanding opportunity for their entire race now sensed the world contracting around them. It started with their own profession. After several decades of double-digit growth, the population of black lawyers actually shrank during the Depression era, even while the total number of attorneys in the country increased. In the cities where most of them practiced, conditions were especially dire for a black lawyer trying to build a practice. One survey of black professionals found that median African American lawyer incomes dropped by almost one-third between 1932 and 1936—a far larger drop than for any other profession surveyed. The explanation was not hard to find. Sadie Alexander told a group of middle-class listeners that "[y]ou . . . have largely attained whatever degree of economic independence you enjoy because of the support of the masses." "[W]hen the masses of our people are unemployed as they are today," she argued, "neither doctors nor lawyers can collect fees." But the reversal hit lawyers especially hard, and many among the younger generation began casting about for explanations. Some, like Davis, were soon in open revolt against the late-Victorian ideals of hard work, thrift, and saving that had traditionally provided a bedrock identity for black lawyers.[20]

Born in 1903, Davis was the son of a prominent Georgia Republican politician and newspaper publisher and attended Morehouse College and Amherst before studying law at Harvard. Davis might have looked forward to a hopeful future even amidst the reversals of the Depression. Initially, he teamed up with the experienced lawyer A. T. Walden, who was building a career that mirrored those of his black lawyer counterparts to the North. Walden would soon become a core figure in a cross-racial elite group of Atlantans who claimed to represent the interests of the local black and white communities while they cautiously moved the city's racial politics into the modern era. Walden already had two decades of wide-ranging experience in the Georgia courts, and stated publicly that an attorney's race mattered little in the courtroom, so long as the black lawyer adopted "an attitude which evinces the pleader's adherence to the highest ideals of the profession."[21]

Ben Davis soon broke with his mentor, and with just about everything in his previous life, after coming to court to take on his first civil rights case. The case involved Angelo Herndon, a Communist organizer who was charged with a capital crime under an anti-insurrection statute for helping to organize an interracial demonstration for poor relief in Atlanta. The case soon became another cause célèbre that would eventually draw in the NAACP, the ILD, and a host of civil liberties advocates. It would go to the Supreme Court twice before Herndon gained his legal freedom.[22]

In January of 1933, Davis entered an Atlanta courtroom to defend Herndon, and emerged as a member of the Communist Party USA. Both Davis and his biographer later wrote that his startling transformation had its roots in Davis's growing dissatisfaction with his father's eroding position in Republican politics, and in slights that he endured in Jim Crow Atlanta. Yet such things hardly distinguished Davis from other black contemporaries, such as his law school classmate, Delaware lawyer Louis Redding, who excoriated Republican machine politics and defended Communists in 1930s courtrooms without joining them. Davis remained comfortably ensconced in the city's black bourgeoisie as Herndon's case proceeded to trial. He helped organize young professionals into an advocacy group, and found the time to continue his starring role in the southern black tennis circuit. The local black press dubbed him "Prince of the Clay Courts" for his enthusiasm and reputation at the sport, and Davis finally put down his racket only as the rush of preparation for Herndon's trial began to overwhelm him. His conversion experience can only be understood as part of a larger story of black law practice in which the young lawyer was embedded.[23]

In Herndon, Davis had found a client who was the polar opposite of Willie Brown. He spoke and wrote quite clearly, and was sure about the viewpoint through which he wanted his trial to be seen. Born into poverty in a small town in southern Ohio, Herndon had joined the Communist Party two years earlier and seemed to find his voice as a dedicated party organizer in Alabama and Atlanta. Judging by his autobiography and his statement at trial, he was also a fairly doctrinaire Depression-era Marxist and believed that his upcoming trial was a simple exercise of capitalist control to stamp out cross-racial working-class unity. When Davis, assisted by his fellow black lawyer John Greer, offered to defend him, Herndon agreed to have them, but only if they would cooperate with the ILD. Davis and Greer consented, and thus bound themselves to a trial strategy that required them to let their radical client do things in court that clashed directly with the professional self-image of the black bar. As ILD theorist William Patterson stated it: "A lawyer has to concern himself only with the juridical aspects of the case. . . . It is the worker defendant who uses the court as his forum." Moreover, Herndon had the bad (or good) luck to be tried in the only U.S. state that still prohibited criminal defendants from testifying under oath in their own defense. Instead, he could only make an unsworn statement to the jury that would not be subject to cross-examination. Because he was being tried in Georgia, Herndon would have the opportunity to make what amounted to a speech in court. He was determined to use it to remove all doubt about how he wanted to be represented.[24]

The ILD's decision to defend Herndon with two black lawyers was key to what would happen in the subsequent trial, for it added the race of the lawyers to the radicalism of their client as the central drama of the proceeding. Like Charles Houston would do later that year, Davis came to court expecting to make headway against the customs of courtroom space that marked black people as inferior. Like Houston, Davis would also enter a southern courtroom and hear racial epithets voiced in open court by his fellow lawyers and judges, and expected to face united opposition from the bench and bar. But Houston encountered a different courtroom when Judges Alexander and McLemore took charge of Crawford's trial and made it clear that the black defense team was to be treated like white men and folded into the local professional community. Davis was not so lucky. He would try his case in front of Lee Wyatt, an inexperienced judge brought in from the rural counties that constituted the base of political support for the segregationists who dominated state-level politics in Georgia. Davis would also face John Hudson, a veteran prosecutor with a decade of experience with headline-grabbing cases, and who was determined to use Herndon's case as a stepping-stone to higher office. Moreover, Davis affiliated himself with the ILD, which, in the aftermath of Scottsboro, had become synonymous in the minds of many white southerners with interracial rape, miscegenation, and promiscuity.[25]

The trial that followed was a struggle for Davis, not so much to put on an adequate defense of his client, but rather simply to be treated like an equal inside the courthouse. The central issue at the trial was whether Herndon's possession of Communist literature, coupled with his leadership role in the poor relief march, was sufficient evidence of revolutionary activity to violate the anti-insurrection law. On that score, Davis's antagonists offered both resistance and red-baiting—for instance, refusing to qualify Davis's expert witnesses' testimony about the Communist literature. However, Wyatt, at least, gave up some ground. The judge, for instance, ended the proceedings with an unexpectedly fair jury charge that raised serious questions about whether Herndon had taken enough concrete steps toward immediate revolution as to violate the statute. Wyatt took a risk in staking out that ground. In fact, his jury charge was more protective of Herndon's Communist advocacy than either the Georgia Supreme Court's interpretation of the statute or the U.S. Supreme Court's emerging First Amendment "clear and present danger" test that provided Herndon with his best chance for freedom.[26]

The most heated exchanges of views at trial concerned the proper racial etiquette to be used inside the courtroom. Perhaps sensing what was to come, Angelo Herndon's first lawyer, H. A. Allen, who had been content to incur the wrath of the local community by affiliating with the ILD, bowed out of the case once it became clear that he had to appear in court alongside black attorneys. Judge Wyatt probably had never seen a black lawyer in his courtroom before, and he quickly marked Davis as a racial inferior rather than a professional equal. Davis later recalled that when he rose to make a motion which challenged the exclusion of African Americans from the grand jury pool, Wyatt denied his motion without even hearing argument or evidence. The jurist's reason for doing so was that "[n]othing you'd say wouldn't make no difference nohow." After the judge reluctantly allowed evidence on both the grand and petit juries, he turned his back when Davis began his own argument. A series of angry exchanges between judge and defense lawyer ensued, when Davis insisted on being treated as a white lawyer would. Things went no better with the prosecuting attorneys. Hudson, the lead prosecutor, marked Davis as a social inferior by referring to him as "Young Ben" inside the courtroom, forgoing even polite appellations such as "my opponent" or "the attorney for the defense" that white southern lawyers used to avoid calling their black colleagues "Mister."[27]

The proceedings would devolve into an intense struggle over racial language. For instance:

> E. A. Stephens [assistant solicitor]: Officer Watson, or Mr. W. B.
> Martin, I don't recollect which, brought this nigger, Angelo
> Herndon, to the solicitor's office.
> Attorney Davis: Mr. Stephens refers to the defendant as "nigger." Your
> Honor . . . it is prejudicial to our case.
> The Court [Wyatt]: I don't know whether it is or not; but suppose you
> refer to him as the defendant.
> . . .
> Stephens: I will refer to him as "negro" which is better; he gave the
> name of Alonzo Herndon—Angelo Herndon; he is the darkey with
> the glasses on.[28]

By this time, the possibility of cross-racial professionalism was long gone, and the trial was now marked by one episode after another of open race-baiting by the prosecuting attorneys, punctuated by cynical responses from a disbelieving Davis. Even Judge Wyatt was reported to have used the term "nigger" in the courtroom. When Herndon rose to make his speech to the jury, charging that the trial was part of a larger effort by "the capitalist class to stir up all this race hatred between Negro and white workers," it seemed to confirm all of what Davis had experienced in his first criminal trial. That night Davis joined the Communist Party. He would return to court to deliver a fiery sermon in front of a packed interracial audience that began with an angry attack on Hudson and charged that "[t]he state's only plea is a prejudiced cry of 'nigger.'" Jurors turned their backs on him. Not surprisingly, they found his client guilty and fixed the penalty at eighteen to twenty years in prison.[29]

The Angelo Herndon case held up an inverted image to the Depression-era trials that raised attorneys like Alexander, Hastie, Houston, and Thurgood Marshall to national prominence. Years later, Davis would say that "[f]irst credit for recruiting me [to the CPUSA] goes not to the Communists but to the savage white supremacy assaults of the trial Judge, Lee B. Wyatt." The example of A. T. Walden, Davis's mentor, as well as his colleagues to the north, seemed to promise that early encounters with moderate judges would provide the professional glue that would bind them to local communities of white lawyers, but Davis received the opposite message. John Hudson, the prosecutor, threatened him with disbarment later that year and ran him out of town before embarking on a career that would see the publicity-hungry former prosecutor defend Ku Klux Klan members who were accused of flogging an interracial group of labor organizers. Hudson would be assisted in the Klan defense by H. A. Allen, the same lawyer who had originally signed on to defend Herndon's Communist advocacy but withdrew rather than appear in court alongside black lawyers. Judge Wyatt, for his part, returned to rural Georgia, was elected to another term, and then embarked on an improbable and paradoxical career. He would eventually be appointed to the state supreme court and cap his career as the presiding judge at the Nuremberg prosecutions of Nazi officials who had been responsible for safeguarding German racial purity. The searing experience of Davis's first civil rights case left him with little in common with such men.[30]

Davis had been effectively expelled from the networks of white lawyers and judges who were so crucial to the early careers of his black colleagues. For the next decade and a half, he remained connected to his counterparts at the respectable black bar, a constant reminder of a point of view that was not their own. Within months of the Herndon trial he was debating Marxist theories of law with his friend Houston and told the Howard vice-dean that he had much to communicate, "which will add greatly to your political education." Davis escaped the mounting legal repression in his native Georgia for New York City, where he became a popular civil rights advocate and served two terms as a Communist member of the city council. Thurgood Marshall would later recall that as late as the 1940s, "Ben Davis used to come to our [NAACP] conventions. We were very friendly."[31]

Such relationships, however, were soon overtaken by events in the larger world. In 1956, when Davis replied in response to an inquiry from Harvard Law School's alumni magazine, he gave an update on his recent doings. He had recently emerged from prison, having served most of a five-year sentence imposed in 1949 under the Smith Act, for teaching and advocating Marxism-Leninism. That result was a replay of his own first major case as an attorney, but this time with Davis as the defendant rather than the lawyer. While he continued to make small contributions to the law school's alumni fund, his own license to practice law had been revoked, completing his exile from the interracial community of lawyers that once seemed to promise so much. "I know little of my classmates," he confessed to the alumni office. "I presume none of them—or few of them—would touch me, so to speak, with a 10-ft. pole." Nonetheless, he still expressed fondness and admiration for former schoolmates such as William Hastie, by then a federal judge, who remained exemplars of a different idea of representation. He remained fully conscious of the contingent set of events that had set them on a path so different from his own.[32]

In Chicago, lawyers like Earl Dickerson waited out the courtroom disputes that defined the Depression-era careers of their colleagues to the east. Chicago's black lawyers were somewhat insulated from those disputes by the political patronage jobs that protected them from their full force. Two years after hanging out his shingle in 1921, for instance, Dickerson threw himself into political organizing for a successful Democratic candidate for mayor. That resulted in a job in the corporation counsel's office. He returned to private practice a few years later, but by 1933 his standing with the party was such that he received an appointment as an assistant attorney general. Dickerson's marriage of public and private life was typical for black lawyers in Chicago, most of whom took advantage of that city's nascent black political machine to move back and forth easily between mutually reinforcing government and private roles. Truman Gibson recalled that one of his early experiences in learning the ropes of Chicago practice was showing up for a case prepared for courtroom work but being told to be quiet, since his political connections had already decided the case in favor of his client.[33]

The defining courtroom performances for Chicago's black bar would not come until the late 1930s, when the *Hansberry v. Lee* racially restrictive covenant case finally brought Dickerson, Gibson, and others to national prominence well after the debate over racial representation had subsided. Still, the Chicago lawyers were not completely insulated from the controversy over the role of the black lawyer in a civil rights courtroom. Dickerson opened the NAACP's 1933 convention with a fiery speech that criticized the group for excessive legalism—an unmistakable reference to his colleague William Hastie's recent appearance in a suit against the University of North Carolina, where the organization had hailed Hastie's professionalism in a southern courtroom as its latest triumph.[34]

"The Whole Trial Was a Frameup"

At the moment that Ben Davis was fleeing Atlanta for more hospitable legal climes, the crisis of representation was coming to a head in its largest and most public episode. It centered on a case that at first had seemed like the greatest triumph for the black bar to date—Charles Houston's defense of George Crawford in late 1933. There, the defense team had emerged from the Loudoun County Courthouse as the embodiment of a new world of racial possibility. Yet a distinct unease remained within black communities that sometimes looked at cases from different vantage points than did their lawyers. Percival Prattis of the Associated Negro Press expressed it when he wrote to Walter White to say that "I wish both you and Charlie [Houston] . . . might have been able to see the public reaction to the course you elected to follow." The trial strategy seemed "to the public either surrender or prudent compliance." Questions remained unanswered: "What! No defense of Crawford? Where are those [Boston] alibi witnesses? What about Paul Boeing? Didn't the Association . . . suggest that Boeing was a pervert and the possible murderer?" Everyone knew that Houston had saved Crawford's life, but an undercurrent of disquiet remained. It focused on the unconstitutionality of the jury selection and Crawford's possible innocence. What was emerging was a battle that would not be waged between the mainstream civil rights bar and the ILD, but rather almost entirely within the respectable civil rights community itself, drawing in civil rights advocates and civil libertarians from around the country.[35]

Prattis struggled to express a view that could be heard in local black communities around the country. Lawyers like Houston claimed to represent those communities, but that remained a difficult thing to do even in Loudoun County, where black people had perhaps the largest stake in the outcome of Crawford's trial. "The colored people are not talking about this case to anyone," one black paper reported before trial. "They never know but what they say may be used against them." In fact, the local prosecutor subpoenaed many of them in advance of trial as material witnesses and put Crawford's girlfriend in jail, prompting trepidation among local African Americans. No one in the county would house the defense team, which commuted forty miles each day from Washington, D.C. During the trial, local blacks showed their support by crowding the courthouse and integrating the seating after the defense lawyers challenged courtroom segregation. Clearly, they were grateful that Houston had come. One local couple even gave their baby, born just before the trial, the middle name of "Houston" in honor of the lawyer's appearance in a county where the only black professional was the local doctor. Again and again, they called Houston back to help them with their legal disputes as the years passed. What exactly they thought of the emerging controversy over Crawford's trial, however, remained impossible to tell.[36]

As the controversy unfolded, it would come to focus on George Crawford himself, who had the chief claim on Houston's loyalty, according to lawyers' ethical standards. One news account called Crawford "a man almost forgotten as his personality is dwarfed into nothingness by things more vital to the actors in this drama," but the unlettered defendant knew how to manipulate the imagery surrounding the case to his advantage. At the trial, he projected an image of jovial simplemindedness and beamed at friends when they identified him in court as having been in the county at the time of the murders. He and his former paramour "smiled broadly as they exchanged glances" when she took the stand as the principal witness against him. He effectively defused the moment of greatest tension at trial when Paul Boeing took the stand and Crawford bowed in homage to his patrician former employer and "removed the atmosphere of horror [that] the prosecution evoked." When Houston argued to the jury that Crawford was a "homeless hungry dog" who tried to rob the Boeing home while under the domination of his co-conspirator, Charlie Johnson, it reinforced what the jurors believed they had seen in the courtroom. Following the jury's recommendation of a life sentence, Crawford "radiated happiness as he assured Judge McLemore that he had nothing to say" and shook hands with his lawyer, while the prosecution seemed content to let him plead guilty to the murder of Boeing's maid in exchange for a second life term.[37]

A month after his conviction, Crawford did something unexpected. He began to talk critically about his trial to a public that had been primed to view his case through the lens of Scottsboro. The NAACP itself had promoted such a viewpoint when it sent an investigator named Helen Boardman to Virginia. Boardman reported that Crawford would have probably been lynched if he had been caught inside the state after a prominent white woman had been murdered in her home. Boardman then published an article in *The Nation* entitled "The South Goes Legal," which helped crystallize sentiment among Crawford's supporters that the outcome of any criminal trial in Virginia was a foregone conclusion—a means of accomplishing through law what used to be done through mob violence. The life sentence and accompanying praise for the defense team helped tamp down that sentiment, but it flared up again shortly after the trial when a story appeared on page one of the *Norfolk Journal and Guide* entitled "Crawford Not Satisfied with His Trial." According to the reporter, Crawford had consented to an interview, and charged that Boston alibi witnesses had not been called, that the witnesses who placed him in Virginia at the time of the murders were lying, and that the prosecutors beat him in Boston and made up the purported confession. "The whole trial was a frameup," Crawford was quoted as saying, although he said that his lawyers had done their best under difficult circumstances.[38]

Crawford's words would roil civil rights politics for the next year and a half. Boardman, along with Martha Gruening, another NAACP staffer, now went public in *The Nation* with her belief that the trial was evidence that southern communities were now substituting law for lynching. Houston's actions had made the NAACP into "the South's best tool in establishing such a procedure," which would send Crawford to jail for life based on flimsy evidence and brazen violations of his constitutional rights. In this and subsequent articles, the investigators argued that the defense team had failed to pursue Crawford's Boston alibi, declined to cross-examine unreliable Virginia witnesses, refused to pursue Boeing as an alternate suspect, and had passed up a very good chance of having the verdict reversed on appeal based on the grand and petit jury exclusion issues. They went so far as to find Crawford's alibi witnesses, who signed affidavits reaffirming their original stories.[39]

Houston and his chief trial assistant, Leon Ransom, published a reply in the *Nation* that strongly implied that Crawford was guilty, and described their approach to the trial as an example of "social statesmanship." Loudoun County whites would have nullified any court order to put African Americans on juries, they contended, but after observing the black defense team's professionalism and its conduct of the case, "both white and colored now report race relations in the county [are] better than ever before." The black lawyers had represented the interests of both blacks and whites in Loudoun County, who now endorsed gradual progress toward calling black people for jury duty. The defense lawyers had adequately represented Crawford as well, they contended, because he did not want to appeal the jury issues and take a chance on a death sentence in a second trial.[40]

Houston and Ransom's article prompted a deluge of responses. Representative white and black men, like Judge McLemore and P. B. Young, the conservative publisher of the *Journal and Guide* rushed to defend them, while others, ranging from black intellectuals and prominent lawyers, to civil libertarians, questioned or condemned their actions. Many argued that Crawford's possible guilt and the NAACP's desire for goodwill did not excuse Houston from his obligation to put on a vigorous defense of his client. Even before Boardman and Gruening went public, Houston and the defense team had been peppered with questions when they spoke to black audiences who were puzzled about the trial strategy. Now letters and articles spilled over into subsequent issues of *The Nation* as well as *The Crisis*, the *New Masses*, and even pamphlet literature. Black newspapers reprinted the Boardman/Gruening essay and Houston and Ransom's reply, as well as Crawford's cryptic letters that failed to explain his own position, and kept their readers updated on the latest developments in the controversy. A year after Crawford's interview, the argument was still raging. Houston endured taunts from the audience at an NAACP banquet in New York, while sixteen prominent intellectuals, including Ralph Bunche, E. Franklin Frazier, and Sterling Brown, signed an open letter to the NAACP asking the organization to provide a better explanation for Houston's conduct or admit that he had been incompetent to handle the case.[41]

The Crawford controversy quickly became a debate over who exactly the black lawyers had represented in that Virginia courtroom, and each side came to depend on Crawford to represent its viewpoint. Houston's critics began to write Crawford in his jail cell to ask him to clarify his comments. However, it turned out that getting Crawford's viewpoint was not so easy. For one thing, his handwriting was hard to understand. A letter commenting on a conversation with his lawyers and his guilty plea reads (with interpolation added to aid in comprehension):

But one thing I *could* [not] understand [was] Why I *did* [not] have my Witnesses he [Houston] state they would do know good so I told him they Would have dun just as much good as those that testifie a gin me. . . . so I told [the] Judge I gest I Will Plead Guilter Because he [Houston] had left me and said he dun Wash his hand up Witch me.

Indeed, the NAACP usually had Crawford's letters typed out and sometimes even reworded to aid in translation.[42]

Observers who heard Crawford speak, by contrast, tended to hear a very articulate person. For instance, the transcript of his plea hearing, containing Crawford's answers to the judge's questions about the *Journal and Guide* interview, reads:

> Those fellows came there to see me, but I did not talk with them about my case. They just came there and discussed it and started asking me how I come out in the trial. I asked who they were, and some of the fellows said that they were newspaper men. I didn't know them. They asked me if I had a fair trial, and I said that I left everything up to my lawyer.

The reporter who conducted the interview wrote that Crawford "speaks intelligently, has a keen sense of humor and is keenly logical in his conclusions." After observing his testimony at the Boston extradition hearing, Boardman called him "an impressive witness on his own behalf." Even the oral Crawford, however, proved hard to grasp. Under fire for the interview, the *Journal and Guide*'s editors finally conceded that the quoted interview, although correct in all the "essential details," was not a verbatim transcript of his words.[43]

A year after the interview, Houston led an interracial group of news reporters to Crawford's cell to get the last word on the case straight from the defendant's mouth. Typically, it produced more confusion. "I'm through talking," Crawford announced; "lots of things have been said [that] I didn't say." After prodding, he would only say that Houston had done his best and that lies had been told at the trial. The result was a dispute in which each side invoked Crawford's words, with good reason, in support of its own theory of what had happened in that courtroom.[44]

Frustrated by his inability to get Crawford to speak clearly, Houston did something that made the controversy into a referendum on a much larger set of issues. He got Crawford to write out a statement admitting his guilt and stating that his lawyers had done everything they could at trial. Crawford gave Houston permission to release it to the public. But Houston declined to do it, thinking that the statement would seem coerced. Instead, he began drafting an article for the NAACP that would explain the facts of the case as he saw them, to support his "social statesmanship" interpretation of the trial—that the defense team's conduct had built up goodwill among white lawyers, judges, and moderate leaders in Virginia. Uncomfortable about putting out a statement that seemed self-serving and perhaps disloyal to his former client (despite Crawford's permission), he asked the NAACP's Roy Wilkins to edit it and suggested that Wilkins or Walter White sign it. The article appeared in two long excerpts in *The Crisis* in early 1935, unsigned by anyone and titled simply "The George Crawford Case: A Statement by the N.A.A.C.P."[45]

The unsigned statement purporting to represent the views of the NAACP appeared as the organization was debating its future, and ensnared the Crawford defense team in a much larger controversy. For several years, a group of younger activists and intellectuals, led by the economist Abram Harris Jr., had been urging the NAACP to reorient its program away from civil rights litigation in favor of a new one that emphasized economic advocacy on behalf of black workers and farmers, unity with the white working class, and decentralization of power to take the organization closer to the people. The NAACP's board appointed Harris as the head of a committee to propose a new program for the organization, but the board tabled his more radical recommendations in the fall of 1934. The organization remained stalemated on which way to go. Houston had positioned himself as the leading exemplar of what he called the "undecided middle group" who wanted to find common cause with both the old guard and the reformers. Indeed, within a few years, along with much of the black bar leadership, he would emerge as a leading exponent of marrying the NAACP's past traditions with the social democratic promise of the future. But the Crawford case did just the reverse, and for many it made the black defense team a symbol of everything that was wrong with the organization's seemingly muddled program.[46]

The Crawford controversy now effectively united people on both sides of the fault line within the NAACP. A wide range of people questioned whether the black defense lawyers' interactions with their white counterparts in that Virginia courtroom—startling as they were to southern mores—could be said to represent any viewpoint other than their own. Traditionalists believed that the defense's less-than-aggressive trial strategy and failure to appeal signaled an abandonment of the organization's forceful legal advocacy of black equality. Reformers believed that these same things meant that the organization was choosing to mollify respectable whites when it should be organizing working-class blacks. Both groups found an outlet for their views in a self-published pamphlet distributed to NAACP members in advance of the organization's 1935 convention, as the controversy over the association's future remained unresolved. Titled *The Crawford Case: A Reply to the "N.A.A.C.P.,"* it set out Boardman and Gruening's views of the trial, in the form of the investigators' detailed response to the two-part, unsigned series in *The Crisis*. The pamphlet's introduction was signed by a variety of NAACP members and leaders, ranging from resolute traditionalists such as longtime board member Joseph P. Loud, who opposed any reorientation of the organization's priorities, to equally resolute critics of the association's traditions such as lawyer-activist Loren Miller, to well-known figures such as the writer J. A. Rogers and the explorer Matthew Henson.[47]

Titling their introduction "Who Is the N.A.A.C.P.?" the motley group concurred on one thing: the problem with the unsigned *Crisis* article was one of representation. It had been written solely from the point of view of the lawyers who litigated that case. A close examination of the facts, however, revealed another perspective, which Boardman and Gruening had now brought to the attention of the NAACP's rank and file. "These facts," the authors intoned, "speak for themselves"—the implication being that the lawyers did not represent Crawford, or the desires of local African American communities around the country.[48]

Facts, of course, would never resolve the controversy, for it was simply the latest, and most public, episode in an ongoing controversy that had been building ever since the ILD's attack on the distinction between law and lynching coincided with the rise of a new group of black lawyers who seemed to breathe life into the possibility that courts could be islands of freedom in a world of segregation. The controversy over racial representation had now become a means for activists, intellectuals, and others to talk about a much larger set of issues concerning the future of African Americans, and of the venerable organization that claimed to represent them. As usual, people continued to talk past one another on the best way to represent the race, and political positions remained jumbled. The only thing that everyone could agree on was that black lawyers had come to symbolize something much larger than themselves. Old NAACP stalwarts like former national field secretary William Pickens continued to doubt Crawford's guilt, while Houston reported that "even a member of my own family is not satisfied" with the defense team's version of the story. After more than a year of conflict and argument defined as much by differing points of view as anything else, he should have expected nothing less.[49]

8

The Strange Journey of Loren Miller

IN LATE June of 1935, two of the nation's best-known black lawyers set out from New York for the long trip to the annual meeting of the NAACP in St. Louis, where they seemed to be on a collision course. Loren Miller arrived in St. Louis as a local celebrity and a hero to the critics of the organization's traditions. His popularity there was due to his writings in the intellectual press and his nationally syndicated newspaper columns, where for a decade he had subjected his fellow black lawyers to a withering barrage of criticism. His main complaint was the charge that black attorneys represented nothing more than the voice of a self-interested middle class, and certainly not the voice of the race as a whole. Lately, he had been coming to believe that Charles Houston personified everything that had stoked his ire for the past decade.

Houston had walked a fine line since the Crawford controversy broke into the open. One of his greatest assets was his courtroom persona and his ability to metaphorically stand in for the rest of his race inside the courthouse. But for an increasingly vocal group of younger critics like Miller, such courtroom performances, powerful as they might be, only marked off his distance from the economic difficulties of working-class blacks in Depression-era America. At the St. Louis meeting, it would be Houston's job to explain to an increasingly volatile NAACP membership how his civil rights work meshed with the pressing needs of local black communities. Houston took up the challenge in St. Louis, but failed to convince Miller.

The rebellious young lawyer left the convention disgusted at what he had seen there. "Houston intends to resolve it [the new NAACP program] into a mandate for a new orgy of legalistic performances," he complained in the pages of the *New Masses*.[1] Nonetheless, Houston soldiered on, and six months later he persuaded the Maryland Court of Appeals to uphold the desegregation of that state's law school. In the aftermath of that victory, letters of congratulations poured into the offices of Houston and his co-counsel, Thurgood Marshall, including one that lustily encouraged them to "carry your battle on" in the courts. "I believe that if you can you will be able to make a serious breach in the whole structure of inadequate facilities," the writer continued. It must have been among the most jolting of the many they received, for it was signed by Loren Miller.[2]

A little more than a decade after the St. Louis meeting, the two lawyers who once seemed to represent opposing views of minority group identification would argue alongside each other in the Supreme Court in the racially restrictive covenant cases. Early in his career, Miller had seemed to speak with the voice of the voiceless—black lawyers and communities shut out of the dreams of economic progress that helped launch the careers of lawyers like Houston and Raymond Alexander in the late 1920s. He honed that voice in the multiracial, multiethnic politics of Depression-era Los Angeles where black and Japanese communities crafted parallel responses to a world bounded by residential segregation. After a visit to the Soviet Union, Miller seemed to hit his stride as he built up a national audience for his caustic views of the current state of American civil rights politics. By the mid-1930s, he had become a well-known figure in black politics and wanted to take his view of race and the law to a wider audience in the mainstream press.

That project, however, was delayed by three decades, during which time Miller became one of the country's leading civil rights lawyers. When Random House finally published his magnum opus in 1966, entitled *The Petitioners: The Story of the Supreme Court of the United States and the Negro*, Miller placed Houston's litigation at the center of a heroic narrative, and popularized that story just as the civil rights movement was searching for historical predecessors. The following decade, Richard Kluger would work from *The Petitioners'* framework when he wrote *Simple Justice*, the book that introduced generations of Americans to the history of the African American struggle for legal equality. What brought Houston and Miller back together again was the same thing that once caused them to embody conflicting images of representation—their shared identity as lawyers struggling to represent the interests of the rest of their race. As a younger man, Miller had done all he could to usher in the crisis of representation. It seems only fitting that as an established lawyer, he would also point the way out.[3]

A Reluctant Lawyer

Years after he was first admitted to the bar, Loren Miller remembered that "I really . . . wasn't enamored of the law, to put it mildly." That fact put him in good company, and was key to the startling evolution that made him into a central figure in two very different periods of American racial politics. Like Raymond Alexander and Charles Houston, Miller came to prominence in the last half of the 1920s with a vision of what the black lawyer was all about. But unlike them, his words set him at odds with the dreams of the leaders of the African American bar.

Born in 1903 to a black father and a white mother, Miller adopted a black cultural identity while attending college at the University of Kansas. He first made his mark as a writer, not a lawyer, in an essay that won first prize in one of the literary contests sponsored by *The Crisis* magazine that marked a high point in the Harlem Renaissance. "At last you have come to college. You are going to be a lawyer," it began. The prospect was not an exciting one. In college the writer discovers other loves— "Poetry, Philosophy," and the humanities, and begins to admire the work of black writers and artists like Langston Hughes. Despairing of ever possessing their gifts, he turns to law by default. "You plunge into law. You secretly loathe it." Although the writer continues to dabble with "bitter little sketches, tragic bits of verse," he realizes that "[y]ou must be but little more than a shyster lawyer." Resigned to the practice of law, the route that Raymond Alexander and others took to prominence stretches out before him, and he makes clear what he thinks of it. "You will be pushed down to preying on police court characters, loose women and gamblers, with perhaps a small share of legitimate business." The details match closely enough with Miller's own life that the essay reads less like fiction than it does the autobiography of a reluctant lawyer.[4]

It would not be an exaggeration to say that many of the central figures who helped bring about the Depression-era crisis in representation were unenthusiastic lawyers. Harvard law graduate John P. Davis first came to prominence as a Harlem Renaissance figure, where he won honorable mention in an essay contest sponsored by *Opportunity* magazine, managed *The Crisis*, helped organize the one-issue avant-garde black literary magazine *Fire!!!*, and obtained a graduate degree in literature from Harvard. He applied to law school only after his career as a writer had fizzled, and established an uneven record there while continuing to work on his literary essays. Davis soon put literature behind him, improved his grades, and obtained one of the coveted places in Felix Frankfurter's public utilities seminar that served as a prime training ground for New Deal lawyers. After graduating, he quickly put those skills to good use in becoming a trenchant critic of the race discrimination being written into New Deal legislation. As the decade passed, however, he moved further and further away from law work and capped his career by organizing the National Negro Congress as the principal leftist alternative to the NAACP. The black Communist politician Ben Davis confessed that he "had never been too keen on the law" and was "much more enamored of the arts." He remembered that he studied law only because his father pushed him to do it. Ben Davis worked for a time in journalism before reluctantly trying his hand at his chosen profession. Miller recalled that "in those days a Negro [with education] could be a doctor, lawyer or schoolteacher—and that's about all." To lawyers like these, law seemed like the province of responsible men and women whose true calling lay elsewhere.[5]

The source of this discontent, as with many political disputes, was generational. Figures like John Davis, Loren Miller, and Ben Davis went to college in the middle of the 1920s rather than the 1910s, and that made all the difference. By that time, younger black professionals and intellectuals were in active revolt against their predecessors' Victorian ideals, which had celebrated hard work, thrift, savings, and success in the market economy as the route to responsible manhood. Many were drawn to literature, consumer culture, and cultural nonconformity rather the idea of the self-made man that had helped lawyers only half a decade older to understand their successes and failures in the profession. They came to law with a smoldering sense of discontent with the values that animated lawyers like Charles Houston and Raymond Alexander.[6]

These lawyers' displeasure with their chosen profession would soon become far more widely shared, and the event that brought about that transformation was the onset of the Great Depression. The Depression marked off a clear divide between two groups of black lawyers separated by only a few years of age. Lawyers who started practicing in the early 1920s had often established themselves in the profession by decade's end. Figures like Alexander, Earl Dickerson of Chicago, and Houston spent most of the 1920s building their reputations. They experienced law as an opportunity to gain some upward mobility, particularly as the migration of African Americans out of the post–World War I South seemed to provide an ever-expanding potential clientele. For a lawyer coming to the bar at the end of the decade, however, the profession seemed to offer only downward mobility that quickly spiraled into a crisis of professional identity.

What were lawyers to do about the crisis that hit them harder than so many others? Loren Miller had more time to think about these reversals than most, and would come to renewed prominence in the early Depression era with an essay that provided an answer. After studying at the University of Kansas and Howard, Miller graduated from Washburn Law School in 1928. He stayed in Kansas for a year and a half and practiced law in a place where "the depression was really an old story . . . by 1929," as he later remembered. Like the inhabitants of most agricultural states, Kansans struggled economically through the 1920s, and few black lawyers there would have dreamed of prosperity. When his sister died in Los Angeles, Miller came out for the funeral and found that he could not go back to Kansas. He stayed because of the sense of possibility that had drawn African Americans to the city ever since W. E. B. Du Bois had praised black Angelenos' comfortable lifestyles in the pages of *The Crisis*.[7]

The "California myth," as Miller later called it, had much material support in 1920s Los Angeles. The city's growing African American Central Avenue business district was the centerpiece of a community that had recently showcased its prosperity by hosting the 1928 national NAACP convention. Miller put his struggles as a lawyer in Kansas behind him and found a new life in the city as an editor and writer for the local black press. He completed a hundred-page draft of a novel and renewed his friendship, struck up earlier in the decade, with Langston Hughes. But he had arrived just as his adopted hometown began to experience its own economic slide, and soon turned his thoughts back to the struggles of his old profession.[8]

"Western Writer Flays Negro 'Professionals,'" announced the *Philadelphia Tribune*, introducing Miller's latest broadside to its readers in July of 1931. Miller had published an article in *Opportunity* magazine about the effect of the Depression on black professionals, and then excerpted it in a press release that was picked up by black newspapers across the country. "Only a few years ago," he wrote in an unmistakable reference to the 1920s-era pronouncements of lawyers like Houston and Alexander, "the professional man . . . believed that he could build up an ever increasing clientele by securing superior training, equipping finer offices and relying on Rotarian 'service' ideals." That self-interested theory of racial progress, however, depended on "prosperity for the worker" and had vanished with the onset of the Depression. Professionals were now supporting the Urban League's petitions for jobs, but that support was based on the "far fetched possibility" that reemployed black workers would confer more patronage on professionals, who would, in turn, "evolve a black capitalist class which will . . . employ the black workers." Similarly, professionals' campaign for "civil, political and citizenship rights" seemed far less radical than it had before, since the worker "takes the view that his ills are purely economic and is less grateful for political victories than he might be."[9]

At this point in his life, Miller had turned his displeasure with his chosen profession into an embrace of the Socialist Party, although he would soon move further to the left. Two factors produced that result. The first was the growing acrimony between the NAACP and the ILD that had emerged in the aftermath of the Scottsboro trials. "I was a bitter end Socialist up to the Scottsboro Case," he later remembered, "and had never had any truck with the Reds until that time." In the ILD's Marxist theories of legal defense, Miller seemed to find something that appealed to his sense of youthful iconoclasm. The other factor that moved him significantly to the left was a chance to see communism up close. In June of 1932 he set sail along with the poet Langston Hughes and other young black luminaries for a land that seemed to promise both danger and opportunity for a rebellious generation of African Americans: the Soviet Union.[10]

Race and Nationality in Los Angeles and Russia

Geography played a key role in allowing Miller to find his own particular voice on matters of racial representation—the racial geography of Los Angeles, to be exact. Race looked different in a city whose composition often surprised people from other parts of the country. "When you got on a streetcar, you could see this spectrum of humanity," Pauli Murray vividly remembered from her first encounter with California, where she worked for a short time with Miller in Los Angeles before moving on to Berkeley. "I began then thinking of minorities rather than just the black-white situation." Dovey Johnson Roundtree recalled that "I'd known of the unique racial mix of Southern California" before she arrived there in 1945 to lobby for fair employment legislation. "But statistics, however carefully compiled," could not capture the "human face" of that city's complicated racial politics. As the city had suburbanized over the previous several decades, its white residents had used a variety of means—most famously racially restrictive covenants—to isolate the black and Japanese American communities who clustered near one another around Central Avenue. African Americans and those of Japanese descent, while experiencing citizenship differently, often borrowed ideas from each other as they plotted their way out of the residential and economic segregation that hemmed them in. That sense of inhabiting a city composed of various national groupings, proceeding on parallel paths to equality, weighed heavily on Miller's mind as he struggled to come to grips with what he saw in the Soviet Union.[11]

Years later in a private letter, Miller tried to recapture what had made the radical left so attractive to a worldwide generation of young people in the post–World War I era.

> Remember that we had been bitterly disappointed in the 1920's; that the brave new world promised by Woodrow Wilson had not materialized. . . . We sensed that there was an impending change in the offing—at first we did not call it by its after-acquired name of fascism. . . . We were alarmed by the seeming dominance of what FDR would later call the Economic Royalists . . . because they were, or seemed to be, remaking the world to their shortsighted order in which Privilege and Money were gods.

"So we enlisted," he sighed with the cares of middle age now weighing on him, "or dallied with the thought of enlisting, with them [the Communists] ostensibly to eliminate poverty and racial prejudice but over and beyond that for the purpose of making a world in which we would be free." By the 1950s, that point of view seemed hopelessly naïve to Miller, but even as an older, anticommunist civil rights lawyer he could look back at the leftist dreams of his youth with a combination of wistfulness and regret.[12]

As the Depression deepened, that brand of utopian radicalism appealed mightily to a younger generation of African Americans. Pauli Murray viewed Russian life as a grand "social experiment in action" from her vantage point in 1930s New York. It would be an "opportunity of a lifetime" to have the chance to see it, she believed at the time. Murray was offered a chance to go in 1932 as part of a group of African Americans who were supposed to act in a Soviet film about American race relations. She reluctantly stayed home to finish her studies. "I always envied them that trip," she later recalled, "and almost cursed the fates which left me at home to study boring books." As late as 1937, John P. Davis would deliver a radio address during a trip to the Soviet Union, wishing long life to "the Union and Stalin" in the midst of the Russian dictator's purges and show trials. Even older lawyers like Raymond and Sadie Alexander, who were too established in their profession to feel such sentiments, found themselves somewhat moved. After a stopover in Russia during a 1931 European vacation, Raymond returned to deliver an excited address to a large local audience, describing a place where neither the "capitalist class" nor the "professional class, doctors and lawyers" were in charge, but rather the "people who work in factories and who earn their daily bread by using their hands." Miller was eventually drawn to the Soviet Union by the film project that had proved so tempting to Murray. In June of 1932 he embarked for Russia along with a number of younger writers and intellectuals such as Langston Hughes, the leftist activist Louise Thompson, future *New York Post* writer Ted Poston, *Amsterdam News* journalist Henry Lee Moon, and Harlem Renaissance figure Dorothy West.[13]

Like other African American visitors to the Soviet Union in that era, what most impressed Miller and his colleagues was the connection between race and nationality in that country. In a well-chronicled story, the film project soon fizzled because of the ineptitude of their hosts and the Soviet authorities' desire for American governmental recognition. But that failure gave part of the group a chance to travel to central Asia as compensation for their disappointment, and to observe the Soviets' treatment of that country's national minorities. Astonished at what they viewed as the resolution of the problem that bedeviled American race relations, the group issued a joint message to the workers of Uzbekistan that praised their hosts for success on the issue.[14]

Miller assumed "intellectual leadership" of the leftist core of the group who traveled to Asia, according to Moon, and remained remarkably consistent in his views of Russia's racial politics as most of the film group drifted back to America with a variety of impressions of what they had seen there. For his part, he became a staunch defender of the Communist Party position that African Americans in the "black belt" southern counties where they constituted a majority were an oppressed "nation" in need of self-determination. The doctrine was worked out in Moscow in 1928 and 1930 as an outgrowth of the Communist International's position on Russian national minorities, and the black belt thesis struck most African Americans as an oddity. Even the black American Communist Harry Haywood, who later claimed credit for the policy, initially thought it was a fallacy. Not so with Loren Miller. "I cannot emphasize too much," he wrote, "the tremendous impression made on me by the success of the policy of self determination for minor nationalities" in the Soviet Union. "Nothing impressed me more," he declared.[15]

The Comintern position on race and nationality seemed so clear to Miller when it seemed so opaque to other black Americans because he was inspired not by the South, but by his adopted hometown of Los Angeles. The Soviet Union that he observed was busy reimagining the various cultural and language groups under its rule as "nations" working their way toward modernity in a way that would refute the idea that races were inherently unequal in their capacity for progress. Soviet leaders were eager to show off those imagined communities, and one such display had a profound effect on Miller. Invited with the film group to view a Soviet commemoration in Moscow, he sent a quick dispatch to newspapers back home in an effort to capture the rush of impressions that threatened to overwhelm him. "Perhaps few Negroes realize that Russia is inhabited by a wide variety of races and nations," he wrote, "ranging from fair-haired, blue [eyed] men to dark Tartars and Mongols." "Speakers on this occasion were representatives of various of the more than 100 nationalities embraced in this nation," and "[e]ach

offered enthusiastic praise for the manner in which the minorities problem has been solved and recited the immense advances made by his
own people in the new order."[16]

That vision of a country comprising a multitude of polyglot races
and nations bore little resemblance to the southern region whose comparison to Russia seemed far-fetched to most black Americans as they
scratched their heads over the black belt thesis. What would occupy
Miller's thoughts for the next several years was the comparison between
the vision of the future he had seen in Russia and the discriminations
he experienced every day at home. But home was not the South of the
black belt debate. In fact, Miller confessed to having so little experience
with southern life that he wanted to go there and "ride on a Jim Crow
car because I want to see how it feels." Home was a place closer at hand,
where multiracial, multilingual communities of color were borrowing
visions of nationalism and progress from one another. It was his own
neighborhood near Central Avenue. "[W]e lived in a neighborhood, surprisingly enough, where most of our neighbors were Japanese," Miller's
son would later recall, in explaining his father's long-term fascination
with multiracial democracy.[17]

Miller returned to his old haunts in December of 1932 and to his job
as city editor of the *California Eagle,* eager to help transform the community that had seemed like a multiracial capitalist utopia three years before
into a multiethnic Communist one. He got married in February 1933 to
Juanita Ellsworth, a Los Angeles social worker, but friends and associates complained of hearing little from him. In response, Miller gave a
terse answer: "the radicals. You can well imagine that I have been in
their hands ever since my return from the Soviet Union." From Southern California to San Francisco, and especially in the Los Angeles area,
he became a much sought-after speaker when churches, civic organizations, and professional groups needed someone to interpret Soviet ex-
periments in race and economic life as a possible future for Americans
experiencing the lowest point of the Depression. In prepared speeches,
prearranged debates with representatives of business interests, and
even one appearance with Albert Einstein, he met with both curiosity
and enthusiasm from audiences across the color line. "Ever since you
talked at Royce Hall," a representative of UCLA's Young Women's Christian Association wrote him, "students have been clamoring to hear you
again."[18]

Courtrooms were the last place that reluctant lawyers like Miller wanted to be, and his Soviet sojourn had given him a new language to express that antipathy. From Moscow, he had reported on the arrival of "Mrs. Ada Wright, mother of two of the Scottsboro boys," whose appearance at a celebration in Red Square seemed to signal that the ILD had made the domestic "Negro problem" into a "world issue." Upon his return from Russia, Miller gladly accepted an invitation to lend his writing skills to an article in the *Daily Worker,* the Communist Party's organ. Urging an ILD colleague in Oregon to continue the leftist group's fight against its chief rival's legalism, he wrote that "[s]uch constant and vigorous attacks on the NAACP will do much to root out its rapidly vanishing influence."[19]

Still, Miller could never quite escape the sense of obligation that came with his lapsed membership in the legal profession. Somehow he managed to avoid joining the Communist Party, and the networks that defined his life in Los Angeles were solidly middle class. His wife was a social worker and a prominent member of Delta Sigma Theta sorority. (Miller wrote literary criticism in the Kappa Alpha Psi journal, although from a Marxist perspective.) His employer at the *Eagle,* the pioneering black woman journalist Charlotta Bass, was a skeptic of interracial working-class agitation in that period. Burton Ceruti, the black NAACP lawyer who led the 1920s Los Angeles restrictive covenant litigation, had died prematurely several years before. When his community called on Miller to use his professional training to help out, he responded despite his misgivings. The local NAACP chapter listed him as a paid-up member as of December 1933. By the following year, he was a member of the chapter's legal committee and collected complaints for the committee about police brutality. Later, he served as a lead attorney in a lawsuit against a drugstore for refusing to serve black patrons. Such activities, however, remained few and far between.[20]

If law work was duty, writing was passion for lawyers like Miller, and he found an ever-expanding audience for that passion upon his return from Russia. His vivid Associated Negro Press (ANP) dispatches with such exotic bylines as Berlin, Tiflis (later Tbilisi), Tashkent, Odessa, and of course Moscow, had made him a familiar figure in black communities across the country. Now, through articles that reached a national audience via the ANP, and through agreements like one with the Southern Newspaper Syndicate to run his column in three southern

black papers, Miller slowly expanded the audience for his thoughts beyond his base in Los Angeles. By the time *Opportunity*'s editors brought
out a special 1934 issue highlighting the thoughts of young writers on
the future of the race, Miller seemed like the natural person to present
the CPUSA point of view. His essay titled "One Way Out: Communism"
presented his mature view that the black belt program was the only way
to create the multiracial nirvana that he had seen in the Soviet Union.
By the following year, Miller and Ben Davis had become chief editors
of the Crusader News Agency, the leftist alternative to the ANP. Miller's
column for the radical wire agency, titled "The Way Out," channeled his
writing into black newspapers around the country.[21]

The final breakthrough came in the middle of 1935, when Miller
signed on as a writer for the leftist journal the *New Masses* and moved to
New York. It was a noteworthy thing for a black writer to join the staff
of a white intellectual journal, even a leftist one, and the national African American press eagerly reported the move and excerpted Miller's
writings from his new post. Once ensconced in New York, Miller applied Marxist analysis to everything from white philanthropy to Socialist Party politics to the writings of W. E. B. Du Bois. His *New Masses* post
made him a popular guest lecturer in New York, and he spent much of
his free time talking to student groups, professionals, YMCA groups, and
just about anyone who would listen about the promise of a Communist
future. When the *New Masses* needed someone to cover the NAACP's
upcoming St. Louis convention, Miller seemed like the obvious choice.
He initially demurred but later gave his reluctant assent.[22]

The St. Louis meeting was a "crossroads" for the NAACP, according
to the leading account of its history. Its membership and sources of
funds had been hit hard with the onset of the Depression. Its most visible black leader, W. E. B. Du Bois, had resigned in a huff the year before, complaining of the group's lack of an affirmative program and
its muzzling of his dissenting views on segregation. In NAACP chapters
around the country, a younger, more aggressive, "new crowd" was forming that would challenge the old guard with a more confrontational style
of protest. The new crowd was finding outlets for its frustration, most
significantly in the proposed National Negro Congress that John P. Davis
was busy organizing to pursue the leftist economic program that had
been rejected by the NAACP's board. The association's leaders felt the
pressure. Houston warned Walter White that the only means "to keep

[Davis] from running off with the show . . . is for the Association to put on a bigger and better performance of its own" in St. Louis.[23]

The 1935 NAACP convention would be a battle of images, its leaders believed, waged to prevent younger members and activists from deserting the organization en masse for more sympathetic ground. But Houston himself was part of the image problem, with the dispute over his performance in the Crawford courtroom symbolizing much of what was wrong with the organization for both traditionalists and reformers. As the NAACP prepared to put its best face on the convention, Martha Gruening and Helen Boardman arrived in St. Louis by bus, with numerous copies of their self-published pamphlet responding to the unsigned *Crisis* articles, and its multiauthored introduction asking "Who Is the N.A.A.C.P.?" With momentum for the National Negro Congress now building, there was speculation that distribution of the pamphlet to the attendees would have "considerable influence in swinging the reorganization of the NAACP to the left."[24]

Loren Miller arrived at the NAACP convention as an influential voice in the battle of images. His Crusader News Agency column ran in the local black newspaper, and his ideas were so familiar there that he was often introduced as "the Loren Miller." In St. Louis, he saw the association put on speakers on subjects like the black union movement and economic discrimination in New Deal programs. He also saw Houston outline the organization's new legal program, ranging from a proposal to attack union discrimination to the trial court victory, only one week before, in the effort to desegregate the University of Maryland's law school. An hour after arriving back home in New York, Miller settled down to write his wife about what he had seen. "The convention muddled along with a great many left promises and really nothing to indicate that the NAACP intends to do more than make a few gestures," he wrote. He had grown so impatient with the proceedings that "[t]oward the end I refused to be polite any longer and broke out with some acute and acid observations."[25]

Those impressions would soon reach a wider audience in a blistering attack on the NAACP published in the *New Masses*. Assessing the St. Louis proceedings, Miller announced that the new program was too vague to commit the organization to economic work, and likely to be given a conservative interpretation by the association's cautious leadership. Moreover, that leadership's "chief lieutenant to aid in carrying out the new program is Charles Houston, a Washington attorney." "Little remains to be said about his opportunistic outlook," Miller continued, "after Martha Gruening's expose . . . of his handling of the Crawford case." At the convention, Houston had "harped on court action" in explaining how lawyers could represent the movement, and even his union discrimination proposal would produce nothing more than "legalistic performances" of a kind that he had given before. The NAACP was beset by many problems, he argued, and Houston embodied them all.[26]

With the publication of his *New Masses* essay, Miller seemed to hit his stride in his decade-long effort to bring his own particular voice to bear nationally on matters of race and representation. The noted journalist Roi Ottley told the readers of his *Amsterdam News* column that "Loren Miller's article concerning the N.A.A.C.P. in last week's New Masses should be required reading." Roy Wilkins stopped in on Miller in a cautious effort to make peace with his organization's fiercest internal critic, but Miller dismissed their parley as talk of "cabbages and kings." The two had traded barbs in the black press earlier that year. Miller remained unappeased, and had planned to do a follow-up article to his combative post-convention piece called "California's Crawford Case." The article would explain how the association continued to pursue useless reformist legalism.[27]

A few months later, Miller prepared to depart for Los Angeles, confident that he had done all he had set out to do in New York. "Working on New Masses has been a swell thing for me," he wrote to his wife. "I have learned more than you imagine about writing since I have been here. Things that I hope to put to good use." He believed that the *New Masses* project had made him into a better writer, given him a larger audience for his thoughts, and would generate more work once he returned home. He was near to placing an article in the *American Spectator,* and was now planning to reach a white audience in the pages of journals such as *The Nation,* the *New Republic,* and *Survey Graphic.* He had become what he had wanted to be a decade earlier: a well-known writer, with a distinct antipathy toward law.[28]

Thus it must have seemed like a bolt from the blue when, just a few months later, Charles Houston opened the stack of letters congratulating him on his appellate victory in the Maryland law school case and found one signed by Loren Miller. Not only did the writer approve of the NAACP's success in the case that Houston had highlighted at the

1935 convention, but he gushed with praise for the victory as a significant breakthrough in the struggle against entrenched inequality. Houston must have concluded that something had happened to his onetime
critic in the six months that separated the St. Louis meeting from the
Maryland appellate victory. It had. Loren Miller had begun to practice law.[29]

Entering the Market

Like many other political transformations, the one that would alter both
the law and the historical memory of the civil rights movement had a
profoundly material cause. Miller was nearly thirty-three years old when
he left New York for home. He had been married for over two years and
had very little money. For the last six years, he had led a vagabond existence that befitted a writer more than someone with the relatively rare
gift of a professional degree. Even Miller conceded that before he took
the *New Masses* post, most people thought of him as "Topeka's bad boy
and a rather sad example of how a young man should *not* waste his talents." While the New York work finally brought respect and greater
fame, it brought little else. "We did not have the cost of a telegram in the
New Masses till," recalled an editor from that period. Miller's wife even
had to send him the cost of postage for the letters he mailed home. His
fellow Soviet travelers Ted Poston and Henry Lee Moon would soon
find more-stable platforms for their writing in the white press and the
NAACP's national office, but little of that type of support existed in Los
Angeles. What the city did have was a magnetic pull that drew in almost twenty-five thousand more black migrants to the Central Avenue
district even during the Depression. It was also a place where Miller's
name was well known, and he returned there expecting that his New
York fame would translate into Los Angeles clients. He believed that
practicing law would simply be a way to pay the bills so that he could
take his *New Masses* work to the next level. So Miller took his first steps
on the path he had struggled to avoid since his 1926 essay, beginning
what he had called the "plunge into law."[30]

By opening his law practice in January of 1936, Miller immersed
himself in something he had defined himself against for the previous
decade—the market for lawyers' work. He also immersed himself in
a set of common experiences shared by black lawyers as far away as

Chicago, Cleveland, Philadelphia, and Washington, D.C. He became part of what could be called the "migration generation" of black lawyers, born near the turn of the century, entering the profession between the two world wars, and making their careers in urban areas as African Americans migrated out of the rural South. These were the lawyers—like Chicago's Earl Dickerson, Baltimore's Thurgood Marshall, Philadelphia's Sadie and Raymond Alexander, and Washington, D.C.'s Charles Houston and William Hastie—who would become the legal arm of the civil rights establishment as the movement began to take shape in the 1930s, 1940s, and 1950s.

What Miller found when he hung his shingle at Vernon and Central avenues was office practice of the kind that was the bread and butter of urban black lawyers around the country. He occupied himself with very practical day-to-day disputes that arose in his community. Divorces and probate matters came his way, and every now and then a case that brought him to court. His courtroom work, such as it was, remained eclectic. In one case, he represented a man who believed that he had been wrongly evicted from his room at the YMCA. In another, he represented the family of a man killed in an automobile accident when the driver was brought up before a coroner's jury. In yet another, he appeared on behalf of a truant officer who was accused of indecent exposure in a movie theater. He once appeared in a dispute between two people who racked up over one hundred dollars in court fees in a dispute over ownership of a dog that Miller called "Skeeter" inside the courtroom, producing angry objections from his opponents, who wanted Miller to call him "Rusty." The matter was finally resolved by expert witnesses.[31]

This was work that left little time for the intellectual debates and political activism that had occupied him for the past decade. After nine months of practice, he had enough business to open an office with Ivan R. Johnson, an old friend from Washburn Law School. The association also brought him closer to the black establishment, as Johnson had been a lawyer with the Golden State Mutual Life Insurance Company, the first black insurance company in the state and a pillar of the self-reliant local black business community. After half a decade of practice, Miller's account books made it clear that he occupied himself with a high volume of small-fee matters. In most cases, his regular fees ranged from two dollars (most likely for an initial consultation) to twenty-five dollars as a retainer for a divorce. About once a month, an estate matter might bring in a hundred or two hundred dollars at a time, which provided about half his income. There was money to be made from such activities—an average monthly net of $280.91 during 1942. In addition, his wife, Juanita Ellsworth, also brought in a regular salary from her job as a social worker at the Bureau of County Welfare. This kind of practice, income, and spousal arrangement made him fairly typical for an urban black lawyer of his time.[32]

It took constant hustling to keep up the volume of small-fee work that could support a lawyer in his type of urban practice, and writing now took a back seat to earning. When Miller tried to make time for more-ambitious writing projects, he found it hard to complete them. A year into his law practice, he submitted a review of Margaret Mitchell's *Gone with the Wind* to the *New Masses* but struggled to finish it, even with the input of a local Communist acquaintance. When the editor of *Kansas* magazine invited him to write an agitprop story of his midwestern youth that "exemplifies or demonstrates the class conflict in this region," Miller jumped at the chance. But he quickly put it off until he could take a vacation, confessing that "I am so busy earning a living that I have little time for literary endeavors at the present time."[33]

Earning a living meant interacting with clients, and Miller found himself enmeshed in a web of relationships that made practicing law seem far different from what he had always imagined. People came to him after they had been turned away from bars, lunch counters, and restaurants because of their race. Others came with matters of personal freedom, such as a client who wrote to express "my appreciation for the wonderful way that you conducted my trial." "I don't believe that there is another attorney in miles [who] could exceed your speech, and realizing that, that speech is the only thing that save [sic] me, I take great pleasure in writing my many thanks." She pledged to pay his fee as soon as she had the money and to spread the word about his talents. If client representation was based in self-interest and exploitation, it did not seem that way once one was inside the everyday world of lawyers, clients, and very practical causes.[34]

Miller channeled his remaining literary impulses into his continuing newspaper work, but that was an enterprise very different from the writing projects that had engaged him before. In 1933, Miller and his cousin, Leon Washington, had founded the *Los Angeles Sentinel* as a competitor to the *Eagle*. Miller wrote short unsigned editorials for the weekly paper, while Washington served as its publisher. The paper was distributed free of charge, styled itself as "independent," and was supported by advertising from the businesses that congregated along Central Avenue. "Patronize your local merchant," the paper's editorial page intoned to its readers. These businesses included the same black doctors, insurance agents, pharmacists, real estate agents, funeral directors, and cleaners who produced the probate work that now provided Miller with his most stable source of revenue. The *Sentinel*'s brief editorials tended to take on the issues that were of most concern to the community's middle-class black leadership—local political candidates, civic improvement, and disputes with city authorities—although it devoted some attention to national politics.[35]

Although the letter to Houston signaled the onset of Miller's change of heart, his Communist politics died a slow death. As he became more firmly embedded in the new network of relationships that came with his professional duties, he had little time or energy to devote to Marxist projects. Among those new relationships was that with Augustus Hawkins, a young New Dealer assemblyman whom the *Sentinel* supported when he had unseated the reliable black Republican Fred Roberts in 1934. Hawkins's almost impossibly wide political coalition was a draw for Miller, as it included everyone from white supporters of Upton Sinclair's Socialist Democratic politics to black voters just beginning to shift out of the Republican column. Nine months after opening his law practice, Miller signed on to manage Hawkins's bruising 1936 rematch with Roberts. But he quickly saw his own leftist politics become a liability when Roberts and the rival *Eagle* accused him of being a "Russian trained" campaign manager and a "Communist." Miller was indeed continuing to praise the Soviet Union in speeches to local groups, but his candidate won handily as local voters shifted decisively to the Democrats. Within a year, Miller himself entered Democratic politics as a candidate for the party's county central committee.[36]

After the Hawkins campaign, Miller seemed to confine his Marxist politics to sporadic attempts to write for national publications like the *New Masses,* and even those appeared to die out after 1937. The Communist Party received nary a mention in the *Sentinel*'s editorial pages, save for periodic rebuttals to charges that civil rights activists were unthinking tools of the CPUSA. An unsigned 1940 editorial went a bit further, inveighing against "secret agents of Stalin" who were attempting to manipulate African Americans. In the late 1930s, Miller signed on as a supporter of the leftist National Negro Congress, but his involvement seemed to quickly wane. As late as July 1939, he added his name to an open letter being circulated to writers and intellectuals that protested against the equation of the Soviet Union with the fascist governments. By 1943, he was lamenting to a friend that the disbanding of the Comintern meant that "the Soviet Union will put its name to a peace that will restore status quo in colonial areas." The letter marked the end of the vision of multiracial democracy that he saw, or believed he saw at any rate, in Moscow in 1932. Miller's 1943 lament was a validation of a process that had been in motion for over half a decade.[37]

Miller, as one might expect, remembered his political transformation differently when he told the story to an oral history interviewer near the end of his life. By then, he had told it many times to FBI agents and others when his past Communist writings repeatedly endangered his present civil rights politics. Recalling his time at the *New Masses,* he said that "I didn't like the magazine" and claimed that the CPUSA controlled its content. He simply wrote what his superiors wanted, he remembered. He now recalled that his transformation began even before his move to New York, and that he quit the *New Masses* because he disliked its leftist politics. Yet his private letters to his wife from New York brim with enthusiasm for the political positions he asserted in print, as did the letter he wrote home following the St. Louis meeting. The same was true of his speeches and articles in everything from conservative black newspapers to radical publications. At the time, Miller's main complaint about the editorial policies of the magazine was that its editors failed to publish "more theoretical articles" informed by rigorous Marxist theory, rather than those that had "direct agitational value." Miller heartily endorsed the agitation, but wanted it backed up by more theory.[38]

Nothing significant happened in the interim between Miller's arrival in Los Angeles and his forceful endorsement of Charles Houston's Maryland victory several months later—neither the various shifts of CPUSA policy that drove so many into, and out of, radical politics, nor anything significant in national civil rights politics. What had changed was not the world around Miller, but Miller himself. After years of denial, he had begun to ply his trade, and one of the first cases to walk through his door was that of two black men who had been humiliated at being denied service at a local drugstore. He took their case and entered the world of his onetime adversaries. He now began to see everything from a different point of view.[39]

Miller's political transformation went largely unnoticed outside his adopted hometown, but he would soon come to renewed national prominence. He did it in the typical way, with high-profile courtroom work that brought office practitioners like himself to the attention of the larger public. It began with a case involving a man whom the white press derided as a "crazed Negro" but whose lurid case held immense symbolic significance for black Angelenos. In February 1938, George Farley shot and killed two deputy marshals when they arrived to evict him from his home near Central Avenue. "Here I is. Come an' get me!" he reportedly shouted, and held off a phalanx of police reinforcements with an antique rifle until multiple bullet wounds and tear gas finally subdued him. He was indicted for capital murder.[40]

Farley's only hope was a story that Loren Miller crafted once he signed on to defend the presumably doomed man. "Facts in my possession," Miller announced in the press, would show that Farley was a hardworking homeowner who had paid off his mortgage in 1929, receiving the deed as well as assurance that, as Farley stated at the subsequent trial, "it was one of the best kinds of deeds and that nobody could ever take the place from me unless I mortgaged it or sold it." Unbeknownst to him, however, the house had been auctioned for less than one hundred dollars to a white purchaser to satisfy an unpaid street assessment bond, and the purchaser had then sold it to another white buyer, who arrived with the deputies to evict Farley. Unable to comprehend what was happening, Farley claimed to remember nothing more until after the deputies lay dead. As one might expect, the *Sentinel* publicized Miller's case, and the story struck a nerve. Two thousand people showed up at a mass meeting to support the defense. They also packed the courtroom during the subsequent trial, where "the whole front row" of spectators openly sobbed and cried as Miller argued his theory to the jury, which returned a verdict of double manslaughter rather than murder.[41]

It was Miller's first major trial, and his theory of the case was no accident, for the image of whites suddenly showing up to dispossess blacks who believed they owned their homes, free and clear, was a familiar one in Los Angeles. Only six years before, the local community had finally resolved one such incident that brought heartbreak and tragedy before its end. It had started in 1905, when a local property owner named Lulu Letteau placed legal restrictions on more than one hundred residential lots near Forty-first and Central, providing that their ownership would revert to her if they were ever owned or occupied by African Americans. Decades after blacks began moving in without objection, Letteau's heirs sued to retake the homes from their current owner/occupants. The lead defendant, William Long, died because of the stress brought on by the case, while the city's leading civil rights lawyer, Burton Ceruti, who had represented him, succumbed to heart failure. The dispute wasn't resolved until 1932, when the appellate courts finally rejected the heirs' remaining claims. But the problem remained. It turned out that in the late 1920s, whites had banded together to restrict the entire neighborhood west of Central Avenue. Much of that neighborhood had now become predominantly black after the influx of Depression-era migrants. The new black residents now stood in danger of losing their homes as whites organized to stem the tide. George Farley's rifle-toting response to what seemed like white perfidy made him into the new face of resistance in the local community. By saving Farley's life, Miller now also became that face. In fact, his next major case after Farley's involved a black couple who had been forced from their home and hired Miller to get them back in.[42]

Miller's new role as the face of the movement against racial restrictions put him in an uncomfortable position, for he had long believed that law mattered little in remedying race and class inequality. As late as March 1939, he chided a correspondent that "[w]e both know that the real reason for the poverty of poor Negroes and poor whites is an outworn system of economic relations." Within months of penning that statement, he was in the middle of a dispute that was drawn in explicit black-white terms and in which law mattered a great deal. Homeownership was the bedrock of prosperity in a city that had drawn in black migrants ever since Du Bois had called local African Americans "the most beautifully housed group of colored people in the United States." Los Angeles had an unusually high percentage of black homeowners at the beginning of the decade—almost one-third of local African Americans owned homes—which nearly matched the ownership rate among local whites. As Miller was drawn into the restrictive covenant controversy in the middle of 1939, he was drawn as well into a deep engagement with something he had never cared much about—the technical details of law.[43]

By 1939, California restrictive covenant law required a good deal of competence from a lawyer. Miller's predecessors at the city's civil rights bar had already forced judges to reach for broad equity powers to enforce racial restrictions. Some restrictions were imposed in the form of defeasible fees, which allowed a person to control the future use of his or her land when deeding it to another person. Other restrictions were in the form of servitudes, which were promises made by neighboring landowners that restricted the future uses of multiple pieces of land.[44] For technical reasons, by the 1920s whites who wanted to impose racial restrictions were likely to create them in the form of servitudes, which required dozens or hundreds of landowners to come together to agree that no nonwhites could live on their lots. It took a good deal of coordination to do this, so it was easy to get part of it wrong. California was different from many other states because it would not enforce a restriction on a home unless the homeowners got it exactly right with respect to that particular lot, even if they had properly restricted all the neighboring homes.[45] Moreover, with the influx of black migrants that continued unabated during the Depression, neighborhoods sometimes changed overnight. Once whites agreed to restrict an area, it often happened that the area would be surrounded by black residents, or that African Americans would succeed in buying many of the restricted homes, as they did west of Central Avenue. If the purpose of the original restrictions was frustrated by later events, courts might refuse to enforce them.[46]

Miller later recalled that "pretty soon when other lawyers got them [covenant cases] they simply referred them to me because they were rather technical." This was because a lawyer in a covenant case had to take on the painstaking job of going down to the registry of deeds and checking the details of dozens or perhaps hundreds of land transactions—whether they had been signed by the proper parties, registered properly with the county, and a host of other details that determined whether the legal requirements had been met. To argue that conditions had changed in the neighborhood, the lawyer had to collect deed information and witness testimony about what had happened over a long period of time on a large number of home lots. Once Miller was drawn into the covenant cases, this was exactly the type of work he began to do. He always preferred the more straightforward argument—that racial restrictions violated the Fourteenth Amendment—but California courts had long rejected that theory. He raised it in every case, but he spent most of his time in a more painstaking process of parsing the relevant precedents for loopholes and assembling evidence to exploit them. "Negro lawyers had become ingenious," he remembered, and "had found all sorts of technical means to invalidate these . . . covenants." That strategy won him his first covenant case, when he persuaded a local judge to invoke the changed conditions rule to invalidate the restrictions that kept his clients out of their home. That case turned on a hotly disputed point of law—whether, in deciding if conditions in the area had changed, the court should look only at East Fiftieth Street, where white residents claimed that they had resisted all black encroachments, or at the entire area west of Central, where there was no dispute about black inroads into restricted neighborhoods.[47]

During World War II, the volume of Miller's covenant work increased, and by the end of the war he reemerged as a nationally important civil rights figure. He made common cause with ACLU lawyer A. L. Wirin in the fight against restrictions on Japanese American property ownership, and his covenant cases became relevant to lawyers around the country. Wartime migrations of African Americans pushed up against covenant restrictions in many cities, but Los Angeles was ground zero for the process. Suburbanization had happened early on the city's west side, and successive generations of local black lawyers had struggled with covenant litigation since the late 1910s. One national survey counted twenty covenant cases in that city at the close of the war, far outstripping those in other cities. Miller had a hand in just about all of them. When the NAACP decided to convene a national meeting to coordinate covenant strategy in the middle of 1945, Miller suddenly emerged from the obscurity of his West Coast practice. He happily accepted an invitation to come to the Chicago meeting and recommended that the association push forward with the approach that would become the core of its strategy. By now, Miller was tired of his years of technical litigation, and he wrote Thurgood Marshall that "I think that the primary job for us is to devise ways and means of securing a United States Supreme Court test and of presenting some [of] the appeals on the broadest possible social and economic grounds." That fall, when Miller finally got a local judge to rule in his client's favor on Fourteenth Amendment grounds, congratulation letters poured in from all over the country.[48]

It was good lawyer's work, and it was soon rewarded with fame and recognition from a profession in which he had always been something of an outsider. The NAACP added him to its national legal committee in 1945. He quickly became a popular speaker in Los Angeles and around the country when liberal advocacy groups, civic associations, professional organizations, and even real estate agents' associations needed someone to speak on intergroup relations. After years of struggling to write, and rejections when he finally got something finished, he now contributed articles to *Survey Graphic,* the *Lawyers Guild Review,* and *The Crisis.* From virtually nowhere, he won election to the second vice presidency of the National Bar Association, trouncing his opponent by a vote of 86–23 after the Chicago faction threw its support behind him. When Miller expressed modest surprise at the honor, C. Francis Stradford wrote from Chicago to tell him that "[y]ou may be assured that if you have received any support from me, it was because of the very fine record you have made as a lawyer."[49]

The crowning achievement of his covenant work took place a little over two years later, when he appeared in the Supreme Court alongside a lawyer whose first major desegregation victory had prompted Miller's blistering attack on the NAACP ten years before: Charles H. Houston. It was as stunning a reversal of positions as any in the chronicles of civil rights politics, although both men seemed to take it in stride. In the coming years, more honors followed for Miller—including selection for the NAACP's national board, close friendships with liberal politicians and judges throughout the state, and eventual appointment as a judge in his adopted hometown.

There is a good deal of irony in the fact that Miller's own maturation as a lawyer seemed to confirm all that he had believed in his youth. There was in fact a relationship between law and politics, and Miller's turn to law had changed his politics. Practicing law brought a steady income, took him inside the everyday world of the middle-class clients whom he had once scorned, and left little time for the intellectual and political projects that once engaged him. It connected him to both middle-class blacks and to liberal white politicians and judges who would help sort out their claims. For most of his adult life, Miller had written and spoken about what it meant to represent his race in court. But he had done little of that in practice until, forced by necessity, he turned to the only means of making a living at his disposal. In cases like George Farley's, Miller began to experience the rush of energy that was familiar to black lawyers as far away as Philadelphia, Chicago, and Baltimore, as the local community came to court and rallied around the black lawyer who now seemed to personify their hopes and desires. He also felt useful, and could see the practical results of his technical mastery of law, as the controversy about black residency on the west side of Central Avenue reached its peak in the mid-1940s.

Miller shared much with his fellow black lawyers as they began to steer their way out of the crisis that had buffeted them in the mid-1930s. They were pushed toward respectability, in part, by the same thing that drew Miller to the practice of law in the first place—material progress. With the continued influx of black residents to Los Angeles and other large cities during World War II, the volume of Miller's small-fee work only increased, and by 1946 he was reporting nearly $7,500 in profits from his practice. This put him well above the national median for solo practitioners of any race. Many of his old friends from the Depression-era left found themselves in similar positions. His fellow Soviet travelers Poston and Moon stopped in on him in the early 1940s and reported back to Roi Ottley that Miller was "living high on the hog nowadays." Prentice Thomas, an old friend from the pacifist left, was now working as a lawyer in the NAACP's national office. When Miller wrote to Thomas and poked fun at Thomas's "rapid rise in the world," his friend quickly fired back. Hailing Miller as a "former fellow sufferer," Thomas added that "I hope that by this time you are living off the fat of the land and are still championing the great cause of the people." It was more than a joke for Miller and Thomas. Both men were doing what black lawyers had always done—connecting themselves to powerful whites and representing the interests of poor blacks. It was a paradoxical role that, as a younger man, Miller swore to never take on. But as a practicing black lawyer, he found it inescapable.[50]

Miller and Thomas's experiences were not atypical. Much was changing in the nation's civil rights politics as the 1930s drew to a close, helping to smooth out the crisis in racial representation. Guided by Charles Houston and his successor, Thurgood Marshall, the NAACP's national leadership grew surer of itself. Buoyed by a series of Supreme

Court victories in the late 1930s and early 1940s, Marshall, not yet forty years old, had grown into a powerful figure in the association's national office. His legal victories gave him the autonomy to hire a new generation of lawyers onto its national staff. Among them were a group of younger black lawyers who grew into nationally important figures— Constance Baker Motley and Robert L. Carter, both of whom would eventually become federal judges, and many other lawyers for whom the NAACP became a stepping-stone to prominence. An organization that had come under fire from a younger generation of blacks who questioned its lawyers' representativeness once again became a place for lawyers to dream of bigger things. Within a decade, however, those dreams would yet again come under assault as a new generation of activists raised what was now one of the oldest questions in American racial politics.

9

The Trials of Pauli Murray

IN THE fall of 1941, Pauli Murray arrived in Washington, D.C., for her first year of study at Howard Law School, wanting nothing more than to represent her race in its legal battles with segregation. Murray described her civil rights advocacy as motivated by "an almost pathetic loyalty to [my] racial group," and she was eager to demonstrate it. The incident that had set her on the path to law was a simple trip south the previous year to see her relatives, which led to her arrest aboard a segregated bus in Virginia. At the time, Murray was in the midst of a personal crisis caused, in part, by her inability to fit in, particularly in public places where her racial and gender appearance often seemed ambiguous. When Murray emerged from prison several days after the arrest to testify in court, it seemed as though a new world had opened to a woman who had always felt profound discomfort in southern public space. "When prisoners speak," she wrote in her diary, "the air is electric with silence." Murray was experiencing the rush of energy that was a quite familiar feeling to lawyers like William Hastie, Leon Ransom, and Thurgood Marshall. Courtroom etiquette allowed her to perform a role that would be denied just outside the courthouse door. Those feelings only grew stronger as she watched NAACP lawyers come to court for further proceedings in her case. The following year, she began her legal studies at Howard and earned top honors there, placing her in line to join the distinguished group of its leading graduates who used their training in service of the NAACP.[1]

But Murray was, at best, a representative woman, not a representative man, and the civil rights courtroom remained off-limits to even as accomplished a woman as Sadie Alexander. In fact, Murray was a poor choice even as a representative woman of her race. She had arrived at Howard with her personal crisis still unresolved. Behind the confident façade of the civil rights crusader lay a person in the middle of a crisis of identity. Typically, at Howard she found herself once again out of place, and she would soon coin a phrase to describe what had been bothering her since the mid-1930s. She called it Jane Crow. Two decades later, she helped Congress name it as sex discrimination, and less than a decade after that Ruth Bader Ginsburg would place Murray's name on a brief that convinced the Supreme Court to elevate what once had seemed like Murray's own personal complaint to the status of constitutional doctrine.

Murray's contributions to American law and politics grew out of a crisis of identity that had been building throughout the 1930s. In her world, the two main racial groups were blacks and whites, but as the decades wore on Murray began to feel representative of neither group. More significantly, in a world where people had to identify themselves as men and women, Murray felt as though she was something else. The civil rights courtroom, she thought, would be a powerful weapon in reclaiming her own personal autonomy, and in defending the rights of a race that, in her younger years, she claimed to represent. In law school she would come to question that representativeness, and put together a legal theory to back up her new conclusions. Jane Crow was like Jim Crow, she decided. At first, almost no one believed her, but as the years passed, more and more people did.

The Roots of Jane Crow

More than anything else, Pauli Murray's idea of Jane Crow was driven by her growing sense that she moved through the world as a lonely individual, hemmed in by the bounds of group identity, although it would take her a while to name and act on that impression. Like Jane Bolin and Loren Miller, she was evidently of mixed-race origin. While Bolin and Miller seemed untroubled by their biracial parentage and comfortably assumed a black identity, Murray's racial background always seemed to give her trouble even though her parents both identified as African Americans. Often, the problem stemmed from her North Carolina family, whose range of complexions, eye color, and hair textures caused her to describe it as a "United Nations in miniature." Born in Baltimore in 1910, Anna Pauline Murray was raised by her grandparents and her Aunt Pauline in Durham following her mother's death and the onset of her father's emotional problems. Some of her North Carolina relatives were the descendants of two local white slave owners and an enslaved woman named Harriet, while others proudly claimed Irish nobility and northern free blacks among their ancestors. In 1938, Murray would publish a poem called "Mulatto's Dilemma," where she wrote eloquently about the problem of racial ambiguity in a world of segregation; but she was no "tragic mulatto," that common figure in American literature who was disastrously torn between two racial identities. She eventually claimed her white slave-owning ancestors along with many other streams of descent. During one of the periodic crises where her ambiguous identity tripped her up, she wrote a well-received family narrative called *Proud Shoes,* claiming that heritage as a source of strength.[2]

Again and again, Murray seemed to cross the racial lines that both blacks and whites used to make sense of their complicated world of race. In Durham, her multihued family lived just outside the main settlement of blacks in the city's West End. Some of her earliest memories were of the uneasy relationship between her family and their black neighbors, who lived on either side of a marshy stretch of land that marked the imaginary boundary between them. Going to a high school several miles away in black "Hayti," which E. Franklin Frazier called the "capital of the black middle class," presented her with a "problem of status," she later wrote. It accentuated her uneasy place in a community where being a member of "a light skinned minority among the kids at school" already made her feel uncomfortable. Upon moving to New York to finish high school and prepare for Hunter College, she once again found herself on the wrong side of a color line. She moved in with the family of her cousin Maude in Queens but soon found out that her complexion was a problem. Maude's family was very light-skinned and had moved to a white neighborhood where few people asked questions about their racial ancestry. When the slightly darker and curly-haired Murray showed up, however, the neighbors became uneasy. Murray returned to Maude's house for college but soon moved on to the Harlem YWCA. During one of her periodic personal crises, she noted, resignedly, that the doctors at a Long Island hospital "tried to palm me off as a Cuban" to avoid trouble.[3]

Later, when Murray finished law school and moved to Los Angeles with her sister for a short time, the two women unwittingly moved to an apartment that was slightly over the line that separated a black neighborhood from a white one just as an intense battle was raging over restrictive covenants. Her sister, who had a lighter complexion, prompted quizzical stares, and the neighbors began an investigation of their racial status that culminated in a demand that the women move out. Murray wrote a satirical column in Loren Miller's *Los Angeles Sentinel* where she skewered whites' efforts to make color into racial identity.[4]

Like many other black Americans, it was in public space where Murray often felt the bite of segregation, but she seemed to feel it more keenly than most. As a child she quickly learned the intricate rules that governed how she should look at and speak to whites and blacks in Durham, depending on whether they were old or young, sitting on their front porches or not, and many other rules that defined race in the small community where she seemed to know everyone. The most difficult problem arose when she had to interact with strangers. Her "first unnerving encounter with the race problem" occurred when she was about nine years old and returning by train to Durham with her Aunt Pauline. They stopped in Norfolk, Virginia, to change trains, and her aunt, who had broken her glasses, mistakenly left Murray in the white waiting room while she went to check on their train connection. The two had attracted little notice when they were together, since her aunt was light enough to pass for white. Once alone, however, Murray was quickly "surrounded by a circle of white faces" as a group of men tried to figure out her racial identity. Her aunt returned in time to rescue her, and got her into the Jim Crow car, where one of the white onlookers soon barged in to inspect Murray one more time.[5]

Murray's invention of the term "Jane Crow" to describe the illogic of sex discrimination was partly motivated by her ongoing struggles with boundaries that sorted people by color. In Durham, for instance, she later remembered that rather than riding the segregated streetcars, she walked when visiting other parts of town. Once Murray left for college, she dreaded her return trips home. Generally they were by bus, and "[t]he bus was the quintessence of the segregation evil," where drivers publicly humiliated black passengers under the gaze of "privileged white spectators, who witnessed our shame." During the bus trip that resulted in her arrest in Virginia, one observer commented that she seemed "neither white nor black" and "spoke like neither." People on the bus simply didn't know how to place her. Years later, she invented the pen name of "Peter Panic" for her satirical newspaper column where she lambasted both Jim Crow and what she called Jim's "mate—Jane Crow."[6]

Murray's move to New York to attend Hunter College temporarily dampened those concerns, but it created a new set of problems. The move placed her firmly in the midst of a community of younger African Americans who were in open revolt against the cultural mores of their elders. Soon after her arrival in 1928, she put aside the expectation that she would prepare for a career in teaching (which was also one of the standard routes to law for black women) and found herself drawn to literature classes instead. Living at the Harlem YWCA for two years and attending an all-women's college, she was soon immersed in a series of same-sex networks that often fostered gender ambiguity in that period. Murray arrived in Harlem when that neighborhood's vibrant 1920s culture of sexual and gender nonconformity was still in full force. She entered into a hasty and brief marriage but soon discovered that "when men try to make love to me, something in me fights." She lost fifteen pounds in her first two years of college and would remain malnourished for decades because of her constant state of near poverty. The round-faced, feminine girl from her 1927 high school graduation picture looked quite different half a decade later. With her slight figure and small stature, Murray began to take on the appearance of a teenaged boy and discovered something new about herself. As she wrote later, "unsophisticated people" sometimes thought of her as a "girl who should have been a boy, and react to me as if I were a boy." She wore her hair short and liked to wear pants in an era when women still wore skirts as a mark of their gender.[7]

Traveling, which had been such a source of discomfort in the South, now became a way to assert an ambiguous racial and gender identity. As early as 1931, she began a series of road trips, often with other women, where she sometimes dressed like a Boy Scout and was happy to be commonly mistaken for one. That year, she took a trip to New England with a friend, Dorothy Hayden, which apparently resulted in their being arrested and remanded to the custody of the Bridgeport (Connecticut) Protective Association. The association's director, amused by the women's pluck, wrote them when they got back to New York and wished them courage in their future traveling adventures. That same year, she caught a ride to California in a friend's car, thinking that she might settle and find work there. Along the way, she composed her first published poem, called "Song of the Highway," celebrating the road as a metaphor for the expanse of America. When Murray arrived, she received a letter saying that her Aunt Pauline was ill. So she decided to come back east. With almost no money, Murray began what turned out to be a harrowing trip back to New York, among the thousands of hoboes who rode the rails during the Depression. Dressed in "scout pants and shirt, knee-length socks, walking shoes, and a short leather jacket," she masqueraded as a boy during a dangerous ride home while evading rough characters, armed railroad guards, and physical injury from jumping trains.[8]

The California trip would see her invent an androgynous literary personality, and eventually a new name, to capture what she experienced on the road. Thrilled at her accomplishment, she penned a partly fictionalized account of her return trip and got it published in the anthology entitled *Negro,* edited by the heiress and art patron Nancy Cunard. In that story, two characters, a boy named Pete and the unnamed, presumably male, narrator make the dangerous rail trip back from California. Murray helped get Cunard interested in her story by sending along a diary of her gender-bending adventures on the road, accompanied by a photo of "Pete," which ran alongside the story. It was a photo of Murray herself, dressed in Boy Scout–style attire. When Cunard received the photo, she pronounced it "the BOY itself" and happily agreed to Murray's request to conceal the sex of the author. When *Negro* was published in 1934, Murray's essay was accompanied by an ambiguous byline. The woman who, up to that time, had gone by the name "Pauline" now shortened it to the more gender-neutral "Pauli," which she would retain for the rest of her life. The essay may have been a declaration of independence of another sort, as Cunard told her that "[y]ou are the only one in the book not represented by a purely *racial* piece of writing."[9]

Despite the name change, Pauli Murray seemed to be headed for the conventional social work–oriented circles that were often the starting points for black women who went into law. In New York and North Carolina, where people knew her well, she seemed to have little trouble being accepted as an educated black woman who moved in social reform circles. She graduated from Hunter in 1933 and got a job selling subscriptions for *Opportunity*, the Urban League's magazine—a position that would have been tough to relinquish during the Depression. But her years of malnourishment caught up with her when she fell ill and had to resign twelve months into the job. Her doctor prescribed rest and a more wholesome environment and secured a place for her at Camp Tera in upstate New York. The camp was the first New Deal camp for unemployed women, which Eleanor Roosevelt had pushed the government to establish as an alternative to the famous Civilian Conservation Corps (CCC) camps. Camp Tera, dubbed a "she-she-she" camp by many, brought Murray back inside the women's networks that had been so influential during her initial years in New York. There she met Peg Holmes, a white camp counselor who was about her age and shared her literary interests, and the two women developed a deep friendship. Murray, however, provoked the ire of the camp's director because of her relationship with Holmes, her possession of Communist literature, and her failure to stand at attention when the First Lady visited the camp. She left after a few months. In February of 1935, she found herself back in New York City, looking for work, and rooming with friends.[10]

Murray's relationship with Holmes only deepened her tendency to associate travel with race and gender boundary-crossing. With not much else to do, the two women hopped a freight train in April for a five-week journey to Nebraska and back. Once again, Murray experienced the rush of being in places where no one knew her. As she and Holmes hitchhiked, did chores for food, and were sometimes held in custody as vagrants, Murray invented the name "Pan" for Holmes in her diary, probably to go along with the "Pete" or "Peter" persona she adopted in her California travel narrative—the boy (often played a young woman in contemporary plays and cinema) who stayed forever young. She took time to have a "[s]erious talk with Peg re: P-P relationship" as the bond between the women now seemed clearly one of desire as well as friendship. Once again, Murray took delight in the reactions of observers who sometimes "thought I was a Boy Scout," or, uncertain of her race, mistook her for an Indian. As usual, a white authority figure intervened to break up the idyll. When she arrived in Roseville, Illinois, she was "[r]efused service," and was "[h]eld & questioned next morning" by the sheriff. "Race again," she concluded.[11]

Murray continued to be accepted in black and white social reform circles in New York as a respectable, albeit leftist, black woman, but by the late 1930s she was wracked by inner turmoil. It had been building since the summer of 1935, just after she and Holmes returned from their trip, and was probably related to dissention in their relationship. The problem stemmed from what Murray called her "inverted sex instinct—wearing pants, wanting to be one of the men, doing things that fellows do, hating to be dominated by women unless I like them." Murray simply felt like a man—or at least like the post-pubescent boy she was sometimes mistaken for—and was having trouble accepting the societal imperatives that forced her to live like a woman. By then, she recognized that "my greatest attractions have been toward extremely feminine and heterosexual women"—women who thought of themselves as well-adjusted heterosexuals and were often surprised at their attraction to Murray. During her years in New York, she had gone through a series of emotional breakdowns, usually after such relationships either ended or were frustrated. She had been hospitalized for one such breakdown in December of 1937, and would be again a little over two years later. Her 1940 hospitalization was precipitated by the usual factors, but now she also cited "anxiety over welfare of two fatherless cousins" whom she could neither support nor guide to responsible manhood. Her two cousins, Joshua, who was also her godson, and James, each about a decade younger than Murray, had recently moved in with her. In addition, she had two aging aunts, one of them her foster mother, who would soon need Murray to support them in retirement. Murray was expected to play the role of the male breadwinner in an extended family that had none, and she found it to be a poor fit and overwhelming.[12]

The key to Murray's dilemma, and to her recognition of what she would later call Jane Crow, was her naming of her problem as "inverted sex instinct," or what her companion, Adelene McBean, called "sex inversion." Murray came of age at a time when the term "homosexuality," as a condition, or perhaps an identity, was just taking hold among scientists who helped to popularize the term, and less certainly among Americans who sometimes applied it to themselves. Typically, she resisted what were now becoming conventional categories of identity. She grudgingly applied the term "homosexual" to the general class of people like herself, but went on to say that many homosexuals "irritate me," and asked: "Why cannot I accept the homosexual method of sex expression, but insist on the normal first?" She consulted doctor after doctor but refused to accept the emerging medical theory that unconventional sexual desires were psychological in cause. Instead, she asserted, again contrary to her doctors' advice, that her desires and sexuality had a glandular cause, or later, that she might be a hermaphrodite with hidden male sex organs. Murray could write movingly (in the privacy of her diary) about her relationship with a woman who could "put her fingers on the wounded places and they would heal" at times of crisis. But she could also reject the advice of one frustrated paramour, who told Murray that "there definitely are three classes of human beings: the true man, the true woman, and the homosexual." Since "the third class" is "where you belong . . . [w]hy try to change yourself?" her lover pleaded. But Murray continued to resist the label.[13]

As she grew older, Murray would find that conventional binaries of identity—black and white, and heterosexual and homosexual, could not capture her unique experience of moving through the world. She still felt "proud of my Negro blood" but attributed at least part of her emotional difficulty to the irrationality of color lines that seemed to be present everywhere, even in New York. With regard to her sexuality, she reached back to the ideas of turn-of-the-century sexologists, who had studied what they called "sexual inversion" rather than modern homosexuality. The sex invert, so the theory went, was not necessarily someone who desired intimate relationships with a person of their own sex. It was someone who acted like a member of the opposite sex—for instance, a woman who dressed like a man, was aggressive sexually, was attracted to feminine partners, and seemed generally masculine. That these women often chose other women as the objects of their desire was not that important to the sexologists. What was important was that they assumed the role of the opposite sex. The causes were thought to be congenital, and some scientists speculated that it might be associated with hermaphroditism.[14]

In naming herself as a sex invert rather than a homosexual, Murray found solace in these older ideas that seemed more in tune with how she moved about in society. What she wanted most of all, she believed, was "monogamous married life"—just with herself in the masculine role. For Murray, to accept herself as a conventional homosexual was just as oppressive as trying to remain as she was and be heterosexual. Instead, she preferred what she called "experimentation on the male side."[15]

Male and female, like black and white, were categories that Murray found inescapable. Murray felt as though she was a man because she seemed to feel a compulsion to perform like a man as she moved through mid-twentieth-century America. Manhood seemed to have less to do with physical construction than it did with how one acted, and Murray felt the need to act like a man. But the problem was that she was imprisoned in a body that made many people treat her as a woman. She would spend much of the decade consulting doctor after doctor about her idea that perhaps she was a man in a woman's body (with hidden male sex organs), or perhaps she could adjust to life on the male side with an injection of male hormones. She found herself duplicating what men did in life, and decided that what drove her most in life was what she called a "desire to be male." Murray wanted to do the things that men do, and eventually she decided that what she wanted to do most was something that was men's work at the time—performing in the civil rights courtroom. She would soon put a name to the societal rules that frustrated that desire.[16]

Murray's crisis of identity had deepened by the end of the decade, and she moved a step closer to her fateful bus trip when she set out for New England in early 1940. By then, she needed relief from a host of troubles. She had a new job, this time as the coordinator for a planned "National Sharecroppers Week," sponsored in part by the Socialist Party–affiliated Workers Defense League. As usual, she had little money and was emotionally overwhelmed by her new commitment. Her new job left her with neither the time nor the financial resources to meet her extended family responsibilities. She was also seeking hormone treatments to help right her gender imbalance.[17]

So she took to the road again, but what had once been a way to escape from social conventions now turned into a nightmare. Police officers found her wandering in Rhode Island, dressed in what they described as men's clothing, and distraught over the disappearance of a woman friend—probably Peg Holmes. They returned her to the custody of the New York City police, who transferred her to Bellevue Hospital for psychiatric treatment. Nearly ten years before, she had set out for New England with Dorothy Hayden, before being picked up by local authorities and remanded to the custody of slightly amused Connecticut social service workers who sent her back to New York City. This trip ended differently. She was no longer a youth in search of freedom, but rather a person of responsibility who would soon enter a profession with its own means of enforcing compliance with conventional mores. The unfortunate end to her 1940 trip would haunt her for the next thirty years.[18]

The Making of a Civil Rights Lawyer

By the latter part of the decade, events seemed to be conspiring to push Murray into a career in law or another profession. Many black women often came to law school after getting a secure foothold in teaching or social work, but Murray hadn't gotten much purchase in any line of work. She had drifted through a series of jobs at the Works Progress Administration, and through an identification with the Lovestoneite wing of the New York left to a growing admiration for Norman Thomas and the Socialists. Her respectable North Carolina family, always at war with her New York bohemianism for Murray's allegiance, now intervened. She worried intensely about her foster mother, Aunt Pauline, as well as her Aunt Sallie, whose need for support still lay unresolved. Her two younger cousins would soon move in with her. Murray would give them what she called "'parently' care" and tried to get them through school and into responsible jobs. By that time, she was living in Harlem, sharing a room with Adelene McBean—"my girl-friend," as she told her aunts. McBean was becoming "just like a mother to both of the boys," who slept in an adjoining room. Murray enjoyed taking her cousins out on the town, "me in slacks like the rest of them." She was now nearing thirty years of age and making only about twenty-five dollars a week. Murray was drawn to professional life partly for the same reasons that men were—as a means of making a living in a world increasingly burdened with responsibility.[19]

It was with this prospect in her near future that Murray inserted herself into civil rights history by taking her first steps toward applying for graduate school at the University of North Carolina in late 1938. Murray planned to return to Durham and care for her aunts while completing her graduate training in the social sciences. In deciding to return to her native region, she made herself part of the local civil rights movement. For half a decade, Durham's self-described young "radicals" had dreamed of renewing the fight to integrate the university's graduate school, ever since William Hastie electrified the town with his courtroom performance in Thomas Hocutt's unsuccessful case. Murray cast her lot with the radicals, and later named herself as one in a letter to a member of the city's cautious old-guard black leadership. She also talked to Hocutt before deciding to seek her graduate training in the South. As the black and white press picked up the story of her decision to integrate the university, and students and faculty debated it, Murray wrote letters to everyone from the university's president to Franklin Roosevelt himself to plead her case. She then released the correspondence to the national black press in an effort to embarrass the officials whose private racial liberalism was belied by their public actions.[20]

The NAACP's national office seemed like it might be interested in Murray's case at first, but apparently Thurgood Marshall later told Murray that her long residence out of state might make her case less than compelling to a court. Limited resources permitted the organization to take only the strongest cases. In addition, her letter-writing campaign seemed calculated to put off the university's racially moderate president, Frank Graham, as well as the state's political leaders— the type of allies the NAACP had cultivated in the Crawford case and in many other controversies since its founding. Roy Wilkins believed that Murray's letter-writing campaign was, "to say the least, not diplomatic," and strongly opposed NAACP involvement in the case, while Marshall was less concerned about this as a potential problem. Walter White sided with Marshall, while Charles Houston sympathized with Wilkins. There was an element of personal competition in the dispute, for Wilkins and Marshall would later clash over their relative degrees of responsibility for legal matters. In any event, the issue of Murray's residence quickly rendered that problem superfluous. So Murray's first encounter with civil rights law fizzled out, but she soon hungered for more.[21]

Much has been made of the NAACP's decision not to pursue Murray's case. When prodded by an interviewer nearly forty years later, Murray recalled that when she met with Marshall to talk about her case, "[h]e might have implied" that "I was too maverick" for the organization. According to this interpretation, Roy Wilkins "thought that Murray posed a terrible risk to the NAACP" and "decided to stop Pauli Murray by any means necessary." After learning of the risk from Wilkins, Marshall may have told Murray that her sexual identity posed too great a risk to the organization, or perhaps that her leftist connections disqualified her. In either case, the argument goes, her personal

qualities made her too unconventional for the conservative organization to take on as a plaintiff. Thus, it is likely that the NAACP's purported reasons for not taking her case were simply a cover for what
Marshall may have told her privately, and the organization's cautious
leadership alienated an eager plaintiff who would have jump-started its
stalled North Carolina desegregation program.[22]

In 1939, however, Murray seemed to believe that her New York
residence was the only thing holding the NAACP back, and she was
probably right. She tried to apply to North Carolina's state law school
later that year and told an acquaintance that "I do not have the technical residence in North Carolina to make my case a sure-fire one, and
the NAACP is too short of funds to spend money on a weak case." She
spent much of the next year trying to dig up a plaintiff with North
Carolina residency. When she found one potential applicant, she told
him that she had met once again with Marshall and that "he seemed
anxious to find a good case in North Carolina, providing such a case
could be used effectively from every legal point of view."[23]

Marshall had good reason to be cautious about the issue of her
residence. Murray had been in New York for over ten years by this
point and had shown little desire to move back to North Carolina before she contacted the university. Her situation differed from those of
other potential NAACP plaintiffs who had left their home states for
college and work, because there was little objective evidence that any
place other than New York was her permanent residence. At the time of
Murray's application, the NAACP had just spent several years getting
state and federal rulings that southern states could not send their black
residents to other states for graduate study. In the association's most
recent Supreme Court victory, *Missouri ex rel. Gaines v. Canada,* handed
down just two months before the probable date of her meeting with
Marshall, the Court had explicitly based its ruling on the state's assumption of an obligation to educate "negroes resident in Missouri," and on
the "separate responsibility of each State" to provide equal protection to
its own residents. Indeed, the NAACP's ability to win the case turned on
this division of responsibility. This was hardly the opportune moment to
try to convince a court that North Carolina had a constitutional obligation to educate a black applicant from New York, particularly when
there was integrated education available to Murray in her own state of
residence.[24]

It is unlikely that, during their meeting, Marshall said or implied that Murray was personally unfit to represent the NAACP. The two of them maintained a good relationship after their meeting, and their actions at the time were inconsistent with that proposition. She was confident enough of Marshall's support to get him to write her a strong recommendation letter for Howard Law School. "Keep this to yourself," he told her, "because we do not usually write letters of recommendation for anyone." When Murray earned top honors in law school, she believed that she was a strong candidate for a position on Marshall's legal staff at the NAACP and spent years dreaming of that possibility before reluctantly giving it up. If Marshall had indicated that Murray's gender persona seemed unconventional enough that it disqualified her from representing the NAACP in court as a plaintiff, she would hardly have expected that he would hire her and send her into southern courtrooms where even black male NAACP lawyers walked a fine line between professionalism and acts that might inspire violence. As for her former connection with the Lovestoneite left, that might have been of concern if the NAACP focused on it, but her contemporary actions do not support this interpretation. It was certainly true that Murray was not entirely convinced that her New York residence should bar her from desegregating the University of North Carolina. But Murray was not yet a lawyer, and any good lawyer in 1939 would have seen that her decade-plus of out-of-state residence was a problem, given the Supreme Court's reasoning in *Gaines*.[25]

Murray quickly found herself back in the NAACP's sights as a plaintiff, and this time she was sure that the association's leaders would back her. They did so enthusiastically, with Roy Wilkins leading the way. The cause was her 1940 arrest aboard a segregated bus in Virginia. Wilkins found out about the arrest and quickly wired back to Virginia: "Please render every assistance possible to Pauli Murray arrested in Petersburg for alleged Bus-Jim-Crow law." He was eager to have the NAACP's name associated with what he called "the Pauli Murray bus case." In fact, Wilkins was angry that the Workers Defense League, which was assisting with the defense, was taking credit for it. In response, he maneuvered to get Murray's case played up prominently in the black press to buttress the NAACP's reputation. Murray's appeal for help also elicited a strong positive response from White, who felt that "[w]e should by all means go into this case." Marshall concurred, and promised that the association's National Legal Committee would back the efforts of Murray's local NAACP lawyers. Charles Houston wrote that "[i]t looks like a good case." "Certainly here is a plaintiff who will stick," he added. The lawyers believed that Murray's bus case had the potential to go to the Supreme Court. Only one year had passed since her University of North Carolina case had petered out, but the NAACP's leaders were eager to have her as a plaintiff in a high-profile case. None of them seemed to care about—or even be aware of—any personal characteristics that should give them pause.[26]

Murray's bus segregation case would take her one step closer to becoming a lawyer. It arose entirely by accident and grew out of her unfortunate 1940 hospitalization. Murray emerged from Bellevue Hospital in March of that year, under the watchful care of McBean, and the two women began the long bus trip to Durham to spend Easter weekend with Murray's aunts. Murray was cautious, as usual, about subjecting herself to the public gaze when traveling in the South, but her recent difficulties would have made her even more careful. She later wrote that her problems were caused, in part, by her being "equally uncomfortable (in public) in pants as well as dresses." "In pants, it is difficult to make persons believe she is not a boy; in dresses," even her friends thought she looked out of place. One fellow passenger on the bus trip even mistook her for a boy. Her gender identity still seemed ambiguous when she traveled among strangers, but what had once been a source of exhilaration had now become a prison from which she was desperate to escape. "I've just about come to the end of my rope," she had pleaded with one doctor the previous fall. To make matters worse she was coming south. So when the two women became uncomfortable with segregated seating as they traveled through Virginia, Murray was somewhat shy and reticent about challenging segregation, at least according to her original story of what had happened on that bus—a story that has sometimes been ignored by historians eager to find a heroic Murray.[27]

The trouble began in Petersburg, Virginia, when Murray and Mc-Bean decided to move two rows forward because of the uncomfortable and broken seats in the back. Virginia law required that bus companies have separate sections for blacks and whites, and by custom blacks filled the seats from the back while whites filled them from the front. Their new seats still left them behind all the white passengers. The driver responded by shouting for them to move back to their original seats. He had previously rebuffed Murray's polite request to move forward. McBean called out from the back of the bus to tell him that she was ill and would not move, while Murray told him that their present seating was in keeping with both custom and segregation law. The driver summoned two local police officers, and the two women explained their plight to them. The officers worked out a compromise that had them move one row back, but McBean was not through. She told the officers that if her seat broke again she would move forward, and she demanded an apology from the driver, who mumbled something conciliatory. As everyone prepared for the bus to depart, the driver handed out note cards to the white passengers, but not the black ones, in case they needed to describe the incident to the authorities. When Murray asked why the black passengers did not get cards, the driver recalled the officers, who arrested the two women for disorderly conduct. McBean, overcome by her protest and arrest, fainted and was taken to the hospital before the two women landed in the local jail.[28]

When Murray emerged from jail the following Tuesday to testify at the initial hearing in her case, she found herself speaking to an overflow crowd in a civil rights courtroom. It was an emotional experience, and she now began to describe herself as a lawyer representing a cause rather than a victim of an abusive driver who wouldn't even let her take a segregated seat. In a courtroom packed with hundreds of black and white observers straining to see the two black women who flouted local laws and customs, Murray took the witness stand in a place that seemed to have "all the flavor and excitement of a much talked about movie." A marked change had come over Murray since the time of her arrest, and a world that had been closing in on her for months began to open up again. The same woman who privately described her attitude on the bus as "appeasement" to segregation in contrast to McBean, who was bent on "civil disobedience," now began to talk differently in public. That new confidence was shaped by her awareness of Gandhian civil disobedience techniques, which both McBean and Murray had been discussing before they left New York. Although the bus dispute had come about by accident, once they reached jail a new awareness slowly began to overtake Murray. Using civil disobedience techniques, she and McBean tried to convert the surly jailhouse deputy and their fellow black prisoners to their cause. By their second night behind bars, they had decided to contact the NAACP to seek help, and wrote up a detailed account of the bus incident for their lawyers. A local NAACP member in Petersburg had already contacted the national office, and two local black lawyers showed up at the jail that Sunday to talk with them about the Virginia bus segregation statute. Murray now began to view their troubles as a means of challenging segregation law.[29]

When they appeared in the Petersburg Recorder's Court to answer the charges, Murray was in firm command of the legal proceedings— or at least desired to be. McBean had little experience with southern life and was still shaken up by the incident. She would spend the next week under a doctor's care, and Murray alone took the stand. As their NAACP lawyers showed up to defend them, the two women now faced an additional charge—that they had violated the state bus segregation law. What Murray saw in that courtroom was a crowd that filled all the seats and spilled over along the walls, evenly divided among blacks and whites. Some 250 people were jammed into a room designed to hold only 200. Word had spread of their arrest over the weekend, and the crowd "witnessed the trial with intense interest," according to Murray. She likened the proceedings to a Hollywood movie and fed off what she described as an "electric" atmosphere in the courtroom. During her testimony, she "laid stress on the real crux of the dispute—our refusal to stand by and see open discrimination of Negro passengers without protesting." The local judge assessed a small fine after the hearing, and Murray and McBean caught the next bus out of Petersburg to continue their ride to Durham. Murray now laid plans to use their de novo trial the following month as an "educational" exercise where her own actions in the courtroom would represent those of southern African Americans who had little voice in their government. Murray was not the first African American to experience the drama of a courtroom performance and to sense its effect on a local community. That had been in the air at least since Hastie's appearance in court in Durham seven years earlier. But to her, the feeling was new, and she liked it.[30]

That feeling was only reinforced when Murray observed her African American defense team as they prepared for trial in a southern courtroom. She now believed that the second hearing could replicate what had happened during her testimony in the recorder's court, and would be the first step in creating a movement that "catches the imagination of the Negro masses." Murray had probably been reading Krishnalal Shridharani's 1939 text on Gandhi's methods, *War without Violence*, which was becoming influential among the socialist left at the time. She remained a strong NAACP supporter, as always, and now she saw a way to combine the program of her socialist friends in New York with that of mainstream civil rights groups. She fired off enthusiastic letters to her leftist friends and her lawyers. She now argued that when her case came to trial, she would be representing the masses of African Americans, and that her performance would inspire them to join the fight against segregation. When her NAACP lawyers traveled to Howard Law School for a mock argument in preparation for her de novo hearing, Murray came too. She later recalled that she "almost drooled" at the sight of her lawyers practicing for their courtroom appearance, and she longed to join in as both lawyer and client.[31]

By now, Murray believed that she was firmly in control of their new strategy. She told friends that McBean remained a "wounded stifled bird" as a result of her first contact with southern segregation and was having trouble lifting her spirits. As Murray charged ahead with her furious correspondence, sometimes without her friend's input, she remarked that McBean "just lets the articulate explosive fellow go ahead." Although the names of both women often appeared at the bottom of their effusive letters to friends, acquaintances, and their lawyers, sometimes only Murray's signature appeared, and at other times they were signed "Pauli (for Pauli and Mac)."[32]

The first step in making their court appearance into an inspiration for a mass movement was to get their story into the black press. But there was one problem. In Murray's original story of what had happened on the bus, she had said and done nothing that challenged bus segregation, while McBean spoke nearly all the words that got them in trouble. So she embellished her story to mesh with her new theory of the stakes behind the trial. Murray and MacBean granted an interview to the local black paper, the *Carolina Times*, where a new story emerged. Now it seems that rather than politely telling the driver that their seating conformed to segregation law and practice, Murray had barraged the driver with "legal questions" about the bus company's policies and "threatened to invoke the services of the NAACP, and to call out the legal forces of the 14th amendment, the Constitution and the Supreme

Court." When the officers boarded the bus, Pauli, the "honey-tongued, legal mind" of the two, accosted one of them and then redirected her "machine-gun fire" of questions to him, and invoked "the 14th Amendment, the Constitution and the Supreme Court" in support of her cause. Murray "proceeded to plead the case" that she would make in court even before she exited the bus. While the driver and officers remained dumbfounded, the two black women, "using Mahatma Ghandi's [*sic*] technique with the British Lion, just sat—and sat." Murray, in a letter to a friend in New York, pronounced the new story a "humorous but essentially accurate" account of what she had said to the *Times*. Her new story made the bus incident into a dramatic legal challenge to segregation from the start, with Murray playing the lead role in a Gandhian exercise. Decades later, when composing her autobiography, she would return to a version much closer to the original story.[33]

The de novo trial, however, proved to be a disappointment. The local judge convicted Murray and McBean of disorderly conduct but dismissed the charge that involved the segregation statute, which removed the most likely avenue for an appeal. Her local lawyers were eager to pursue the case, but the NAACP's national legal committee declined to put the organization behind any further efforts, given the trial judge's careful ruling. This was the association's usual stance in a bus or train dispute if a conviction was based on disorderly conduct rather than segregation law. McBean and Murray, "blazing with silent resentment" over the loss of the opportunity to put their new ideas into practice, chose to return to the local jail rather than pay the fine—at least until friends decided to bail them out. Returning to New York, Murray now faced up to something she would have had to deal with had she been able to continue her effort to integrate the University of North Carolina. Earlier that year, she had admitted to herself that she could never again live in her native region. Her unconventional sexual identity remained an unmanageable problem even in New York. Now Murray found that she could barely tolerate the need to conform to southern mores even during her short stay in Durham. While there, Murray had written that she and McBean were "truly alien souls" in the South. She begged off her friends' suggestions that she remain in the region to continue the fight. Within a short time, however, she would find a way of renewing the legal struggle that she believed had been frustrated in Petersburg.[34]

Over the next year, she was drawn more and more toward law as a means of doing something useful in life, and of supporting herself. Back in New York, she renewed her association with the Workers Defense League and got involved in the legal defense campaign for Odell Waller, a black Virginia sharecropper who was sentenced to death for shooting his white landlord during a dispute over shares of the harvest. On a fund-raising tour of Richmond for Waller's defense, she ran into Thurgood Marshall and Leon Ransom, who were in town to raise money for the defense of an interracial rape case. With a bit of bravado, Murray told Ransom that she was now thinking of becoming a lawyer herself. To her surprise, Ransom encouraged her to apply to Howard Law School, where he taught. A few weeks later, she took him up on his offer and began the application process. She thought that she would specialize in either labor law or "the legal techniques used by the NAACP in its consistent attack upon racial inequality." In a longer essay setting out what she hoped to accomplish as a lawyer, she argued that "while this attack must be led by legal discussion and skirmishes, it must be reinforced by militant and direct action"—the position she had begun to formulate during her bus case. She also added, cryptically, that "I also think that the woman attorney has a unique contribution to make to the profession." Nonetheless, she remained undecided on law and took the following summer off to write in isolation, where she completed her first short story and sent it off to *Harper's*. But then a letter arrived offering her admission to Howard and a scholarship, and Murray made a decision that would change her life and affect the course of American law.[35]

Finding Jim Crow's Twin

Pauli Murray would find more than she was looking for when she arrived at Howard Law School in the fall of 1941. What she was looking for was a way to represent her race in its struggle with legal segregation, and a means to gain some autonomy in a world where she never seemed to quite fit in. Twice during the previous eighteen months, she had come close to representing her race in court. This was her third try, and she quickly began to establish a law school academic record that seemed likely to set her on that path. At her first court hearing in Petersburg, she had felt a sense of control in public space that she had not experienced in a long time, and she now seemed to be on her way to a repeat of that experience, but this time as an NAACP lawyer. Nonetheless, for Murray, Howard was a place full of contradictions. "Howard Law School equipped me for effective struggle against Jim Crow," she later wrote, but "it was also the place were I first became conscious of the twin evil of discriminatory sex bias, which I quickly labeled Jane Crow."[36]

Murray was not the first person to struggle with the question of what happened when a black woman tried to join the fraternity of lawyers. For nearly two decades, lawyers like Ruth Whitehead Whaley and Sadie Alexander had worked hard to put a name to what exactly happened when the "New Negro Woman," as Whaley called her, joined the profession. Alexander still felt that the prejudices against women in the profession were "so subtle that it is difficult to state them with any assurance." Murray felt differently. Pauli Murray had come of age among a younger generation of African Americans, and she had a set of gender expectations very different from those of women lawyers who were only a little older. Black women who came to Howard law in the 1940s remembered it as an unwelcoming place for women, although they did not come up with a full-blown legal theory to describe it, as Murray did. What set Murray apart, even from contemporaries, was that she came to law school in the middle of an unresolved crisis of identity. At the end of her first year of study, she described her emotional condition as "unbearable in its present phase." The following year, she found herself in the hospital once again, this time after an affair with an undergraduate woman student. Murray still felt like a sex invert—a man trapped in a body that made people treat her like a woman. If she saw the world differently than did lawyers like Whaley and Alexander, she presented the same problem to the male lawyers around her—the discomforting presence of a woman's body in a man's courtroom.[37]

By the time Murray arrived at Howard Law School, the civil rights courtroom had moved to the forefront as a metaphor for everything that happened there. That shift had begun in the aftermath of the Howard defense team's performance in the Crawford case, and accelerated with the arrival of professor James Nabrit Jr. in 1936. Nabrit soon introduced Howard's famous civil rights course. It was taught seminar style, with students expected to participate in intense research and debate of the type that a lawyer might do before arguing in an appellate court.

Outside of class, students matched wits with NAACP lawyers in mock arguments. Houston returned there for a dry run before his Supreme Court argument in *Gaines*. Those students who performed well could expect to have a prominent role in the NAACP's legal cases. Murray saw one of the mock arguments during the preparations for her bus case, and later recalled that the experience "made law school almost a must for me." What she found when she actually enrolled at Howard was something else—a place of intense masculine competition. "[S]traight out machismo" is how Murray later described the culture there. What Howard offered to ambitious young men was the confidence that they could come to court and be treated "like white men" even in the United States Supreme Court—to use Judge McLemore's evocative language from the Crawford litigation.[38]

Murray's presence at the school became a problem for her fellow male students, she believed, because her academic performance made her the logical choice for the highest honorific the school could confer on a student—election as chief justice of Howard's Court of Peers. Students had organized the Court of Peers in 1932, and it served as the school's honor society. Each law school class elected two representatives to the court. The top student usually served as chief justice, and the position was a logical entrée into NAACP work. James Tyson had served as the first chief justice before graduating and later going off to work on the Crawford trial. Thurgood Marshall succeeded him. Now Pauli Murray seemed to be the logical choice. She had been elected to the Court of Peers and was ready to take the next step. Her scholastic performance was so strong that she now expected to break the record for the highest academic average in the school's history. Leon Ransom called her a "legal genius." Two decades later William Hastie, the law school's dean during Murray's third year of school, remembered her as "the best student the law school had ever had." But Murray was a woman, even though she kept "wanting to be one of the men, [and] doing things that fellows do." Murray had bested every man in the school at the task that defined their worth as lawyers. When it came time to name her as chief justice for her third year of law school, they hesitated.[39]

Murray received other signs that "I was not recognized as a member of the fraternity of lawyers who would make civil rights history." Ransom, for instance, had recruited her to Howard, and worked hard to keep her in school when her relationship with the undergraduate student threatened to endanger her future at Howard. Nonetheless, Murray recalled that her "real awakening" to the problem of sex discrimination happened only a few weeks into law school, when Ransom invited all the male first-year students to a smoker at his house for a legal fraternity. When she confronted Ransom about the exclusion of women, he simply laughed and told her that women could form their own sorority. That would have been a futile endeavor, since there was only one other woman law student at Howard, and that student dropped out before the end of the year. Murray also had problems with William Robert Ming Jr., a young professor from Chicago who was on his way to a distinguished career as a civil rights lawyer. Only two or three days into the first semester, Ming opined in class that "we don't know why women come to law school anyway, but since you're here. . . ." Murray fumed but kept her tongue. She sat in frustrated silence as the "deeper voices" of the men drowned out hers in classroom debate. During her third year of law school, she decided to follow in the tradition of Howard's leading graduates who often went to Harvard for graduate work. Harvard's law school, however, did not admit women, and Murray began a campaign to persuade the school to reverse its admissions policy. Harvard stood fast, but at Howard her continued academic success could not be overlooked. After much delay the students finally elected her to the chief justice position that she coveted. Instead of being a place to reclaim some personal autonomy, Howard turned out to be just one more place where she had to fight for room to assert her own unique identity.[40]

Murray had taken a step closer to the idea of Jane Crow when she was drawn into what she called "non-violent direct action" during her second year. The catalyst was the arrest of three undergraduate women students after a dispute over service at a lunch counter. Student discontent with segregation bubbled over, and disaffected students formed a Civil Rights Committee to organize a response. Murray, who was living in an undergraduate dormitory, quickly became a leader and legal adviser to the group, which settled on a direct-action response and debated the philosophy that should guide their movement. The students soon launched a nonviolent sit-in that broke the color line at a whites-only cafeteria near campus. The following year they renewed their sit-ins and temporarily desegregated a downtown cafeteria. Murray also took heart when four students who had been involved in the Civil Rights Committee staged a sit-in aboard a segregated bus in northern

Virginia. But momentum was lost when university administrators ordered a stop to the protests. Murray spent the last part of her time at Howard in meetings with university officials to try to get them to reverse the ban on protests, and in a futile effort to build student support for a test case under a nineteenth-century local public accommodations law. If the direct-action movement was a casualty of the university's decision, so was Murray's coveted goal of attaining the highest grade-point average in the history of the school. With little time to study for exams, her grades plummeted.[41]

If Murray lost one cherished goal in the student protests, she gained a legal theory that would affect the rest of her life. The protests forced her to think deeply about something that had long been one of her core concerns—discrimination in public space. As the protests gathered steam, Murray was also working on her long paper for the civil rights seminar. In that paper, her lifelong preoccupation with the ambiguity of the color line, her association of travel with freedom, her struggle with sexual identity, and her experience as legal adviser to the student protesters would all come together in a theory of discrimination that she would use to come up with the idea she called Jane Crow. Student papers in the seminar often dealt with cutting-edge issues that NAACP lawyers encountered in practice. In Murray's paper, she concluded that it was time to ask the Supreme Court to overrule *Plessy v. Ferguson*. At the time, NAACP lawyers were slowly chipping away at the legal foundations of separate but equal, but held back from arguing that segregation laws and practices were unconstitutional on their face. Murray later recalled that the male students greeted her call to overturn *Plessy* with "hoots of derisive laughter." But Murray's call to attack segregation head-on was not the most contentious part of her thesis. What was most controversial about Murray's paper was the theory she came up with to accomplish that objective.[42]

Murray contended that segregation was unconstitutional because it violated the Thirteenth Amendment, which had abolished slavery, despite the fact that the Supreme Court had long held that the amendment applied only to conditions that closely resembled involuntary servitude. Murray, however, argued that the essence of slavery was that it violated an individual's personal autonomy—the freedom to move about and control one's own fate without being locked into a predefined status. To demonstrate that, she would not focus on segregated schools or the Fourteenth Amendment, which would eventually provide the basis for the ruling in *Brown v. Board of Education*. Rather, she believed that the essence of segregation was another type of discrimination that had long conflicted with her deeply held sense of personal freedom and which she had spent a year trying to fit into her Gandhian vocabulary—segregation in travel and public accommodations.[43]

Murray's image of the victim of discrimination was that of the lonely dissenter, hemmed in by social constraints that prevented her from fully participating in the life of her community. It was decidedly autobiographical. Her legal brief against Jim Crow began by asserting that "[t]he most precious of all rights known to free men are those which affect the individual in terms of his personal status in the community." Segregation, she argued, violated what she called "personal rights," which are those that govern the interactions between "the individual" and "the rest of the community." Chief among those personal rights was what she called "freedom of locomotion, freedom in the use of public accommodations on the basis of equality with other members of the body politic." Personal relationships were the key thing that civil rights law protected, she argued, and her brief launched into an extended defense of that idea. The Thirteenth Amendment, she argued, abolished slavery, but in doing so, it also abolished what was the essence of slavery—the "wall of legal restrictions" embodied in pre–Civil War state and federal law, that controlled the movement of enslaved people and cut them off from social interaction with whites. The Fourteenth Amendment, she argued, merely elaborated at greater length the same objectives that Congress tried to establish in the Thirteenth. Both amendments, she argued, had been proposed and ratified to protect the personal rights that had been denied by the legal system that governed slavery.[44]

The centerpiece of Murray's brief against segregation was her approach to discrimination in public space. It was in public places, she argued, that Americans sought to lock individuals into predetermined categories based on personal appearance. With that idea, she launched into an extended defense of the constitutionality of the 1875 Civil Rights Act, which banned discrimination in public accommodations, and of the Constitution's application to public accommodations more generally. By the logic of the Thirteenth Amendment, the Constitution applied in full force to public and private attempts to deny access to public accommodations based on race. Under the Fourteenth Amendment's guarantees of equality and due process, race discrimination in public accommodations was an "arbitrary classification" based on race. It was a "fixed and arbitrary" benchmark which locked people into unchangeable categories. Having established that the Constitution applied in full force to protect the "personal right" to interact with others in public accommodations, she believed, it was only a short step to invalidating all segregation laws and practices that cut blacks off from social interaction with whites. As in so many things, Murray was somewhat ahead of her time. Half a century after she proposed it, legal scholars, historians, and others began to reclaim the Thirteenth Amendment as a charter of freedom protecting a wide range of injuries to personal autonomy, including those visited specifically upon women—a project that continues to this day.[45]

A few months after her graduation in June 1944, Murray sent her completed thesis on to Leon Ransom, along with a note informing him that "this is the first installment of 'Who Killed Jim Crow?'" "I might ask you now," she added, "how do I go about killing *'Jane Crow'*—prejudice against sex." Murray believed that she was a good candidate for a job at the NAACP, where she might get a chance to put into practice the ideas she had formulated in her paper. "Maybe five years from now I'll be arguing Plessy v. Ferguson before the old boys up there" in the Supreme Court, she told her friend Caroline Ware. As yet, she had no comparable institutional location from which to attack Jane Crow. But she had a theory. Sex discrimination was like race discrimination. Both were denials of the fundamental "personal right" of the individual to interact with "the rest of the community." They were arbitrary, for both types of discrimination "classifie[d] persons in such a manner [that] they cannot change their conduct" to remove them.[46]

While she was finishing her thesis, she was also putting her campaign for admission to Harvard into full gear. "I would gladly change my sex to meet your requirements," she told Harvard's law faculty, "but since the way to such change has not been revealed to me, I have no recourse but to appeal to you to change your minds." She spoke truer than her correspondents knew. For years, she had been consulting doctors to explore the possibility that she had hidden male sex organs, or perhaps that an injection of male hormones could make her feel more like the man she wanted to be. "Very recent medical examination reveals me to be a functionally normal woman with perhaps a 'male slant' on things," she told the Harvard authorities.[47]

Murray now had an idea that she would push for the rest of her life, and to great effect. Jane Crow was much the same thing as Jim Crow. Sex discrimination was like race discrimination. Both kinds of distinctions should be legally actionable for the same reasons—that they violated the personal autonomy of the individual. Two decades later, that idea would place her at the center of the equality debates of the 1960s. When Congress had to decide whether to add sex discrimination to the Civil Rights Act of 1964, she was there. When lawyers and judges had to decide whether the Fourteenth Amendment covered sex as well as race, she was there.[48]

It was a theory born from her own struggles with categories that seemed to do violence to Murray's own sense of self—sometimes black and white, but far more often men and women. More and more, she wanted to perform a role that was denied to her simply because of the vagaries of her own physical appearance. Personal identity, to her, was more about how one acted than how one looked, and her own crisis of identity seemed to reach a head when she decided that she wanted to act like a civil rights lawyer and to represent her race in court. But that was a task reserved for representative men, as she found out during her years at Howard. As the years passed, she would become more and more convinced that she didn't fully represent any particular group, especially the unified voice of a race. Feminist politics, too, would eventually leave her feeling marginalized and alone. She would eventually come to rely on the term "human rights" as a more universal term than civil rights. In 1944, the idea that Jane Crow was like Jim Crow was a marginal position, but over time it would become conventional for many mainstream Americans. Its origins, however, lay in part in the unconventional life of a black woman lawyer struggling to resist what, to most people around her, seemed like just plain common sense.

10

A Lawyer as the Face of Integration
in Postwar America

In December of 1952, and again almost exactly a year later, an integrationist drama played itself out before the justices of the United States Supreme Court. It involved a case that was argued twice in that period, *Brown v. Board of Education*, and this particular drama focused on the two lawyers who seemed to personify the stakes behind the litigation: Thurgood Marshall, the NAACP's chief lawyer, and the courtly southerner John W. Davis, perhaps the most prestigious lawyer in the country, who had chosen to lend his ample talents to the defense of school segregation. "Legal Giants to Vie in Segregation Case," announced the *Washington Post* on the eve of the first argument, accompanied by the paired photographs of the two lawyers that would become the iconic image of the case in both the black and white press. Marshall was glad to be seen as Davis's equal and did everything he could to promote the comparison. He told reporters a story that quickly became a staple of civil rights lore—that as a young man, he had skipped classes at Howard Law School to watch Davis argue cases before the Supreme Court. Marshall made a point of asking Davis to lunch before they would meet as adversaries in court, despite strong objections from his own staff. He also told the press that he had stayed up nearly all night to "edit out the snide cracks" about the white southern lawyer that Marshall's assistants had inserted into the NAACP's briefs.[1]

According to Davis's biographer, during both of the *Brown* arguments the two lawyers would "whisper sallies and exchange humorous stories" across the boundary of race, just as they were asking the justices to decide what those bounds should be outside the courtroom. They even appeared together in a joint photograph that also became news and, later, history. After Marshall's eventual victory in the case, the first call of congratulations reportedly came from a despondent Davis himself. The octogenarian lawyer sank into depression after the Court's decision and died within a year, sure that his world was slipping from his grasp—seemingly unaware that the lawyerly interactions between himself and his black adversary were as sure a sign as any of the true nature of that slippage.[2]

The Marshall-Davis story proved so intriguing for midcentury Americans because it seemed to encapsulate a larger set of changes overtaking the country in the two decades that succeeded World War II. For the previous sixty years, Americans had placed more and more physical distance between racial groups, particularly in public places like neighborhoods, schools, restaurants, and theaters, where one might meet strangers of a different race. Now that world was in danger of falling apart, as a nascent civil rights movement began to push back at the barriers that divided Americans by race. Many whites recoiled from the threatened changes, and withdrew from the neighborhoods, schools, and public facilities that had once seemed so important in their lives. For southerners like Davis, the whole thing seemed even more disconcerting. Davis could be friendly to blacks if the relationship was paternalistic, and he privately confessed his belief in the "anatomical" and "intellectual" differences between the races that constituted unmistakable signs that blacks and whites should remain socially separate from one another. Yet, when presented with a black man in the shape of a lawyer, Davis put on a display of public racial egalitarianism that he would have found impossible to maintain in another setting. For Davis, it was something new, but to Marshall this was just the latest, and largest, stage on which to perform a role that he had begun to play in the courtrooms of rural Maryland nearly two decades before.[3]

Integration was often a frightening process for postwar Americans, and Marshall was self-conscious about showing whites, including the justices of the Supreme Court, how they might navigate it. In that project, he was not alone. As the 1940s bled into the 1950s, black lawyers moved into unprecedented public roles in governmental agencies, blue-ribbon commissions, civic associations, law firms, and the judiciary. Each year seemed to bring yet another breakthrough, avidly followed in the press, as professional norms allowed black lawyers to interact with whites in ways that seemed unimaginable a decade earlier. For the lawyers, the dizzying changes seemed to bring to fruition everything they had desired for the past two decades, and more. By now, the professional breakthroughs of lawyers like Marshall seemed to merge seamlessly with the dreams of the rest of the race.

Marshall and his colleagues' unprecedented triumphs were of immense symbolic importance for blacks and whites alike, but therein lay an enduring paradox of group identity. For both the white liberals who invited black lawyers to join their ranks and the masses of African Americans who cheered that process on, integration was based on the idea that the lawyers represented the larger racial group. But it was also true that professional integration was possible only because of the increasing distance between the lawyers and the communities they still claimed to represent. An old problem soon reasserted itself. By the early 1960s, a new cry could be heard everywhere—from the counsels of the NAACP to the cities around the country where African Americans now dreamed of being a majority. Eventually, Americans of a wide range of political perspectives would join in. That cry was community control. At its core, the new idea was that the representatives of a minority group had to be closer to the people themselves, and lawyers of Marshall's generation seemed to be moving further and further away. Within half a decade of his most famous triumph, Marshall was in danger of losing his relevance in a rapidly changing American politics of race.

From Thurgood Marshall's complicated interactions with John W. Davis to the election of an African American lawyer as president of the United States, the same question would swirl around the appearance of black attorneys in public life. In a world where society required them to have professional bonds with whites and still stand in for blacks, who exactly did they represent in an era where group loyalty still played an unmistakable role in public life? As Americans worked through their complicated views of racial authenticity, they would often map their desires and fears onto the body of a public figure that became ubiquitous in postwar American politics: the black lawyer.

A Glass of Milk for Democracy

On August 9, 1948, a lunch counter clerk at the Washington National Airport refused to serve a glass of milk to a black passenger who was changing planes there, and brought down the censure of the federal bureaucracy upon his head. The Justice Department began drafting an opinion to decide whether the Civil Aeronautics Administration (CAA) could ban discrimination at the facility. Maverick Republican senator Wayne Morse jumped into the fray and challenged President Truman to take action on the issue. Eleanor Roosevelt wrote an editorial that condemned race discrimination at the airport. Only a month and a half after federal officials learned of the incident, the CAA issued its order banning discrimination based on "race, color or creed" at the facility. Discrimination in the airport's facilities had been the subject of controversy for years, but federal officials were moved to decisive action by the identity of the passenger who was denied service. It was Philadelphia lawyer Sadie T. M. Alexander, who had recently completed her service as one of only two black members of President Harry Truman's blue-ribbon Committee on Civil Rights. Being refused service at a lunch counter was nothing new for Alexander, but she was sure that what had once seemed like a mere personal affront was now an attack on America's "democratic way of life," as she put it in a letter demanding action from Truman. Now it seemed as though the full weight of American democracy was behind her when she stepped up to that counter to ask for service.[4]

For a decade leading up to the National Airport incident, one barrier after another had seemed to fall for lawyers like Alexander, but the rapid pace of change could be uncomfortable for blacks as well as whites. As early as 1943, Charles Houston fell victim to the shifting politics of race. That year, he was unexpectedly defeated in a contest for the presidency of the National Bar Association. By rights, he should have won the election in a walk, since the convention was held in Baltimore, and lawyers from his hometown, nearby Washington, D.C., were expected to predominate. Regional bloc voting often determined the outcome of the elections. It didn't hurt that his father, William Houston, was a former NBA president and that he was endorsed by the civil rights establishment. But Houston encountered "resentment" from the Washington bar, according to news reports, and lost narrowly to the Kentuckian Charles Anderson. One clue to the strange result is a letter that Anderson wrote two years later, complaining that "a large number of the membership of the Association are mindful of Charlie's lack of interest in Bar Affairs, except at Convention time." At the time, William Hastie also came in for censure for his involvement in white professional groups and lack of attention to the NBA. The bar association's national secretary, Sadie Alexander, harshly criticized Hastie, but within a few years she found herself in the same position. For years, she and her husband had been the bar association's two most prominent members, but by the early 1950s she confessed that she had so little contact with the NBA that she had no idea what it was actually doing.[5]

In May of 1946, Detroit lawyer George W. Crockett Jr. prompted a testy exchange of letters between himself and the National Bar Association leadership when he resigned from the editorial board of the association's journal and announced that he was letting his membership lapse. "At the time of its founding," Crockett reluctantly concluded, "the National Bar had a definite purpose which it alone could serve," but there was no longer any need for a national black bar group given that the white bar was integrating. Crockett conceded the need for local black bar groups in southern locales where white associations excluded them, but beyond that he stood his ground. His letter made explicit something that had been in motion for nearly a decade. The National Lawyers Guild, an organization of liberal lawyers, had welcomed black lawyers into its ranks since its founding in 1937. Now, everywhere outside the South, barriers to entry into white bar associations were falling, and black lawyers had recently broken through the American Bar Association's nearly three-decade-long effort to keep them out.[6]

The most important factor that pushed black lawyers across racial lines was the New Deal political realignment itself, which brought African American voters into the Democratic column and, significantly, a few dozen symbolically placed black administrators into the federal government. Dubbed the "Black Cabinet," the group included a few lawyers, the most important of whom was Hastie himself, who served as an assistant solicitor in the Interior Department, where his work led to his appointment as a district judge in the U.S. Virgin Islands. Few of the Black Cabinet, however, had any high-profile public responsibilities. Important as they were, their presence did little to challenge the public norms of cross-racial interaction. All that would begin to change during World War II, when the Fair Employment Practices Committee (FEPC) gave a few important black lawyers the opportunity to come to Washington and assume an unprecedented public role.[7]

Earl Dickerson was the most prominent of the black lawyers who crossed over into the white world through their work at the FEPC. Dickerson had broken barriers two decades before, as the first black graduate of the University of Chicago Law School. After his bar admission, he alternated between private practice and stints as a Democratic appointee to successive legal jobs in local and state government in Chicago. He was lucky enough to get in on the ground floor when the Liberty Life Insurance Company was organized in the 1920s, providing him with an alternative source of income and a fallback during periods when his law practice faltered. Dickerson was a key member of the legal team that took the racially restrictive covenant case of *Hansberry v. Lee* to the Supreme Court. But Dickerson's lawyerly persona emerged from Chicago Democratic politics rather than the disciplining space of the courtroom. Compared with lawyers like Houston and Raymond Pace Alexander, he was a bit rough around the edges. Dickerson, for instance, asked one witness at the *Hansberry* trial a question that would have left many black lawyers aghast: "Are you a member of the Ku Klux Klan?" Nonetheless he was in the middle of a typical journey of an elite black lawyer in the 1940s. He won election as an alderman in Chicago in 1939, and by 1941 he was eager to move on to larger things.[8]

President Roosevelt created the FEPC in 1941, in response to labor leader A. Philip Randolph's threat to lead a March on Washington to protest against discrimination in the armed forces and defense industries. Dickerson quickly emerged as the dominant figure in the six-man committee, where he served alongside RCA business executive David Sarnoff, representatives of the AFL and CIO, a moderate white southerner named Mark Ethridge, and the black labor activist Milton Webster. By executive order, President Roosevelt had banned discrimination based on "race, creed, color, or national origin" in defense industries and government service. In an example of his well-known wartime experimentalism, Roosevelt had given the committee a vague mandate to "receive and investigate complaints of discrimination in violation of the provisions of this order and . . . take appropriate steps." As the geographically scattered, unpaid FEPC committee members tried to decide what to do, it was Dickerson who convinced the FEPC to interpret its vague mandate in ways that proved extremely controversial—holding hearings where the committee would call in leaders of industry and labor. With no actual enforcement powers, the real purpose of the hearings was to embarrass recalcitrant employers and unions into taking action.[9]

As an FEPC committee member, Dickerson interacted with whites in a way that few African Americans, or whites for that matter, would have thought possible before. According to the leading account of the FEPC's history, he "approached the hearing[s] as a trial lawyer would, often pressed witnesses with determined single-mindedness and copious, time-consuming reiteration." As the committee scheduled hearings in Los Angeles, Chicago, and New York, Dickerson got into frequent disputes with his fellow committee members over his style, and sometimes arrived in advance of hearings as a one-man investigative team, calling whites to the carpet even before formal proceedings started. "I was more aggressive than ever in my life in those days," he recalled. Brushing aside the fears of other committee members, he decided to attend the committee hearings in Birmingham, Alabama. Reality intruded when a six-foot, four-inch federal marshal met the Chicago black lawyer as he stepped off the plane in Alabama, to protect him from violence. As opponents organized to rein in Dickerson and his committee, Roosevelt disbanded the original FEPC in the spring of 1943 and formed a new committee, in which the conservative Norfolk newspaper publisher P. B. Young would replace Dickerson.[10]

Prior to his FEPC appointment, Dickerson's accomplishments had drawn little notice outside Chicago's local civil rights community and the NAACP, but his aggressive committee work made him into a force to be reckoned with across racial lines. Hastie now recommended the Chicago lawyer to the Department of Justice for a high-level appointment. By that time, however, that possibility was becoming ever more remote. By late 1941, Dickerson's aggressive FEPC tactics had given the FBI a questionable opening wedge to launch an investigation of his loyalty under the Hatch Act, which prohibited federal employees from becoming members of organizations that advocated the overthrow of the government. Like Charles Houston, Dickerson became the subject of an FBI probe that would continue on and off again for years. Dickerson had to content himself with the presidency of the National Bar Association, which came in due course in 1945. The real breakthrough would be six years later, when he became the first black lawyer to serve as president of a white bar association, the National Lawyers' Guild.[11]

Nonetheless, Dickerson left behind an agency whose investigative machinery made it into the natural starting point for black lawyers trying to expose their talents to a wider audience. Younger lawyers like former NAACP attorney Frank Reeves and Philadelphia's Maceo Hubbard parlayed staff jobs at the FEPC into careers as civil rights lawyers. George Crockett joined the reorganized FEPC as its first hearing commissioner, setting in motion a process that would lead him to conclude that the NBA was now irrelevant.[12]

Even experienced lawyers like Charles Houston found themselves in uncharted racial territory as the result of FEPC service. Houston joined the committee in 1942 as an investigating attorney to help with a hearing on the southern railway industry, then publicly broke with Roosevelt and resigned when the president forced a cancellation in the planned hearing. Nonetheless Roosevelt later appointed him to the committee itself when the aging P. B. Young stepped down in 1944. The following year, Houston resigned again when President Truman stopped the committee from ordering the Washington, D.C., Capital Transit System to cease discriminating against black workers. This time, Houston's resignation made headlines in both the black and white press, as he and Truman exchanged dueling open letters with their contrasting accounts of the dispute. In the half decade that remained to Houston before his untimely death from overwork in 1950, he would remain a nationally known civil rights figure on both sides of the color line.[13]

By the mid-1940s, Washington had become the type of destination for black lawyers that it had been for their white counterparts since the days of Daniel Webster—a place to branch out beyond the confines of local and group affiliation and connect to something larger. William Hastie found that out when he resigned his Virgin Islands judgeship in 1939 to become dean of Howard Law School. He did not remain in private life for long. Concerned about black support in the 1940 elections, President Roosevelt appointed Hastie to a new post as civilian aide to the secretary of war, to help manage race relations within the military effort. Like Houston, the former Howard dean got into a dispute with the political establishment. He made headlines when he resigned in 1943 over his frustration with continued discrimination and segregation in the war effort, and returned to his post as dean of Howard Law. But that did not stop his advancement at a time when successive Democratic presidents were looking for representative leaders as a way to maintain black electoral support. President Truman nominated him for the governorship of the Virgin Islands in 1946, and the personal bond between the two men grew during a three-day presidential visit to the islands in early 1948. Hastie returned the favor by working himself to exhaustion trying to secure the black vote for Truman that fall. "I had never participated in party politics," Hastie later recalled, but his personal interactions with the president, and Truman's civil rights initiatives, changed his mind. After Truman's unlikely electoral victory, the president made him the first black judge of the federal court of appeals.[14]

"Democracy" was the watchword that was on the lips of both blacks and whites in these professional integrationist struggles. As the war against Nazism turned into a Cold War against totalitarian dictatorship, lawyers joined other liberal Americans in linking the civil rights struggle to the language of democracy. Earl Dickerson and Loren Miller found that language to be useful in struggles to integrate everything from bar associations to political gatherings. Dickerson told his Chicago colleagues that they were content to "preach Democracy . . . but never practice it" after they decided to meet at a country club that excluded black patrons. For others, Gunnar Myrdal's *An American Dilemma: The Negro Problem and Modern Democracy* provided the rhetorical link between American democracy and racial integration. Myrdal's immensely influential work had a deceptively simple thesis: that the "Negro problem" was really a "problem in the heart of the [white] American"—a moral and psychological dilemma brought on by the conflict between the egalitarian "American Creed" and the inegalitarian American practice.[15]

Within months of its publication, *An American Dilemma* found its way into Pauli Murray's ongoing conversation with Eleanor Roosevelt. Murray, during her efforts to get into the University of North Carolina, had struck up an acquaintance with the First Lady, and the two women maintained a sometimes brutally honest friendship. When Murray was drawn into the Howard sit-in movement during her last year of law school, she asked for Roosevelt's help, telling her that the protests were a straightforward application of "Myrdal's analysis of the American Creed and the internal conflict within the minds of individual white Americans." Myrdal's ideas also quickly became a standard citation for Raymond Pace Alexander in his speeches and writings about racially exclusive bar associations. As both Murray and Alexander realized, if the real objective was to appeal to the psychological and moral compass of whites whose beliefs were belied by their actions, then there were few better means to use than the example of representative blacks.[16]

Spurred by a variety of impulses, a select group of black lawyers joined with sympathetic whites in converging on a race relations project as World War II drew to a close, and few people better exemplified that trend than Philadelphia lawyer Sadie T. M. Alexander. Alexander began to make the transition to the white world in 1947, when the political space opened by Harry Truman's Fair Deal suddenly replaced the National Bar Association as the focus of her public life. Up to that time, she had remained a loyal Republican in a city where the GOP machine still dominated black and white politics. All that began to change when Truman, motivated by a combination of personal belief, political calculation, and Cold War competition for the allegiance of people of color around the world, moved with unprecedented forcefulness on civil rights. When Truman, spurred by a meeting with Walter White and other civil rights leaders, dusted off an old Roosevelt-era proposal to appoint a blue-ribbon Committee on Civil Rights, Sadie Alexander was surprised to find her name on the list of appointees to the committee.[17]

The appointment to the Truman Committee was a transformative experience for a lawyer who had just about reached the limit of what she could do inside the black professional world. As one of her correspondents put it, "[e]ven though the men of the National Bar Association would not elect you president, because you are a woman, at least the President of the United States acknowledges your worth." The reason for that presidential acknowledgment was the unavoidable politics of group identity in postwar America. "[S]he was a Negro, a woman, and a northerner," remembered presidential aide Philleo Nash, in explaining her appointment. Truman adopted what Nash called a "Noah's Ark" approach to committee membership. He appointed two representatives from every group that might be interested in its work: two women, two university presidents, two corporate executives, two southerners, two African Americans, and more. (Former Urban League head Eugene Kinckle Jones was the other black member.) As the committee met in full session ten times, heard from dozens of witnesses, and corresponded with hundreds of advocacy groups, Alexander kept up her contacts with civil rights leaders like Walter White and A. Philip Randolph, to ensure "that I rightly anticipated the tenor of the American colored people."[18]

The committee's famous 1947 report, *To Secure These Rights*, recommending a variety of new federal civil rights initiatives, emerged from a relatively easy consensus among its members about how to define

America's race problem. They were guided to that consensus almost from its first meetings in Washington, when Sadie Alexander "testily raised the question whether the committee members could eat together" during their lunch break. That casual lunch break broke the color line at the dining room of the Mayflower Hotel. After one incident where a waiter physically blocked Alexander from accompanying her white colleagues to their table, committee chair Charles Wilson, president of General Electric, exclaimed: "I never thought this could happen to a woman like you." The committee was also influenced by a well-publicized series of lynchings and other violent incidents in the South that continued as it deliberated. On the few issues that were contentious, committee members tended to act as representatives of their own constituencies. Alexander, for instance, refused to cede ground to her southern colleagues on federal funding for segregated schools and explained that if she had acted any differently, "the people of my own racial group would not feel that I had sufficiently protected their interests."[19]

For the most part, however, the committee was guided to its results by a Myrdalian framework that by now had become second nature to its members. After a pivotal meeting, the committee's staff put the final touches on its report, which began with a long introductory section setting out the core "American ideal" of "freedom and equality for all men" and listing the many areas where the nation failed to live up to its founding creed. The report told the many Americans who perused its pages that "[t]he pervasive gap between our aims and what we actually do is creating a kind of moral dry rot which eats away at the emotional and rational basis of democratic beliefs." By some estimates, about one million copies of the report reached the American public through printing and serialization. As Harry Truman made civil rights a part of the Fair Deal program, and scored an improbable electoral victory in the fall of 1948, it seemed to Alexander and those like her that American democracy and their own professional aspirations were moving forward, hand in hand.[20]

"You Would Hardly Know the Place"

Writing to an acquaintance in the early 1950s, Sadie Alexander noted with evident pride that "Philadelphia has made many changes in the last few years. . . . [Y]ou would hardly know the place." "There are four colored lawyers in the District Attorney's office," a black man was in charge of city procurement, and "[t]he Sheriff of Philadelphia has as his private secretary a colored girl." Not far away, William Hastie was sitting as the first black federal court of appeals judge, although that was also the source of continuing tension. Raymond Alexander, joined by other local black lawyers, had opposed Hastie's nomination since it would deprive Alexander of his first, and probably last, chance to become a federal judge. William Coleman Jr., who had clerked for Supreme Court justice Felix Frankfurter, had just broken the color bar when he obtained a job at a local corporate law firm. Yale Law School graduate A. Leon Higginbotham Jr. would soon arrive at the district attorney's office and would go on to cofound a firm that produced multiple federal judges.[21]

Similar trends were in motion in other cities. In New York, Thurgood Marshall and Jane Bolin's names had been batted about for a judgeship after Congress decided to expand the federal judiciary. Bolin was a member of the wrong political party, and Marshall's chances were apparently sunk by his failure to smooth the feathers of the local black Democratic machine. Chicago's Earl Dickerson would soon head the National Lawyers' Guild, although after that he turned away from active law practice to devote himself to the black insurance company he helped launch in the 1920s. In Los Angeles, Loren Miller was becoming a pillar of the Fair Deal wing of the state Democratic Party. He allied himself with future governor Edmund "Pat" Brown Sr. and would end his career as a local judge, which was, incidentally the antithesis of what the younger Miller had imagined for himself. It seemed like the decade had finally brought to fruition these lawyers' dreams of representing their race in the larger world of American life. Like just about every idea of racial representation that had preceded it, that vision was destined to fail.[22]

As early as 1942, Dickerson could sense that something was wrong. By that time, the pugnacious lawyer who had served as a Chicago Democratic alderman since 1939 was making national headlines because of his aggressive confrontations with white witnesses at the FEPC hearings. Despite his new prominence, or more exactly because of it, he discovered that his position in Chicago's black politics was eroding. In 1942, his fellow black lawyer William Dawson would turn what should have been Dickerson's greatest asset into a liability. That year, Dawson and

Dickerson faced off in a bitter primary contest for a symbolically important Chicago congressional seat. Dickerson's wily rival defeated him
handily, employing a series of code words that spelled the end of Dickerson's career in local black politics. Dickerson was a "silk stocking"
and a "high hat," Dawson's camp charged, and was married to a white
woman (both Dickerson and his wife were light skinned). Dickerson
moved through the white world with ease, and scandalized his white
colleagues by dropping in for lunch when the local bar group integrated
its eating facilities. Dawson charged that such things made Dickerson
an inauthentic representative of the Chicago wards that were fast becoming a bastion of black political strength. The charges stuck, and
Dawson's camp repeated them the following year in getting the local
black ward committee to deny Dickerson renomination for his own
aldermanic seat. At the moment of his greatest national prominence,
Dickerson had suddenly lost the black Democratic base that had sustained his career for almost two decades. He would remain a forceful
presence in local civil rights politics almost until his death, at age ninety-
five, in the mid-1980s. But his career as a viable political candidate was
finished.[23]

In 1952, a local black activist took the time to write to Sadie
Alexander, to assure her—if she needed any additional assurance—
that "the race will be represented without being compromised" with
Alexander as a member of Philadelphia's newly formed Commission on
Human Relations. For Alexander, it had been a whirlwind half-decade
since the release of the Truman Committee's report. Speaking invita-
tions had poured into her office, and she had traveled around the
country—at least, as much as her family and professional responsibilities
would allow her—giving speech after speech to church groups, civic
organizations, and others. Her standard speech argued that the "gap
between what we state we believe . . . and how we act . . . is creating a
kind of moral dry rot which eats away our real democratic beliefs." After
the 1948 elections, she and her husband had moved firmly into the
Democratic Party, and both joined the liberal coalition led by Philadelphia lawyers Richardson Dilworth and Joseph Clark Jr., which ousted
the Republican machine and took control of the city government in 1951.
Raymond won election to the City Council as part of the liberal Democratic takeover. With their political base in the black North Philadelphia
neighborhood where they had lived for decades and their connections to

the governing coalition, the Alexanders seemed to personify the restless ambitions of an assertive and growing black community.[24]

Sadie Alexander quickly found it difficult to live up to the expectations that were heaped upon both herself and her husband. Among other things, the commission's job was made more difficult by the state of 1950s civil rights law, which was fast being outstripped by the expectations of African Americans, in Philadelphia and elsewhere. The commission's job was to "enforce all statutes and ordinances prohibiting discrimination against persons because of race, color, religion or national origin" and to "conduct educational programs" for the "promotion of understanding" between different racial and ethic groups. But it was only empowered to "hold public hearings . . . and make public its findings." For enforcement, it had to turn to other city departments. Even with willing allies like Clark and Dilworth, it was often hampered by statutory limitations. An early case involving an allegation that a hospital had a blanket ban on black technicians petered out because the hospital was a charitable entity and thus exempt from the applicable statute. Other promising cases went by the wayside for similar reasons.[25]

The commission's main weapon was a familiar one to lawyers like Sadie Alexander—it was the Myrdalian argument that discrimination went against the nation's core principles, and thus local businesses and neighborhood leaders ought to do the right thing. "As constituted under the Charter," its executive director noted reluctantly, "the Commission's primary powers are those of a moral and persuasive nature backed up by law." Within those limits, it often acted vigorously. It hired an administrative staff that investigated each complaint and, if valid, tried to resolve the issue through moral suasion. It negotiated with neighborhood leaders to get breakthrough black families into housing on white blocks, and even worked to calm tensions between a Jewish family and their Catholic neighbors. Legal enforcement actions, however, were few.[26]

By 1963, Sadie Alexander had risen to the chair of a human relations commission that now included younger luminaries such as Harvard law graduate Christopher Edley Sr. But that was not a good year to be a representative Negro in urban politics. Tensions rose sharply between black residents and local authorities in cities across the country, surprising even seasoned civil rights advocates. Looking out over Philadelphia that summer, Alexander told an expectant city that "[w]e are caught in a people's revolution." To her, it seemed as though initiative in race relations had shifted from the representatives to the people them-selves. That process had been set in motion, oddly enough, by Leon Sullivan—the pastor of her husband's church. Sullivan had come to Philadelphia in 1950 as minister of the historic Zion Baptist Church. Ten years after throwing himself into a variety of local civic improve-ment initiatives, Sullivan saw a city where both industry and white residents were leaving, and where many of the remaining jobs seemed out of reach to black residents because of explicit color bars. In re-sponse, Sullivan began a series of activities that would make him inter-nationally famous, and it all started with a critique of the local civil rights establishment that, unavoidably, amounted to a rebuke of Sadie Alexander.[27]

Leon Sullivan saw a city where moral suasion had little force and law was ineffective in remedying persistent racial inequality. By 1960, he had formed a group that called itself the Four Hundred Ministers, which launched boycott campaigns against selected local businesses, demand-ing that they promote and hire specific numbers of black workers into higher-level jobs. "There was never a formal organization," Sullivan later wrote; "[n]o minutes were kept and there was no treasurer, no elected leader"—an assertion that also appealed to the ministers' fear of legal liability. Sullivan claimed that the Selective Patronage campaigns represented the shadowy, dispersed power of hundreds of thousands of black consumers who took things into their own hands when the race leadership failed at its appointed task.[28]

For their first campaign, Sullivan and his colleagues organized a boycott of the Tasty Baking Company, a local manufacturer still re-membered fondly by young Pennsylvanians of that era for its Tastykake sweet pastries. The human relations commission investigated the com-pany and concluded that there was no "intentional" discrimination at work in the company. The ministers disagreed, and within a few months selective patronage forced the popular company to hire several black workers into jobs previously held only by whites, and to take other ac-tions to integrate its workplace. Over the next year, the ministers used the legitimate threat of mass black consumer action to force company after company to hire and promote black workers into white-occupied jobs, including companies that the commission had investigated to no avail. Then, at the height of his influence, Sullivan turned away from the boycotts to begin the work that would make him famous—job-training programs for urban youth, and black-owned local business and residential development.[29]

Far more disturbing than Sullivan's growing influence was the emergence of a rival within the local black bar itself—the sharply dressed and confrontational Cecil B. Moore. The Temple University law graduate had set up shop as a criminal lawyer in 1954, and largely shared the liberals' agenda of desegregating the city's public institutions and its private workforce. Where Moore differed from his rivals was almost entirely in his style of group affiliation. In fact, he seemed to go out of his way to define his style in opposition to the man he displaced as the city's leading black criminal defense lawyer—Raymond Pace Alexander. Moore had a genius for antagonizing the kind of white professionals who had played a key role in the rise of lawyers like Alexander. Inside the courtroom, he quickly became legendary for insisting that everyone, from the police officers to the judges, was a racist, and for extreme dilatory tactics designed to wear down the prosecution. Local black lawyers like William Coleman and Leon Higginbotham remembered him as a man whose antics could get his client sentenced to twenty years in prison, "yet people think he's a great lawyer because he really gave that goddamn white judge hell." Others claimed that he was the most effective criminal defense lawyer in the city.[30]

Moore's move to the center of the city's racial politics began with a symbolic repudiation of Sadie and Raymond Alexander. In January of 1959, the city's black establishment celebrated yet another breakthrough when the governor appointed Raymond Alexander as the first black judge to sit on the Philadelphia Court of Common Pleas. The Alexanders soon moved out of the North Philadelphia home that they had occupied for decades and into a suburban-style house in the Mount Airy section of the city. The new owner of their old home at Seventeenth and Jefferson streets was none other than Cecil B. Moore. In the coming years, Moore would publicly deride Sadie Alexander and Christopher Edley as "part-time Negroes" who had little contact with the black residents of North Philadelphia. Moore also threw his lot in with a faction inside the local NAACP chapter that tried to oust its traditional professional leadership. For a while, the professionals held them off under the leadership of the younger and energetic A. Leon Higginbotham Jr. But in December of 1962, Moore finally claimed the presidency and converted an organization that had once negotiated with the city's liberals into an engine that could turn out masses of protesters for controversial demonstrations that its critics feared would turn violent.[31]

In 1963, the conflict over race leadership reached a new level as frustration mounted among local activists over the scarcity of black workers at unionized city construction sites. That year, Moore threw up an NAACP picket line around a school construction site and shut it down, after Raymond Alexander had called the NAACP president's bombastic statements "an insult to the Negroes of this area." Curtis Carson, who got his start as a lawyer in Sadie Alexander's office, appeared on a local radio show to charge that his former mentor and her husband "do not represent the Negro people of Philadelphia."[32]

Carson's charges were soon taken up by the Four Hundred Ministers. In September, Raymond Alexander issued an open letter to the ministers, because of reports that they would shift their activism to the local schools. The common pleas judge called on them to hire "one or better two, highly trained and experienced men or women in the field of primary and secondary education" to study the problem before taking action. The Four Hundred quickly struck back with their own open letter, issued "so that the community might have the assurance that no one person has the power to shut the mouths of 400 Negro preachers." "The Honorable Judge," they continued, "speaks in [sic] behalf of the Negro cause and suggests methods used by the white cause." "The Negro has been studied enough," they concluded. It was time for action by the people themselves. For Sullivan himself, that action would soon shift to local community development, leaving it to Moore to demonstrate who really represented his race in Philadelphia.[33]

Moore provoked his last major confrontation with Raymond Alexander by taking on the cause that stood as Alexander's greatest loss as a civil rights lawyer—the desegregation of Girard College, a boarding school in North Philadelphia that educated only "poor male white orphans" by the terms of the bequest that had created it in the nineteenth century. In the mid-1950s, Alexander, with the support of the city council and the human relations commission, had taken a case against the Girard Trust, which was administered by the city, up to the United States Supreme Court before claiming a temporary victory. But on remand, the city's Orphans' Court reorganized the trust to eliminate city involvement in order to make Girard immune from Fourteenth Amendment claims—an action that was upheld in the appellate courts.[34]

Seven years later, Moore decided to revive the dispute. In the middle of 1965, he began leading confrontational daily rallies in front of the whites-only school, resulting in a continuous standoff with the local police. To defuse the stalemate, Governor William Scranton agreed to appoint lawyers acceptable to Moore to bring a new lawsuit in exchange for an end to the protests. After a complicated set of maneuvers, in 1968 the Third Circuit Court of Appeals finally affirmed a ruling that Girard's practices violated the Fourteenth Amendment, and the school announced that it would admit black pupils. At a "peace rally" at the college, Raymond Alexander returned to his old neighborhood and heard some boos when he spoke to the crowd, while Moore, uncharacteristically, urged unity with his rival. He could afford to be magnanimous. In 1960, Moore had been a somewhat marginal figure in a city that boasted the most prestigious group of black lawyers in the country, but now he was the kingmaker in local civil rights politics. He had done it all by raising a simple question of representation.[35]

While the Third Circuit finally resolved the Girard controversy, its lone black member, Judge William Hastie, sat out the escalating legal confrontations, secure in the role he had carved out for himself as the nation's representative black man in the judiciary. As a younger lawyer, he had come up with innovative theories inspired by the Legal Realist thinkers to defend black protesters who boycotted white-owned businesses that did not employ or promote African Americans. At the time, he and his fellow protesters defended their actions against criticism inside the NAACP by advocating for "intelligently controlled racialism" among Negroes. Three years after he took the bench, however, *Jet* magazine asked: "What happened to Hastie?" "Once rated No. 1 race crusader in the nation," the black weekly magazine's editors concluded, "today he is almost a forgotten man."[36]

As a judge, Hastie cultivated an image that made him almost indistinguishable from his white colleagues. In the early part of his judicial career, he rarely sat on a Third Circuit panel that heard a controversial race relations case. In the one notable case where he did, involving black taxi drivers who sued their union for race discrimination, the panel unanimously ruled against the black plaintiffs—even when existing Supreme Court precedent seemed to call for the opposite result and when, as a lawyer, he had seemed to endorse the opposing position. Three years later, the Fifth Circuit would cite Hastie by name in choosing to follow the approach of Hastie's panel and reject black unionized workers' claims.[37]

In the latter part of his career, Hastie let other judges write the opinions when the Third Circuit ruled in favor of minority civil rights claims. When Attorney General Robert F. Kennedy pushed for Hastie's nomination to the Supreme Court in early 1962, Chief Justice Earl Warren and Justice William O. Douglas opposed the move because they thought—perhaps mistakenly, it turns out—that Hastie was a judicial conservative. Kennedy's interest in Hastie prompted Assistant Attorney General Nicholas Katzenbach to review Hastie's opinions. Katzenbach recalled that afterward, he concluded that "the first black justice should be someone with whom blacks identified far more than they would with Hastie." Later in the decade, Hastie developed a keen interest in black nationalist radicals. During a speech at Temple University, when a student accused the judge of being an apologist for the establishment, Hastie interrupted him to correct the young man's obvious mistake. "I am not an apologist for the establishment," he replied. "I am the establishment." He was not speaking metaphorically.[38]

In the middle of the 1950s, Pauli Murray also found herself in an unaccustomed role as the symbolic representative of an oppressed group (two intersecting groups, in fact), although that would soon change. After struggling to establish herself as a lawyer, she had gotten a job at a prestigious New York law firm, Paul, Weiss, Rifkind, Wharton and Garrison. She was the only black lawyer at the firm and one of only a few women. Murray had also been engulfed in what Loren Miller and Sadie Alexander called a "miasma of fear" as they exchanged cautious letters about 1950s Cold War culture. Earlier in the decade, she had applied for a job at a law compilation project for Liberia that was sponsored by Cornell University. Wary university officials, however, had rejected her because of concerns about her past leftist connections. In response, she wrote a well-received book called *Proud Shoes: The Story of an American Family,* a history of her multiracial boundary-crossing forebears. Publicly, Murray claimed that *Proud Shoes* was motivated by her fear of being labeled a Communist. But since the time of her 1948 New York bar application, another fear always lurked beneath the surface. Murray worried intensely that a character investigation would show that in 1940, Rhode Island authorities had taken her into custody, disoriented and wearing what they described as men's clothes, and transferred her to the New York police, who committed her to Bellevue. When the job at Paul Weiss materialized, she jumped at the chance to get some well-deserved stability and kept uncharacteristically silent about her belief that the head of her practice group, Simon Rifkind, was prejudiced against women lawyers. "No crusade is in order," she wrote to her friend Caroline Ware, "just quiet outstanding work that comes to his attention."[39]

Behind Murray's comfortable position at the firm as the diligent representative of women—and to a lesser extent, black lawyers—lay the discontent with the constraints of group identity that had emerged in law school. It would soon come to the fore. She had rejoiced over the decision in *Brown v. Board of Education,* and published an effusive letter about it in the *New York Times,* but read the decision as the confirmation of the theory of discrimination that she had worked out at Howard. Murray also fired off a letter to her law school adviser, Leon Ransom, arguing that it was now time to revive the federal public accommodations law, the Civil Rights Act of 1875, and strike the "last big blow" against segregation, by attacking "private discrimination." "Private discrimination" meant something very specific to Murray. It was the core of the idea she had broached in her law school thesis—that discrimination was wrong because it made personal appearance into racial identity. She was also reviving another idea that she had developed there. In 1958, she renewed her sometimes friendly, sometimes wary relationship with Roy Wilkins, who had now risen to executive secretary at the NAACP. Murray struck a nerve with Wilkins by writing a letter about a newspaper article that had suggested that the respected civil rights group had lost its mass appeal. Wilkins took the time to pen a six-page detailed reply defending his program. But Murray felt justified in her own friendly criticism. "My trademark is my independence and emphasis on the individual" she told the NAACP's chief executive, arguing that racial unity was no reason for silence. As she stated in a letter to a segregationist southern politician, she wanted people to relate to her as "one Negro stripped of his label, and see him merely as a human being."[40]

At a time when black lawyers of her age were often relegated to the sidelines of the equality debates of the 1960s, Murray was moving toward the center. She did it, of course, in an unconventional way. By that time, group unity and nationalism were becoming an important basis for civil rights politics, but Murray was moving in the other direction.

It began, appropriately enough, in Africa. After several years of diligent work at Paul Weiss, Murray decided that corporate law was not for her and answered an advertisement for an experienced lawyer to teach constitutional law in newly independent Ghana. In February of 1960, Murray set sail for Africa, joining the exodus of black American expatriates who found something attractive about Ghanaian leader Kwame Nkrumah's experiment in African nationhood. She sailed into Monrovia harbor, her first stop in Africa, full of hope, but found instead a city with an "air of neglect over buildings like the Post Office." In Ghana, things seemed better, but it was still a disorienting experience. She had come to teach constitutional law at the behest of a government that she believed was becoming more and more lawless. A side trip to Leopoldville to render aid to South African foes of apartheid left her relieved at the familiar climate and architecture but appalled at the segregation. Another side trip to Europe made her feel at home among "pink faces and Western clothing." She took to signing her increasingly depressed diary entries "An American in Ghana" and composed an unpublished article on her experiences entitled "A Question of Identity." Murray's Ghanaian sojourn has been criticized as an exercise in Cold War conformity to American foreign policy objectives, but in reality something else was at work. She stated publicly, based on her experience in Ghana, that Africans had good reason to be skeptical of American foreign policy, and Murray would soon disappoint her Cold War liberal friends on the subject of Vietnam. What was happening was a fissuring and fracturing of identity that had been in the works since the 1950s, and it would continue when Murray arrived home in the summer of 1961.[41]

Back in the United States, Murray obtained a fellowship to pursue a doctorate in law at Yale, where she wrote a dissertation on the "Roots of the Racial Crisis," but she was soon distracted by other concerns. In 1962, friends invited her to serve on a subcommittee of President Kennedy's blue-ribbon President's Commission on the Status of Women. Murray's subcommittee asked her to draft a memorandum on legal strategies for achieving equality, which placed her in the middle of an intense debate between two groups of activists, each of whom claimed to speak for the interests of women. One group wanted the commission to endorse the proposed Equal Rights Amendment (ERA), which its supporters believed would sweep away protective labor legislation that prescribed minimum wages, maximum hours, and other occupational limitations for women's work. The other group wanted to preserve protective labor laws. Murray drafted a memorandum that reached for common ground in the fractious debate. Working from ideas she had been ruminating since the 1940s, Murray proposed that the commission de-emphasize the ERA and instead endorse a litigation approach modeled on the NAACP's Fourteenth Amendment strategy, which would allow different groups of women to be treated differently. The commission's final report drew on Murray's approach to the problem and quoted extensively from her memorandum. As the decade wore on, her position would gradually bridge the divide between the two groups of advocates.[42]

Murray played much the same role when civil rights groups and some women's advocates were at loggerheads over a proposed amendment to the draft Title VII of the 1964 Civil Rights Act, which would add sex discrimination to the bill. At the behest of friends, Murray wrote a memorandum that was sent to every member of Congress, arguing that that the word "sex" should stay in the statute, because it protected the interest of "Negro women" who had been left out of the debate. Once again, Murray was a key player in resolving a debate between advocates who saw themselves as speaking for cohesive groups. By now, she was moving toward the position that she would assert in a 1965 law review article that she coauthored with Mary Eastwood—that race and sex discrimination were objectionable because they both violated what she was beginning to call "human rights"—the right of the individual to be free of constraints that kept her from full participation in society. It was derived from the decidedly autobiographical theory that she had worked out in her law school thesis. By the late 1960s she seemed to be pushing it everywhere, from the ACLU, where she helped draft the brief in the influential Fifth Circuit decision in *White v. Crook*, which invalidated the exclusion of women from juries in Alabama, to the National Organization for Women, which she cofounded. By then her once-controversial approach to sex discrimination, if not the theory behind it, was becoming mainstream. When Ruth Bader Ginsburg finally persuaded the Supreme Court to elevate sex discrimination to a constitutional claim, she would place Murray's name on the brief as a progenitor of her ideas.[43]

In racial politics, too, Murray seemed to slip between emerging categories of sixties-era group affiliation. Roy Wilkins, for one, was coming to see her as an unusual kind of pest. At a time when Wilkins faced a challenge from a group of self-proclaimed "Young Turks" who wanted the interracial organization to stress group loyalty among blacks, Murray pushed from the opposite direction. She produced a steady stream of open letters, speeches, and opinion pieces on current racial politics that, at one point, led Wilkins to recommend that the NAACP's leadership issue some form of public rebuke to her. In 1963, she ratcheted up the debate by publicly criticizing the March on Washington for excluding women from its leadership positions, earning a standing ovation with a speech to the National Council of Negro Women on the issue. When march organizer A. Philip Randolph agreed to speak at the National Press Club, where women were forced to sit in the balcony, Murray wrote yet another public letter noting that "[s]urely Mr. Randolph is aware" that both race and sex segregation "are equally insulting and do violence to the human spirit." By the end of the decade, she seemed to be constantly at cross-purposes with advocates of group politics. A position as an administrator at Benedict College, a black institution in South Carolina, proved to be short-lived after she alienated many of her fellow staffers. A faculty position at Brandeis came next, now that she was in possession of a Yale J.S.D. But that brought her into conflict with black nationalist students who now saw her as a representative of white values, not black ones. At the ACLU and in NOW, she was increasingly embittered at being marginalized by younger, radical feminists who "have caused me to begin to reassess my entire relationship to the women's movement."[44]

By now, she was forming a consistent story about her ongoing difficulty fitting herself inside group-based advocacy. Writing of her troubles at Brandeis, she noted that "this challenge has in it elements of Ghana, Benedict, Yale, Howard and even Harvard." By this time, she was reluctantly concluding that "to the degree that I am 'unique' I seldom fit into accepted modes of thinking and patterns of operation." Although Murray would make headlines one last time when she left Brandeis for the seminary and became one of the nation's first ordained women Episcopal priests, she now thought that she would end her life on the margins of civil rights politics when she rightly belonged in the center. "Whatever have been the sensitivities that have kept me in obscurity are obviously part of my nature," she wrote. From the perspective of civil rights politics, circa 1970, that was true. It would be another generation before Murray's unusual sexual identity, her iconoclastic perspective on group identity, and her dissenting civil rights politics, would appeal to twenty-first-century Americans and become relevant to their own lives. History had finally caught up with her. By then, however, Murray had passed from the scene. She exited this world in 1985, leaving behind younger women she had influenced, such as Eleanor Holmes Norton and Marian Wright Edelman, as well as an autobiography that veiled the deep personal conflicts that were the source of her profoundly influential ideas.[45]

A New Frontier for Representation

In January of 1961, President John F. Kennedy reviewed a Coast Guard Academy honor guard during his inaugural parade and saw something that led him to open a new chapter in the story of racial representation. "There wasn't a black face in the entire group," he told his young staffer Richard Goodwin afterward. "That's not acceptable." In response, Kennedy's aides began to assemble lists of hundreds of educated African Americans who were qualified for appointment to higher-level federal posts, which inevitably included a number of well-placed lawyers. Earl Dickerson initially seemed to be in line for a post in the Commerce Department, but that was apparently scuttled by Dawson's opposition and Dickerson's own controversial past. Washington's Frank Reeves, the former NAACP and FEPC staffer, had campaigned hard for Kennedy, and moved into a short-lived position as special assistant to the president before resigning amid accusations of questionable financial dealings. More successful were San Francisco lawyer Cecil Poole, who became the U.S. attorney for the Northern District of California, and Detroit lawyer Wade McCree Jr., who became a federal judge and later solicitor general of the United States, as well as a less experienced group of lawyers whom the Kennedys gave their start in public life. Among them were Ohio lawyer Roger Wilkins, Roy's nephew, who was working in low-level private practice when he was surprised by an invitation to come work at the U.S. Agency for International Development before becoming assistant attorney general at age thirty-three. The following year, New York's Clifford Alexander Jr., almost as youthful, arrived in Washington for a job at the National Security Council before moving to the White House staff and eventually to the chairmanship of the Equal Employment Opportunity Commission. He would eventually become secretary of the army in the Carter administration.[46]

During Kennedy's first year in office, a bright, young Massachusetts lawyer named John Garrett Penn simply walked into the Justice
Department building, looking for work, and wound up interviewing with
a deputy assistant attorney general. After a heated argument over his
qualifications, he was offered a position in the Tax Division, and rose to
become a federal judge. That same year, Howard law graduate Walter
Washington was toiling away at the National Capital Housing Authority
when Robert Kennedy dropped in unannounced to tell him that "my
brother wants to know if you'd be interested in serving as the executive
director of this outfit." A surprised Washington said yes, and his new
position eventually placed him in line to become the first black mayor
of the District of Columbia. In 1962, Leon Higginbotham, still fending
off Cecil Moore's faction inside the Philadelphia NAACP, received an
appointment to the Federal Trade Commission and later became a federal judge, incidentally clearing the path for Moore to rise to the top in
Philadelphia's civil rights politics. William Hastie should have been the
elder statesman among the new brand of Kennedy-era race leaders. By
the time a Supreme Court vacancy opened up, however, Hastie's style
of leadership seemed so anachronistic that Assistant Attorney General
Burke Marshall thought that Hastie, who had campaigned tirelessly for
Harry Truman in 1948, was a Republican.[47]

Thurgood Marshall would eventually assume the role that might
have been Hastie's, but only after a period of strife and turmoil. Marshall remained the most famous black lawyer in America, but a com-
plex reality lay hidden behind his public image as "Mr. Civil Rights." He
got the title honestly, as one of the chief field operatives of an NAACP
whose organizational base lay in its numerous chapters, particularly in
the South, where so many other avenues of protest were cut off. From
the time of his earliest cases in Maryland, Marshall played the joint role
of lawyer and community organizer in small towns and rural counties,
where his professional role gave him some protection from white reprisals. When Marshall became the NAACP's chief lawyer, he slipped into
a role that required one to log thousands of miles of often-dangerous
travel in a typical year, patiently nurturing local chapters, taking their
measure, and deciding which places were most likely to support a legal
challenge to segregation in the face of local repression. But things
changed markedly in the 1950s. He spent more and more time in the
NAACP's national office in New York as the appellate stages of the *Brown*

litigation began to consume his energy. After that historic victory, Marshall left even brief writing to subordinates.[48]

It was black support that made Marshall one of his race's chief bridgeheads to the white world, and African Americans took great pride in his new prominence. But Marshall's relationship to his rank-and-file constituency was changing. He was now increasingly in demand as a fund-raiser in an era when the NAACP desperately needed support from well-heeled white contributors to ward off attacks by southern politicians and defend the victory in *Brown*. During one period in 1956, he received an invitation for a fund-raising banquet in St. Paul, collected an honorary degree from the New School for Social Research, and was showered with additional honors by everyone from a black war veterans' group to civil liberties organizations. In addition, he remarried in December 1955 after the death of his first wife. Marshall would soon have two young sons, and had earned a well-deserved break from life on the road. When the Montgomery bus boycott began to gather steam during that month, Marshall was about to leave for his honeymoon, and he soon departed. It was his assistant, Robert Carter, who would coordinate with Alabama lawyer Fred Gray on the initial strategic decisions that would help a previously unknown twenty-six-year-old minister named Martin Luther King Jr. to eventually declare victory over the local authorities.[49]

In the middle of the year-long bus boycott, when King arrived as a hero at the NAACP's 1956 convention, reporters quoted Marshall as dismissing him as a "boy on a man's errand." Decades later, Marshall would grudgingly concede King's oratorical gifts, but still refused to admit his importance in territory that Marshall had once claimed for his own. "As an organizer, he [King] wasn't worth diddley-squat," he opined. With the *Brown* victory in hand, Marshall appeared on the cover of *Time* magazine and was the NAACP's ambassador to the public at large. He now moved in rarefied circles. He could sense younger, more mass-based activists gaining on him, and he didn't like it.[50]

Just as disquieting was the presence of a rival within the NAACP's national office. Howard law graduate Robert Carter had played the role of the diligent number two on the NAACP's legal staff after Marshall hired him in the mid-1940s, all the way through the victory in *Brown*, but now the relationship between the men was fraying. Darker skinned, less polished, and more brusque than Marshall, Carter was endowed

with fewer of the qualities that made his mentor such an effective con-
duit to a professional world controlled by whites. Inside the changing
world of black politics, however, it was a different matter. By the mid-
1950s, the two men sometimes disagreed, with Carter more attuned to
the mood of impatient younger African Americans, and Marshall more
distant, as their fellow NAACP lawyers would later recall. When a segregationist Alabama judge ordered the NAACP to turn its membership
lists over to state authorities in 1956, Marshall wanted to comply. Carter,
however, vowed to defy the order. The NAACP board backed Carter, and
the Supreme Court eventually validated Carter's position when it decided the issue.[51]

By then, Marshall had already moved to separate himself from his
former protégé. Formally, the NAACP's legal staff actually consisted of
two separate entities—the NAACP itself, and the tax-exempt NAACP
Legal Defense and Educational Fund Inc. (the LDF). In response to an
Internal Revenue Service probe, in 1956 Marshall took steps to ensure
that the two organizations would have separate boards and legal staffs. He
made Carter general counsel of the NAACP, while he himself remained
head of the LDF. The move also allowed Marshall to become more independent from the NAACP and its constituency. Nonetheless, many
NAACP insiders were surprised when Marshall eventually selected one of
his white assistants, Jack Greenberg, rather than Carter, to succeed him
as chief lawyer for the LDF. The relationship between the three lawyers
would be forever altered by their contrasting interpretations of that
fateful decision.[52]

Carter was also more race conscious than his former mentor, and
assembled an interracial cast of young, sometimes radical lawyers who
pushed a series of groundbreaking cases challenging school segregation
in the North rather than the South. In the mid-1960s, he shared the
views of the nationalist Young Turks within the organization who
wanted to oust Roy Wilkins from its leadership. Carter and his staff
were coming to believe that they were battling what he would later call
"white supremacy"—entrenched white racial attitudes that would simply not go away. He eventually resigned his post because of a dispute
with the NAACP board over an article by one of his subordinates, Lewis
Steel, which seemed to charge that the Supreme Court justices (including the Court's newest member, Thurgood Marshall) were simply "nine
men in black who think white." Carter would go on to cofound the

National Conference of Black Lawyers, which saw itself as the legal ad-junct to the emerging black nationalist movements of the late 1960s. He himself became a federal judge, appointed by President Nixon to the Dis-trict Court in Manhattan in 1972. Thirty-four years later, Carter would earn a stinging rebuke in the pages of the liberal *New Republic* when he published an autobiography asserting his nationalist position that the NAACP/LDF's legal campaign was—and should have remained—a black-led enterprise. When Marshall commented, in the aftermath of the 1960 sit-in movement, that "the kids are serving notice on us that we're mov-ing too slow," he could see the potential for a contrary example in his own former protégé.[53]

When Robert Kennedy began to consider Marshall for an appoint-ment to the federal judiciary, Marshall made a show of being noncom-mittal, but in reality he needed the liberal Washington establishment as much as it needed him. In the early years of his administration, John Kennedy had established a civil rights record that caused even his sympathetic historian, Arthur Schlesinger Jr., to confess ambivalence in the privacy of his diary, if not in his subsequent history of Kennedy's administration. Kennedy was personally committed to civil rights and had made unprecedented progress in his black appointments, but the black voters who had helped elect him wanted to see more. For his part, Marshall was living in New York and unsure of his next move. He had been talked about as a candidate for political office in the increas-ingly black electoral wards in the city, but Marshall decided—rightly enough—that this was not a good path for him. A federal judgeship might have been his a decade earlier if he had been willing to cooperate with the local black Democratic machine, but this, too, did not suit his style. In 1961, Carter was now being talked about as a rival for the seat on the federal bench in New York. The Kennedys offered another route, al-though Marshall made it clear that he would only accept an appoint-ment to the more prestigious Second Circuit Court of Appeals rather than the District Court. When Marshall was finally confirmed as a judge after an initial recess appointment in 1961, he gained a lifetime appointment that meshed with his family responsibilities, and removed himself from an increasingly fractious world of civil rights movement politics.[54]

Marshall's new post made him a symbolically attractive figure for successive Democratic presidents. As early as 1962, Robert Kennedy had come to believe that putting a black justice on the Supreme Court would burnish the administration's flagging civil rights credentials like nothing else, domestically and around the world. President Johnson saw it too, and persuaded Marshall to leave the appellate court for the job of solicitor general in 1965, then engineered the resignation of Justice Tom Clark so he could name Marshall to the Supreme Court in 1967. Musing to Doris Kearns, Johnson confessed that Marshall's nomination was one of his last chances to do something for African Americans who had made so much effort to "register and vote for the people who'd do a good job for them" but continued to be frustrated by barriers to equality. What Johnson saw in the waning years of his presidency was that appointing a black justice would change the nature of the Court from an institution where blacks had been "Petitioners"—as Loren Miller titled his 1966 history of blacks and the Court—to one where they had political representation. For Marshall's part, he was now even more insulated from the black politics that he had negotiated and sometimes sidestepped for over a decade. But in spite of this, indeed because of it, questions of representativeness became all the more pressing for the nation's first black Supreme Court Justice.[55]

After a period of adjustment, Marshall settled comfortably into the new role. In a 1973 case where the Court upheld the requirement of a fifty-dollar fee for a bankruptcy filing, for instance, Marshall invoked his unique experience in a heartfelt dissent. He reminded his colleagues that "no one who has had close contact with poor people can fail to understand how close to the margin of survival many of them are." More significant was his draft opinion in *Regents of the University of California v. Bakke,* where he observed, acidly, that the Court had never had a black "Officer of the Court" and only had "three Negro law clerks." His biographer Mark Tushnet credits the draft, after it was reshaped a bit, with convincing Harry Blackmun to join the justices who voted to uphold some forms of affirmative action. One of Marshall's last acts as a justice was to ask a lawyer who was arguing a search and seizure case, "Was the defendant in this case by any chance a Negro?" producing an embarrassed answer in the affirmative. Within the Court's deliberations, Marshall's stories of his experiences as a black man who had grown up under Jim Crow were one of the things that his colleagues remembered most about him. It was not self-evident that a black justice should act this way. Indeed, Marshall's judicial persona was a deliberate rejection of the one pioneered by William Hastie, who began his judicial career in one period of racial politics and was unfortunate enough to end it in a quite different era.[56]

By the time that Clarence Thomas succeeded Marshall as the lone black member of the Supreme Court, the role that Marshall had pioneered had become so well worn that the new black justice found it impossible to escape, despite the popular perception that he had set himself against claims of racial loyalty. He made it clear that he shared his predecessor's view that a significant part of his role was to speak for those whom the politics of race have marginalized within the Court. Although an ardent critic of race-based government practices, Thomas, for instance, took the time to write separately in a ruling on school desegregation early in his tenure. Lauding state-sponsored historically black colleges as representing "the highest attainments of black culture," he made clear his caution about a ruling that would endanger them. In the context of pre-college education, too, Thomas has gone on record to distinguish himself from his conservative allies in emphasizing that black schools "can function as the symbol and center of black communities." More than any other justice in the Court's history, including Marshall, Thomas makes a point to cite black writers such as Frederick Douglass and W. E. B. Du Bois to ensure that their thoughts are made part of the record of the Court's deliberations. As scholars such as Randall Kennedy and Angela Onwuachi-Willig have argued, Justice Thomas undoubtedly views himself as a "race man" on the Court, to put it in terms that Marshall himself would have understood, although there are evident reasons to criticize the uses to which Thomas has put that racial politics.[57]

When Sonia Sotomayor was nominated for a Supreme Court seat that would make her the Court's first Puerto Rican justice, it seemed inevitable that the main questions that would swirl around her nomination centered on whom she would represent in the complicated racial politics of judging. It was a question that grew out of the paradox of group identity for lawyers in a racially stratified society. It was a question that had been around at least since John Mercer Langston had to decide which race he belonged to before he could become a lawyer. It was asked of Charles Houston and Thurgood Marshall as they rose to prominence in American life. And it had inspired many to seek out clear and definite answers. Harvard law professor Derrick Bell would ask it of the NAACP's school desegregation cases, and would use the answer to work his way toward the beginnings of a new jurisprudential theory known as Critical Race Theory.[58] It would continue to dog the footsteps of the nation's first successful black presidential candidate, whose success in politics was premised on his ability to appeal to whites and at the same time lodge himself in a civil rights narrative that his own ancestors had never experienced. It was a question without an answer, as Marshall of all people understood better than most. But that, of course, would not stop Americans from continuing, as they always had done, in their quest to find one.

Conclusion: Race and Representation in a New Century

ON AN unusually warm night in early November 2008, an immense, wildly enthusiastic crowd gathered in Chicago's Grant Park to watch the acceptance speech of an African American former civil rights lawyer who had just been elected president of the United States. Some acknowledgment of history seemed to be required, and the president-elect kept the expected references to civil rights history, like his tone, measured to capture the significance of the moment. Barack Obama had first drawn national media notice in 1990, when he was elected as the first black person to head the prestigious *Harvard Law Review*—the same institution that had helped launch Charles Houston's career seven decades before, when Houston became its first black editor. In his election-night speech, Obama kept most of the historical references indirect, paraphrasing both Martin Luther King Jr. and Abraham Lincoln before finally invoking the story of a 106-year-old black woman who could not vote early in her life but lived long enough to cast her ballot in a presidential election won by an African American. Rev. Jesse Jackson, the most serious black contender for the presidency before Obama, and a direct connection to civil rights history, stood in the audience, weeping. For the moment it seemed—at least to the flag-waving crowd in the park—that "America is a place where all things are possible," as the president-elect phrased it, a place where a black man could be the chief representative of a nation that practiced African slavery at its founding.

It is tempting to frame this story solely as the end point of a struggle begun by Houston and others for a world where citizenship rights would not be circumscribed by race. That struggle, of course, is an un-deniable part of the significance of that November evening, as Obama himself acknowledged to the cheers of the crowd. The president-elect stood on the shoulders of those Americans who had the courage to stand up, or sit down, to force their country to acknowledge that humanity had no racial bounds. He stood on the shoulders of those lawyers who had the courage to come to court not knowing whether that simple act would inspire violence or simple professional camaraderie, as Marshall knew so well. He also stood on the shoulders of judges and jurors who sometimes had the courage to risk their reputations in their local com-munities to acknowledge the justice of those claims. Since that election evening, Americans have argued themselves to a draw over the question of whether the 2008 presidential election was the end point of civil rights history, or perhaps just one more step on a longer journey. They have argued about whether the nation is now "post-racial" or not, and about the amount of racism that still exists, conscious or unconscious. They have argued about the persistence of gaps between racial groups in income, educational advancement, and health at a time when the boundaries and composition of those groups seem more fluid than ever. Important as these questions are, they are all matters that would have been familiar to late twentieth-century Americans.

Perhaps it is time to turn the page to a different story—particularly in an era when the civil rights movement lies more than a generation in the past. History, the story of the past, is inevitably written in the pres-ent. Our own present circumstances provide an opportunity to tell a story that has become familiar to many Americans—the story of the struggles of blacks and whites during the civil rights era—in an unfamiliar way. Protest, repression, struggle, acquiescence, agency, and powerlessness have long been familiar themes to Americans as they have worked to preserve the memory of the movement for racial equality and add depth and texture to the nation's knowledge of its past. These familiar themes appear in the story told in these pages, as they would in any ac-count of the nation's racial history, but they are not the main subjects of the narrative presented here. Instead, the story told here has focused on the divided minds of Americans, black and white, as they have strug-gled with the question of who exactly could represent a minority group in the give-and-take of American racial politics. That story has been told through the collective biography of a contentious and diverse group of African American civil rights lawyers.

Americans began to talk of the "representative colored man" in the middle of the nineteenth century, and they have continued to speak about that idea, in one form or another, up until the present time. It was an idea born of the deep ambivalence of both black and white Americans, as they wrestled with the question of whether African Americans were part of the diverse group of peoples united as one nation. Representatives were those black people who seemed to breathe hope into the notion that American citizenship could cross racial lines. They were those black people who had obtained enough education to become doctors, dentists, schoolteachers, ministers, and lawyers. Their very existence seemed to give lie to the claim that an entire race lacked the intellectual and emotional capacity to be full citizens. From the beginning, lawyers were a special case of racial representation. A successful black lawyer had to speak in the language that judges and jurors could understand, and until relatively recent times nearly all those judges and jurors were white. At the same time, the whole idea of representation was premised on the notion that the lawyers stood in for the rest of their race.

In the nineteenth century, no one seemed to personify the dilemma of representation better than John Mercer Langston. In Ohio, he was admitted to the bar as a white man. In Kentucky, Union soldiers worried about his racial identity. Throughout the postbellum South, the immaculately dressed, urbane lawyer sought to uplift former slaves by telling them that he was one of them. He had learned the subtleties of race as an up-and-coming lawyer in an Ohio township with no black residents, where he made a comfortable life for himself by convincing white Democrats that he could be their ablest representative in court, while at the same time working for civil and political rights for Ohio's free black population. After the Civil War, as he rose higher and higher in Republican politics and eventually represented his native Virginia in Congress, he would be dogged by a question that would be asked of civil rights lawyers for the next century—whether he was inauthentic. For some, Langston seemed to stand too far away from his black constituents as their civil rights began to erode. Langston was soon joined by the first generation of African Americans who struggled to get admitted to the bar and practice their trade in an era when people were not sure that an African American could be an equal citizen, much less an officer of the court.

In the twentieth century, the civil rights courtroom slowly etched itself into American memory as a place where worthy representatives of a unified minority group made claims on a society that often did not want to hear them. But, in a lesser-known story, that same courtroom also stood at the center of a debate over race and representation, as a generation of black lawyers came to court and demanded to be treated like white men—even if things were different just outside the court- house. At times the entire nation seemed to be watching, as when Charles Houston came to Loudoun County, Virginia, not knowing whether his or his client's life was in greater danger. At other times, the stage for the drama was a small community, as when a gangly, light-skinned, youth- ful lawyer named Thurgood Marshall showed up in rural Maryland communities that had never seen anyone like him before. Sometimes it was just a community of a few dozen, as Pauli Murray learned when she arrived at Howard Law School wanting to do what men do in a civil rights courtroom, and left with a theory of discrimination that still re- verberates through American culture.

Others asked a different question, and inevitably turned to the problem of authenticity. This was particularly true of a younger genera- tion of African Americans during the Great Depression who did what youth do everywhere—rebelled against their elders. No one did it with more aplomb than Loren Miller, and his conversion from reluctant law- yer to civil rights advocate would affect both civil rights law and history. As the classical phase of the civil rights era reached its zenith, a new set of race leaders came to the fore. They were integrationists, not separat- ists, and their cry was community control. Their emergence spelled the death of the classical civil rights lawyer as well, as the question of repre- sentation once again reasserted itself. Lawyers who only a few years be- fore had seemed like brave representatives of a repressed minority group now seemed inauthentic. But then a new group of black lawyers emerged, as the changing politics of Washington during the Kennedy-Johnson years once more put black lawyers into a context where no one had seen anyone like them before. The story of those years remains to be written.

What of civil rights lawyers and representation in the twenty-first century? Many lawyers have turned to the historic work of the NAACP, to search for new models for an old craft. Lawyers for other minority groups now model themselves on the work of the NAACP. Lawyers for conservative political groups do also. But the era when a minority civil rights lawyer could come to court and transfix an entire community now lies far in the past. Ambitious and socially conscious young people often dream of doing something else, as a young African American lawyer did when he passed up the opportunity to become a prominent civil rights attorney and went into Illinois politics instead. As he rose to the presidency, one could see questions of racial representativeness emerge again and again. As he sought to convince black and white primary voters that he was both familiar and new, the writer Debra Dickerson charged that he was not really black, since he was not descended from West African slaves.[1] During his time as president, activists and intellectuals have asked over and over again whether he has a "black agenda." Others pointed to his unusual background in asserting that he does not represent mainstream America.

These are old questions, asked in a new context. They might have been appropriate if Barack Obama had remained a representative of a mostly black constituency, as were most of the civil rights leaders and black politicians who preceded him. But somehow they seemed slightly off center, as Americans of all races, and people around the world, struggle to understand the past and present of a seemingly atypical black man who has come to public prominence. It is certainly too early to know for sure the questions to ask of race in a new century, and of the president who encapsulates the complexity of American racial politics in his own pedigree. But it is not too early to identify one enduring theme that has reasserted itself—the question of authenticity, asked of an African American who seems unlike those around him. That, too, is a question that Thurgood Marshall would have understood completely, for it encapsulates something seemingly unavoidable in the American politics of race.

Notes

Abbreviations

PEOPLE

CHH	Charles H. Houston
JML	John Mercer Langston
LM	Loren Miller
PM	Pauli Murray
RPA	Raymond Pace Alexander
STMA	Sadie T. M. Alexander
TM	Thurgood Marshall

NEWSPAPERS

AN	*Amsterdam News* (New York)
BAA	*Afro-American* (Baltimore)
CD	*Chicago Defender*
LAS	*Los Angeles Sentinel*
LAT	*Los Angeles Times*
NJG	*Journal and Guide* (Norfolk)
NYT	*New York Times*
PC	*Pittsburgh Courier*
PT	*Philadelphia Tribune*
WP	*Washington Post*

ARCHIVAL COLLECTIONS

AMDP	A. Mercer Daniel Papers. Moorland-Spingarn Research Center. Howard University.
BDPH	Benjamin Davis Collection. Harvard Law School.
BvBPY	Brown v. Board of Education Collection. Sterling Memorial Library. Yale University.

CHHP	Charles H. Houston Papers. Moorland-Spingarn Research Center. Howard University.
DNP	Dallas Nicholas Papers. University of Maryland Law School.
EBDP	Earl B. Dickerson Papers. Chicago Historical Society.
ESSP	Edith Spurlock Sampson Papers. Schlesinger Library, Radcliffe Institute for Advanced Study. Harvard University.
HUA	Howard University Archives. Moorland-Spingarn Research Center. Howard University.
JGTP	James Guy Tyson Papers. Moorland-Spingarn Research Center. Howard University.
JMBP	Jane Matilda Bolin Papers. Schomburg Center for Research in Black Culture. New York, N.Y.
JMLP	John Mercer Langston Papers. Franklin Library. Fisk University. Nashville, Tenn.
LARP	Leon A. Ransom Papers. Moorland-Spingarn Research Center. Howard University.
LMP	Loren Miller Papers. Huntington Library. San Marino, Calif. (original box numbers, not accessioned)
LSRMP	Laura Spelman Rockefeller Memorial Papers. Rockefeller Archive Center. Sleepy Hollow, N.Y. (by series, box and folder, e.g., S3.8-B101-F1019)
NAACPP	Papers of the NAACP. Manuscript Division, Library of Congress. Washington, D.C. (by volume, series and box, e.g., Vol2-SerL-B253)
NAACPPmf	Papers of the NAACP (microfilm edition). Frederick, Md.: University Publications of America, 1988.
NARA	National Archives and Records Administration. College Park, Md.
PMP	Pauli Murray Papers. Schlesinger Library, Radcliffe Institute for Advanced Study. Harvard University.
RHTP	Robert Heberton Terrell Papers (microfilm edition). Manuscript Division, Library of Congress. Washington, D.C.
RPAP	Raymond Pace Alexander Papers. University of Pennsylvania Archives and Records Center. Philadelphia.
RPP	Roscoe Pound Papers. Harvard Law School.
STMAP	Sadie Tanner Mossell Alexander Papers. University of Pennsylvania Archives and Records Center. Philadelphia.
WLHFP	William LePre Houston Family Papers. Manuscript Division, Library of Congress. Washington, D.C.

Introduction

1. Thurgood Marshall, "The Reminiscences of Thurgood Marshall," in Mark V. Tushnet, ed., *Thurgood Marshall: His Speeches, Writings, Arguments, Opinions, and Reminiscences* (Chicago: Lawrence Hill Books, 2001), 416, 418; Brett Zongker, "Marshall's Legacy Takes Center Stage," Associated Press, 6/8/2010, http://www.ap.org/.

2. *Baltimore Sun*, 8/29/1995. For assertions that the University of Maryland rejected Marshall, see Howard Ball, *A Defiant Life: Thurgood Marshall and the Persistence of Racism in America* (New York: Crown Publishers, 1998), 45; Randall Walton Bland, *Justice Thurgood Marshall: Crusader for Liberalism; His Judicial Biography* (Bethesda, Md.: Academica Press, 2001), 5; Carl T. Rowan, *Dream Makers, Dream Breakers: The World of Justice Thurgood Marshall* (Boston: Little, Brown, 1993), 45–46; Michael D. Davis and Hunter R. Clark, *Thurgood Marshall: Warrior at the Bar, Rebel on the Bench*, rev. ed. (New York: Citadel Press, 1994), 47. For assertions that Marshall did not apply, see Juan Williams, *Thurgood Marshall: American Revolutionary* (New York: Random House, 1998), 52–53; Rawn James Jr., *Root and Branch: Charles Hamilton Houston, Thurgood Marshall, and the Struggle to End Segregation* (New York: Bloomsbury Press, 2010), 16. Mark Tushnet declined to take sides. Marshall was sometimes cagey with interviewers on the subject but did confess to Richard Kluger that he never applied. Richard Kluger, Handwritten Notes of Interview with Thurgood Marshall, B4, BvBPY.

3. The classic work on the problem of experience is Joan W. Scott, "The Evidence of Experience," *Critical Inquiry* 17 (1991): 773–797.

4. C. Vann Woodward, *The Strange Career of Jim Crow*, 3rd rev. ed. (New York: Oxford University Press, 1974).

5. Eric Foner, *Reconstruction: America's Unfinished Revolution, 1863–1877* (New York: Harper & Row, 1988), 611–612.

6. David A. Hollinger, "Cultural Pluralism and Multiculturalism," in Richard Wrightman Fox and James T. Kloppenberg, eds., *A Companion to American Thought* (Cambridge, MA: Blackwell, 1995), 162.

7. It has become common to accuse the NAACP's mostly black legal team of ignoring the desires of local black communities in their push for desegregation. See, for example, Charles M. Payne, " 'The Whole United States Is Southern!' *Brown v. Board* and the Mystification of Race," *Journal of American History* 91 (2004): 83, 90. For thoughtful rejoinders, see Patricia Sullivan, *Lift Every Voice: The NAACP and the Making of the Civil Rights Movement* (New York: New Press, 2009), 211–216, 404–405; Mark V. Tushnet, *The NAACP's Legal Strategy against Segregated Education, 1925–1950* (Chapel Hill: University of North Carolina Press, 1987), 146–158.

8. Actually, the story is even more complicated than this. Not only were Americans confused about whether the representative Negro was supposed to

be "authentically" black; they were even confused as to what they meant by "representation." Representation might mean any one of several things. The central idea might be that (1) the representative is authorized by the minority group to advocate for its interests, (2) the representative resembles the larger group, (3) the representative symbolically stands in for the larger group, or (4) the representative speaks for the larger group. All these meanings shade into one another, and it is impossible to maintain a clear distinction between them. This is what Hanna Pitkin's famous work on the subject shows, as Martha Minow points out in an insightful essay. Martha Minow, "From Class Actions to 'Miss Saigon': The Concept of Representation in the Law," in Susan Sage Heinzelman and Zipporah Batshaw Wiseman, eds., *Representing Women: Law, Literature, and Feminism* (Durham, N.C.: Duke University Press, 1994), 8–43.

9. United States v. Carolene Products, 304 U.S. 144, 152 n. 4 (1938).

10. The analysis here is indebted to Dylan C. Penningroth, "The Claims of Slaves and Ex-Slaves to Family and Property: A Transatlantic Comparison," *American Historical Review* 112 (2007): 1039, 1041–1045; and Walter Johnson, "On Agency," *Journal of Social History* 37 (2003): 113–124.

11. See, for example, Derrick A. Bell Jr., "Serving Two Masters: Integration Ideals and Client Interests in School Desegregation Litigation," *Yale Law Journal* 85 (1976): 470–516; Lani Guinier, "From Racial Liberalism to Racial Literacy: *Brown v. Board of Education* and the Interest-Divergence Dilemma," *Journal of American History* 91 (2004): 92, 97; Adam Fairclough, "The Costs of *Brown*: Black Teachers and School Integration," *Journal of American History* 91 (2004): 43, 43–44, and nn. 1–2 (collecting examples of the genre); Robert Rodgers Korstad, *Civil Rights Unionism: Tobacco Workers and the Struggle for Democracy in the Mid-Twentieth-Century South* (Chapel Hill: University of North Carolina Press, 2003); Glenda Elizabeth Gilmore, *Defying Dixie: The Radical Roots of Civil Rights, 1919–1950* (New York: W. W. Norton, 2008); Kevin Boyle, "Labour, the Left and the Long Civil Rights Movement," *Social History* 30 (2005): 366–372 (collecting examples of the genre); Penny M. Von Eschen, *Race against Empire: Black Americans and Anticolonialism, 1937–1957* (Ithaca, N.Y.: Cornell University Press, 1997); Risa L. Goluboff, *The Lost Promise of Civil Rights* (Cambridge, Mass.: Harvard University Press, 2007).

12. See, for example, Charles M. Payne, *I've Got the Light of Freedom: The Organizing Tradition and the Mississippi Freedom Struggle* (Berkeley and Los Angeles: University of California Press, 1995); John Dittmer, *Local People: The Struggle for Civil Rights in Mississippi* (Urbana: University of Illinois Press, 1994); Jacquelyn Dowd Hall, "The Long Civil Rights Movement and the Political Uses of the Past," *Journal of American History* 91 (2005): 1233, 1239–1250. By contrast, newer work that explores the civil rights movement outside the South has often organized itself around themes other than authenticity. For example, Thomas J. Sugrue, *Sweet Land of Liberty: The Forgotten Struggle for Civil Rights in*

the *North* (New York: Random House, 2008); Nancy MacLean, *Freedom Is Not Enough: The Opening of the American Workplace* (Cambridge, Mass.: Harvard University Press, 2006); Matthew J. Countryman, *Up South: Civil Rights and Black Power in Philadelphia* (Philadelphia: University of Pennsylvania Press, 2006); Robert O. Self, *American Babylon: Race and the Struggle for Postwar Oakland* (Princeton, N.J.: Princeton University Press, 2003); Jeanne Theoharis and Komozi Woodard, eds., *Freedom North: Black Freedom Struggles outside the South, 1940–1980* (New York: Palgrave Macmillan, 2003).

13. Daniel J. Sharfstein, "Crossing the Color Line: Racial Migration and the One-Drop Rule, 1600–1860," *Minnesota Law Review* 91 (2004): 592, 603, quoting W. E. B. Du Bois, *Dusk of Dawn: An Essay toward an Autobiography of a Race Concept* (New Brunswick, N.J.: Transaction Books, 1992), 153.

14. See, for example, Isabel Wilkerson, *The Warmth of Other Suns: The Epic Story of America's Great Migration* (New York: Random House, 2010).

15. RPA, "The Negro Lawyer" [c. 1947], 7, 14, B96-FF44, RPAP.

16. For a summary of the trend, see Mark Brilliant, *The Color of America Has Changed: How Racial Diversity Shaped Civil Rights Reform in California, 1941–1978* (New York: Oxford University Press, 2010), 13–14, nn. 46–52.

17. For a recent example, see the contrasting efforts of the Supreme Court justices to mobilize civil rights history in *Parents Involved in Community Schools v. Seattle School District No. 1,* 551 U.S. 701 (2007).

1. The Idea of the Representative Negro

1. RPA, The Significance from a Standpoint of Reflecting Racial Adjustment of 3 Major Cases Now in Litigation in the American Law Courts in Which the Negro Plays a Material Part (1925), pp. 1, 16–17, 17–18, 18, 19 (emphasis in original), B95-F15, RPAP.

2. RPA, A Challenge to North Philadelphia Men, pp. 5–8 (1926), B95-F17, RPAP.

3. *WP,* 6/7/2008; John Mercer Langston, *From the Virginia Plantation to the National Capitol* (New York: Kraus Reprint, 1969); JML to Frederick Douglass, 4/16/1855, in C. Peter Ripley and Jeffrey S. Rossbach et al., eds., *The Black Abolitionist Papers,* vol. 4 (Chapel Hill: University of North Carolina Press, 1991), 281.

4. Langston, *From the Virginia Plantation,* 11–36; Arnold Rampersad, *The Life of Langston Hughes,* vol. 1, *I, Too, Sing America* (New York: Oxford University Press, 1986), 6–9; Stephen Middleton, *The Black Laws: Race and the Legal Process in Early Ohio* (Athens: Ohio University Press, 2005), 42–55, 243–244.

5. Lane v. Baker, 12 Ohio 237 (1843); William Cheek and Aimee Lee Cheek, *John Mercer Langston and the Fight for Black Freedom, 1829–1865* (Urbana: University of Illinois Press, 1989), 131.

6. Langston, *From the Virginia Plantation*, 125.

7. Paul Finkelman, "Prelude to the Fourteenth Amendment: Black Legal Rights in the Antebellum North," *Rutgers Law Journal* 17 (1986): 415–482; Davison M. Douglas, *Jim Crow Moves North: The Battle over Northern School Segregation, 1865–1954* (New York: Cambridge University Press, 2005), 12–60.

8. Catherine M. Hanchett, "George Boyer Vashon, 1824–1878: Black Educator, Poet, Fighter for Equal Rights, Part One," *Western Pennsylvania History* 68 (1985): 205, 208; Charles Sumner Brown, "The Genesis of the Negro Lawyer in New England: Part I," *Negro History Bulletin* 22 (April 1959): 147, 148; Kevin M. Burke, "Avenging *Dred Scott:* Chief Justice Roger Taney, John Rock and the War to Redefine a Nation" (unpublished paper, in author's possession); George A. Levesque, "Boston's Black Brahmin: Dr. John S. Rock," *Civil War History* 26 (1980): 326, 334.

9. *Minutes and Address of the State Convention of the Colored Citizens of Ohio, Convened at Columbus, January 10th, 11th, 12th, and 13th, 1849* (Oberlin, Ohio: J. M. Fitch's Power Press, 1849), 8; Cheek and Cheek, *John Mercer Langston*, 114, 232.

10. Hanchett, "George Boyer Vashon," 212 (emphasis in original); J. Harlan Buzby, *John Stewart Rock: Teacher, Healer, Counselor* (Salem, N.J.: Salem County Historical Society, 2002), 51, 111; Roberts v. City of Boston, 59 Mass. 198 (1849); James Oliver Horton and Lois E. Horton, *Black Bostonians: Family Life and Community Struggle in the Antebellum North* (New York: Holmes & Meier, 1999), 60; Albert J. von Frank, *The Trials of Anthony Burns: Freedom and Slavery in Emerson's Boston* (Cambridge, Mass.: Harvard University Press, 1998), 42–43.

11. Horton and Horton, *Black Bostonians*, 60–61; Langston, *From the Virginia Plantation*, 126–131.

12. Langston, *From the Virginia Plantation*, 132.

13. *Ibid.*, 133–134.

14. Daniel J. Sharfstein, *The Invisible Line: Three American Families and the Secret Journey from Black to White* (New York: Penguin Press, 2011); Langston, *From the Virginia Plantation*, 139–143, 156–170.

15. Nell Irvin Painter, *Exodusters: Black Migration to Kansas after Reconstruction* (New York: W. W. Norton, 1992), 15, 16; Eric Foner, *The Fiery Trial: Abraham Lincoln and American Slavery* (New York: W. W. Norton, 2010), 256, 330–331. Nineteenth-century black Americans may have been influenced by Emerson's famous idea of representative men, although they quickly went beyond it. For prominent examples of the genre, see William Wells Brown, "Representative Men and Women of the Race," in his *The Rising Son* (Boston: A. G. Brown, 1874), 418–552; John Mercer Langston, "A Representative Woman—Mrs. Sara K. Fidler," *A.M.E. Church Review* 6 (July 1887): 461–475; and *The Negro Problem: A Series of Articles by Representative American Negroes of To-day* (1903; New York: Arno Press, 1969).

16. *New York Daily Tribune*, 2/7/1865, p. 8; Levesque, "Boston's Black Brahmin." A contemporary illustration shows Rock as dark-skinned with

wavy hair, and the 1850 census lists him as a "mulatto." The *Tribune* author may have gotten carried away in his description of Rock's hair. *Harper's Weekly,* February 25, 1865, p. 124; Free Inhabitants of the South Ward of the City of Camden, Seventh Census of the United States, 1850, M432, Schedule 445, NARA.

17. John Mercer Langston, *The World's Anti-Slavery Movement, Its Heroes and Its Triumphs: A Lecture Delivered at Xenia, O., Aug. 2, and Cleveland, O., Aug. 3, 1858* (Oberlin, Ohio: Shankland & Harmon, 1858), 6, 12 (emphasis in original); John Mercer Langston, "The Oberlin Wellington Rescue," *Anglo-African Magazine* 7, no. 1, July 1859, 209–216.

18. Foner, *Fiery Trial,* 252; Langston, *From the Virginia Plantation,* 198–217; "From the Anglo African," *Elevator,* May 12, 1865, *Black Abolitionist Papers* (online edition); John Mercer Langston, "Citizenship and the Ballot," in Langston, *Freedom and Citizenship* (Washington, D.C.: Rufus H. Darby, 1883), 110.

19. Bradwell v. State, 83 U.S. 130 (1872); John Oldfield, "The African American Bar in South Carolina, 1877–1915," in James Lowell Underwood and W. Lewis Burke Jr., eds., *At Freedom's Door: African American Founding Fathers and Lawyers in Reconstruction South Carolina* (Columbia: University of South Carolina Press, 2000), 116–129; Irvin C. Mollison, "Negro Lawyers in Mississippi," *Journal of Negro History* 15 (1930): 38, 41; Peggy Lamson, *The Glorious Failure: Black Congressman Robert Brown Elliott and the Reconstruction in South Carolina* (New York: W. W. Norton, 1973), 21–33; Hanchett, "George Boyer Vashon," 208.

20. Langston, *From the Virginia Plantation,* 224–230; "From the Anglo African," *Elevator,* May 12, 1865, *Black Abolitionist Papers* (online edition).

21. Cheek and Cheek, *John Mercer Langston,* 441; Langston, *From the Virginia Plantation,* 232–274; Langston, "Citizenship and the Ballot," 105, 110.

22. Kate Masur, *An Example for All the Land: Emancipation and the Struggle over Equality in Washington, D.C.* (Chapel Hill: University of North Carolina Press, 2010); William S. McFeely, *Frederick Douglass* (New York: W. W. Norton, 1991), 260; Painter, *Exodusters,* 28.

23. Maxwell H. Bloomfield, *American Lawyers in a Changing Society, 1776–1876* (Cambridge, Mass.: Harvard University Press, 1976); William Francis Cheek III, "Forgotten Prophet: The Life of John Mercer Langston" (Ph.D. diss., University of Virginia, 1961), 96–97 (emphasis removed); Walter Dyson, *Howard University: The Capstone of Negro Education* (Washington, D.C.: Graduate School, Howard University, 1941), 219.

24. Bloomfield, *American Lawyers,* 331, 332, 336; Dyson, *Howard University,* 36.

25. Langston, *From the Virginia Plantation,* 318–503; Cheek, "Forgotten Prophet," 244–335.

26. Benno C. Schmidt Jr., "Principle and Prejudice: The Supreme Court and Race in the Progressive Era. Part 3," *Columbia Law Review* 82 (1982): 835,

841, 845; R. Volney Riser, *Defying Disfranchisement: Black Voting Rights Activism in the Jim Crow South, 1890–1908* (Baton Rouge: LSU Press, 2010), 12–40.

27. Langston, *From the Virginia Plantation,* 510–511; Frederick Douglass, *Address by Hon. Frederick Douglass, Delivered in the Metropolitan AME Church, Washington, D.C., Tuesday, January 9, 1894, on the Lessons of the Hour* (Baltimore: Thomas & Evans, 1894), 20, 21. The amendment would also have reduced the size of a state's representation in the federal government in proportion to the number of adult male voters it disfranchised. Thus it would allow a state to disfranchise a portion of its male population, as long as it was willing to have its federal representation also reduced.

28. JML, "Our Emancipation, Our Progress," pp. 5, 6, B2-FF15, JMLP; Langston, *From the Virginia Plantation,* 521–534; Cheek, "Forgotten Prophet," 373–375; Willard B. Gatewood, *Aristocrats of Color: The Black Elite, 1880–1920* (Bloomington: Indiana University Press, 1990), 336.

29. Robert H. Terrell, The Virginia Constitution before the Supreme Court, 5/25/1904, pp. 2–4, R2-F223, RHTP; *WP,* 4/5/1904, p. 11; Jones v. Montague, 194 U.S. 147 (1904); Selden v. Montague, 194 U.S. 153 (1904).

30. Irvin C. Mollison, "Negro Lawyers in Mississippi," *Journal of Negro History* 15 (1930): 38, 42; Maxwell Bloomfield, "From Deference to Confrontation: The Early Black Lawyers of Galveston, Texas, 1895–1920," in Gerald W. Gawalt, ed., *The New High Priests: Lawyers in Post–Civil War America* (Westport, Conn.: Greenwood Press, 1984), 153; Oldfield, "African American Bar in South Carolina," 117–118; D. Augustus Straker, *First Annual Address to the Law Graduates of Allen University* (Atlanta: Jas. P. Harrison, 1885); Thomas Calhoun Walker, *The Honey-Pod Tree: The Life Story of Thomas Calhoun Walker* (New York: John Day, 1958), 66; Judith Kilpatrick, "(Extra)ordinary Men: African-American Lawyers and Civil Rights in Arkansas before 1950," *Arkansas Law Review* 53 (2000): 299, 345–81; Joseph Gordon Hylton, "The African-American Lawyer, the First Generation: Virginia as a Case Study," *University of Pittsburgh Law Review* 56 (1994): 115, 162–163. The University of South Carolina's law school admitted black students for a period during Reconstruction, as did the University of Maryland Law School for a few years in the 1880s. W. Lewis Burke Jr., "The Radical Law School: The University of South Carolina School of Law and Its African American graduates, 1873–1877," in Underwood and Burke, *At Freedom's Door,* 90–115; David Skillen Bogen, "The First Integration of Maryland School of Law," *Maryland Historical Magazine* 88 (1989): 39.

31. Mollison, "Negro Lawyers in Mississippi," 38, 42–43, 64–65; Oldfield, "African American Bar in South Carolina," 120; Hylton, "African-American Lawyer," 149; Bloomfield, "From Deference to Confrontation," 158; Tom Dillard, "Scipio A. Jones," *Arkansas Historical Quarterly* 31 (1972): 201; Walker, *Honey-Pod Tree,* 71; *Thirteenth Census of the United States, Taken in the Year 1910. Vol. 4: Population, Occupation Statistics* (Washington, D.C.: Government Printing

Office, 1913), 434–613; RPA, "The Negro Lawyer" [c. 1947], 7, 14, B96-F44, RPAP.

32. Walker, *Honey-Pod Tree*, 74, 77; Dillard, "Scipio A. Jones," 206, 212; Kilpatrick, "(Extra)ordinary Men," 353.

33. Buck Colbert Franklin, *My Life and an Era: The Autobiography of Buck Colbert Franklin*, John Hope Franklin and John Whittington Franklin, eds. (Baton Rouge: LSU Press, 1997), 197, 198, 200; Tomiko Brown-Nagin, *Courage to Dissent: Atlanta and the Long History of the Civil Rights Movement* (New York: Oxford University Press, 2011); Riser, *Defying Disfranchisement*; Richard C. Cortner, *A Mob Intent on Death: The NAACP and the Arkansas Riot Cases* (Middletown, Conn.: Wesleyan University Press, 1988); Riser, *Defying Disfranchisement*, 101–111; J. Clay Smith Jr., *Emancipation: The Making of the Black Lawyer, 1844–1944* (Philadelphia: University of Pennsylvania Press, 1993), 146–147, 278–280.

34. Peter Vickery, "The Genesis of the Black Law Firm in Massachusetts," *Massachusetts Legal History* 5 (1999): 121, 138–145; Clarence Contee Jr., "Lewis, William H[enry]," in Rayford W. Logan and Michael R. Winston, eds., *Dictionary of American Negro Biography* (New York: W. W. Norton, 1982), 396–397; Robert N. Strassfield, "How the Cleveland Bar Became Segregated: 1870–1930" (paper presented at the annual meeting of the American Society for Legal History, November 2006); *Chicago Tribune*, 12/4/1897, p. 16; Smith, *Emancipation*, 371–372; CHH, Tentative Findings re: Negro Lawyers (Jan. 23, 1928) (revised), p. 6, S3.8-B101-FF1019, LSRMP.

35. Arna Bontemps and Jack Conroy, *They Seek a City* (Garden City, N.Y.: Doubleday, Doran, 1945), 83; Gwen Hoerr McNamee, "'Without Regard to Race, Sex or Color': Ida Platt, Esquire," *CBA (Chicago Bar Association) Record* 13 (May 1999): 24; Evan J. Albright, "William Henry Lewis: Brief Life of a Football Pioneer: 1868–1949," *Harvard Magazine* 108 (Nov.–Dec. 2005): 44–45; Dennis Clark Dickerson, "Gaius Charles Bolin: First Black Graduate of Williams College," n.d., B3, JMBP; Transcript of Interview of Jane Bolin by Jean Rudd with Lionel Bolin, 6/4/1990, pp. 2, 37–38, B1-FF2, JMBP; Interview of Sadie Alexander by Walter M. Phillips, Philadelphia, 10/20/1976, p. 1, B1-FF19, STMAP.

36. Aubrey Robinson Jr., "Terrell, Robert Herberton," in Logan and Winston, *Dictionary of American Negro Biography*, 585–587; Lester C. Lamon, "Church, Robert Reed, Sr.," in *ibid.*, 109–111.

37. Robert H. Terrell, Remarks of Judge Robert H. Terrell at a Banquet in His Honor, 2/5/1906, pp. 2, 4, 5, R2-F257, RHTP.

38. William H. Lewis, "An Address Delivered before the House of Representatives of Massachusetts," in Fitzhugh Lee Styles, *Negroes and the Law* (Boston: Christopher Publishing House, 1937), 204; David McBride, "Mid-Atlantic State Courts and the Struggle with the 'Separate but Equal' Doctrine: 1880–1939," *Rutgers Law Journal* 17 (1986): 569, 581.

39. JML, "Our Emancipation, Our Progress," p. 3, B2-FF15, JMLP.

40. Thomas J. Sugrue, *Sweet Land of Liberty: The Forgotten Struggle for Civil Rights in the North* (New York: Random House, 2008), 87–250; Davison M. Douglas, *Jim Crow Moves North: The Battle over Northern School Segregation, 1865–1954* (New York: Cambridge University Press, 2005), 123–166; LM, Let Tomorrow Come, p. 2, B14, LMP; *LAS*, 1/30/1936, p. 1.

41. Robert L. Carter, *A Matter of Law: A Memoir of Struggle in the Cause of Civil Rights* (New York: New Press, 2005), 15; William T. Coleman Jr., with Donald T. Bliss, *Counsel for the Situation: Shaping the Law to Realize America's Promise* (Washington, D.C.: Brookings Institution Press, 2010), 7–8; Truman K. Gibson Jr., with Steve Huntley, *Knocking Down Barriers: My Fight for Black America* (Evanston, Ill.: Northwestern University Press, 2005), 40; Vincent P. Franklin, *The Education of Black Philadelphia: The Social and Educational History of a Minority Community, 1900–1950* (Philadelphia: University of Pennsylvania Press, 1979), 69.

42. Interview of Sadie Alexander by Walter M. Phillips, Philadelphia, October 20, 1976, p. 5, B1-FF19, STMAP; RPA, "The Struggle against Racism in Philadelphia from 1923 to 1948," 2/15/1950, p. 4, B97-FF19, RPAP.

43. Constitution of the Harvard Negro Club, B18, WLHFP; CHH to Miss Catherine, n.d., *ibid.;* Memorandum for Use of the Harvard Union, 11/20/22, *ibid.*

44. Nell Painter, "Jim Crow at Harvard: 1923," *New England Quarterly* 44 (1971): 627–634; Raymond Pace Alexander, "Voices from Harvard's Own Negroes," *Opportunity* 1 (1923): 29; Raymond Wolters, "The New Negro on Campus," in Werner Sollors, Caldwell Titcomb, and Thomas A. Underwood, eds., *Blacks at Harvard: A Documentary History of African-American Experience at Harvard and Radcliffe* (New York: NYU Press, 1993), 197.

45. RPA, Address Topics before the Congregation of the Synagogue Temple Beth Hillel, 1/15/71, B100-FF3, RPAP.

46. Alexander, "Voices from Harvard's Own Negroes"; *New York World*, 4/10/23, V2-SerL-B253, NAACPP.

47. Alexander, "Voices from Harvard's Own Negroes"; RPA to George W. Maxey, 1/10/1933, Scrapbook 1931–1935, RPAP.

2. Racial Identity and the Marketplace for Lawyers

1. C. Francis Stradford, "Changes in the Law Wrought by Economic and Social Forces," in *Addresses Delivered before the Fifth Annual Convention of the National Bar Association* (Philadelphia: National Bar Association, 1930), 8, 9; RPA, "Our Local and National Bar Associations: Their Aims and Purposes" [c. 1930], B95-FF18, RPAP; George W. Lawrence to RPA, 4/26/1932, B85-FF20, RPAP. Lawrence, as NBA secretary, was relaying Heslip's comments to NBA members.

2. CHH to TM, 9/21/1935 V1-Admin-C81, NAACPP.

3. J. Clay Smith Jr., *Emancipation: The Making of the Black Lawyer, 1844–1944* (Philadelphia: University of Pennsylvania Press, 1993), 105–108, 191–354, 624–637; RPA, "The Negro Lawyer" [c. 1947], 7, 14, B96-F44, RPAP.

4. CHH, Tentative Findings re: Negro Lawyers (Jan. 23, 1928) (revised), p. 6, S3.8-B101-FF1019, LSRMP.

5. Peter Vickery, "The Genesis of the Black Law Firm in Massachusetts," *Massachusetts Legal History* 5 (1999): 121–145; Robert N. Strassfield, "How the Cleveland Bar Became Segregated: 1870–1930" (paper presented at the annual meeting of the American Society for Legal History, November 2006); Robert Blakely, with Marcus Shepard, *Earl B. Dickerson: A Voice for Freedom and Equality* (Evanston, Ill.: Northwestern University Press, 2006), 45–46; Gwen Hoerr McNamee, "'Without Regard to Race, Sex or Color': Ida Platt, Esquire," *CBA (Chicago Bar Association) Record* 13 (May 1999): 24; Peter Vickery, "African American Attorneys in Late Nineteenth and Early Twentieth Century Massachusetts" (1997; unpublished manuscript, in author's possession), 22; Clarence Contee Jr., "Lewis, William H[enry]," in Rayford W. Logan and Michael R. Winston, eds., *Dictionary of American Negro Biography* (New York: W. W. Norton, 1982), 396; Timothy N. Thurber, "Brooke, Edward," in Henry Louis Gates Jr. and Evelyn Brooks Higginbotham, eds., *African American Lives* (New York: Oxford University Press, 2004), 99.

6. Smith, *Emancipation*, 552–566; Clater W. Smith to Dallas Nicholas, 6/16/1941, B9B1a, DNP; CHH, Tentative Findings (revised), p. 14; A. M. Burroughs, "The Importance of Local Bar Associations," in *Addresses Delivered before the Fifth Annual Convention*, 23, 27.

7. Interview of Earl Dickerson by Robert Blakely, Chicago, 9/22/1983, pp. 3–4, CHH to Walter L. McCoy, 2/16/1926, B2, WLHFP.

8. Geraldine R. Segal, *Blacks in the Law: Philadelphia and the Nation* (Philadelphia: University of Pennsylvania Press, 1983), 76–83; Carter G. Woodson, *The Negro Professional Man and the Community* (New York: Johnson Reprint Corp., 1970), 196–239; CHH, Tentative Findings (revised), p. 14; William Henri Hale, "The Career Development of the Negro Lawyer in Chicago" (Ph.D. diss., University of Chicago, 1949), 58–59, 62–67; RPA, "The Negro Lawyer" [c. 1947], B96-FF44, RPAP; Interview of Judge William H. Murphy Sr. by Kenneth W. Mack, Baltimore, 1/21/1997; Charles H. Houston, "The Need for Negro Lawyers," *Journal of Negro Education* 4 (1935): 49–52.

9. Martin Summers, *Manliness and Its Discontents: The Black Middle Class and the Transformation of Masculinity, 1900–1930* (Chapel Hill: University of North Carolina Press, 2004), 1–2.

10. Genna Rae McNeil, *Groundwork: Charles Hamilton Houston and the Struggle for Civil Rights* (Philadelphia: University of Pennsylvania Press, 1983), 22–53; William L. Houston to CHH, 9/21/1912, B7, WLHFP; Charles H. Houston, "Notice and Hearing as a Condition Precedent to Governmental Action. Preliminary Report" (S.J.D. thesis, Harvard Law School, June 1923).

11. Kenneth W. Mack, "Rethinking Civil Rights Lawyering and Politics in the Era before *Brown*," *Yale Law Journal* 115 (2005): 256, 284–287, 312–316; CHH to Leonard Outhwaite, 11/20/1927, S3.8-B101-FF1018, LSRMP.

12. CHH, Tentative Findings (revised), p. 14; United States Internal Revenue Form 1040, Individual Income Tax Return, Charles Houston (1929), B19, WLHFP; Leonard Outhwaite, Memorandum of Interview with Charles H. Houston, 11/15/1927, p. 1–2, S3.8-B101-FF1018, LSRMP; CHH to Leonard Outhwaite, 1/5/1928, *ibid.*; McNeil, *Groundwork*, 70.

13. CHH to Leonard Outhwaite, 4/7/1928, S3.8-B101-FF1018, LSRMP; "Annual Catalogue 1938–1939, with Announcements for 1939–1940 sessions," *Howard University Bulletin* 18 (April 30, 1939): 222; McNeil, *Groundwork*, 111–113. For the popular assertion that Houston taught a civil rights course and that Marshall took it, see, for example, James Haskins, *Thurgood Marshall: A Life for Justice* (New York: Henry Holt, 1992), 32. For further documentation of my claims about Houston's transformation of Howard and his 1928 report, see Mack, "Rethinking Civil Rights Lawyering and Politics," 284–287, 312–316.

14. W. B. Donham to Victor M. Cutter, 6/8/1920, B18, WLHP.

15. CHH to Leonard Outhwaite, 1/19/1928, S3.8-B101-FF1018, LSRMP; CHH, Memorandum for Dean Holmes, 7/16/1930, p. 2, B1357, HUA; CHH, Memorandum to Student Body, 10/20/1932, B1387, HUA; CHH, Memorandum to President Johnson from Vice-Dean Charles H. Houston re Reorganization of School of Law, Howard University, 2/20/1933, pp. 3, 5, B1209, HUA; "The School of Law 1936–1937 with Announcements for 1937–1938 Sessions," *Howard University Bulletin* 16/3 (December 15, 1936): 19; CHH to Leonard Outhwaite, 4/7/1928, S3.8-B101-FF1018, LSRMP.

16. Return of Births, in the City of Philadelphia, Under My Care for the Month of October 1897, 7/17/1930, B1-FF47, RPAP; Registration Card [World War I draft], Reel PA202, M1509, NARA; Mack, "Rethinking Civil Rights Lawyering and Politics," 309, n. 188; CHH, Tentative Findings (revised), p. 10. Although documents from the early twentieth century show Alexander's birth date as 1897, later in life he began to list his birth year as 1898—an assertion picked up in some biographical accounts of his life.

17. RPA, A Short Biographical Sketch of the Life of Raymond Pace Alexander, Philadelphia's Young Colored Lawyer [c. 1925], B1-FF14, RPAP; *PT,* 03/27/1925, p. 1; *PT,* 03/25/1925, p. 1; David A. Canton, *Raymond Pace Alexander: A New Negro Lawyer Fights for Civil Rights in Philadelphia* (Jackson: University Press of Mississippi, 2010), 30–34; August Meier and Elliott Rudwick, "Attorneys Black and White: A Case Study of Race Relations within the NAACP," *Journal of American History* 62 (1976): 913–946.

18. *PT,* 5/24/1924, p. 1; *PT,* 10/24/1925, p. 1; *PT,* 10/31/1925, p. 4; Commonwealth v. Thomas, 127 A. 427 (Pa. 1925).

19. *CD,* 8/15/1925, p. 2; *AN,* 8/25/1926, p. 9; *BAA,* 8/13/1927, p. 1; *CD,* 8/11/1928, p. 1; *AN,* 8/7/1929, p. 2; STMA, Acceptance Speech of the Posthu-

mous Award to the Late Judge Raymond Pace Alexander, 8/21/1975, B72-F12, STMAP; RPA to Charles W. Anderson and Sidney R. Redmond, 1/4/1944, B86-F8, RPAP; C. W. Anderson to STMA, 12/13/1945, p. 2, B48-F23, STMAP; Smith, *Emancipation*, 556–562.

20. *Addresses Delivered before the Fifth Annual Convention*, 33, 35, 38, 39.

21. RPA, A Short Biographical Sketch of the Life of Raymond Pace Alexander, Philadelphia's Young Colored Lawyer [c. 1925], B1-FF14, RPAP.

22. *Ibid.*, 1.

23. *Ibid.*, 2–6.

24. *Ibid.*, 10–13, 14.

25. *Ibid.*, 14–26.

26. *Ibid.*, 26.

27. James V. Catano, *Ragged Dicks: Masculinity, Steel, and the Rhetoric of the Self-Made Man* (Carbondale: Southern Illinois University Press, 2001), 10–11, 94–95. Among other elements of his story, Raymond Alexander's account of his chance meeting with John R. K. Scott is fictionalized. Scott was a friend of Alexander's father, and Alexander got the job in Scott's office through family connections. John R. K. Scott to Brigadier General F. H. Osborn, 10/5/1942, B9-FF21, RPAP.

28. Interview of Earl Dickerson by Robert Blakely, Chicago, 9/7/1983; Blakely and Shepard, *Earl B. Dickerson*, 11, 14–15. The college professor was almost certainly black, whereas Dickerson's other fortuitous benefactors, like those of Alexander and William Houston, were often white.

29. *WP*, 12/21/1952, p. M17.

30. STMA, "The Doom of the Self-Made Man," B71-FF21, STMAP; Richard J. Walsh, "The Doom of the Self-Made Man," *Century* 109 (December 1924): 253; Irvin G. Wyllie, *The Self-Made Man in America: The Myth of Rags to Riches* (New York: Free Press, 1954), 169.

31. Buck Colbert Franklin, *My Life and an Era: The Autobiography of Buck Colbert Franklin*, John Hope Franklin and John Whittington Franklin, eds. (Baton Rouge: LSU Press, 1997), 136–137; Horace I. Gordon, "The Problem of the Negro Lawyer." *Education* 2, no. 2 (April 1936): 4, 6, 8; S. D. McGill, "Problems Facing the Negro Lawyer in the South," [1940], 4, B85-FF3, RPAP; CHH, Tentative Findings (revised), pp. 7–9, 14; Woodson, *Negro Professional Man*, 231–235; John Caswell Smith, "Kaleidoscope in Court," *Opportunity* 17 (January 1938): 15; Meier and Rudwick, "Attorneys Black and White," 916; Roger Lane, *William Dorsey's Philadelphia and Ours: On the Past and Future of the Black City in America* (New York: Oxford University Press, 1991), 173; D. Augustus Straker, "The Negro in the Profession of Law," *A.M.E. Church Review* 8 (1891): 178, 181; Joseph Gordon Hylton, "The African-American Lawyer, the First Generation: Virginia as a Case Study," *University of Pittsburgh Law Review* 56 (1994): 107, 145–146.

32. "Black Lawyers," in Philip S. Foner, ed., *The Black Panthers Speak* (Philadelphia: J. B. Lippincott Co., 1970), 14–16.

33. Robert H. Terrell, The Lawyer's Relation to Business Development (n.d.), p. 9, R2-F526, RHTP; CHH to Leonard Outhwaite, 5/7/28, s3.8-B101-F1018, LSRMP; Tomiko Brown-Nagin, *Courage to Dissent: Atlanta and the Long History of the Civil Rights Movement* (New York: Oxford University Press, 2011), 29.

34. RPA, [Untitled Biographical Essay], 1/14/1949, B1-FF5, RPAP.

35. W.E.B. Du Bois, *The Philadelphia Negro: A Social Study* (Boston: Ginn and Co., 1899), 114–115; Woodson, *Negro Professional Man,* 191.

36. Lane, *William Dorsey's Philadelphia,* 135–136, 156, 174–182; Vincent P. Franklin, *The Education of Black Philadelphia: The Social and Educational History of a Minority Community, 1900–1950* (Philadelphia: University of Pennsylvania Press, 1979), 58–59.

37. A. Mercer Daniel, History of Howard Law School, Appendix—Graduates of the Howard University School of Law from 1871 to 1970 (n.d.), p. 10, B177–02, AMDP.

38. *The First Colored Directory of Baltimore, Md.,* 23rd ed. (Baltimore: Robert W. Coleman, 1935–1936); George W. Evans to Howard Hucles, 7/19/1941, B9A1, DNP; Dallas Nicholas to National Assn. of Schools & Publishers, 1/17/1933, *ibid.;* Dallas Nicholas to Calvert Bank, 2/17/1936, *ibid.;* Dallas Nicholas to Olivia C. Handy, 9/24/1935, *ibid.;* Dallas Nicholas to Raymond Pace Alexander, 1/29/1945, box 1A1, DNP; Dallas Nicholas to Raymond Pace Alexander, 1/7/1937, *ibid.;* Dallas Nicholas to STMA, 6/21/1939, *ibid.;* Maryland State Tax Return, Dallas Nicholas (1941), box 2A1, DNP; Maryland State Tax Return, Dallas Nicholas (1945), *ibid.;* Telephone Interview of Judge John R. Hargrove by Kenneth W. Mack, Baltimore, 1/1/1997.

39. STMA, "[Reminiscences of a Career in Law]" (1972), p. 1, B72, STMAP; Hargrove, Mack Interview; Murphy, Mack Interview; RPA to Dallas Nicholas, 3/8/1945, B1A1, DNP.

40. *The Crisis* 10 (May 1915): 8; CHH to Maceo W. Hubbard, 3/27/1926, B2, WLHFP; William L. Houston to CHH, 10/30/1909, B7, *ibid.;* William L. Houston to CHH, 4/30/1909, *ibid.;* William L. Houston to CHH, 10/30/1909, *ibid.;* William L. Houston to CHH, 10/17/1909, *ibid.;* Allan H. Spear, *Black Chicago: The Making of a Negro Ghetto, 1890–1920* (Chicago: University of Chicago Press, 1967), 61, 189; Smith, *Emancipation,* 371–372.

41. William L. Houston to CHH, 10/30/1909, B2, WLHFP; McNeil, *Groundwork,* 230; CHH to W. A. C. Hughes, 5/15/1943, DNP; United States Internal Revenue Form 1040, Individual Income Tax Return, Charles Houston (1925), B19, WLHFP; *ibid.* (1926).

42. Blakely, *Earl B. Dickerson,* 41–49, 66–92, 93–110, 148–149; Interview of Earl Dickerson by Robert Blakely, Chicago, 12/15/1983.

43. *Philadelphia Record,* 12/10/1945; *Philadelphia Inquirer,* 12/10/1945; *Philadelphia Evening Bulletin,* 12/10/1945.

44. *PT,* 10/24/1925, p. 1; RPA to CHH, 11/9/1939, B163/7-FF4, CHHP; George Cooper, *Poison Widows: A True Story of Witchcraft, Arsenic, and Murder*

(New York: St. Martin's Press, 1999); Trial Transcript, State of New Jersey v. Ralph Cooper et al. (1951); [Profits and Loss Statement] From September 3, 1928, to September 2, 1929, Inclusive, B26-FF3, RPAP.

45. RPA to Carl Murphy, 5/2/1949, B1-FF5, RPAP; Raymond Pace Alexander, "Days of Glory," *Central High School Alumni Journal* 2/2 (May 1953): 3, 16–17.

46. Compare, for example, Letter to Mary Beatty Brady, 3/5/1946, B1-FF5, RPAP, with RPA to Michael Bradley, 7/15/1947, B10-FF4, RPAP.

3. The Role of the Courtroom in an Era of Segregation

1. *Philadelphia Public Ledger,* 2/10/1932, Scrapbook 1931–1935, RPAP; *PT,* 2/25/1932, *ibid.*

2. *Philadelphia Record,* 2/25/1932, *ibid.; Philadelphia Evening Public Ledger,* 2/24/1932, *ibid.; Philadelphia Daily News,* n.d., *ibid.*

3. J. Clay Smith Jr., *Emancipation: The Making of the Black Lawyer, 1844–1944* (Philadelphia: University of Pennsylvania Press, 1993), 128–148, 101–368; Jerold S. Auerbach, *Unequal Justice: Lawyers and Social Change in Modern America* (New York: Oxford University Press, 1976), 14–129. California repealed its statute limiting law practice to white males in 1878. Maryland courts continued to uphold that state's similar law until 1885, when they reversed course and admitted the state's first black lawyer. Three years later, the statutory racial prohibition was formally dropped. David S. Bogen, "The Transformation of the Fourteenth Amendment: Reflections from the Admission of Maryland's First Black Lawyers," *Maryland Law Review* 44 (1985): 939, 1043.

4. "Louis L. Redding, Civil Rights Attorney," *Harvard Law School Record,* November 13, 1952; Carter G. Woodson, *The Negro Professional Man and the Community* (New York: Johnson Reprint Corp., 1970), 198–220, 219; RPA, "The Negro Lawyer" [c. 1947], B94-FF44, RPAP.

5. Record, Vol. 1, Commonwealth v. Corrine Sykes (Phila. Ct. Oyer & Terminer 1945), at 114a–117a, B46-FF5, RPAP.

6. Sadie T. M. Alexander, "The Best of Times and the Worst of Times," *University of Pennsylvania Law Alumni Journal* 12 (Spring 1977): 19.

7. Dallas Nicholas to Paul B. Mules, 3/22/1943, B9B1a, DNP; reel 2, frames 369, 622, 625, Trial Transcript, Hansberry v. Lee, Docket 25116 (1939), Vault 50076, Illinois Supreme Court, Microfilm Department.

8. CHH to Walter White, 6/22/1933, P8-SA-R6-F795, NAACPPmf; Walter White to CHH, 6/23/1933, *ibid.,* frame 794; Interview of Z. Alexander Looby by John Britton, Nashville, TN, 11/29/1967, pp. 4–5, 15, MSRC; Raymond Pace Alexander, "Blacks and the Law," *Negro History Bulletin,* May 1971, pp. 109, 112. This is not to say that Alexander was treated exactly like a white lawyer. He had to sit in the black section of the segregated courtroom.

9. *NJG,* 11/11/1933, p. A1; PM and Adelene McBean to Attorneys Valentine and Cooley, 4/2/1940, p. 1, B4, PMP.

10. Robert L. Carter, "A Tribute to Justice Thurgood Marshall," *Harvard Law Review* 105 (1991): 33, 40–41.

11. PM, "Judge Denies Casting Reflections on Negro," B1, PMP; *CD,* 8/1/1936, p. 1; *CD,* 8/14/1937, p. 2; Constance A. Cunningham, "Homer S. Brown: First Black Political Leader in Pittsburgh," *Journal of Negro History* 66 (1982): 304, 307; CHH to RPA, 7/20/1936, B9-FF5, RPAP.

12. Michael A. Musmanno to RPA, 3/16/1950, B10-FF17, RPAP; RPA to Andrew M. Bradley, April 29, 1950, *ibid.;* In re Girard's Estate, 127 A.2d 287, 318 (Pa. 1956) (Musmanno, J. dissenting), *rev'd,* Commonwealth v. Board of City Trusts, 353 U.S. 230 (1957); In re Girard College Trusteeship, 138 A.2d 844, 854 (Pa. 1958) (Musmanno, J. dissenting), *cert. denied,* Commonwealth v. Board of City Trusts, 357 U.S. 570 (1958); Interview of Earl Dickerson by Robert Blakely, Chicago [10th Interview].

13. Thurgood Marshall, "Reminiscences of Thurgood Marshall," in Mark V. Tushnet, ed., *Thurgood Marshall: His Speeches, Writings, Arguments, Opinions, and Reminiscences* (Chicago: Lawrence Hill Books, 2001), 422; Interview of Loren Miller by Lawrence B. de Graaf, 3/3/1967, Oral History 174, Center for Oral and Public History, California State University, Fullerton; *Collier's,* 2/23/1952, p. 29.

14. Marshall, "Reminiscences of Thurgood Marshall," 415–416, 421–422; CHH, Tentative Findings re: Negro Lawyers (Jan. 23, 1928) (revised), p. 12, S3.8-B101-FF1019, LSRMP; CHH to Alfred Z. Reed, 5/30/1931, B1458, HUA.

15. Clark Flint Kellogg, *NAACP: A History of the National Association for the Advancement of Colored People,* vol. 1, *1909–1920* (Baltimore: Johns Hopkins University Press, 1967), 58, 63; August Meier and Elliott Rudwick, "Attorneys Black and White: A Case Study of Race Relations within the NAACP," *Journal of American History* 62 (1976): 913, 931; H. Viscount Nelson, *Black Leadership's Response to the Great Depression in Philadelphia* (Lewiston, N.Y.: Edwin Mellen Press, 2006), 201.

16. Meier and Rudwick, "Attorneys Black and White," 930–933; Mark V. Tushnet, *The NAACP's Legal Strategy against Segregated Education, 1925–1950* (Chapel Hill: University of North Carolina Press, 1987), 32.

17. CHH, Tentative Findings re: Negro Lawyers (Jan. 23, 1928) (revised), pp. 6–7, S3.8-B101-FF1019, LSRMP; *Proceedings of the National Bar Association at Its Seventh and Eighth Annual Meetings* (Chicago: Chicago Review Publishing Co., [1933]), 71, 73.

18. *Philadelphia Evening Public Ledger,* 2/24/1932, 1931–1935 Scrapbook, RPAP; *Philadelphia Daily News,* 3/24/1932, *ibid.; Philadelphia Evening Public Ledger,* 4/1/1932, *ibid.; Philadelphia Inquirer,* 4/25/1950.

19. *Philadelphia Evening Public Ledger,* 3/29/1932, 1931–1935 Scrapbook, RPAP; *Philadelphia Independent,* 3/20/1932, *ibid.; Franklin Repository,* 2/25/1932, *ibid.; NJG,* 2/27/1932, p. 5; *PC,* 2/27/1932, p. A1.

20. *PT,* 2/18/1932, pp. 1, 2; *PT,* 2/25/1932, p. 1; *BAA,* 3/19/1932, p. 2.

21. *Philadelphia Inquirer*, 2/25/1932, 1931–1935 Scrapbook, RPAP; *Philadelphia Evening Public Ledger*, 3/8/1932, *ibid.; Franklin Repository*, 2/25/1932, *ibid.*

22. *Philadelphia Evening Bulletin*, 7/1/1952; *Philadelphia Inquirer*, 7/2/1952.

23. *Philadelphia Public Ledger*, 2/10/1932, 1931–1935 Scrapbook, RPAP; *Philadelphia Daily News*, 3/24/1932, *ibid.; Philadelphia Evening Public Ledger*, 3/28/1932, *ibid.; Philadelphia Evening Public Ledger*, 3/29/1932, *ibid.; Philadelphia Evening Public Ledger*, 2/24/1932, *ibid.*

24. *Philadelphia Daily News*, 3/29/1932, 1931–1935 Scrapbook, RPAP; *Philadelphia Inquirer*, 3/30/1932, *ibid.; Philadelphia Evening Public Ledger*, 3/30/1932, *ibid.; Philadelphia Daily News*, 3/30/1932, *ibid.*

25. *PT*, 4/7/1932, p. 1; *Philadelphia Evening Public Ledger*, 4/1/1932, 1931–1935 Scrapbook, RPAP; *Philadelphia Record*, 3/31/1932, *ibid.; Philadelphia Daily News*, 4/1/1932, *ibid.; Philadelphia Evening Bulletin*, 4/1/1932, *ibid.*

26. *PC*, 12/3/1932, p. 9; George W. Maxey to RPA, 1/11/1933, 1931–1935 Scrapbook, RPAP.

27. George W. Maxey to RPA, 6/1931, 1931–1935 Scrapbook, RPAP; *The Nation*, 1/6/1932, p. 7.

28. Commonwealth v. Brown, 164 A. 726, 728–730 (Pa. 1933); *PT*, 3/30/1933, pp. 1, 15.

29. *NJG*, 1/14/1933, p. A1; Kramer Hosiery v. American Federation of Full Fashioned Hosiery Workers, 157 A. 588, 598–603 (1931) (Maxey, J., dissenting); RPA to George W. Maxey, 1/10/1933, 1931–1935 Scrapbook; George W. Maxey to RPA, 1/7/1933, *ibid.;* George W. Maxey to RPA, 5/4/1933, *ibid.;* George W. Maxey to RPA, 1/11/1933, *ibid.;* George Maxey to RPA, 5/4/1933, *ibid.*

30. Hubert T. Delaney to RPA, 2/6/1935, B9-FF4, RPAP; STMA to William H. Lewis Jr., B7-FF6, RPAP; George W. Maxey to STMA, 11/2/1942, B6-FF18, STMAP.

31. Amy MacKenzie, "Walter White on Lynching," *Interracial Review*, September 1946; RPA to Ben Richardson, 4/10/1946, p. 2, B86-FF12, RPAP.

32. RPA, The Thomas Mattox Extradition Case, B47-FF19, RPAP; Opinion of the Court, Commonwealth *ex rel* Mattox v. Superintendent of County Prison (Pa. Sup. Ct. 1942), *ibid.*

33. *Philadelphia Inquirer*, 7/2/1952; RPA, The Thomas Mattox Extradition Case, B47-FF19, RPAP; RPA to Clare Gerald Fenerty, 9/1/1942, B47-F16, RPAP; Opinion of the Court, Commonwealth *ex rel* Mattox v. Superintendent of County Prison (Pa. Sup. Ct. 1942), B47-FF19, RPAP.

34. Opinion of the Court, Commonwealth *ex rel* Mattox v. Superintendent of County Prison (Pa. Sup. Ct. 1942), B47-FF19, RPAP; RPA to J. Schneyer Clearfield, 11/19/1942, B47-FF15, RPAP.

35. RPA, "Address Topics before the Congregation of the Synagogue Temple Beth Hillel" (1971), p. 6, B100-FF3, RPAP; *PT*, 11/26/1933, p. 1; *PT*, 5/2/1935, p. 2.

36. *Philadelphia Inquirer,* 4/23/1950; RPA to Maggie Hart, 11/3/1968, B61-FF16, RPAP.

37. RPA, A Short Summary of the Life of Raymond Pace Alexander (1966), p. 9, B1-FF8, RPAP.

38. *Ibid.;* George Cooper, *Poison Widows: A True Story of Witchcraft, Arsenic, and Murder* (New York: St. Martin's Press, 1999).

39. *NYT,* 10/29/1939, p. 12; RPA to CHH, 11/9/1939, B163/7-FF3, CHHP.

40. *PT,* 12/7/1939.

41. *Ibid.;* Interview of Gussella Gelzer by Kenneth W. Mack, Philadelphia, 6/23/1999, p. 12; [RPA] to Mary Beatty Brady, 3/5/1946, B1-FF5, RPAP.

42. TM, "Remarks at a Testimonial Dinner Honoring Raymond Pace Alexander, November 25, 1951," in Tushnet, *Thurgood Marshall,* 138, 139; Charles H. Houston, "Commonwealth v. William Brown," *Opportunity* 11 (1933): 109, 110.

4. A Shifting Racial Identity in a Southern Courtroom

1. Helen Boardman, "The South Goes Legal," *The Nation,* 3/8/1933, pp. 258–260; *NYT,* 4/25/1933, p. 19; *NYT,* 4/26/1933, p. 17; *NYT,* 4/27/1933, p. 1; Hale v. Crawford, 65 F.2d 739 (1st Cr. 1933), *cert. denied,* 290 U.S. 674 (1933); *NYT,* 10/29/1933, pp. E1, E6.

2. Glenda Elizabeth Gilmore, *Defying Dixie: The Radical Roots of Civil Rights, 1919–1950* (New York: W. W. Norton, 2008), 95; Lee v. State, 161 A. 284 (Md. 1932); *PT,* 2/11/1932, p. 1; Dan T. Carter, *Scottsboro: A Tragedy of the American South,* rev. ed. (Baton Rouge: LSU Press, 1979), 198; James Goodman, *Stories of Scottsboro* (New York: Vintage Books, 1994), 122; Interview of Charles H. Houston by Edward Mazique, 12/1949, B208/3-FF31, William L. Patterson papers, Moorland-Spingarn Research Center, Howard University.

3. Joseph Gordon Hylton, "The African-American Lawyer, the First Generation: Virginia as a Case Study," *University of Pittsburgh Law Review* 56 (1994): 107, 150; Maxwell Bloomfield, "From Deference to Confrontation: The Early Black Lawyers of Galveston, Texas, 1895–1920," in Gerald W. Gawalt, ed., *The New High Priests: Lawyers in Post–Civil War America* (Westport, Conn.: Greenwood Press, 1984), 151, 165; Joseph Gordon Hylton, "Negotiating the Boundaries of Jim Crow: Black Virginia Lawyers on the Eve of the Civil Rights Era" (unpublished paper, November 2006, in author's possession), 4, 9; Carter G. Woodson, *The Negro Professional Man and the Community* (New York: Johnson Reprint Corp., 1970), 192–193; Irvin C. Mollison, "Negro Lawyers in Mississippi," *Journal of Negro History* 15 (1930): 45, 53–55.

4. John Oldfield, "The African American Bar in South Carolina, 1877–1915," in James Lowell Underwood and W. Lewis Burke Jr., eds., *At Freedom's Door: African American Founding Fathers and Lawyers in Reconstruction South Carolina* (Columbia: University of South Carolina Press, 2000), 116, 123; S. D. McGill,

The Problems Facing Negro Lawyers in the South (1940), B85-FF35, RPAP; Bloomfield, "From Deference to Confrontation," 165; Benjamin Davis, *Communist Councilman from Harlem: Autobiographical Notes Written in a Federal Penitentiary* (New York: International Publishers, 1969), 45.

5. Mark V. Tushnet, *Making Civil Rights Law: Thurgood Marshall and the Supreme Court, 1936–1961* (New York: Oxford University Press, 1994), 52; Mahala Ashley Dickerson, "Jet-Propelled into the Law," in J. Clay Smith Jr., ed., *Rebels in Law: Voices in History of Black Women Lawyers* (Ann Arbor: University of Michigan Press, 1998), 29, 30; Mollison, "Negro Lawyers in Mississippi,", 56–57.

6. Kenneth W. Mack, "Rethinking Civil Rights Lawyering and Politics in the Era before *Brown,*" *Yale Law Journal* 115 (2005): 256, 316; Gilbert Ware, *William Hastie: Grace under Pressure* (New York: Oxford University Press, 1984), 10–34, 48–50; Gilmore, *Defying Dixie,* 257–258.

7. Gilmore, *Defying Dixie,* 257–258; Ware, *William Hastie,* 51–52; August Meier and Elliott Rudwick, "Attorneys Black and White: A Case Study of Race Relations within the NAACP," *Journal of American History* 62 (1976): 913, 940, and n. 103.

8. Ware, *William Hastie,* 53; Walter White, *A Man Called White* (New York: Viking Press, 1948), 158–159.

9. Tushnet, *Making Civil Rights Law,* 62; Constance Baker Motley, *Equal Justice under Law: An Autobiography* (New York: Farrar, Straus and Giroux, 1998), 75–76.

10. *WP,* 11/7/1933, p. 1; CHH to Walter White, 4/21/1933, P8-SerA-R6-F582-85, NAACPPmf.

11. Helen Boardman and Martha Gruening, *The Crawford Case: A Reply to the "N.A.A.C.P."* (New York: Helen Boardman and Martha Gruening, 1935); *NYT,* 12/24/1933, p. E7.

12. Virginius Dabney to Walter White, 10/30/1933, P8-SerA-R7-F103, NAACPPmf; "Change in Va. Sentiment Is Annoying," *BAA,* 12/16/1933, p. 2, *ibid.,* F351; *Loudoun Times-Mirror,* 10/26/1933, p. 1.

13. Letter to Editor, *The Nation,* 4/5/1933, p. 375; *WP,* 11/2/1933, p. 24; *WP,* 11/5/1933, p. 1; *WP,* 11/7/1933, pp. 1, 2; *NJG,* 11/11/1933, p. 1.

14. *Loudoun Times-Mirror,* 11/9/1933, p. 2; *WP,* 11/8/1933, p. 17.

15. *WP,* 11/5/1933, p. 1; *Richmond Times-Dispatch,* 11/7/1933, B108/2-F25, JGTP; White, *Man Called White,* 155.

16. *WP,* 11/20/1933, p. 13.

17. [Deposition of Helen Boardman], 2/2/1933, P8-SerA-R6-F308-10, NAACPPmf.

18. CHH and Edward P. Lovett, Confidential Memorandum on Trip to Leesburg, Va., 3/13/1933, P8-SerA-R6-F505, NAACPPmf; CHH to Walter White, 3/12/1933, p. 3, F467, *ibid.;* CHH to Walter White, 3/8/1933, p. 1, F432, *ibid.*

19. *Loudoun Times-Mirror,* 11/9/1933, p. 1; *ibid.,* p. 2; *ibid.,* pp. 1, 6.

20. JML, "Our Emancipation; Our Progress; and Our Future," B2-FF15; JMLP; Douglas Freeman to Walter White, 11/02/1933 P8-SerA-R7-F140-41, NAACPPmf; Virginius Dabney to Walter White, 10/30/1933, F103, *ibid.;* Walter White to Edward Lovett, Leon Ransom, and James Tyson, 10/30/1933, F99, *ibid.*

21. CHH to Walter White, 6/22/1933, P8-SerA-R6-F795, NAACPPmf; *NJG,* 11/11/1933, p. 1; CHH to Walter White, 11/10/1933, P8-SerA-R7-F190, NAACPPmf; Trial Transcript, Virginia v. Crawford, at 14–15.

22. Virginius Dabney to Walter White, 10/30/1933, P8-SerA-R7-F103, NAACPPmf; Walter White to Edward Lovett, Leon Ransom, and James Tyson, 10/30/1933, p. 2, F99–100, *ibid.;* Daisy Lampkin to Walter White, 11/3/1933, *ibid.,* F147; Douglas Freeman to Walter White, 11/2/1933, *ibid.,* F140.

23. *Loudoun Times-Mirror,* 1/5/1967; John Henry Alexander (n.d.), J. R. H. Alexander Vertical File, Thomas Balch Library, Leesburg, Va.; *Loudoun Times-Mirror,* 11/23/1933, pp. 1, 3; *ibid.,* 11/2/1933, p. 1; *NJG,* 11/11/1933, p. 1.

24. In re—J. R. J. Alexander Memorial Service (January 3, 1967), Thomas Balch Library, Leesburg, Va.; CHH to Walter White, 11/10/1933, P8-SerA-R7-F190, NAACPPmf.

25. Virginius Dabney to Walter White, 11/3/1933, P8-SerA-R7-F142, NAACPPmf; Walter White to Douglas Freeman, 11/10/1933, F174, *ibid.;* Walter White to CHH, 11/14/1933, F195, *ibid.*

26. *Proceedings of the National Bar Association at Its Seventh and Eighth Annual Meetings* (Chicago: Chicago Review Publishing Co., [1933]), 73; CHH to Walter White, 10/17/1933, P8-SerA-R6-F905, NAACPPmf; CHH to Douglas Freeman, 11/11/1933, R7-F182, *ibid.*

27. CHH to Douglas Freeman, 11/11/1933, P8-SerA-R7-F182, NAACPPmf.

28. *NYT,* 4/30/1933, p. E1; Carter, *Scottsboro,* 192–239; Goodman, *Stories of Scottsboro,* 118–146; CHH to Walter White, 3/12/1933, p. 3, P8-SerA-R6-F467, NAACPPmf.

29. Walter White to Douglas Freeman, 11/10/1933, P8-SerA-R7-F174, NAACPPmf; CHH to Douglas Freeman, 11/11/1933, F182, *ibid.*

30. CHH to Editor, *Richmond News Leader,* 11/9/1933, p. 1, P8-SerA-F164, NAACPPmf; *Loudoun Times-Mirror,* 11/9/1933, p. 1; *NJG,* 11/18/1933, p. 1.

31. CHH to Editor, *Richmond News Leader,* 11/9/1933, p. 1, P8-SerA-F164, NAACPPmf.

32. Walter White to Roy Wilkins, 12/15/1933, P8-SerA-R7-F331, NAACPPmf; *NJG,* 12/16/1933, p. A27; Trial Transcript, Virginia v. Crawford, p. 540.

33. *Loudoun Times-Mirror,* 10/19/1933, p. 1; "Offers Alibi Fighting Return to Virginia for Double Murder," 2/10/1933, P8-SerA-R6-F368, NAACPPmf; Boardman and Gruening, *Crawford Case,* 23–24; "Mystery and Motive behind Move to Get Negro for Virginia Murder," 2/3/1933, P8-SerA-R6-F333, NAACPPmf.

34. Boardman and Gruening, *Crawford Case,* 19–27; Joint Affidavit of Leon A. Ransom and James G. Tyson, 6/6/193, B108/2-F34, JGTP; CHH to Walter

White, 11/27/1933, P8-SerA-R7-F264, NAACPPmf; Trial Transcript, Virginia v. Crawford, pp. 405–408.

35. Roy A. Seaton, Interview by Charles Houston, Leon Ransom, Edward Lovett, and James Tyson, Middleburg, Va., 11/24/1933, p. 1, B108/2-F34, JGTP; CHH to Walter White, 11/10/1933, P8-SerA-R7-F190, NAACPPmf; *Loudoun Times-Mirror,* 12/7/1933, pp. 1, 6; *WP,* 12/12/1933, p. 2; Walter White to Butler Wilson and J. Weston Allen, 3/7/1933 P8-SerA-R6-F430-31; Walter White to P. B. Young, 3/14/1933, F469, *ibid.;* Joint Affidavit of Leon A. Ransom and James G. Tyson, 6/6/1933, pp. 3–5, B108/2-F34, JGTP.

36. George Crawford to Walter White, 7/1/1933, P8-SerA-R6-F828, NAACPPmf. Some commentators assert that Crawford told his lawyers that he was guilty, more or less along the lines of the statement that the prosecutor had obtained in Boston. See, for example, Rawn James Jr., *Root and Branch: Charles Hamilton Houston, Thurgood Marshall, and the Struggle to End Segregation* (New York: Bloomsbury Press, 2010), 10. However, Houston was quite guarded, in both public and private, about what exactly Crawford told him in that important conversation.

37. Boardman and Gruening, *Crawford Case,* p. 19; Walter White to Roy Wilkins, 12/15/1933, P8-SerA-R7-F332, NAACPPmf; Walter White, "George Crawford: Symbol," *The Crisis* 41 (January 1934): 15; Walter White to Helen Boardman, 1/18/1934, P8-SerA-R7-F500, NAACPPmf; CHH to J. Weston Allen and Butler Wilson, 2/12/1934, F519, *ibid.*

38. *Loudoun Times-Mirror,* 12/14/1933, p. 4; Trial Transcript, Virginia v. Crawford, pp. 16–23, 41, 42–289; 190, 204–207, 212–214, 216–228; *WP,* 12/31/1933, pp. SM3, 15; Lester Hill, Interview by Charles Houston and James Tyson, Middleburg, Va., 11/28/1933, p. 1, B108/2-F34, JGTP; Boardman and Gruening, *Crawford Case,* pp. 7–8; *NYT,* 12/13/1933, p. 48; *WP,* 12/13/1933, p. 5. Houston did, however, aggressively challenge one witness, Robert Hutchins, who testified that Crawford bragged about doing the murders, and another witness who clearly had manufactured his story at the last minute. He had to challenge Hutchins, for if the jury believed him, Crawford would certainly have received a death sentence.

39. *WP,* 12/13/1933, p. 5; Walter White, [Notes on Crawford Trial], 12/13/1933, P8-SerA-R7-F333-46, NAACPPmf; *Loudoun Times-Mirror,* 12/7/1933, pp. 1, 6; *ibid.,* 12/14/1933, pp. 1, 4; Trial Transcript, Virginia v. Crawford, pp. 111–119.

40. Walter White, [Notes on Crawford Trial], 12/13/1933, P8-SerA-R7-F333-46, NAACPPmf; Trial Transcript, Virginia v. Crawford, pp. 87, 128, 155–157, 212, 225, 231, 243–244; Walter White to Roy Wilkins, 12/15/1933, p. 2, P8-SerA-R7-F351, NAACPPmf.

41. "Commissioner Who Passes on 'Negro Intelligence' Has Hard Time Reading Names," *BAA,* n.d., P8-SerA-R7-F332, NAACPPmf; Trial Transcript,

Virginia v. Crawford, pp. 49–52, 228–229, 289–290; Walter White, [Notes on Crawford Trial], 12/13/1933, P8-SerA-R7-F333-46, NAACPPmf.

42. *Loudoun Times-Mirror,* 12/21/1933, p. 4; Transcript, Virginia v. Crawford, pp. 396–411.

43. Transcript, Virginia v. Crawford, pp. 296–378. The prosecution actually put three confessions into evidence. The first one was recorded on the two-part transcript, and that confession effectively determined the admissibility and relevance of all three.

44. Transcript, Virginia v. Crawford, pp. 356–361, 501–509; Walter White to Roy Wilkins, 12/14/1933, p. 1, P8-SerA-R7-F332, NAACPPmf.

45. Transcript, Commonwealth of Virginia v. Crawford, pp. 473, 474–496, 516.

46. *Ibid.,* pp. 516, 517, 519, 524, 526.

47. "'Homeless Dog' Plea Saves Life of Crawford," *Afro-American,* n.d., B108/2-F25, JGTP; *WP,* 12/31/1933, pp. SM3, 15; Walter White to Virginius Dabney, 12/18/1933, P8-SerA-R7-F365, NAACPPmf; *NJG,* 12/23/1933, pp. 1, 15.

48. Transcript, Virginia v. Crawford, pp. 537, 538, 540, 541; *CD,* 11/18/1933, p. 1; *CD,* 12/16/1933, p. 1; "Crawford Case Ends in Legal Love Feast," B108/2-F25, JGTP.

49. Walter White to CHH, 12/18/1933, P8-SerA-R7-F358, NAACPPmf; George Crawford—Symbol, F248–54, *ibid.;* White, "George Crawford"; Douglas Freeman to Walter White, 12/18/1933, F389, *ibid.; NYT,* 12/24/1933, p. E7; *WP,* 12/31/1933, pp. SM3, 15.

50. Lee v. State, 161 A. 284 (Md. 1932); Norris v. Alabama, 294 U.S. 587 (1935).

51. Genna Rae McNeil, *Groundwork: Charles Hamilton Houston and the Struggle for Civil Rights* (Philadelphia: University of Pennsylvania Press, 1983), 115–118; *WP,* 12/16/1933, p. 15; Walter White to John Galleher, 12/22/1933, P8-SerA-R7-F386, NAACPPmf.

52. *NJG,* n.d., B173/14-F20, LARP; Frank Raflo, *Within the Iron Gates: A Collection of Stories about Loudoun* (Leesburg, Va.: Loudoun Times-Mirror, 1988), 348–353; Virginius Dabney to CHH, 3/19/1940, B163/30-F15, CHHP; *Richmond Times-Dispatch,* 3/13/1940, F8, *ibid.*

53. Lisa Lindquist Dorr, *White Women, Rape, and the Power of Race in Virginia, 1900–1960* (Chapel Hill: University of North Carolina Press, 2004), 103, 105, 151; CHH, Memorandum re: Samuel Legions, 2/20/1942, B163/24-F10, CHHP; CHH to J. R. H. Alexander, 4/30/1942, F11, *ibid.;* CHH, Memorandum re: Samuel Legions Case, 4/8/1942, *ibid.;* CHH to Colgate W. Darden, 6/3/1942, F13, *ibid.; Washington Evening Star,* 6/15/1932, F23, *ibid.;* CHH to Samuel Legions, 6/16/1943, *ibid.;* Legions v. Commonwealth, 23 S.E.2d 764 (Va. 1943).

5. *Young Thurgood Marshall Joins the Brotherhood of the Bar*

1. Thurgood Marshall, "The Reminiscences of Thurgood Marshall," in Mark V. Tushnet, ed., *Thurgood Marshall: His Speeches, Writings, Arguments, Opinions, and Reminiscences* (Chicago: Lawrence Hill Books, 2001), 419; Mark V. Tushnet, *Making Civil Rights Law: Thurgood Marshall and the Supreme Court, 1936–1961* (New York: Oxford University Press, 1994), 10; [File Cards of Thurgood Marshall on his Legal Cases], Vol1-PartC-B-438-F1, NAACPP; Daniel Becker, "Segregated City: Black Lawyers in the 1950s," *Washington Lawyer,* Sept. 2001, p. 29.

2. "Remembering the Fourth Circuit Judges: A History from 1941 to 1998," *Washington & Lee Law Review* 55 (1998): 471, 514–519; Myers v. Anderson, 238 U.S. 368 (1915); Benno C. Schmidt Jr., "Principle and Prejudice: The Supreme Court and Race in the Progressive Era, Part 3," *Columbia Law Review* 82 (1982): 835, 866 n. 139; *Baltimore Sun,* 12/14/1922, p. 7; Fountain v. State, 107 A. 554 (Md. 1919).

3. Sherrilyn A. Ifill, *On the Courthouse Lawn: Confronting the Legacy of Lynching in the Twenty-first Century* (Boston: Beacon Press, 2007), 14–15, 30–55.

4. Tushnet, *Making Civil Rights Law,* 8–9; Juan Williams, *Thurgood Marshall: American Revolutionary* (New York: Random House, 1998), 22–60.

5. *BAA,* 12/12/1931, p. 8; Lee v. State, 157 A. 723, 725 (Md. 1931); Lee v. State, 161 A. 284 (Md. 1932); *BAA,* 12/16/1933, p. 12; CHH to Bernard Ades, 12/7/1933, B163/36-F17, CHHP.

6. Clater W. Smith to Dallas Nicholas, 6/16/1941, B9B1a, DNP.

7. *BAA,* 12/16/1933, p. 12; CHH to Bernard Ades, 12/7/1933, B163/36-F17, CHHP; *BAA,* 11/04/1933, p. 11. The picture of Ades and his attorneys can be found in Joseph E. Moore, *Murder on Maryland's Eastern Shore: Race, Politics and the Case of Orphan Jones* (Charleston, S.C.: History Press, 2006), 159.

8. Lee v. State, 157 A. 723 (Md. 1931); Lee v. State, 161 A. 284 (Md. 1932); *Baltimore Sun,* 10/24/1933, B163/36-F14, CHHP.

9. Moore, *Murder on Maryland's Eastern Shore,* 204–206; Ifill, *On the Courthouse Lawn,* 50–54.

10. Statement of the ILD on the Ades Case Decision, 4/2/1934, p. 2, B163/37-F1, CHHP; CHH to TM, 1/25/1934, B163/36-F24; TM to CHH 12/14/1933, *ibid.,* F17; CHH to TM, 1/25/1934, *ibid.,* F24.

11. *BAA,* 3/10/1934, p. 23; In re Ades, 6 F. Supp. 467, 477, 479–481 (D. Maryland 1934); Statement of the ILD on the Ades Case Decision, 4/2/1934, p. 2, B163/37-F1, CHHP.

12. *BAA,* 3/10/1934, p. 23; In re Ades, 6 F. Supp. at 480–81; *BAA,* 12/15/1934, p. 16; Vernon Pedersen, *The Communist Party in Maryland, 1919–57* (Urbana: University of Illinois Press, 2001), 61–62; Moore, *Murder on Maryland's Eastern Shore,* 213–214.

13. Aaron Borden to CHH, 3/19/1934, B163/36-F29, CHHP.

14. Moore, *Murder on Maryland's Eastern Shore*, 212.

15. Lawrence M. Friedman, *American Law in the Twentieth Century* (New Haven, Conn.: Yale University Press, 2002), 84–85; R. J. Valentine and R. H. Cooley to TM, 4/19/1940, P15-SerA-R17-F592, NAACPPmf.

16. Ifill, *On the Courthouse Lawn*, 15; Fountain v. State, 107 A. 554, 555 (Md. 1919).

17. *WP*, 10/16/1934, p. 26; *WP*, 12/8/1934, p. 11; *BAA*, 12/15/1934, p. 16.

18. Williams, *Thurgood Marshall*, 29, 65–66; *WP*, 7/26/1934, p. 3; *CD*, 8/4/1934, p. 3; *WP*, 4/5/1935, p. 6; Gross, Mrs. Corine [notecard], V1-Part C-B438-F1, NAACPP.

19. TM to Walter White, 12/12/1934, P8-SerA-R11-F525-26, NAACPPmf; TM, re: State vs. William Carter [memorandum], 12/18/1934, December 18, 1934, *ibid.*

20. TM to Roy Wilkins, 12/18/1934, P2-R3-F648, NAACPPmf; TM, re: State vs. William Carter [memorandum], 12/18/1934, December 18, 1934, *ibid.*

21. TM to Roy Wilkins, 12/18/1934, P2-R3-F648, NAACPPmf; TM, re: State vs. William Carter [memorandum], 12/18/1934, *ibid.;* TM to CHH, 12/18/1934, Vol1-AdminFile-C196, NAACPP.

22. *BAA*, 12/22/1934, p. 6; *WP*, 12/18/1934, p. 19; "N.A.A.C.P. Lawyer Probes Rape Case in Frederick, Md.," *BAA*, n.d., P2-R5-F346-47, NAACPPmf.

23. TM to Roy Wilkins, 6/7/1935, P8-SerA-R12-F447, NAACPPmf; *PC*, 4/20/1935, p. 8; TM, re: State vs. James Poindexter [memorandum], 6/7/1935, P8-SerA-R12-F448-50, NAACPPmf; Roy Wilkins to TM 6/3/1934, P8-SerA-R12-F444, NAACPPmf; Poindexter to NAACP, 5/22/1935, *ibid.*, F445-46.

24. Roy Wilkins to TM, 6/30/1935, P8-SerA-R12-F451, NAACPPmf; TM to Roy Wilkins, 6/7/1935, P8-SerA-R12-F447, NAACPPmf; TM, re: State vs. James Poindexter [memorandum], 6/7/1935, P8-SerA-R12-F448-50, NAACPPmf.

25. *BAA*, 5/4/1935, p. 5; TM to Walter White, 9/11/1934, P8-SerA-R11-F387, NAACPPmf.

26. *BAA*, 5/4/1935, p. 5; Robert P. McGuinn to TM, 8/15/1935, P2-R4-F183, NAACPPmf; David Skillen Bogen, "The First Integration of Maryland School of Law," *Maryland Historical Magazine* 88 (1989): 39, 42–44. The out-of-state scholarship commission was headquartered at 4 East Redwood Street, the same building where Marshall, like many local black lawyers, had his office. It sent one of its members to the trial to testify in support of the NAACP. There is a good chance that Judge Soper was tacitly supporting the lawsuit, in cooperation with the local black bar. Robert P. McGuinn to TM, 8/15/1935, P2-R4-F183, NAACPPmf; *NJG*, 4/13/1935, p. 5.

27. TM, Memo, n.d., P3-SerA-R13-F659, NAACPPmf; R. A. Pearson to Harold Arthur Stevens, 7/26/1933, *ibid.*, F159; R. A. Pearson to Juanita E. Jackson, 2/19/1934, *ibid.*, F166; Stenographer's Record, Murray v. Pearson, p. 129; Tushnet, *Making Civil Rights Law*, 11, 14.

28. Marshall, "Reminiscences of Thurgood Marshall," 418–419; Richard Kluger, *Simple Justice* (New York: Vintage Books, 1977), 189; *BAA*, 6/22/1935, pp. 1, 7.

29. Stenographer's Record, Murray v. Pearson (Baltimore City Court, June 18, 1935), pp. 1–116, 117.

30. *BAA*, 6/22/1935, p. 7; Tushnet, *Making Civil Rights Law*, 14. The *Baltimore Afro-American*'s report of the trial states that the "ox cart" remark was made by the law school dean rather than LeViness, presumably during the trial testimony—an assertion picked up in some historical accounts of the case. But that remark does not appear in the trial transcript, and the *Afro* article describes the remark in its report on the closing argument, not the trial testimony. The reporter probably just inserted the wrong name into that paragraph.

31. Walter White to Elizabeth Gilman, 11/13/1935, P3-SerA-R13-F608, NAACPPmf; Walter White to Elizabeth Gilman, 11/20/1935, p. 2, *ibid.*, F619.

32. Transcript of the Shorthand Report of the Proceedings, etc., Pearson v. Murray, No. 53 (Ct. App. Md., November 5, 1935), at 2, *ibid.*, R14-F155; TM to CHH, 12/6/1935, *ibid.*, R13-F627.

33. Walter White to Elizabeth Gilman, 11/13/1935, P3-SerA-R13-F608, NAACPPmf.

34. TM to Walter White, 9/10/1934, P8-SerA-R11-F339, NAACPPmf; Karen Lesla Williams Gooden, *A Cross Bourne: A Biography of Judge James Franklyn Bourne, Jr.* (Virginia Beach, Va.: Donning Co., 1993); B. V. Lawson to C. Y. Trigg, 8/2/1934, P8-SerA-R11-F494, NAACPPmf; TM to Walter White, 9/10/1934, *ibid.*, F389; TM to Walter White, 9/26/1934, *ibid.*, F408; *Baltimore Sun*, 12/16/1924, p. 28.

35. *CD*, 8/4/1934, p. 3; *NJG*, 8/4/1934, p. 2.

36. TM to Walter White, 9/11/1934, P8-SerA-R11-F387, NAACPPmf; TM to Walter White, 9/21/1934, *ibid.*, F401; TM to Walter White, 9/26/1934, *ibid.*, F408.

37. State of Maryland vs. Charles Flory [memorandum], 5/7/1935, *ibid.*, F549; TM to CHH, 10/17/1935, *ibid.*, F575; TM to Roy Wilkins, 10/17/1935, *ibid.*, F574. Mattingly along with his colleague Judge William Loker presided over both the criminal and civil trials.

38. B. V. Lawson to TM, 10/15/1935, P8-SerA-R11-F561, NAACPPmf; *BAA*, 2/1/1936, p. 5; *NJG*, 2/8/1936, p. 5.

39. Transcript, Commonwealth of Virginia v. Crawford, p. 516; James L. McLemore, Letter to Editor, *The Nation*, 8/8/1934, p. 159; *NJG*, 1/27/1934, p. 7.

40. City of Greenwood v. Peacock, 384 U.S. 808 (1966); Cox v. Louisiana, 348 F.2d 750 (5th Cir. 1965); City of Clarksdale v. Gertge, 237 F. Supp. 213 (D. Miss. 1964), *rev'd*, Smith v. City of Drew, 360 F.2d 283 (5th Cir. 1966).

41. J. L. Chestnut Jr. and Julia Cass, *Black in Selma: The Uncommon Life of J. L. Chestnut, Jr.* (New York: Farrar, Straus and Giroux, 1990), 183; Solomon Seay Jr., *Jim Crow and Me: Stories from My Life as a Civil Rights Lawyer* (Montgomery, Ala.: New South Books, 2008), 42–44.

6. A Woman in a Fraternity of Lawyers

1. *NYT*, 7/23/1939, p. 7; *LAT*, 7/23/1939, p. 3; *Cleveland Call & Post*, 8/3/1939, p. 8; *AN*, 7/29/1939, p. 1; *BAA*, 7/29/1939, p. 1; Jacob Panken, Remarks on the Induction of Justice Bolin, 7/24/1939, B3, JMBP; *NYT*, 5/14/1993, p. B8; *NYT*, 1/10/2007. To protect client anonymity, pseudonyms will be used for client names mentioned in this chapter.

2. STMA to Jane M. Bolin, 7/25/1939, B6-F12, STMAP; Sadie T. M. Alexander, "Women as Practitioners of Law in the United States," *National Bar Journal* 1 (1941): 56–64; PM to Jane Bolin, 2/14/1978, B1-F5, JMBP.

3. See, for example, Jacqueline A. McLeod, "Persona Non-Grata: Judge Jane Matilda Bolin and the NAACP, 1930–1950," *Afro-Americans in New York Life and History* 29 (January 2005): 7–29; Helen LaVille and Scott Lucas, "The American Way: Edith Sampson, the NAACP, and African American Identity in the Cold War," *Diplomatic History* 20 (Fall 1996): 565–590; Kevin K. Gaines, "Pauli Murray in Ghana: The Congo Crisis and an African American Woman's Dilemma," in Kevin K. Gaines, *African Americans in Ghana: Black Expatriates and the Civil Rights Era* (Chapel Hill: University of North Carolina Press, 2006), 110–135; Virginia Drachman, *Sisters in Law: Women Lawyers in Modern American History* (Cambridge, Mass.: Harvard University Press, 1998), 199–211; Glenda Elizabeth Gilmore, *Defying Dixie: The Radical Roots of Civil Rights, 1919–1950* (New York: W. W. Norton, 2008); Nancy MacLean, *Freedom Is Not Enough: The Opening of the American Workplace* (Cambridge, Mass.: Harvard University Press, 2006), 119–154.

4. Panken, Remarks on the Induction of Justice Bolin; *AN*, 7/29/1939, p. 10; *BAA*, 7/29/1939, p. 2; *BAA*, 8/19/1939, p. 16; Letter to the Editor, *AN*, 12/2/1939, p. 14; Jessie Carney Smith, Undated Biographical Sketch of Jane Bolin, B3, JMBP; *CD*, 8/19/1939, p. 18.

5. "Interview with Sadie Tanner Mossell Alexander," 10/12/1977, p. 5, B1-F20, STMAP; *BAA*, 7/25/1931, p. 5; *BAA*, 3/5/1938, p. 9; Christine Ann Lutz, "'The Dizzy Steep to Heaven': The Hunton Family and the Atlantic World, 1850–1970" (Ph.D. diss., Georgia State University, 2001), 278; Edith Spurlock Sampson, These Things I Remember Well, p. 4, B1-F1; Jane Bolin, [Untitled Speech at Dedication of Bust of W. E. B. Du Bois], [1957], pp. 2–3, JMBP; *CD*, 9/30/1939.

6. Ruth Whitehead Whaley, "Closed Doors: A Study in Segregation," in Venetria K. Patton and Maureen Honey, eds., *Double Take: A Revisionist Harlem Renaissance Anthology* (New Brunswick, N.J.: Rutgers University Press, 2001), 17, 19; Zephyr Abigail Moore, "Law and Its Call to Women," in J. Clay Smith Jr., ed., *Rebels in Law: Voices in History of Black Women Lawyers* (Ann Arbor: University of Michigan Press, 1998), 13, 14; Bolin, [Untitled Speech at Dedication of Bust of W. E. B. Du Bois], p. 3.

7. STMA to Dorothy L. Freeman, 4/18/1946, B49-F42, STMAP; "Interview with Sadie Tanner Mossell Alexander," 10/12/1977, pp. 4–7.

8. *PT*, 6/21/1924, p. 9; *BAA*, 6/20/1935, p. A3; *BAA*, 7/25/1931, p. 5.

9. Pauli Murray, *Song in a Weary Throat: An American Pilgrimage* (New York: Harper & Row, 1987), 283; CHH to Leonard Outhwaite, 5/7/1928, S3.8-B101-F1018, LSRMP; Katie McCabe and Dovey Johnson Roundtree, *Justice Older Than the Law: The Life of Dovey Johnson Roundtree* (Jackson: University of Mississippi Press, 2009).

10. *BAA*, 7/25/1931, p. 5; *CD*, 5/31/1924, p. A7; Lutz, "'Dizzy Steep to Heaven,'" 282; Republican Candidate for Assembly, 19th Assembly District: Jane M. Bolin, B3, clippings file, JMBP; Publicity Material on Elsie Austin, B13-F18, STMAP; [Untitled Data Sheet on Chicago Black Woman Lawyers], *ibid.;* David Hepburn, "Edith Sampson Speaks for America," *Our World,* February 1951, B2-F45f, ESSP; STMA, "Remarks of Sadie T. M. Alexander, Esq. At Luncheon Honoring Her Fifty Years in the Practice of Law," 5/24/1979, p. 3, B72-F17, STMAP.

11. *BAA*, 7/25/1931, p. 5; Alexander, "Remarks," pp. 2–3; Linda K. Kerber, *No Constitutional Right to Be Ladies: Women and the Obligations of Citizenship* (New York: Hill & Wang, 1998), 170.

12. Murray, *Song in a Weary Throat,* 277; *BAA,* 2/21/1959, B1-F6, JMBP; *WP,* 2/14/1977, pp. B1, B8; *BAA,* 7/25/1931, p. 5; "Edith Sampson Speaks for America"; J. D. Ratcliff, "Edith Sampson . . . Thorn in Russia's Side," *United Nations World* 5 (March 1951): 24, 25.

13. Sadie T. M. Alexander, "The Best of Times and the Worst of Times," *University of Pennsylvania Law Alumni Journal* 12 (Spring 1977): 20–21; Alexander, "Remarks," pp. 3–4.

14. Alexander, [Reminiscences of a Career in Law], pp. 1–3; STMA to Dorothy L. Freeman, 4/18/1946, B49-F42, STMAP; Sadie T. M. Alexander, "Forty-five Years a Woman Lawyer," *The Shingle* 35 (June 1972): 127; *BAA,* 7/25/1931, p. 5; Transcript of Interview of Jane Bolin by Jean Rudd with Lionel Bolin, 6/4/1990, pp. 13–14, B1-F2, JMBP.

15. Drachman, *Sisters in Law,* 85–93, 259; Beatrice Doerschuk, *Women in the Law: An Analysis of Training, Practice and Salaried Positions* (New York: Bureau of Vocational Information, 1920), 41–45; Murray, *Song in a Weary Throat,* 272.

16. Barbara Watts Goodall to STMA, 10/15/1947, B51-F6, STMAP; Edith Spurlock Sampson, "Legal Profession Followed by Nation's Best Known Socialites," in Smith, *Rebels in Law,* 17; Eunice H. Carter to STMA, 4/26/1939, B13-F18, STMA; STMA to Eunice H. Carter, 4/28/1939, B13-F17, *ibid.;* Elsie Austin to STMA, B13-F18, *ibid.*

17. Alexander, "Forty-five Years a Woman Lawyer," 126, 127; [Reminiscences of a Career in Law], pp. 1–2.

18. Alexander, "Forty-five Years a Woman Lawyer," 127.

19. "Interview with Sadie Tanner Mossell Alexander," 10/12/77," pp. 6–7.

20. *Ibid.,* p. 7.

21. "Interview with Sadie Tanner Mossell Alexander," 10/12/77, p. 6; Alexander, "Best of Times and the Worst of Times," 19–20.

22. Alexander, "Forty-five Years a Women Lawyer," 126; Charles Houston, Tentative Findings re: Negro Lawyers (Jan. 23, 1928) (revised), p. 10, S3.8-B101-F1019, LSRMP; Interview of Curtis Carson by Kenneth W. Mack, Philadelphia, 6/11/1999, pp. 1–2.

23. Certificate of Admission to Practice before the Orphans' Court, 10/7/1927, B72-F22, STMAP; STMA, [Reminiscences of a Career in Law], p. 1; "Interview with Sadie Tanner Mossell Alexander," 10/12/1977, p. 6.

24. Divorce Docket, 1926 to 1937, B20-F1, STMAP; Master's Report, James Sterling, also Called James Johnson v. Annie Sterling (Mun. Ct. of Phila. 1944), at 9, B36-F27, *ibid.*

25. Alexander, "Remarks," p. 3; George W. Maxey to STMA, 2/28/1936, B10-F26, STMAP.

26. Ruth Whitehead Whaley, "Women Lawyers Must Balk Both Color and Sex Bias," in Smith, *Rebels in Law,* 50; STMA to Ann Butler, 3/16/1938, B11-F2, STMAP.

27. Ratcliff, "Edith Sampson: Thorn in Russia's Side," p. 25; Jane Bolin, Interview by Jean Rudd, pp. 47–53; *New York Amsterdam Star-News,* 6/14/1941, p. 15; Lutz, " 'Dizzy Steep to Heaven,'" 279, 289; *BAA,* 3/19/1938, p. 9.

28. [Untitled Data Sheet on Chicago Black Women Lawyers], B13-F20, STMAP; To the Committee on Admissions: The Association of the Bar of the City of New York (1943), B1-F3, JMBP; Eunice H. Carter to STMA, 4/26/1939, B13-F18, STMAP.

29. STMA to Jane Bolin, 11/7/1945, B48-F36, STMAP; Interview of Curtis Carson by Kenneth Mack, p. 2; Interview of Clark Byse by Kenneth W. Mack, Cambridge, Mass., 5/17/2000; Charles W. Anderson to Sidney R. Redmond, 11/22/1945, p. 1, B49-F32, STMAP; STMA to Allan Morrison, 12/9/1946, p. 6, B50-F16, STMAP.

30. Interview of Sadie Alexander by Marcia Greenlee, 1/26/1977, in Ruth Edmonds Hill, ed., *The Black Women Oral History Project,* vol. 2 (Westport, Conn.: Meckler Publishing, 1991), 67, 79.

31. Petition for Counsel Fee, Mary J. Goode v. William Goode (Phila. Ct. of C.P. 1943), B35-F22, STMAP; Fitzhugh Lee Styles to STMA, 1/30/1943, *ibid.;* STMA to Fitzhugh Lee Styles, 3/24/1943, *ibid.;* William Cohen to STMA, 5/14/1945, *ibid.;* STMA to Mary Goode, 11/18/1945, *ibid.*

32. Irving J. Katz to STMA, 5/4/1943, B36-F27, STMAP; Annie Sterling to STMA, 8/31/1944, *ibid.;* STMA to Annie Sterling, 9/5/1944, *ibid.;* STMA to Annie Sterling, 9/15/1944, *ibid.;* Master's Report, James Sterling, also Called James Johnson v. Annie Sterling (Mun. Ct. of Phila. 1944), *ibid.*

33. STMA to Dorothy Rolle, 9/2/1942, p. 2, B37-F1, STMAP.

34. Dorothy Rolle to STMA, n.d., B37-F1, STMAP; STMA to Oliver Hill, 5/12/1943, *ibid.;* Oliver Hill to STMA, 5/15/1943, *ibid.;* STMA to Oliver Hill, 5/17/1943, *ibid.;* Oliver Hill to STMA, May 21, 1943, *ibid.;* STMA to Dorothy Rolle, July 2, 1943, *ibid.*

35. Power of Attorney, In re Estate of James Edward Windsor (Orphans' Ct. of Phila. 1942), B32-F4, STMAP; STMA to Jane Du Bois, 6/8/1942, *ibid.;* STMA to Joanne Houston, 4/8/1943, F14, *ibid.;* STMA to Oscar Windsor, 7/14/1943, F13, *ibid.;* STMA to the heirs of James E. Windsor, 10/1/1945, F20, *ibid.;* Rule to Accept or Refuse Partition, In re Estate of Windsor (1947), F26, *ibid.;* Principal of Personal Estate, In re Estate of Windsor (1948), folder 32, *ibid.*

36. William Seraile, *Fire in His Heart: Bishop Benjamin Tucker Tanner and the A.M.E. Church* (Knoxville: University of Tennessee Press, 1998); Brendan Davis et al. v. Arthur Jamison et al. (Phila. Ct. of C.P. 1944), B35-F3, STMAP.

37. STMA to Herbert E. Millen, 1/12/1943, B35-F3, STMAP; Master's Report, Davis v. Jamison (1944), *ibid.;* STMA to Robert K. Greenfield, n.d., F1, *ibid.*

38. STMA to Rev. Michael Dudley, 2/7/1945, B37-F42, STMAP; STMA to Pennsylvania Company, 2/12/1945, *ibid.;* STMA to Jack Findley, 4/4/1945, *ibid.;* George White to STMA, 3/31/1945, B36-F48, *ibid.*

39. STMA to Bartholomew Sicuglienio, 11/3/1944, B37-F29, STMAP; RPA to Julius Langhorne, 8/11/1943, *ibid.;* STMA to J. P. Meehan, 1/30/1942, *ibid.;* STMA, Memorandum to Matthew Bullock, 8/7/1950, B14, *ibid.;* Articles of Incorporation, In re Saints of Grace Church (Phila. Ct. of C.P. 1951), *ibid.;* STMA to William W. Bunn, 11/21/1951, *ibid.;* J. Paul Lyet to STMA, 11/28/1951, *ibid.;* J. Paul Lyet to STMA, 12/12/1951, *ibid.;* STMA to Lori Groomes, 12/17/1951, *ibid.*

40. James Willard Hurst, *The Growth of American Law: The Lawmakers* (Boston: Little, Brown, 1950), 303.

41. National Urban League, *Negro Heroes,* no. 2: *Woman of the Year* (Summer 1948), B1-F3, STMAP; Sixteenth Census of the United States, Vol. 3: The Labor Force, Part 1: United States Summary, Table 62, Race of Employed Persons (Except on Public Emergency Work), and of Experienced Workers Seeking Work by Occupation and Sex, for the United States: 1940, p. 90; Smith, *Rebels in Law,* 286.

42. STMA to Allan Morrison, 12/9/1946, pp. 3, 5, 6, B50-F16, STMAP; STMA to Adrian Bonnelly, 3/15/1944, B6-F24, STMAP.

43. *CD,* 5/10/1947, B7-F137, ESSP; "First Negro Woman to Win State Post," *ibid.;* "Woman Attorney Blazes Second Trail," *ibid.;* "Mrs. Sampson Gets $9,000 Legal Job," *ibid.;* William O. Douglas to Edith Sampson, 5/22/1951, B3-F70, *ibid.;* Hubert H. Humphrey to Edith Sampson, 10/27/1950, B5-F109, *ibid.;* Hepburn, "Edith Sampson Speaks for America"; Dale Kramer, "America's Newest Diplomat," *New Republic,* 1/22/1951, p. 15, B2-F43, *ibid.*

44. Whaley, "Women Lawyers Must Balk Both Color and Sex Bias," 49, 50, 51.

45. Pauli Murray diary, 4/19/1967, B2-F30, PMP.

7. Things Fall Apart

1. *BAA,* 12/12/1931, p. 8; *Philadelphia Independent,* 3/20/1932, 1931–1935 Scrapbook, RPAP; *BAA,* 2/16/1935, p. 1; Kenneth W. Mack, "Law and Mass Politics in the Making of the Civil Rights Lawyer, 1931–1941," *Journal of American History* 93 (2006): 37–62.

2. RPA to William Andrews, 4/22/1931, B85-F18, RPAP; Louis C. Tyree to RPA, 5/9/1931, *ibid.;* Dan T. Carter, *Scottsboro: A Tragedy of the American South,* rev. ed. (Baton Rouge: LSU Press, 1979), 3–103; James Goodman, *Stories of Scottsboro* (New York: Vintage Books, 1994), 3–38; Susan Pennybacker, *From Scottsboro to Munich: Race and Political Culture in 1930s Britain* (Princeton, N.J.: Princeton University Press, 2009), 24–26; RPA to Perry W. Howard, 7/27/1931, B85-F12, RPAP.

3. *AN,* 8/12/1931, p. 20; *Daily Worker,* 7/30/1947, p. 5; Dan Georgakas, "Brodsky, Joseph," in Mary Jo Buhle, Paul Buhle, and Dan Georgakas, eds., *Encyclopedia of the American Left,* 2nd ed. (New York: Oxford University Press, 1998), 108.

4. *What Is the I.L.D.?* (New York: International Labor Defense, 1934), 9, 13; *Labor Defense Manifesto, Resolutions; Constitution Adopted by the First National Conference* (Chicago: International Labor Defense, [c. 1925]), 10; Rebecca N. Hill, *Men, Mobs, and Law: Anti-Lynching and Labor Defense in U.S. Radical History* (Durham, N.C.: Duke University Press), 2008; Mark Solomon, *The Cry Was Unity: Communists and African Americans, 1917–1936* (Jackson: University Press of Mississippi, 1998), 185–206, 219–223, 238–249; Charles Martin, "The International Labor Defense and Black America," *Labor History* 26 (1985): 165, 168.

5. [Minutes of the 1936 Convention of the National Bar Association], 8/6/1936, Afternoon Session, P2-R3-F15, NAACPPmf; *BAA,* 8/16/1930, p. 3.

6. Kevin Boyle, *Arc of Justice: A Saga of Race, Civil Rights, and Murder in the Jazz Age* (New York: Henry Holt, 2004).

7. National Bar Association, *Proceedings of the National Bar Association at Its Seventh and Eighth Annual Meetings* (Chicago: Chicago Review Publishing Co., [1933]), 8–19, 20, 22.

8. *Ibid.,* p. 23.

9. *Ibid.,* 24–28, 30, 31, 32, 33.

10. National Bar Association Elects Heslip President, B85-F20, RPAP; *PC,* 8/15/1931, pp. 1, 4; *Proceedings of the National Bar Association,* 54.

11. *Philadelphia Record,* 2/25/1932, 1931–1935 Scrapbook, RPAP; *PT,* 2/25/1932, p. 1. The Scottsboro defendants seemed to confess during their first trials when, unnerved by the tense courtroom atmosphere, they began to accuse each other of the crime.

12. *PT,* 2/18/1932, pp. 1, 2; *PT,* 3/10/1932, p. 2; *PT,* 3/31/1932, p. 1; *PT,* 4/14/1932, p. 16.

13. *PT,* 11/3/1933, p. 1; *PC,* 12/3/1932, p. A9.

14. George W. Maxey to RPA, 5/41933, 1931–1935 Scrapbook, RPAP; Commonwealth v. Brown, 164 A. 726, 730, 731, and n. 2 (1933); George W. Maxey to RPA, 1/11/1933, 1931–1935 Scrapbook, RPAP.

15. Charles H. Houston, "Commonwealth v. William Brown," *Opportunity* 11 (1933): 109, 111.

16. *Philadelphia Independent,* 3/20/1932, Scrapbook, RPAP.

17. *PT,* 4/27/1933, p. 1; *PT,* 9/28/1933, p. 1; *PT,* 11/9/1933, p. 16; Roy Wilkins to Herbert Millen, 10/10/1933, P3-R8-F250, NAACPPmf.

18. "The Negro and the Courts," *Opportunity* 11 (April 1933): 103.

19. Mack, "Law and Mass Politics," 43; *Cambridge Directory of the Inhabitants, Business Firms, Institutions, Manufacturing Establishments, Societies* (Boston: W. A. Greenough, 1922); *ibid.,* 1927; *ibid.,* 1928; *ibid.,* 1930; John M. Fitzgerald and Otley M. Scruggs, "A Note on Marcus Garvey at Harvard," in Werner Sollors, Caldwell Titcomb, and Thomas A. Underwood, eds., *Blacks at Harvard: A Documentary History of African-American Experience at Harvard and Radcliffe* (New York: NYU Press, 1993), 189, 193; Loren Miller to William T. Smith, n.d., B1, LMP.

20. Note Card, Harvard Law School Quinquennial Catalogue, BDPH; Richard L. Abel, *American Lawyers* (New York: Oxford University Press, 1989), 280; Charles Johnson, *The Negro College Graduate* (Chapel Hill: University of North Carolina Press, 1938), 375; STMA, The Economic Status of Negro Women, [Feb. 1934], B71-F31, STMAP.

21. *PC,* 1/30/1932, p. A3; Tomiko Brown-Nagin, *Courage to Dissent: Atlanta and the Long History of the Civil Rights Movement* (New York: Oxford University Press, 2011); Karen Ferguson, *Black Politics in New Deal Atlanta* (Chapel Hill: University of North Carolina Press, 2002), 265; A. T. Walden, "Problems Confronting the Negro Lawyer in the South," p. 6, B85-F27, RPAP.

22. Charles H. Martin, *The Angelo Herndon Case and Southern Justice* (Baton Rouge: LSU Press, 1976); Kendall Thomas, "*Rouge et Noir* Reread: A Popular Constitutional History of the Angelo Herndon Case," *Southern California Law Review* 65 (1992): 2599.

23. Benjamin J. Davis, *Communist Councilman from Harlem* (New York: International Publishers, 1969), 41, 51–52; Gerald Horne, *Black Liberation / Red Scare: Ben Davis and the Communist Party* (Newark: University of Delaware Press), 26, 31; Louis L. Redding, "I Become a Party Man," *Opportunity* 7 (November 1929): 347–349; Louis Redding to Roy Wilkins, 9/2/1933, B95/8, Joel Spingarn papers, Moorland-Spingarn Research Center; *Atlanta Daily World,* 9/28/1932, p. 1A; *ibid.,* 7/27/1932, p. 5; *ibid.,* 9/4/1932, p. 5.

24. Angelo Herndon, *Let Me Live* (Ann Arbor: University of Michigan Press, 2007), 3–215; Transcript of Record at 70–78, Herndon v. State of Georgia, 295 U.S. 441 (1935); Davis, *Communist Councilman,* 54–55; William L.

Patterson, "The International Labor Defense and Courtroom Technicians," *Labor Defender*, May 1933, p. 54; Joel N. Bodansky, "The Abolition of Party-Witness Disqualification: An Historical Survey," *Kentucky Law Journal* 70 (1981–1982): 92–93.

25. *Atlanta Constitution*, 7/12/1940, p. 24; *ibid.*, 9/10/1931, p. 1.

26. Transcript of Record at 126–137, and especially pages 132–133, Herndon v. State; Thomas, *"Rouge et Noir,"* 2693–2694.

27. Davis, *Communist Councilman*, 62–68; Martin, *Angelo Herndon Case*, 47.

28. Transcript of Record at 60–61, Herndon v. State; the official trial transcript uses the word "darky" instead of "nigger." Davis charged that the transcript was altered when the record was prepared for appeal, an assertion supported by contemporary observers who reported that the prosecution used the word "nigger" as well as "darky," and that Davis obtained rulings on both epithets. The transcription that I have used in the text seems like the most logical way of squaring the official transcript with other contemporary sources. *AN*, 1/25/1933, p. 1; *NJG*, 1/28/1933, pp. A1, 15.

29. Davis, *Communist Councilman*, 73–75; Transcript of Record at 76, 80, Herndon v. State; Martin, *Angelo Herndon Case*, 47 n. 25; *WP*, 1/19/1933, p. 3; *Atlanta Constitution*, 1/19/1933, p. 1.

30. *Ben Davis on the McCarran Act at the Harvard Law Forum* (New York: Gus Hall—Benjamin Davis Defense Committee, 1962), 5; *Atlanta Constitution*, 5/15/1940, p. 1; *NYT*, 2/7/1960, p. 84.

31. Benjamin J. Davis Jr. to CHH, 6/12/1933, B163/26-F9, CHHP; Thurgood Marshall, "The Reminiscences of Thurgood Marshall," in Mark V. Tushnet, ed., *Thurgood Marshall: His Speeches, Writings, Arguments, Opinions, and Reminiscences* (Chicago: Lawrence Hill Books, 2001), 413, 439.

32. Alumni Fund Records of Annual Giving, BDPH; Ben J. Davis to Harrison S. Dimmitt, n.d., BDPH.

33. Interview of Earl B. Dickerson by Robert Blakely and James O. Berry, Chicago, 8/10/1983, p. 4; Truman K. Gibson Jr., *Knocking Down Barriers: My Fight for Black America* (Evanston, Ill.: Northwestern University Press, 2005), 72–73.

34. Jay Tidmarsh, "The Story of *Hansberry:* The Rise of the Modern Class Action," in Kevin M. Clermont, ed., *Civil Procedure Stories*, 2d ed. (New York: Thompson/Foundation Press, 2008), 233; Shifting Lines of Attack to Meet the Needs of the Day, P1-R9-F489, NAACPPmf.

35. Percival Prattis to Walter White, 9/12/1934, P8-SerA-R7-F611-12, NAACPPmf.

36. *NJG*, 11/11/1933, p. 1; Helen Boardman and Martha Gruening, *The Crawford Case: A Reply to the "N.A.A.C.P."* (New York: Helen Boardman and Martha Gruening, 1925), 20; Walter White to Ludwell Denny, 12/19/1933, P8-SerA-R7-F370, NAACPPmf; *BAA*, 12/23/1933, p. 11.

37. "What Happened at Leesburg," *Afro-American*, n.d., B108/2-F25, JGTP; *Loudoun Times-Mirror*, 11/9/1933, p. 2; *ibid.*, 12/14/1933, pp. 1, 4; *WP*, 12/14/1933, p. 5; Trial Transcript, Commonwealth of Virginia v. Crawford (Cir. Ct. Loudoun Co., Va., Dec. 12–16, 1933), pp. 524, 526; *PC*, 12/23/1933, pp. 1, 4.

38. Helen Boardman, "The South Goes Legal," *The Nation*, 3/8/1933, p. 258; *NJG*, 2/10/1934, pp. 1, 8.

39. Helen Boardman and Martha Gruening, "Is the N.A.A.C.P. Retreating?" *The Nation*, 6/27/1934, p. 730; Boardman and Gruening, *Crawford Case*.

40. Charles H. Houston and Leon Ransom, "The Crawford Case: An Experiment in Social Statesmanship," *The Nation*, 7/4/1934, p. 17.

41. A small sample of the voluminous debate includes: *NJG*, 2/24/1934; W. E. B. Du Bois, "The Crawford Case," *The Crisis*, May 1934, p. 149; *The Nation*, 7/18/1934, p. 75; *ibid.*, 8/8/1934, pp. 157–159; *New Masses*, 1/8/1935; *The Crisis* 42 (April 1935): 104; *The Crisis* 42 (May 1935): 147; *CD*, 6/30/1934, p. 10; *NJG*, 7/71934, p. A14; *PC*, 7/7/1934, p. 10; *Washington Tribune*, 2/16/1935, p. 2; *AN*, 3/9/1935, p. 1; *LAS*, 3/28/1935, p. 12.

42. Boardman and Gruening, *Crawford Case*; George Crawford to Walter White, 7/1/1933, P8-SerA-R6-F828, NAACPPmf; George Crawford to Walter White [corrected copy], 7/1/1933, *ibid.*

43. Transcript of Hearing in Circuit Court of Loudoun County, B163/26-F4, CHHP; Boardman and Gruening, *Crawford Case*, 10; *NJG*, 2/17/1934, p. 4.

44. *NJG*, 3/9/1935, p. 1.

45. CHH to Walter White, 2/17/1935, P8-SerA-R7-F677-78, NAACPPmf; Statement of George Crawford, 2/10/1935, *ibid.*, F682; CHH to Walter White, 2/25/1935, *ibid.*, F694; CHH to Walter White and Roy Wilkins, 3/12/1935, *ibid.*, F766–67; CHH to Roy Wilkins, 3/14/1935, *ibid.*, F771-72; CHH to Walter White, 3/4/1935 (telegram), *ibid.*, F716; "The George Crawford Case: A Statement by the N.A.A.C.P.—Part I," *The Crisis* 42 (April 1935): 104; "The George Crawford Case: A Statement by the NAACP—Part II," *The Crisis* 42 (May 1935): 143.

46. B. Joyce Ross, *J. E. Spingarn and the Rise of the NAACP, 1911–1939* (New York: Atheneum, 1972), 218–241; Patricia Sullivan, *Lift Every Voice: The NAACP and the Making of the Civil Rights Movement* (New York: New Press, 2009), 174–175; 203; Jonathan Scott Holloway, *Confronting the Veil: Abram Harris, Jr., E. Franklin Frazier, and Ralph Bunche, 1919–1941* (Chapel Hill: University of North Carolina Press, 2002), 93–103; Mack, "Law and Mass Politics," 55–61.

47. *AN*, 6/22/1935, p. 4; Boardman and Gruening, *Crawford Case*; "Who Is the N.A.A.C.P.?" in Boardman and Gruening, *Crawford Case*, 2.

48. "Who Is the N.A.A.C.P.?"

49. Roy Wilkins to William Pickens, 4/5/1935, P8-SerA-R7-F780, NAACPPmf; CHH to Roy Wilkins, 3/14/1935, *ibid.*, F771.

8. The Strange Journey of Loren Miller

1. LM to Juanita Ellsworth, 6/8/1935, B17, LMP; LM to Juanita Ellsworth, 7/1/1935, *ibid.; New Masses* 16 (July 1935): 12, 13.

2. LM to CHH, 1/24/1936, P3-SerA-R13-F730, NAACPPmf.

3. Loren Miller, *The Petitioners: The Story of the Supreme Court of the United States and the Negro* (New York: Random House, 1966); Richard Kluger, *Simple Justice* (New York: Vintage Books, 1977).

4. Interview of LM by Lawrence B. de Graaf, part 1, p. 2, 3/3/1967, Oral History 174, Center for Oral and Public History, California State University, Fullerton; Loren Miller, "College," in Sondra Kathryn Wilson, ed., *The Crisis Reader: Stories, Poetry, and Essays from the N.A.A.C.P.'s "Crisis" Magazine* (New York: Modern Library, 1999), 237–241.

5. Hilmar Ludvig Jensen, "The Rise of an African American Left: John P. Davis and the National Negro Congress" (Ph.D. diss., Cornell University, 1997), 111, 153, 160–200, 220, 268, 294, 305–306, 313, 479, 510; Official Transcript, John Preston Davis, Harvard Law School; Benjamin J. Davis, *Communist Councilman from Harlem: Autobiographical Notes Written in a Federal Penitentiary* (New York: International Publishers, 1969), 40–44; *LAT,* 5/17/1964, p. E4.

6. Martin Summers, *Manliness and Its Discontents: The Black Middle Class and the Transformation of Masculinity, 1900–1930* (Chapel Hill: University of North Carolina Press, 2004).

7. LM, de Graaf Interview, part 1, pp. 1–2; *The Crisis* 6 (August 1913): 194.

8. Douglas Flamming, *Bound for Freedom: Black Los Angeles in Jim Crow America* (Berkeley and Los Angeles: University of California Press, 2005), 280–295; Langston Hughes to LM, 8/21/1930, B1, LMP; Langston Hughes to LM, Sunday (n.d.), *ibid.*

9. *PT,* 7/30/1931, p. 12; *AN,* 7/29/1931, p. 2; *BAA,* 8/1/1931, p. 20; *Denver Star,* 8/1/1931, B1, LMP; *Kansas City Call,* 8/1/1931, *ibid.;* Press Release, n.d., *ibid.;* Loren Miller, "The Plight of the Negro Professional Man," *Opportunity* 9 (1931): 239, 240, 241.

10. LM to Henry Lee Moon, 2/11/1953, p. 4, B3, LMP.

11. Interview of PM by Genna Rae McNeil, 2/13/1976, p. 75, Interview G-0044, Southern Oral History Program Collection, Wilson Library, University of North Carolina at Chapel Hill; Katie McCabe and Dovey Johnson Roundtree, *Justice Older Than the Law: The Life of Dovey Johnson Roundtree* (Jackson: University of Press of Mississippi, 2009), 82; Scott Kurashige, *The Shifting Grounds of Race: Black and Japanese Americans in the Making of Multiethnic Los Angeles* (Princeton, N.J.: Princeton University Press, 2008), 36–90.

12. LM to Henry Lee Moon, 2/11/1953, p. 2, B3, LMP.

13. Pauli Murray, *Song in a Weary Throat: An American Pilgrimage* (New York: Harper & Row, 1987), 88, 89; "Notes on the San Francisco Conference," 4/27/1945, B73-F1271, PMP; *PT,* 12/16/1937, p. 20; *Richmond Planet,* 11/30/1937;

PT, 12/24/1931, p. 2; Henry Lee Moon, Information on Party of Players en Route to Moscow to Participate in Film on Negro Life in America, 6/11/1932, B1, LMP.

14. Langston Hughes, *I Wonder as I Wander: An Autobiographical Journey* (New York: Hill & Wang, 1956), 65–107; Arnold Rampersad, *The Life of Langston Hughes,* vol. 1, 1902–1941: *I, Too, Sing America* (New York: Oxford University Press, 1986), 236, 242–258; Glenda Elizabeth Gilmore, *Defying Dixie: The Radical Roots of Civil Rights, 1919–1950* (New York: W. W. Norton, 2008), 134–148; Louise Thompson Patterson, "With Langston Hughes in the USSR," *Freedomways* 8 (1968): 152–158. Homer Smith, one of the film group who stayed on in Russia, also wrote a firsthand account of the trip after his return to the United States during the Cold War, but Smith falsified many details of the story to minimize his own involvement. Homer Smith, *Black Man in Red Russia* (Chicago: Johnson Publishing, 1964).

15. Henry Lee Moon, Why I Never Joined the Communist Party, 2/2/1953, p. 33, B3, LMP; Gilmore, *Defying Dixie,* 61–66; Mark Naison, *Communists in Harlem during the Depression* (Urbana: University of Illinois Press, 1983), 17–19; Harry Haywood, *Black Bolshevik: Autobiography of an Afro-American Communist* (Chicago: Liberator Press, 1978), 218–280; LM, [Typescript of Observations on Soviet Union, 1933], B1, LMP; LM to Editor of *Soviet Russia Today,* 4/17/1932, *ibid.*

16. Francine Hirsch, *Empire of Nations: Ethnographic Knowledge and the Making of the Soviet Union* (Ithaca, N.Y.: Cornell University Press, 2005), 101–144, 187–233; *PC,* 8/13/1932, p. A3; *San Francisco Spokesman,* n.d., B1, LMP.

17. LM to Juanita Ellsworth, 9/8/1935, B17, *ibid.;* Interview of Loren Miller Jr. by Kenneth W. Mack, Los Angeles, 3/27/2007, p. 6.

18. LM to Norman McCleod, 3/3/1933, B1, LMP; G. W. Reed to LM, 3/1/1933, *ibid.;* LM to G. W. Reed, 3/3/1933, *ibid.;* LM to W. Henry Thomas, 3/3/1933, *ibid.; PC,* 2/4/1933, p. A6; Fay Allan to LM, 4/12/1933, B1, LMP.

19. *BAA,* 12/3/1932, p. 10; William Patterson to LM, 2/14/1933, B1, LMP; LM to William Patterson, 3/3/1933, *ibid.;* LM, "Mass Protest Saves the Scottsboro Boys," 3/16/1933, *ibid.;* LM to Revels Cayton, 3/3/1933, *ibid.*

20. LM to Frank Crosswaith, 3/3/1933, p. 3, B1, LMP; *PC,* 2/2/1935, p. 9; Anne Barbara Rapp, "A Marginalized Voice for Racial Justice: Charlotta Bass and Oppositional Politics, 1914–1960" (Ph.D. diss., University of California at Santa Barbara, 2005), 60–99; Flamming, *Bound for Freedom,* 224; NAACP Membership Report Blank, 12/15/1933, B1-F17, Vol1-SerG, NAACPP; *LAS,* 7/5/1934, p. 1; *LAS,* 3/14/1935, p. 1.

21. *BAA,* 11/12/1932, p. 2; *Atlanta Daily World,* 10/21/1932, p. 4; *PC,* 9/10/1932, p. 3; *PC,* 12/10/1932, p. 5; Frank Marshall Davis to LM, 12/30/1932, B1, LMP; Loren Miller, "One Way Out—Communism," *Opportunity* 12 (July 1934): 214–217; Crusader News Agency Press Releases 1935–1940 (microfilm), Schomburg Center for Research in Black Culture, New York.

22. *New Masses* 15, no. 3, 4/16/1935, pp. 10–12; *New Masses* 16, no. 5, 7/30/1935, pp. 11–13; *New Masses*, 10/29/1935, pp. 23–24; *CD*, 3/2/1935, p. 14; *BAA*, 4/27/1935, p. 12; *AN*, 5/18/1935, p. 2; LM to Juanita Ellsworth, 6/15/1935, p. 2, B17, LMP.

23. Patricia Sullivan, *Lift Every Voice: The NAACP and the Making of the Civil Rights Movement* (New York: New Press, 2009), 190–236; Beth Tompkins Bates, "A New Crowd Challenges the Agenda of the Old Guard in the NAACP, 1933–1941," *American Historical Review* 102 (1997): 340–377; Jensen, "The Rise of an African American Left," pp. 432–507.

24. *BAA*, 6/29/1935, p. 2.

25. Sullivan, *Lift Every Voice*, 221–223; *New Masses* 16 (July 16, 1935): 12–13; LM to Juanita Ellsworth, 7/1/1935, B17, LMP.

26. *New Masses* 16 (July 16, 1935): 12, 13.

27. *AN*, 7/20/1935, p. 13; *BAA*, 7/27/1935, p. 12; *AN*, 8/3/35, p. 11; *AN*, 8/10/1935, p. 9; LM to Juanita Ellsworth, 7/1/1935, B17, LMP; LM to Juanita Ellsworth, 10/8/1935, *ibid.*

28. LM to Juanita Ellsworth, 10/6/1935, *ibid.;* LM to Juanita Ellsworth, 10/8/1935, *ibid.;* LM to Juanita Ellsworth, 10/16/1935, B17, *ibid.*

29. LM to CHH, 1/24/1936, P3-SerA-R13-F730, NAACPPmf.

30. *LAT*, 5/17/1964, p. E4; LM to Revels Cayton, 3/3/1933, B1, LMP; LM to Juanita Ellsworth, 11/1/1935, *ibid.*, B17 (emphasis in original); "Prologue," in Joseph North, ed., *New Masses: An Anthology of the Rebel Thirties* (New York: International Publishers, 1972), 31; LM to Juanita Ellsworth, 9/8/1935, B17, LMP; Flamming, *Bound for Freedom*, 308; Miller, "College," 241.

31. Account Book, 6/1942 to 1/1944, B1, LMP; *LAS*, 4/16/1936, p. 8; *LAS*, 6/15/1939, p. 1; *LAS*, 10/12/1939, p. 1; *CD*, 4/27/1940, p. 5.

32. *LAS*, 9/3/1936, p. 1; Account Book, 6/1942 to 1/1944; LM to Rosa Farrington, 1/24/1945, B2, LMP; *LAS*, 4/16/1936, p. 4.

33. John to LM, 5/17/1937, B2, LMP; C. E. Rogers to LM, 5/5/1937, *ibid.;* LM to C. E. Rogers, 5/15/1937, B2, *ibid.*

34. *CD*, 3/20/1937, p. 1; *CD*, 8/16/1941, p. 5; Marion Musick to LM, 6/30/1939, B2, LMP.

35. LM, de Graaf Interview, part 1, pp. 8–9; *LAS*, 11/15/1934, p. 1.

36. LM, de Graaf Interview, part 2, pp. 15–17; Flamming, *Bound for Freedom*, 312–329; *LAS*, 6/23/1938, p. A2.

37. *LAS*, 4/18/1940, p. 1; *LAS*, 10/10/1940, p. 1; Lillian Jones to LM, 12/7/1938, B2, LMP; *LAS*, 8/31/1939; Initiating Committee to LM, 7/17/1935, B2, LMP; LM to Initiating Committee, 7/22/1939, *ibid.;* LM to Clore Warne, 5/28/1943, *ibid.*

38. LM to Henry Lee Moon, 2/11/1953, p. 3, B3, LMP; LM, de Graaf Interview, part 1, p. 10; LM to Juanita Ellsworth, 10/6/1935, B17, LMP.

39. *LAS*, 1/30/1936, p. 1.

40. *LAT*, 2/18/1938, p. 1.

41. *CD*, 3/19/1938, p. 1; *LAS*, 5/19/1938, p. 1A; *CD*, 4/2/1938, p. 7; *Atlanta Daily World*, 5/30/1938, p. 5; *LAS*, 6/2/1938, p. 1.

42. Letteau v. Ellis, 10 P.2d 496 (Cal. Dist. Ct. App., 1st Dist. 1932); Flamming, *Bound for Freedom*, 221–225; *LAS*, 10/5/1939, p. 1.

43. LM to Idell A. Bateman, 3/11/1939, B2, LMP; *The Crisis* 6 (August 1913): 194; Kurashige, *Shifting Grounds of Race*, 49.

44. Wayt v. Patee, 269 P. 660 (Cal. 1928); Los Angeles Inv. Co. v. Gary, 186 P. 596 (Cal. 1919); Letteau v. Ellis, 10 P.2d 496 (Cal. Dist. Ct. App., 1st Dist. 1932); Los Angeles Guarantee & Trust Co. v. Garrott, 183 P. 470 (Cal. Dist. Ct. App., 2d Dist. 1919). In the text, I will call these types of restrictions "covenants," as does most of the literature. To be more precise, several different sources of law exist—the law of real covenants, where California law remained quite undeveloped, and the precedents that applied to equitable servitudes and defeasible fees, which the state's courts interpreted broadly.

45. Werner v. Graham, 183 P. 945 (Cal. 1919).

46. Letteau v. Ellis, 10 P.2d 496, 497 (Cal. Dist. Ct. App., 1st Dist. 1932).

47. LM, de Graaf Interview, part 2, pp. 25, 33; *AN*, 12/2/1939, p. 13.

48. Clement E. Vose, *Caucasians Only: The Supreme Court, the NAACP, and the Restrictive Covenant Cases* (Berkeley: University of California Press, 1959), 56–57, 58; TM to LM, 6/26/1945, B4, LMP; LM to TM, 7/2/1945, *ibid.*; TM to LM, 12/11/1945, *ibid.*; PM to LM, 12/8/1945, B2, *ibid.*; Jesse Heslip to LM, 12/13/1945, B2, *ibid.*; William Henry Huff to LM, 12/14/1945, B2, *ibid.*; A. L. Wirin to LM, 1/12/1945, B2, LMP.

49. William H. Hastie to LM, 1/10/1945, B4, LMP; Fred Fertig to LM, 10/23/1947, *ibid.*; LM to City of Detroit Interracial Committee, 5/23/1947, *ibid.*; Loren Miller, "Covenants in the Bear Flag State," *The Crisis* 35 (May 1946): 138–140, 155; Loren Miller, "Covenants for Exclusion," *Survey Graphic* 36 (October 1947): 541–543, 558–559; Loren Miller, "Race Restrictions on Ownership or Occupancy of Land," *Lawyers Guild Review* 7 (1947): 99–111; Transcript of Proceedings at Convention of the National Bar Association, Cleveland, 12/1/1945, B49-F17, STMAP; C. Francis Stradford to LM, 12/22/1945, B2, LMP.

50. 1946 Tax Return, B2, LMP; Richard L. Abel, *American Lawyers* (New York: Oxford University Press, 1989), 302; Roi Ottley to LM, 8/10/1942, B2, LMP; Prentice Thomas to LM, 6/4/1942, B2, *ibid.* Although Miller sometimes practiced with another lawyer, his 1946 practice most closely resembled that of a solo practitioner.

9. The Trials of Pauli Murray

1. Prison [Undated Notes], B4-F85, PMP; Questions Prepared for Dr. Titley, 12/17/1937, B4-F71, *ibid.*; Notes from City Courthouse, 3/27/1940, B4-F86, *ibid.*

2. Pauli Murray, *Song in a Weary Throat: An American Pilgrimage* (New York: Harper & Row, 1987), 7–12, 15, 28; Pauli Murray, *Proud Shoes: The Story of an American Family* (New York: Harper & Bros., 1956), 35–47, 55–58, 275–276; Pauli Murray, "Mulatto's Dilemma (A Poem)," *Opportunity* 16 (1938): 180.

3. Murray, *Proud Shoes*, 8–23; Murray, *Song in a Weary Throat*, 59–60, 69, 71, 74; E. Franklin Frazier, "Durham: Capital of the Black Middle Class," in Alain Locke, ed., *The New Negro* (New York: Atheneum, 1992), 333–340; Interview of PM by Genna Rae McNeil, 2/13/1976, p. 11, Interview G-0044, Southern Oral History Program Collection, University of North Carolina; Questions Prepared for Dr. Titley, 12/17/1937, B4-F71, PMP.

4. Interview of PM by Robert Martin, New York City, 8/15/1968 and 8/17/1968, p. 73–74, B1-F8, *ibid.;* Peter Panic [Pauli Murray], "Little Man from Mars," *LAS*, 7/14/1944, B1-F12, *ibid.*

5. Murray, *Song in a Weary Throat*, pp. 31–32, 37–38.

6. *Ibid.*, pp. 32, 109; Harold Garfinkel, "Color Trouble," *Opportunity* 18 (1940): 144, 146; Peter Panic [Pauli Murray], "Little Man from Mars, *LAS*, 7/14/1944, B1-F12, PMP.

7. PM, McNeil Interview, p. 25; List of Residences, Report of New York FBI Office, 1/10/1967, PM FBI File; John D'Emilio and Estelle B. Freedman, *Intimate Matters: A History of Sexuality in America* (New York: Harper & Row, 1988), 188–201, 223–229; Eric Garber, "A Spectacle in Color: The Lesbian and Gay Subculture of Jazz Age Harlem," in Martin Bauml Duberman, Martha Vicinus, and George Chauncey Jr., eds., *Hidden from History: Reclaiming the Gay and Lesbian Past* (New York: Penguin, 1989), 318–331; Murray, *Song in a Weary Throat*, 76, 213; Summary of Symptoms of Upset, 3/8/1940, B4-F71, PMP; Notes of Interview with Dr. ———, 12/16/1937, B4-F71, *ibid.*

8. Murray, *Song in a Weary Throat*, 77–81; May J. Bull to Girls, 3/30/1931, B4-F84, PMP.

9. Pauli Murray, "From 'Three Thousand Miles on a Dime in Ten Days,'" in Nancy Cunard, ed., *Negro* (London: Wishart & Co., 1934), 90–93; Nancy Cunard to PM, 1/15, n.d. (emphasis in original), B4-F84, PMP. The best analysis of Murray's fictionalized essay remains Doreen Marie Drury, "'Experimentation on the Male Side': Race, Class, Gender, and Sexuality in Pauli Murray's Quest for Love and Identity, 1910–1990" (Ph.D. diss., Boston College, 2000), 69–78.

10. Murray, *Song in a Weary Throat*, 92–98; Jane Kahramanidis, "The She-She-She Camps of the Great Depression," *History Magazine*, February/March 2008, pp. 13–16; List of Residences, Report of New York FBI Office, 1/10/1967, PM FBI File; PM to Eleanor Roosevelt, 12/6/1938, B15-F380, PMP.

11. Murray, *Song in a Weary Throat*, 98–99; Travel Diary, 4/27/1935–5/24/1935, B1-F25, PMP.

12. PM to Mother, 1/10/1940, B10-F253, PMP; PM to Mother, 6/4/1943, *ibid.;* Notes for Interview with Dr. ———, 12/16/1937, B4-F71, *ibid.;* Questions

Prepared for Dr. Titley; Summary of Symptoms of Upset, 3/8/1940, *ibid.;* Memorandum to Dr. Helen Rogers and Mrs. Blount, 3/8/1940, *ibid.;* Murray, *Song in a Weary Throat,* 50; PM to Aunt Sallie and Mother, 8/13/1939, B10-F252, PMP.

13. Notes for Interview with Dr. ———, 12/16/1937; A. McBean, Letter to the Editor, *AN,* 11/25/1939, p. 14; George Chauncey Jr., "From Sexual Inversion to Homosexuality: The Changing Medical Conceptualization of Female 'Deviance,'" in Kathy Peiss and Christina Simmons, with Robert Padgug, eds., *Passion and Power: Sexuality in History* (Philadelphia: Temple University Press, 1989), 87–117; Questions Prepared for Dr. Titley, 12/17/1937, B4-F71, PMP; Summary of Symptoms of Upset, 3/8/1940, *ibid.;* Diary, 5/24/1940, B1-F26, *ibid.;* Unknown to PM, 1/8/1941, B4-F71, *ibid.;* PM to Dr. Richards, 11/4/1939, B4-F71, *ibid.;* Memorandum on PM, 7/13/1942, B4-F71, *ibid.*

14. Questions Prepared for Dr. Titley; Chauncey, "From Sexual Inversion to Homosexuality." Scholars continue to debate the coherence of the sexologists' ideas and whether those ideas affected the thinking of ordinary Americans. Murray, at least, seemed to find much coherence in the sexology that she read.

15. Questions Prepared for Dr. Titley.

16. *Ibid.;* Notes for Interview with Dr. ———, 12/16/1937; PM to Dr. Mazique, 7/29/1944, B4-F73, PMP; Summary of Symptoms of Upset, 3/8/1940. Murray's theories did have some support in the scientific parlance of the day, although the particular doctors she consulted resisted them. See Elizabeth Reis, *Bodies in Doubt: An American History of Intersex* (Baltimore: Johns Hopkins University Press, 2009), 55–114.

17. Application for Federal Employment, 1966, PM FBI File; PM to Mother, 1/10/1940, B10-F253, PMP; PM to Dr. Richards, 11/4/1939, B4-F71, *ibid.*

18. Teletype Transmission from Boston to New York, 1/3/1967, PM FBI file; Notice of Application for Commitment, Department of Hospitals, Division of Psychiatry, Bellevue Hospital, 3/2/1940, B4-F71, PMP.

19. Application for Federal Employment, 1966, PM FBI File; Basis for Investigation, Report of New York FBI Office, 1/10/1967, PM FBI File; An Inquirer to Norman Thomas, 1/26/1939, B102-F1836, PMP; Murray, *Song in a Weary Throat,* 50; PM to Aunt Sallie and Mother, 8/13/1939, B10-F252, PMP; PM to Mother and Aunt Sallie, 8/25/1939, *ibid.;* Memorandum to Dr. Helen Rogers and Mrs. Blount, 3/8/1940, *ibid.*

20. Leslie Brown, *Upbuilding Black Durham: Gender, Class, and Black Community Development in the Jim Crow South* (Chapel Hill: University of North Carolina Press, 2008), 286–289, 318–319; PM to James Shephard, 4/2/1940, B4-F85, PMP; PM to Frank P. Graham, 1/17/1939, P3-SerA-R18-F559, NAACPPmf; PM, Letter to Editor, *BAA,* 1/14/1939, p. 4; PM to Eleanor Roosevelt, 12/6/1938, B15-F380, PMP; PM to Louis Austin, 1/18/1939, B15-F381, PMP; *PC,* 1/28/1939, p. 20; Murray, *Song in a Weary Throat,* 108–112, 115–125.

21. Memorandum to Mr. White from Mr. Wilkins, 1/21/1939, P3-SerA-R18-F566, NAACPPmf; Memorandum to Mr. Wilkins from Mr. White, 1/23/1939, *ibid.,* F568; Memorandum from Mr. Wilkins to Mr. White, 2/2/1939, *ibid.,* F571; Mark V. Tushnet, *Making Civil Rights Law: Thurgood Marshall and the Supreme Court, 1936–1941* (New York: Oxford University Press, 1994), 33–34, 123; Murray, Song in a Weary Throat, 125–126.

22. PM, McNeil Interview, 48; Glenda Elizabeth Gilmore, *Defying Dixie: The Radical Roots of Civil Rights, 1919–1950* (New York: W. W. Norton, 2008), 285–289.

23. PM to Carl DeVane, 10/22/1939, B15-F381, PMP; PM to Gerald Edwards, 4/13/1940, B4-F87, *ibid.*

24. Missouri *ex rel.* Gaines v. Canada, 305 U.S. 337, 348, 350 (1938).

25. TM to PM, 2/26/1941, B15-F384, PMP; TM to Leon Ransom, 2/26/1941, *ibid.;* PM to Caroline Ware, 9/16/1944, in Ann Firor Scott, ed., *Pauli Murray and Caroline Ware: Forty Years of Letters in Black and White* (Chapel Hill: University of North Carolina Press, 2006), 32, 33; PM to Mother, 11/4/1945, B10-F253, PMP.

26. Telegram from Roy Wilkins to H. S. Fauntleroy, 3/28/1940, P15-SerA-R17-F604, NAACPPmf; Memorandum to Mr. Murphy from Mr. Wilkins, 4/5/1940, *ibid.,* F622; Walter White to TM, 4/6/1940, *ibid.,* F626; TM to Robert Cooley, 4/5/1940, *ibid.,* F616; CHH, Memorandum for Walter, Roy and Thurgood, 4/5/1940, *ibid.,* F621.

27. Memorandum on P.M., 7/13/1942, B4-F71, *ibid.;* Gilmore, *Defying Dixie,* 322–324; PM to Dr. Richards, 11/4/1939, B4-F71, PMP.

28. Summary of Facts Leading Up to Arrest of Pauli Murray and Adelene McBean, 3/24/1940, B4-F85, PMP; PM to Dave Clendenin, 3/25/1940, B4-F86, PMP.

29. PM and Adelene McBean to Walter White, 3/29/1940, B4-F85, PMP; PM (for Pauli and Mac) to Jean and Pan, 4/9/1940, B4-F87, *ibid.;* PM to Jean and Pan, 4/2/1940, B4-F86, *ibid.;* Notes from City Courthouse, 3/27/1940, *ibid.;* Summary of Facts Leading Up to Arrest, B4-F85, *ibid.;* Murray, *Song in a Weary Throat,* 138–146.

30. PM (for Pauli and Mac) to Jean and Pan, 4/9/1940, B4-F87, PMP; *PC,* 4/13/1940, *ibid.;* Notes from City Courthouse, 3/27/1940, B4-F86, *ibid.;* PM and Adelene McBean to Attorneys Valentine and Cooley, 4/2/1940, *ibid.*

31. PM to Jean and Pan, 4/2/1940, B4-F86, PMP; PM to Jean and Pan, 4/2/1940, *ibid.;* PM to Morris Milgram, 4/9/1940, B4-F87, *ibid.;* PM and Adelene McBean to Messrs. Valentine and Cooley, 4/10/1940, *ibid.;* PM, McNeil Interview, 64–65.

32. PM to Jean and Pan, 4/2/1940, B4-F86, PMP; PM and Adelene McBean to Walter White, 3/29/1940, *ibid.;* Pauli (for Pauli and Mac) to Jean and Pan, 4/9/1940, B4-F87, *ibid.*

33. Murray, *Song in a Weary Throat*, 138–140; *Carolina Times*, 4/6/1940, B4-F86, PMP; Pauli (for Pauli and Mac) to Jean and Pan, 4/9/1940, B4-F87, *ibid.* A white passenger on the bus later described the incident in a manner that presented Murray as even more passive than she appeared to be in her original story, although he mistook her for a boy. Garfinkel, "Color Trouble."

34. PM to Morris Milgram, 4/29/1940, B4-F85, PMP; PM to Morris Milgram, 5/14/1940, B4-F88, *ibid.;* Tushnet, *Making Civil Rights Law,* 73; PM to Thomas Stone, 5/14/1940, B4-F88, PMP; PM to Jean and Pan, 5/16/1940, *ibid.;* Pauli (for Pauli and Mac) to Jean and Pan, 4/9/1940, B4-F87, *ibid.;* PM and Adelene McBean to Attorneys Valentine and Cooley, 4/21/1940, *ibid.*

35. Murray, *Song in a Weary Throat*, 150–152, 160–166, 177, 180–181; PM to Leon Ransom, 11/30/1940, B15-F384, PMP; PM to Leon A. Ransom, 2/13/1941, *ibid.;* Diary, July 8 and 9, 1941, B1-F26, *ibid.*

36. Murray, *Song in a Weary Throat*, 183.

37. STMA to Dorothy L. Freeman, 4/18/1946, B49-F42, STMAP; Martin Summers, *Manliness and Its Discontents: The Black Middle Class and the Transformation of Masculinity, 1900–1930* (Chapel Hill: University of North Carolina Press, 2004), 155–157, 187–188; Kate McCabe and Dovey Johnson Roundtree, *Justice Older Than the Law: The Life of Dovey Johnson Roundtree* (Jackson: University Press of Mississippi, 2009), 91–92; PM to Joseph Eidelsberg, 7/13/1942, B4-F71, PMP; PM to Mother, 6/2/1943, B10-F253, *ibid.;* Bedside Notes, University Health Service, Howard University, 5/1943, B4-F71, *ibid.*

38. *Howard University Bulletin* 16/12 (April 30, 1937): 9; *Howard University Bulletin* 18 (April 30, 1939): 222; PM, McNeil Interview, pp. 64, 66.

39. *WP*, 5/2/1932, p. 14; Biographical—James G. Tyson, box 108–1, folder 1, JGTP; TM to George W. Crawford, 4/23/1936, P2-R3-NAACPPmf; Murray, *Song in a Weary Throat*, 188, 217–218; PM to Mother, 6/2/1943, p. 3, B10-F253, PMP; Report of Special Agent [Redacted], 1/3/1967, p. 2, PM FBI file; Notes for Interview with Dr. ———, 12/16/1937.

40. Murray, *Song in a Weary Throat*, 183, 184, 219; PM to Mother, 6/2/1943, B10-F253, PMP; PM, McNeil Interview, p. 65; Mary Elizabeth Basile, "Pauli Murray's Campaign against Harvard Law School's 'Jane Crow' Admissions Policy," *Journal of Legal Education* 57 (2007): 77.

41. Howard University Students Demonstrate New Technique, F17, PM Collection, Moorland-Spingarn Research Center; Murray, *Song in a Weary Throat*, 202–208, 222–231, 233–237; Scholastic Record of Murray, Pauli, Howard University, B15-F385, PMP.

42. Tushnet, *Making Civil Rights Law,* 72–76, 120–127; Murray, *Song in a Weary Throat*, 220–222.

43. PM, Should the Civil Rights Cases and Plessy v. Ferguson Be Overruled?, May 1944, B84-F1466, PMP.

44. *Ibid.*, pp. 1, 26, 38, 41–43.

45. *Ibid.*, pp. 32–56, especially 43–44; PM, Outline of Argument that *Plessy v. Ferguson* Should Be Overruled, B84-F1466, PMP; Amy Dru Stanley, "Instead of Waiting for the Thirteenth Amendment: The War Power, Slave Marriage, and Inviolate Human Rights," *American Historical Review* 115 (2010): 732–765, 735–736, nn. 5–7 (collecting citations).

46. PM to Andy, 8/21/1944, B84-F1466, PMP; PM to Skipper, 9/16/1944, in Scott, *Pauli Murray and Carolina Ware*, 33; PM, Should the Civil Rights Cases and Plessy v. Ferguson Be Overruled?, May 1944, p. 44, B84-F1466, PMP.

47. Murray, *Song in a Weary Throat*, 243; PM to A. Calvert Smith, 6/24/1944, B18-F415, PMP.

48. Serena Mayeri, "Constitutional Choices: Legal Feminism and the Historical Dynamics of Change," *California Law Review* 92 (2004): 755; Nancy MacLean, *Freedom Is Not Enough: The Opening of the American Workplace* (Cambridge, Mass.: Harvard University Press, 2006), 119–152; Linda K. Kerber, *No Constitutional Right to Be Ladies: Women and the Obligations of Citizenship* (New York: Hill & Wang, 1998), 185–199.

10. A Lawyer as the Face of Integration in Postwar America

1. *WP*, 12/ 7/1952, p. M10; *Time*, 12/21/1953; Juan Williams, *Thurgood Marshall: American Revolutionary* (New York: Random House, 1998), 214–225.

2. William H. Harbaugh, *Lawyer's Lawyer: The Life of John W. Davis* (New York: Oxford University Press, 1973), 512, 518–519, 529; Williams, *Thurgood Marshall*, 229.

3. Thomas J. Sugrue, *Sweet Land of Liberty: The Forgotten Struggle for Civil Rights in the North* (New York: Random House, 2008), 130–250; Harbaugh, *Lawyer's Lawyer*, 492–495.

4. STMA to Harry Truman, 11/10/1948, B39-F7, STMAP; STMA to Eugene Kinckle Jones, 12/29/1948, *ibid.; New York Herald Tribune*, 12/29/1948, *ibid.; New York World-Telegram*, 12/29/1948, *ibid.;* Part 570.28, Chapter II (CAA), Title IV (Civil Aviation), 12/27/1948, *ibid.*

5. *BAA*, 12/4/1943, p. 15; *NJG*, 12/11/1943, p. A15; C. W. Anderson Jr. to Perry Jackson, 10/16/1945, B48-F33, STMAP; C. W. Anderson to STMA, 9/14/1945, p. 3, F39, *ibid.;* Sidney Redmond to STMA, B48F39, *ibid.;* STMA to Elliott Cheatham, B11-F29, *ibid.*

6. George W. Crockett Jr. to S. R. Redmond, 5/20/1946, B49-F43, STMAP; STMA to George W. Crockett Jr. 6/5/1946, B49-F43, *ibid.*

7. Harvard Sitkoff, *A New Deal for Blacks* (New York: Oxford University Press, 1978), 76–79; Gilbert Ware, *William Hastie: Grace under Pressure* (New York: Oxford University Press, 1984), 81–85.

8. Robert J. Blakely with Marcus Shepard, *Earl B. Dickerson: A Voice for Freedom and Equality* (Evanston, Ill.: Northwestern University Press, 2006), 39–69;

R2-F610, Trial Transcript, Hansberry v. Lee, Docket 25116 (1939), Vault 50076, Illinois Supreme Court, Microfilm Department.

9. Merl E. Reed, *Seedtime for the Modern Civil Rights Movement: The President's Committee on Fair Employment Practice, 1941–1946* (Baton Rouge: LSU Press, 1991), 13–22, 34, 38; Executive Order 8802, 6 Fed. Reg. 3109 (1941).

10. Reed, *Seedtime*, 45, 67–76, 112–113; Interview of Earl Dickerson by Robert Blakely, 8/10/1983, part 2, pp. 1–2; Exec. Order 9346, 8 Fed. Reg. 7183 (1943).

11. William Hastie, Memorandum to Mr. James E. Rowe, March 21, 1942, box 34, James Rowe papers, Franklin D. Roosevelt Presidential Library and Museum, Hyde Park, N.Y.; A. J. Johnson to Director, Federal Bureau of Investigation, 10/1/1941, B154-F18, National Lawyers Guild Records, Tamiment Library, New York University; J. Edgar Hoover, Memorandum for Special Defense Unit, 2/28/1942, CHH FBI file; Blakely, *Earl B. Dickerson*, 148–149.

12. *PT*, 7/30/1991, p. 7A; Interview of Frank Reeves by Robert Wright, 11/28/1969, pp. 1–2, Manuscript Division, Moorland-Spingarn Research Center, Howard University; *NYT*, 9/15/1997, p. B7; Interview of George W. Crockett by James Mosby, 7/9/1970, pp. 1–14, Moorland-Spingarn Research Center; Reed, *Seedtime*, 10, 89, 92, 148.

13. *Seedtime*, 333–337; NJG, 1/23/1943, p. B1; CHH to Harry Truman, 12/3/1945, B163/14-F2, CHHP; *NYT*, 12/8/1945, p. 11.

14. Ware, *William Hastie*, 93–109, 203–204, 213–241; Interview of William Hastie by Jerry Hess, 1/5/1972, pp. 44–48, 51–52, Harry S. Truman Library and Museum, Independence, Mo.

15. Earl Dickerson to Roger Kiley, 10/5/1940, B1-B1, EBDP; Daniel Marshall to LM, 11/171945, B2, LMP; Gunnar Myrdal, *An American Dilemma: The Negro Problem and Modern Democracy* (Norwalk, Conn.: Easton Press, 1993), xliii, 8, 26 (italics removed).

16. PM to Mrs. Roosevelt, 5/4/1944, p. 2, B18-F396, PMP; RPA, "The Negro Lawyer," p. 1, B96-F44, RPAP.

17. Donald R. McCoy and Richard T. Ruetten, *Quest and Response: Minority Rights and the Truman Administration* (Lawrence: University of Kansas Press, 1973), 24, 47–52; Steven F. Lawson, ed., *To Secure These Rights: The Report of Harry S. Truman's Committee on Civil Rights* (Boston: Bedford/St. Martin's, 2004), 12–14.

18. Logan McWilson to STMA, 12/16/1946, B39, 1946–1947 scrapbook, STMAP; Interview of Philleo Nash by Jerry Hess, 2/21/1967, p. 631, Truman Library; STMA to Roland, 10/10/1947, B40-F1, STMAP.

19. William E. Juhnke, "Creating a New Charter of Freedom: The Organization and Operation of the President's Committee on Civil Rights, 1946–1948" (Ph.D. diss., University of Kansas, 1974), 82, 200–201; STMA to Roland, 10/10/1947, B40-F1, STMAP.

20. Lawson, *To Secure These Rights,* 49, 49–54, 158; McCoy and Ruetten, *Quest and Response,* 92–93.

21. STMA to S. Tanner Stafford, 6/3/1952, B11-F24, STMAP; RPA to Marshall Shepard, 9/26/1949, B100-F10, RPAP; William T. Coleman Jr. with Donald T. Bliss, *Counsel for the Situation: Shaping the Law to Realize America's Promise* (Washington, D.C.: Brookings Institution Press, 2010), 132.

22. *BAA,* 8/20/1949, p. 1; *Collier's,* 2/23/1952, pp. 29, 73–74; Blakely, *Earl B. Dickerson; LAT,* 5/17/1964, p. E4.

23. Blakely, *Earl B. Dickerson,* 67–69, 86–92, 146–147.

24. Lenerte Roberts to STMA, 2/8/1952, B40-F27, STMAP; STMA, Radio Speech, KYW, 1/7/1948, B71-F88, *ibid.;* Matthew J. Countryman, *Up South: Civil Rights and Black Power in Philadelphia* (Philadelphia: University of Pennsylvania Press, 2006), 1, 11, 45–46.

25. §§ 4–700, 4–701, chapter 7, Philadelphia Home Rule Charter, 4/17/1951; Recommendation for Closing, Jean Bernice Hude vs. Jefferson Hospital, 9/23/1952, B40-F27, STMAP.

26. George Schermer to STMA, 6/4/1963, B42-F1, STMAP; Report on the Committee on Housing, 8/29/1952, B40-F27, *ibid.;* Report on Cases Not Closed within Thirty Days of Receipt of Charge, Lillian Rose vs. Catholic Neighbors, 7/31/1952, *ibid.*

27. Sugrue, *Sweet Land of Liberty,* 286–290; Mrs. Alexander's Remarks to Advisory Committee, 7/2/1963, p. 1, B42-F1, STMAP; Leon H. Sullivan, *Build Brother Build* (Philadelphia: Macrae Smith, 1969), 44–69; Guian A. McKee, *The Problem of Jobs: Liberalism, Race, and Deindustrialization in Philadelphia* (Chicago: University of Chicago Press, 2008).

28. Sullivan, *Build Brother Build,* 68, 71.

29. Memorandum re: Investigation of Employment Policies and Practices of the Tasty Baking Company, 7/28/1960, B41-F50, STMAP; Sullivan, *Build Brother Build,* 70–97; Countryman, *Up South,* 104–117.

30. *PT,* 4/17/1954; Interview of William T. Coleman Jr. by Kenneth W. Mack, 12/20/2002, tape 2, p. 5; Sam Schrager, *The Trial Lawyer's Art* (Philadelphia: Temple University Press, 1999), 89–101; Joel Moldovsky and Rose DeWolf, *The Best Defense* (New York: Macmillan, 1975), 124–135.

31. *PT,* 2/25/1958, p. 4; *PT,* 6/11/1963, p. 2; Countryman, *Up South,* 95–101, 124–130.

32. Countryman, *Up South,* 136–144; *PT,* 1/22/1963, p. 1; Interview of Curtis Carson by Kenneth Mack, 6/17/1999, tape 2, p. 1; Transcript, Program Broadcast over Radio Station WCAU, 2/8/1963, p. 14, B89-F20, RPAP.

33. RPA, A Plea and Suggestion to the "Four Hundred Negro Ministers" of Greater Philadelphia, 9/13/1963, B98-F43, RPAP; The Plea Was Heard, n.d., *ibid.*

34. "Alexander's Sanguine Stand," *Greater Philadelphia Magazine*, n.d., B35-F4, RPAP; In re Girard Estate, 4 Pa. D. & C.2d 671, (Pa. Orph. 1956), *aff'd*, In re Estate of Girard, 127 A.2d 287 (Pa. 1956), *rev'd sub nom*, Commonwealth v. Board of Directors of City Trusts, 353 U.S. 230 (1957); In re Girard College Trusteeship, 138 A.2d 844 (Pa. 1958).

35. Commonwealth v. Brown, 260 F. Supp. 358 (E.D. Pa. 1966), *rev'd*, 373 F.2d 771 (3rd Cir. 1967), *on remand*, 270 F. Supp. 782 (E.D. Pa. 1967), *aff'd*, 392 F.2d 120 (3rd Cir. 1968); Deborah P. Samuel, "The Fight for Equality: Racial Integration of Girard College" (senior honors thesis, University of Pennsylvania, 1990), 99–102.

36. Kenneth W. Mack, "Rethinking Civil Rights Lawyering and Politics in the Era before Brown," *Yale Law Journal* 115 (2005): 256, 319–325; *Jet*, December 4, 1952, pp. 2, 8–9.

37. Williams v. Yellow Cab Co., 200 F.2d 302 (1952). Syres v. Oil Workers International Union, 223 F. 2d 739, 741 (5th Cir. 1955). The main issue in the case was whether the federal court had jurisdiction to hear the suit under the National Labor Relations Act. As a lawyer, Hastie had advocated for the black boycott movements by arguing that their boycotts were labor disputes under the Norris-La Guardia Act. He also filed an amicus brief for the NAACP in *Tunstall v. Brotherhood of Locomotive Firemen*, arguing that a labor union contract that permitted a union to discriminate against black workers was illegal under the Railway Labor Act. Although both cases are distinguishable from *Williams*, they would seem to incline lawyer Hastie to a set of positions that Judge Hastie repudiated. Mack, "Rethinking Civil Rights Lawyering," 324–325; Motion and Brief for the National Association for the Advancement of Colored People as Amicus Curiae, Tunstall v. Brotherhood of Locomotive Firemen, 1944 WL 42507.

38. Shannon v. HUD, 436 F.2d 809 (3d Cir. 1970); Young v. International Telephone and Telegraph, 438 F.2d 757 (3d Cir. 1971); Contractors Association v. Secretary of Labor, 442 F.2d 159 (3d Cir. 1971); Note, " 'Just One More Vote for Frankfurter': Rethinking the Jurisprudence of Judge William Hastie," *Harvard Law Review* 117 (2004): 1639–1660; Edwin O. Guthman and Jeffrey Shulman, eds., *Robert Kennedy in His Own Words* (New York: Bantam Books, 1988), 115, 116; Nicholas deB. Katzenbach, *Some of It Was Fun: Working with RFK and LBJ* (New York: W. W. Norton, 2008), 57; Memorial Service in Memory of the Honorable William H. Hastie, United States Court of Appeals for the Third Circuit, Philadelphia, 6/18/1976, p. 17, B110/9, William Hastie papers, Harvard Law School.

39. LM to STMA, 5/10/1952, B3, LMP; Murray, *Song in a Weary Throat*, 294–314; PM to Mother, 5/6/1948, B10-F262, PMP; PM to Caroline Ware, 12/2/1956, in Ann Firor Scott, ed., *Pauli Murray and Caroline Ware: Forty Years of*

Letters in Black and White (Chapel Hill: University of North Carolina Press, 2006), 108, 109.

40. NYT, 5/21/1954, p. 26; PM, Diary Entries, 5/17/1954 to 5/24/1954, B1-F27, PMP; PM to Leon Ransom, 5/25/1954, B173/1-F23, LARP; PM to Channing Tobias, 7/4/1958, P21-R20-F89, NAACPPmf; Roy Wilkins to PM, 7/18/1958, *ibid.*, F98; PM to Roy Wilkins, 7/28/1958, *ibid.*, F108; PM to Thomas Waring, 2/14/1959, F150, *ibid.*

41. Murray, *Song in a Weary Throat,* 318–343; Diary Entries, 2/20/1960 to 2/23/1960, 6/30/1960 to 4/10/1961, B2-F29v, PMP; PM to NYT, 8/28/1960, B5-F38, PMP. For a critical assessment of Murray's Ghanaian sojourn, see Kevin K. Gaines, *African Americans in Ghana: Black Expatriates and the Civil Rights Era* (Chapel Hill: University of North Carolina Press, 2006), 110–134.

42. Serena Mayeri, "Constitutional Choices: Legal Feminism and the Historical Dynamics of Change," *California Law Review* 92 (2004): 755, 761–801; Cynthia Harrison, *On Account of Sex: The Politics of Women's Issues, 1945–1968* (Berkeley and Los Angeles: University of California Press, 1988), 126–137; Alice Kessler-Harris, *In Pursuit of Equity: Women, Men, and the Quest for Economic Citizenship in 20th-Century America* (New York: Oxford University Press, 2001), 229–234; *American Women: Report of the President's Commission on the Status of Women and Other Publications of the Commission* (Washington, D.C.: U.S. Government Printing Office, 1963), 147–151.

43. Nancy MacLean, *Freedom Is Not Enough: The Opening of the American Workplace* (Cambridge, Mass.: Harvard University Press, 2006), 118–122; Murray, *Song in a Weary Throat,* 354–368; Pauli Murray and Mary O. Eastwood, "Jane Crow and the Law: Sex Discrimination and Title VII," *George Washington University Law Review* 34 (1965): 232–256; Linda K. Kerber, *No Constitutional Right to Be Ladies: Women and the Obligations of Citizenship* (New York: Hill & Wang, 1998), 185–199. Although Murray broke ground by analogizing sex distinctions to race discrimination, she remained pragmatic in arguing that some sex distinctions might remain legal where a comparable race distinction would not. See Serena Mayeri, *Reasoning from Race: Feminism, Law and the Civil Rights Revolution* (Cambridge, Mass.: Harvard University Press, 2011).

44. Memorandum from Mr. Wilkins to Messrs. Moon, Morsell, 3/5/1959, P21-R20-F130, NAACPPmf; PM to Roy Wilkins, 11/20/1963, *ibid.*, frame 144; PM, Letter to the Editor, *WP,* 8/24/1963, p. A8; Dorothy I. Height, "'We Wanted the Voice of a Woman to Be Heard': Black Women and the 1963 March on Washington," in Bettye Collier-Thomas and V. P. Franklin, eds., *Sisters in the Struggle: African American Women in the Civil Rights–Black Power Movement* (New York: NYU Press, 2001), 83, 89–90; Scott, *Pauli Murray and Caroline Ware,* 144; Diary entry, 11/1/1968, B2-F30, PMP; Diary entry, 11/24/1971, *ibid.* Murray also defended the black militant North Carolina NAACP leader, Robert Williams, after the national NAACP suspended him from his post in 1959 for

advocating violent self-defense for black Southerners. Murray concluded that Williams spoke out of "understandable desperation," and called for him to be censured instead of suspended. PM, Memorandum to Mrs. Daisy Bates, 6/5/1959, p. 3, B127-F2313, PMP.

45. Diary entry, 11/1/1968, B2-F30, PMP; Diary entry, 4/19/1967, *ibid.;* Diary entry, 4/29/1967, *ibid.;* Interview of the Hon. Eleanor Holmes Norton by Kenneth W. Mack, Washington, D.C., May 17, 2011; Marian Wright Edelman, "One Woman's Freedom Movement," *Huffington Post,* June 10, 2011, http:// www.huffingtonpost.com/marian-wright-edelman/one-womans-freedom -moveme_b_875134.html. Murray dropped veiled references to her lost love, Peg Holmes, in each of her signature works: her family narrative, *Proud Shoes,* her poetry collection, *Dark Testament and Other Poems,* and her autobiography. Late in life, she purged some of her correspondence to protect Holmes's privacy. Peg Gilbert to PM, 8/16/69, B96-F1688, PMP; PM to Peg, 3/18/1973, *ibid.;* PM to Peg, 2/8/1977, *ibid.*

46. Richard N. Goodwin, *Remembering America: A Voice from the Sixties* (Boston: Little, Brown, 1988), 4; Nick Bryant, *The Bystander: John F. Kennedy and the Struggle for Black Equality* (New York: Basic Books, 2006), 211–219; Blakely, *Earl B. Dickerson,* 193–194; NYT, 9/1/1987, p. 6; Roger Wilkins, *A Man's Life: An Autobiography* (New York: Simon and Schuster, 1982), 87–93, 176.

47. *Bar Report* (D.C. Bar), 26/1 (Aug./Sept. 1997): 10–11; *ibid.,*24/3 (Dec./ Jan. 1996): 12–13; Guthman and Shulman, *Robert Kennedy in His Own Words,* 115.

48. Patricia Sullivan, *Lift Every Voice: The NAACP and the Making of the Civil Rights Movement* (New York: New Press, 2009), 211; Mark V. Tushnet, *Making Civil Rights Law: Thurgood Marshall and the Supreme Court, 1936–1961* (New York: Oxford University Press, 1994), 311–312; Mark V. Tushnet, *The NAACP's Legal Strategy against Segregated Education, 1925–1950* (Chapel Hill: University of North Carolina Press, 1987), 151.

49. Frank M. Smith to TM (Telegram), 4/30/1956, P17-Supp-R4-F480, NAACPPmf; Honorary Degree to Marshall from New School for Social Research, 6/7/1956, *ibid.,* F481; William K. De Fossett to Roy Wilkins, 9/12/1956, F499, *ibid.;* Williams, *Thurgood Marshall,* 245; Randall Kennedy, "Martin Luther King's Constitution: A Legal History of the Montgomery Bus Boycott," *Yale Law Journal* (1989): 999–1068; Robert Jerome Glennon, "The Role of Law in the Civil Rights Movement: The Montgomery Bus Boycott, 1955–1957," *Law and History* Review 9 (1991): 59, 65–67.

50. Taylor Branch, *Parting the Waters: America in the King Years 1954–63* (New York: Simon & Schuster, 1988), 190; Thurgood Marshall, "The Reminiscences of Thurgood Marshall," in Mark V. Tushnet, ed., *Thurgood Marshall: His Speeches, Writings, Arguments, Opinions, and Reminiscences* (Chicago: Lawrence Hill Books, 2001).

51. Tushnet, *Making Civil Rights Law,* 283–289, 311.

52. Tushnet, *Making Civil Rights Law,* 310–311; Williams, *Thurgood Marshall,* 259–261, 294–295; Interview of Reeves by Wright, p. 15.

53. Robert L. Carter, *A Matter of Law: A Memoir of Struggle in the Cause of Civil Rights* (New York: New Press, 2005), 165–202; Robert L. Carter, "A Reassessment of *Brown v. Board,*" in Derrick Bell, ed., *Shades of Brown: New Perspectives on School Desegregation* (New York: Teachers College Press, Columbia University, 1980), 21–28; Lewis Steel, "Nine Men in Black Who Think White," *New York Times Magazine,* 10/15/1968, p. 53; Interview of Robert L. Carter by Kenneth W. Mack, Cambridge, Mass., 8/16/2004; Book Review, "The Lawyers' Revolution," *New Republic,* March 13, 2006; Bryant, *Bystander,* 283.

54. Arthur M. Schlesinger Jr., *Journals: 1952–2000* (New York: Penguin Press, 2007), 164–165; Williams, *Thurgood Marshall,* 273; *NYT,* 8/11/1961, p. 11; Mark V. Tushnet, *Making Constitutional Law: Thurgood Marshall and the Supreme Court, 1961–1991* (New York: Oxford University Press, 1997), 9–10.

55. Guthman and Shulman, *Robert Kennedy in His Own Words,* 116; Tushnet, *Making Constitutional Law,* 18–25; Doris Kearns, *Lyndon Johnson and the American Dream* (New York: Harper & Row, 1976), 306–307; Loren Miller, *The Petitioners: The Story of the Supreme Court of the United States and the Negro* (New York: Random House, 1966).

56. Tushnet, *Making Constitutional Law,* 5–8, 122–132.

57. Randall Kennedy, *Sellout: The Politics of Racial Betrayal* (New York: Pantheon Books, 2008), 123–131; Angela Onwuachi-Willig, "Just Another Brother on the SCT? What Justice Clarence Thomas Teaches Us about the Influence of Racial Identity," *Iowa Law Review* 90 (2005): 931.

58. Derrick A. Bell Jr., "Serving Two Masters: Integration Ideals and Client Interests in School Desegregation Litigation," *Yale Law Journal* 85 (1976): 470.

Conclusion

1. Debra J. Dickerson, "Colorblind," *Salon,* 1/22/2007, http://www.salon.com/news/opinion/feature/2007/01/22/obama.

Acknowledgments

In these necessarily too-brief acknowledgments I will leave many things out that should be said, but first credit goes to my wife, Lisa A. Jones, whose questions are always harder to answer than those of any other interlocutor, and to my children, Sophia and Nicholas, whose questioning minds constantly force me to think more deeply about what race means in a new century. For intellectual comradeship and guidance, my colleagues at Harvard have been essential, including Chris Desan, Lani Guinier, Charles Ogletree, David Wilkins, Evelyn Brooks Higginbotham, Morton Horwitz, David Barron, Martha Minow, Ben Sachs, Walter Johnson, and Joe Singer. Randall Kennedy has been a friend, supporter, and inspiration since my time as a law student. Three Harvard Law School deans—Elena Kagan, Martha Minow, and Bob Clark—saw this project to completion and provided more support than I would have ever expected. Thanks also to Elena and Martha for sharing your recollections of Thurgood Marshall with me. Colleagues elsewhere have been no less essential, including Daniel Sharfstein, Patricia Sullivan, Ariela Gross, Heather Gerken, Dan Ernst, Al Brophy, Dylan Penningroth, Ian Haney López, Rick Pildes, Gordon Hylton, Laura Kalman, Crystal Feimster, Dani Botsman, and Sam Roberts.

Mark Tushnet and Ariela Gross read the entire manuscript, and their enthusiasm and criticism steered it through its final stages. At every stage of this project, Mark has offered guidance and support based on his unmatched knowledge of Thurgood Marshall. Roger Fairfax graciously agreed to read a partial draft. Tomiko Brown-Nagin, Risa Goluboff, and I have been working along parallel but diverging paths for years. Spencer Overton and I met first as law students, then as fellows at Harvard, and finally as law professors, and at every stage I have appreciated his advice. Arnold Rampersad helped point me toward the Loren Miller papers (then in the family's possession) and provided early encouragement and friendship. The Honorable Robert L. Carter, the late Derrick Bell, and John Payton were all supportive and inspirational, even when we had differing interpretations of civil rights history. Thanks also to David Canton for making our mutual interest in Raymond Pace Alexander into a cooperative enterprise.

In different ways, Bob Dallek, Darlene Clark Hine, Dirk Hartog, Gerald Frug, and Duncan Kennedy encouraged me to think of this book as a way to tell a larger story of American history out of the lives of the particular lawyers who appear in this book. The participants in the workshop on the Long Civil Rights Movement at the Charles Warren Center for Studies in American History at Harvard University also helped me view this project through a larger lens. At the beginnings of this project, David Bogen of the University of Maryland Law School, J. Clay Smith Jr. of Howard Law School, and the late Judge Solomon Baylor of Baltimore offered generous help to a young scholar whose promise was not then apparent. The genesis of the organizing idea for this book came from reading the syllabus for Janet Halley's class on "Representing Social Movements" nearly a decade ago. The ideas and methods that lay behind it began to develop long ago in my graduate seminars with Dirk, and with Nell Painter, and they remain among my most important mentors. Dan Rodgers and Kevin Gaines were teachers whose examples still inspire me. Bob Gordon and Laura Kalman's many works inspired me to think deeply about the lawyers, and both have been generous with their friendship. Behind it all lies the late Betsy Clark, who first opened my eyes to the excitement of history during my time in law school.

Many sources of support have brought this project to completion, but I would like to thank especially Buddy Fletcher, Skip Gates, and the selection committee for the Alphonse Fletcher Sr. Fellowship. I would also like to thank the American Society for Legal History and the William Nelson Cromwell Foundation for fellowship support. Stanford Law dean Larry Kramer helped in the early stages of the book project with a semester as a Visiting Scholar at Stanford Law School. Larry, as well as Michele and Ken Dauber, Arnold Rampersad, Marvina White, and Lydia Klussman, were there with friendship and unparalleled support during a very difficult time. I would also like to thank two Georgetown Law School deans, Alex Aleinikoff and Bill Treanor, for their kind support during my years at their institution. Andrew Taylor, Vincent Haskell and their family opened the doors of their home during numerous research trips to Washington. Drew Faust also provided essential help in reaffirming the importance of this work and my future projects.

Many library staffs have gone out of their way to run down obscure books and articles and provide access to primary sources, but I would like to especially acknowledge the support of the library staffs at Harvard Law School and Georgetown University Law Center. At Harvard, David Warrington and especially Janet Katz went above and beyond the call of duty to make sure that my book came out on time. Adrienne Cannon in the Manuscript Division at the Library of Congress was extremely encouraging at an early stage of this project. Charles Houston Jr. kindly let me see documents pertaining to his father. At the Huntington Library, curator Bill Frank was especially helpful in opening up the Loren Miller papers to me at an early date, as were Halvor Miller and Loren Miller Jr., who kept me up to date on the Loren Miller papers and graciously sat for interviews. The staffs at the University of Pennsylvania Archives and Records Center and the Moorland-Spingarn Research Center have been especially helpful. In particular Mark Lloyd (director), James Curtiss Ayers, and Nancy Miller at the Archives and Records Center went out of their way to accommodate my long period of research in the Alexander papers. At Moorland-Spingarn, Dr. Clifford Muse, university archivist at Howard University, was kind enough to open up previously closed records in the Howard University Archives for my research, and the staffs at the Schlesinger Library at Harvard endured numerous requests for access, photocopying, and other tasks in tracking down the history of women lawyers. I also want to thank my assistant, Wendy Moore, who has helped me in many ways.

Many excellent research assistants have helped immeasurably over the years, including Julia Rindler, Amal Bass, Emily Pollack, Darryl Hazelwood, Laura Jarrett, Ashton Lattimore, Tazneen Shahabuddin, Beverly Vu, Shira Hoffman, Beth Avery, James Chang, Chartey Quarcoo, Greta Gao, Darrell Miller, Amos Jones, and Kami Kruckenberg. Independent scholar Krista Reynen was instrumental in helping with research in the Earl Dickerson papers at the Chicago Historical Society.

Finally, I am grateful for friends who, just by being true friends, helped more than they can imagine, including Joe Davis and Duane Powell, with whom I have spent long hours talking about obscure subjects that no one outside history could expect to be interested in; David Hill and Andre Nobles, some of my oldest friends from law school who never raised their eyebrows about my desire to be a writer and a professor; George Payne and Darrell Andrews, two of my oldest friends in the world who are part of this story and many others; as well as Abe Dorph and Sanjay Misra, who joined me on my journey away from a career in engineering to places none of us expected to go. Also, I would like to acknowledge the friendship of the extended Jones family over the years. No less important are the old and new friends in Washington, D.C., and dear friends in Newton, Massachusetts, who have provided support in the final stages of this project in more ways than they know. You are all part of the story behind the story told in this book.

Index